AMERICAN COMMANDO

**Evans Carlson, His WWII Marine Raiders, and
America's First Special Forces Mission**

JOHN WUKOVITS

NAL
CALIBER

NAL Caliber
Published by New American Library, a division of
Penguin Group (USA) Inc., 375 Hudson Street,
New York, New York 10014, USA
Penguin Group (Canada), 90 Eglinton Avenue East, Suite 700, Toronto,
Ontario M4P 2Y3, Canada (a division of Pearson Penguin Canada Inc.)
Penguin Books Ltd., 80 Strand, London WC2R 0RL, England
Penguin Ireland, 25 St. Stephen's Green, Dublin 2,
Ireland (a division of Penguin Books Ltd.)
Penguin Group (Australia), 250 Camberwell Road, Camberwell, Victoria 3124,
Australia (a division of Pearson Australia Group Pty. Ltd.)
Penguin Books India Pvt. Ltd., 11 Community Centre, Panchsheel Park,
New Delhi - 110 017, India
Penguin Group (NZ), cnr Airborne and Rosedale Roads, Albany,
Auckland 1310, New Zealand (a division of Pearson New Zealand Ltd.)
Penguin Books (South Africa) (Pty.) Ltd., 24 Sturdee Avenue,
Rosebank, Johannesburg 2196, South Africa

Penguin Books Ltd., Registered Offices:
80 Strand, London WC2R 0RL, England

First published by NAL Caliber, an imprint of New American Library,
a division of Penguin Group (USA) Inc.

First Printing, June 2009
10   9   8   7   6   5   4   3   2   1

LIBRARY OF CONGRESS CATALOGING-IN-PUBLICATION DATA:

Wukovits, John F., 1944–
    American commando : Evans Carlson, his WWII Marine raiders, and America's first Special Forces mission/
John Wukovits.
        p.   cm.
    Includes bibliographical references and index.
    ISBN 978-0-451-22692-1
    1. World War, 1939–1945—Campaigns—Solomon Islands.   2. World War, 1939–1945—Commando
operations—Pacific Area.   3. Makin Atoll, Raid on, Kiribati, 1942.   4. Guadalcanal, Battle of, Solomon
Islands, 1942–1943.   5. Carlson, Evans Fordyce, 1896–1947.   6. United States. Marine Corps—Biography.
7. Generals—United States—Biography.   8. United States. Marine Corps. Marine Raider Battalion, 2nd.
9. Special forces (Military science)—History—20th century.   I. Title.
D767.98.W85 2009
940.54'265933092—dc22   2008055329

Set in Fairfield
Designed by Ginger Legato

Printed in the United States of America

PUBLISHER'S NOTE
While the author has made every effort to provide accurate telephone numbers and Internet addresses at the time
of publication, neither the publisher nor the author assumes any responsibility for errors, or for changes that occur
after publication.
    Further, publisher does not have any control over and does not assume any responsibility for author or third-party
Web sites or their content.

To my daughter, Julie,
who always makes me proud

Contents

Preface

As a Pacific War historian, I have long known that the name Guadalcanal evokes memories of gallant clashes and valorous deeds by Army, Navy, and Marine personnel. I was unaware, however, of the Second Marine Raider Battalion's role on that island until coming across an officer's statement explaining how a thirty-day patrol behind Japanese lines altered his views toward the enemy. The man stated that whereas at the start of the patrol he felt compassion, hatred subsequently took over as the dominant emotion.

That led me to investigate this Long Patrol, as it is called in Marine annals. I discovered that, far from being a routine assignment, the Long Patrol rested with the few celebrated missions behind enemy lines in the war against Japan and emerged as a precursor to today's special forces operations. I became familiar with fascinating individuals, from the battalion's commanding officer, Evans F. Carlson, to the Roosevelt family, to the indomitable Transport Maghakian and the other Marine Raiders. I learned that before their actions in Guadalcanal, the battalion executed one of the war's first covert operations with its July 1942 raid at Makin.

Despite the personalities and events, historians have largely overlooked the Second Marine Raider Battalion. One book exists about its raid at Makin, and a 1947 biography of Carlson brought attention to the commander, but other than a few sparse chapters in war summaries, no books have appeared either detailing the exploits of Carlson's Raiders in the Solomons or relating the events of the battalion's yearlong existence.

Two years of research for this book took me to diverse centers. As always, Barry Zerby and the archivists at the National Archives and Record Administration helped immensely in locating official and unofficial accounts. Matthew Hanson at the Franklin D. Roosevelt Presidential Library and Museums at Hyde Park, New York, provided voluminous correspondence between Evans Carlson and the Roosevelt family, as well as placed me in contact with Mary Roosevelt, James Roosevelt's widow. Mary, who offered insightful comments on her husband's role with the Marines, proved most helpful. Tony Magnotta's aid at the Marine Corps Research Center at Quantico, as well as the rest of the able staff, made my time productive at that beautiful center, as did the staff at the Library of Congress. Carmen Miller Michael made available an illuminating collection of letters to and from her brother, Lt. Jack Miller, that currently reside at the DeGolyer Library and Special Collections at Southern Methodist University. The collection's director, Russell L. Martin, offered valuable assistance during my visits to the library.

Other individuals aided my research. Michael J. Zak shared an insightful collection of materials, including papers he wrote at Harvard University and transcripts of interviews and correspondence with prominent Raiders. Two Raiders, Dr. Ervin Kaplan and Frank Kurland, arranged access to past issues of the *Raider Patch*, the United States Marine Raider Association's newsletter, and John McCarthy and others at the Raider Association kindly responded to my inquiries.

Above all, I want to offer a special thanks to the many Marine Raiders who took time, either in person or by telephone, to share their reminiscences with me. The story would have been incomplete without the recollections of the men who were there. I have listed in the book's bibliography the names of each person interviewed as well as the interview dates.

This book would not have been possible without the assistance of my agent, Jim Hornfischer. A polished World War II historian as well as a superb literary agent, Jim understands the needs and demands placed on a writer. He is tops. Jeffrey Ward again designed the outstanding maps that help complement the text, and Mark Chait at New American Library helped remove the rough edges from the manuscript. The examples of my writing mentor, Thomas Buell, and of my Notre Dame history professor and adviser, Dr. Bernard Norling, keep me on the proper path.

I have also been fortunate to enjoy the encouragement of other individuals who exist outside the literary realm. My three daughters—Amy, Julie, and Karen—lend support with their words while I am writing and with their deeds at all times. They make me proud to be a father. My four grandchildren—Matthew, Megan Grace, Emma, and Kaitlyn—offer love and smiles, especially when they know their grandfather is in his "writing cave," as Matthew calls it.

When I most needed a mental boost, Terri Faitel was there with her incisive comments, made all the wiser by her vast researching and educational skills. She scrutinized my manuscript in her typically meticulous manner and offered a cheery word when needed. She helped me more than she realizes, and I am not only thankful for her aid but proud of the work she has accomplished in her own field.

Mostly, my thanks go to four people, only one of whom is still with me. My parents, Tom and Grace, and my two brothers, Tom and Fred, never failed to lend support to my endeavors. I hope always to make them proud of whatever I achieve.

I would like to mention how I determined the rank (private, corporal, and so on) used for each Raider mentioned in the book. Many started with the Raiders in February 1942 as privates, then became privates first class, corporals, and so forth. To eliminate confusion, except in a few cases involving the most important officers (Carlson, Roosevelt, Washburn, and Peatross, for example), I used the highest rank attained by the individual during the scope of the book. For instance, Ray Bauml began as a private in February 1942, but had become a private first class by the Long Patrol in November. He is thus referred to as Pfc. Ray Bauml throughout the book. On the other hand, I refer to Lt. Richard Washburn in the beginning, but Captain Washburn later to reflect his promotion.

AMERICAN COMMANDO

Reaching for the Stars,
but Never Touching Them

Marine Lt. Col. Evans F. Carlson, battling salt spray as he squinted into the stiff ocean wind and brutal breakers, faced his direst crisis. He had brought his Marine Raiders to Butaritari, a small island in the Makin Atoll in the central Pacific, to shock the Japanese with an unexpected raid. He had, instead, been stunned, not so much by the Japanese as by nature itself. Already fatigued from a long day of fighting the enemy on land, Carlson and his small group of Raiders now struggled through heavy surf to reach the submarines waiting beyond the reef to take them safely back to Hawaii.

His own rubber boat had been no match for the waves, which tossed boat and occupants toward shore with alarming ease. Carlson now slumped on the beach, exhausted and wet, and watched the breakers do the rest of their dirty work. One after the other the angry waves flipped rubber boats upside down, slapping exhausted Raiders into the water and swallowing their equipment. Carlson wondered if any of his men would reach their destination.

He had faith in his Raiders, no doubt about that. The Marine publicity machine called them "experts in death, demolition and destruction." The amphibious commander, Maj. Gen. Holland M. Smith, wrote that the Raiders were "the elite of toughness" who "were taught all the tricks of undercover combat; they could out-read a jungle-tracker, climb mountains like billy goats, and out-swim a fish."[1]

Carlson had long had a dream—to train men in his unique system, one based upon fairness and equality, one centered on devotion to the democratic principles that underpinned the nation. For his labors, he had received bitter criticism, much of it from fellow Marine officers, and been labeled a troublemaker.

Now, in this his first test, a debacle loomed. He had no idea how many Japanese remained on the island. He knew most of his men had lost their weapons in the surf and, with them, the ability to defend themselves. He knew that, even if they had rifles, his fatigued men could barely lift them. Surrender, considered anathema to every Marine, suddenly was a frightening possibility.

As nightmarish as that was, Carlson faced a worse specter. One of those weary men beside him on that forlorn beach, the battalion's executive officer, happened to be the president's oldest son.

Would his dream of fashioning a pioneering battalion end here, on the shores of this tiny Pacific outpost?

"His Spirit Is Restless"

To comprehend the uniqueness of the Second Marine Raider Battalion, one must understand the man behind it—Evans Fordyce Carlson. Rarely has a person combined such diverse qualities—an intellectual who loved combat; a high school dropout who quoted Emerson; a thin, almost fragile-looking man who relished fifty-mile hikes; an officer in a military organization who touted equality among officers and enlisted; a kindly individual with the capacity to kill; the product of small New England towns who sought adventure in the vast reaches of the world; a man who believed in decency and love and fairness, but whose actions generated bitterness and hatred and antipathy.

Carlson was the American version of T. E. Lawrence, a contemporary from Great Britain who fashioned a career from adventure, combat, and asceticism. At various times of his life, Carlson exhibited the tendencies of Don Quixote chasing an elusive dream, a cutthroat worthy of making pirates blush, an intellectual on a par with astute minds, an adventurer in the mold of Lawrence of Arabia, a patriot, an Elmer Gantry–style preacher, or a naïve optimist.

Born on February 26, 1896, in Sidney, New York, Carlson could hardly escape such traits, as the lust for adventure had long fueled the Carlson clan. His grandfather panned for gold in the mountains of California, while an uncle maintained law and order in the wilds of Alaska as a United States marshal. Carlson's father, Thomas, had been born in a rude shack in a mining town in the California High Sierras.

During his New England youth, Carlson thrilled to the stories of colonial settlers and their struggles against the Native Americans. He read of the exploits of Maj. Robert Rogers and his Rangers, a special colonial militia that roamed New England's wilderness during the French and Indian War during the mid-eighteenth century and gained a reputation for courage and cunning with their missions deep into enemy territory.

Carlson early developed affection for great literature. He read most of the classics boys his age read, such as James Fenimore Cooper's tales of colonists, soldiers, and Native Americans, but unlike most boys, Carlson also plunged into deep philosophical volumes, especially the essays of Ralph Waldo Emerson. The New England philosopher challenged Carlson's mind with such thoughts as "Do not go where the path may lead, go instead where there is no path and leave a trail"; "A hero is no braver than an ordinary man, but he is braver five minutes longer"; and "None of us will ever accomplish anything excellent or commanding except when he listens to this whisper which is heard by him alone."[2] For the remainder of his life, even during his lengthy march with Chinese military units in the 1930s or the daring mission with his Raiders in 1942, his worn volume of Emerson was a constant companion.

At the same time he inherited from his father, a New England Congregationalist minister, a Christlike code based on decency and a respect for all. Thomas believed that one not only read and studied the lessons of Christ, but that a person lived it in his daily life. As a result, Carlson grew to early manhood driven by a longing to explore new things, to smash through the boundaries that restricted his world, yet guided by his father's spiritual dictates.

Though he loved to read, Carlson felt constricted by the confines of a tiny classroom. The lure of those forests and woods where he could indulge his more primitive tastes, combined with a strong independent streak, pulled him from the textbooks and chalkboards.

After running away from home for three weeks at age twelve, Carlson permanently left in 1910, which some attributed, in part, to a clash with his mother's aristocratic attitudes. His parents stepped aside, realizing they could not prevent their son from departing, even though he was only fourteen years old. When Joetta Carlson told her husband that their son was intent on leaving, he instructed her not to blame herself. "It's no one's fault. Evans is a good boy. But his spirit is restless." The father added, "There won't be peace for him or for us until he breaks away."[3]

After working on a farm and for the Rutland Railroad for two years, in 1912 Carlson joined the United States Army. An Emerson-quoting teenager hardly fit the recruiting poster stereotype for a raw private, but the Army offered Carlson a chance to see the world beyond New England and to experience the adventure that had driven his ancestors. On November 6, 1912, the sixteen-year-old Carlson lied to evade the Army's minimum age regulation of twenty-one and entered as a private.

Within three months Carlson stood in the Philippines, where he helped emplace guns on the island of Corregidor. For three years he labored in various Pacific posts, including Hawaii, showing sufficient talent that he received speedy promotions to sergeant major. When the nation entered the European conflict in April 1917, the Army commissioned Carlson a second lieutenant and assigned him to duty with the Thirteenth Field Artillery Regiment.

Carlson was not your typical officer. In an essay about military ethics, he wrote that officers and men should work for the good of society, not for what benefited them. In a letter to his father, he explained the principles of leadership he tried to follow in commanding his men.

"I love my men but I must keep them working. When the work is over, I must see that they have some recreation. I must always see that they have sufficient food and shelter wherever it is possible. I will lead a man, if he will be led. But I'll get him where he's got to go, even if I have to drive him. I never ask a man to do something I won't do myself. . . . This inspires the confidence of the men. . . . But I must never become too intimate with the men. That is the downfall of many officers. An officer who can mix with his men and show them that he does not feel above them, but still keeps a certain reserve, always holds their respect and loyalty. It is the great secret of leadership and requires a great amount of diplomacy."[4]

The young officer had already formulated some of the guiding tenets that would later appear with the Raiders, as well as exhibited tendencies that distanced him from other officers. In an early efficiency report, his superior officer referred to Carlson's philosophy of managing men as odd, but praised Carlson as a person of character.

He lived up to his reputation. Within a year he had risen to captain in the 334th Regiment, a unit headed overseas. Carlson looked forward to commanding men in battle, but before he reached the front lines the armistice terminated the war.

Carlson resigned from the Army in 1919 to take a job with the California Packing Company, but he never found his niche in the commercial world. He opted to return to service, but when the Army declined to take him back unless he accepted a reduced rank, Carlson turned to the United States Marines. In April 1922, Carlson enlisted as a private in the Marines.

"Well, I'm back—in the service," he wrote to his father. "And believe me, I'm so happy I'm almost moved to tears. Lord, I've fought off the desire to get back into harness but I'd rather be a buck private in the Marines than a Captain [sic] of industry." He added, "My heart is in the service—and here I must stay."[5]

The Marines made things easier for their new enlistee by promoting him to corporal within twenty days. Carlson showed such promise that before the year was out, he proudly wore the trappings of a second lieutenant.

Carlson demanded much of his men and officers, but more from himself. He prodded his officers to treat the men fairly and to live to the highest standards. "Are you honest with yourselves at all times?" he asked. "Do you adhere as rigidly to the code when you are alone as when you are under observation?"[6]

Superiors soon marked Carlson as a man to watch. Brig. Gen. Smedley Butler, a legend in the Marine Corps who commanded Carlson on the West Coast, told a newspaper reporter in answer to the question as to why the Marines were so popular in the nation during the 1920s, "It's because we've [got] a lot of officers like Carlson who take care of the men."[7]

In 1927, the Marines sent Carlson to China, the first of three sojourns in that nation over the next twelve years. He arrived with twelve hundred Marines in February 1927, and quickly became fascinated with Chinese culture and history. The allure would strengthen in later years and help mold his philosophy of command.

Before that, though, three years in Nicaragua exposed Carlson to revolutionary ideas and military tactics. Combined with his later experiences in China, they fashioned the officer who played such a pivotal role in establishing the Marine Raiders.

The Nicaragua Classroom

In May 1930, Carlson landed in Nicaragua as part of the United States' effort to maintain peace and stability in the politically unstable nation. Carlson would train, advise, and lead a native military force called the Guardia Nacional.

Sometimes violent clashes among competing political factions created a volatile situation in the Central American country. The rebel leader Augusto Cesar Sandino, who commanded a powerful militia in northern Nicaragua, led guerrilla attacks against government forces and pillaged towns housing and feeding his opponents. The U.S. government ordered Marines into the areas to protect American interests as well as shore up the Nicaraguan government.

Carlson had to be wary of the men he led. Mutinying Nicaraguan troops had already killed seven Marine officers—mostly in the remote outposts where Carlson would be posted—largely because the officers either treated the Nicaraguans with disdain or refused to understand the native ways. Carlson, however, studied Nicaraguan culture, and he learned to speak Spanish so he could issue orders to the men in their own language and communicate directly to each man without using an interpreter, whose reliability could be in question.

When Carlson arrived at the tiny post at Jalapa in northern Nicaragua to command a group of forty Guardia Nacional, he must have thought he had stepped backward in time to the Army posts that dominated the American frontier in the 1880s. Wooden slabs barricaded the front door to the single building, and rudimentary barriers offered meager protection.

Though isolated, the situation worked to Carlson's advantage by forcing him to rely on his own leadership skills and judgment. Nicaragua thus proved a fertile training ground for Carlson and other young Marine officers. Samuel Griffith, a contemporary of Carlson's who later served with the First Raider Battalion in World War II, said of the South American post, "I was a young officer, I had a lot of responsibility, I had to do things on my own, I had to run my own district, I was my own boss. I think I learned more in the 14 months that I was in Nicaragua—I learned a hell of a lot, about men and animals and the country."[8]

On July 9, 1930, one hundred rebels plundered a village in Carlson's region. Carlson gathered sixteen men, unfazed by the prospects of taking on such a large foe with a diminutive force, and rode out in pursuit.

Early the next morning Carlson spotted the rebel band. He ordered his men to dismount, then led them across a river and through a pasture. At the opportune time Carlson opened fire on the rebels. In a furious ten-minute exchange, Carlson's hardy band killed five rebels and forced the rest to retreat into a forest sanctuary.

For his courage under fire, Carlson earned a Navy Cross and the acclaim of his Nicaraguan soldiers. For the remainder of his tenure in Jalapa, Carlson's steady guidance so kept the violence to a minimum that his superior officer, Gen. Calvin B. Mathews, commended him for keeping his district "singularly free from banditry."[9]

Carlson added to his reputation when he set out alone on a reconnaissance mission against the guerrillas, a twenty-mile ride through rebel-controlled territory near the Honduran border. Carlson traveled to the border and back, shielding a Thompson submachine gun under his serape, knowing that he could at any moment fall into the hands of bloodthirsty opponents. "How's that for guts,"[10] exclaimed an admiring Samuel Griffith of his fellow officer.

Carlson returned to the United States when malignant malaria made it impossible for him to continue his duties, but not before absorbing lessons from the guerrilla warfare in Nicaragua that he would later utilize in the Pacific.

In a 1937 article describing his time in Nicaragua, Carlson focused on five points. The first concerned the proper use of small-unit tactics. Like other Marine officers with service in the country, Carlson recognized the futility of large-unit maneuvers in the wilds of Nicaragua. To fight bands of guerrillas, who favored speedy strikes before disappearing into the countryside, smaller groups of men worked better in the jungles and streams.

"The only successful offensive operations," stated a Guardia officer, "have been by small, very mobile patrols capable of living off the country and of following the bandits wherever they have been able to go."[11]

Combined with the second tactic—concentrate as much firepower on the enemy as quickly as possible—Carlson had the foundations for much of what he advocated later with his Raiders. In the jungles and hills of Nicaragua, success often depended upon establishing superiority in firepower. To achieve this end, most patrols employed a Browning Automatic Rifle (BAR) or Thompson submachine gun, as well as a rifle-grenade launcher. When Carlson encountered the enemy, the men in the front half of his column established a base of fire while the grenade launcher pinned down the rebel forces so they could not escape. In the meantime, the rear half of the column swung to the side to outmaneuver the opposition and attack from the flank.

Adaptation and the use of initiative formed the third lesson. Junior officers like Carlson had to think quickly on their feet, be able to act independently, and trust their judgment. They could not worry that their actions might subsequently be subject to censure; they had to react to the situation at hand and trust that action was preferable to inaction.

Constant movement to achieve surprise constituted another lesson. Carlson preferred mobility and flanking attacks to combat at a fixed position, where he could be pinned down. A speedy, hard-hitting attack demoralized the enemy, who had expected Carlson to wait until being hit before taking action. "You don't stand and slug it out, not in guerrilla warfare anyway,"[12] emphasized Samuel Griffith.

Carlson took his leadership beyond battlefield tactics, though. He believed that his predecessors failed, in part, because of their ignorance about the Nicaraguan people and their culture. "If the leader took an unusual interest in their welfare," Carlson wrote of commanding the Guardia, "and had proved himself to be valiant in battle, his men would follow him with unwavering devotion."[13] From Carlson's perspective, familiarity did not breed contempt; it created unity.

Nicaragua served as Carlson's first military classroom. He only had pieces in place—the rest would be added in China—but his acclaimed 1942 campaign in Guadalcanal would reflect what he learned in Central America.

"He's Something You Don't See Every Day in the Marines"

The 1930s were crucial to Carlson's formation. Besides his time in Nicaragua, he encountered monumental figures in the United States and China who influenced the way he viewed not only the military but society as a whole.

Surprisingly, Carlson developed a friendship with President Franklin D. Roosevelt. Starting in 1935 and lasting until Roosevelt's death ten years later, the two maintained a vast correspondence, which must have been heady stuff for the young Marine.

In 1935, then Captain Carlson received orders posting him to Warm Springs, Georgia, where he served as the second in command of Roosevelt's protective detachment. The president often traveled to the resort, where he believed the heated spring waters benefited his crippled legs.

The affable president took a liking to the introspective Carlson. By early

1936 they had become friendly enough that the president and his wife, Eleanor, invited Carlson and his wife to lunch at Warm Springs. Carlson responded to the humanitarianism of Roosevelt's New Deal policies, and he admired how the president overcame his paralyzing polio to reach the highest office in the land. By the latter half of 1936 an enamored Carlson wrote his parents, "I believe that Roosevelt will prove by virtue of his second administration to be one of the greatest of all our presidents. He has the heart and sympathetic understanding of Lincoln."[14]

Carlson's admiration for Roosevelt deepened the more he was in his presence. Overwhelmed to even be sharing confidences with a man so powerful, Carlson wished to assist him in any way he could. In one of the first letters Carlson sent to the president, addressed to his personal secretary, Missy LeHand, Carlson wrote of his desire to help both the president and his family. "If I can be of any service to the President in any way he can rest assured that I should be happy to do so, and that his confidence will be carefully guarded." He added later, "Incidentally, if I can do anything of a personal nature for the members of his family, or for you, while I am there I hope you will never hesitate to call on me."[15]

Roosevelt accepted his offer in 1937, after Carlson had received orders to China. When Carlson met with Roosevelt on July 15, the president asked Carlson to write him about developments in China, where the Chinese military was engaged in a brutal war with the Japanese. An isolationist Congress constricted Roosevelt's ability to act in foreign matters, but he felt that a reliable pair of eyes in China could relay information he might otherwise not receive from normal diplomatic sources. One way that Roosevelt, the cagy politician, kept a step ahead of opponents was to benefit from diverse streams of information. Carlson could be one of those by quietly sending reports to Roosevelt through Missy LeHand.

"I want you to drop me a line now and then—direct to the White House," Roosevelt told Carlson. "Let me know how you're doing. Tell me what's going on. I suspect there's going to be a great deal going on this summer in China. I'd like to hear what you have to say about it." When Carlson readily agreed, Roosevelt added, "Shall we keep these letters a secret? Just between the two of us? Shall we?"[16]

Years later an officer who served for Carlson wrote, "Carlson was prouder of his relationship with President Roosevelt than of anything else that had ever happened to him."[17] This bond would both help Carlson achieve success with the Raiders and earn the censure of fellow officers.

Volatile political and military strife marked China in the 1930s. Within the country, the Nationalist forces of Chiang Kai-shek had temporarily set aside their squabbles with Mao Tse-tung's Communists to focus on repelling the Japanese. Since 1931, the nations had waged a bitter battle for China, which by 1937 saw the Japanese in control of much of northeast China and most of her important cities and ports, such as Shanghai and Peiping.

Carlson made an immediate impression on fellow Marines and American civilians residing in that nation. He took command of a Marine detachment at Peiping that had amassed an unenviable record of disciplinary actions, and concluded they engaged in frequent drunken brawls because they lacked an understanding for why they were in China. Carlson organized a series of classes to instruct the men in Chinese history and customs and to explain to them why they were posted to the country. A dramatic decline in the number of infractions quickly ensued.

Carlson's desire to learn about China and his natural intellectual curiosity brought him into contact with a collection of writers who traveled the nation. The group conducted weekly meetings, during which the members engaged in lively discussions on philosophy and world politics and debated ways to promote tolerance and justice throughout the world.

Carlson flourished amidst the free exchange of ideas. Edgar Snow, a noted author from the United States who dismissed most military officers as un-educated automatons, told his wife after first meeting Carlson, "He's something you don't see every day in the Marines."[18]

Many in the military would be naturally suspicious of people like Snow, especially when they touted what they claimed were the benefits of Mao Tse-tung's Communists. Carlson's association with the writers' group marked him as a maverick and gained him the distrust of some fellow officers.

Misgivings increased when Carlson studied the Chinese Communists and forged friendships with top leaders. In lengthy discussions, Mao Tse-tung explained to Carlson his military beliefs, which focused on the use of guerrilla warfare to combat the Japanese. A devotee of the influential Chinese military strategist Sun Tzu and his book, *The Art of War*, Mao promoted the employment of speedy strikes by highly maneuverable forces against the points of weakest resistance. Mao's beliefs were summed in the quote

> Enemy advances, we retreat.
> Enemy halts, we harass.

Enemy tires, we attack.

Enemy retreats, we pursue.[19]

Mao also showed Carlson that while the United States was then neutral in regards to the Sino-Japanese conflict, the U.S. government and American industrialists actually aided the Japanese by shipping vast amounts of war supplies to that country. Mao's arguments strongly influenced Carlson, who embarked on an extensive study of the situation.

Chu Teh, one of Mao's top military aides, imparted to Carlson the foundations of his tactics against the militarily superior Japanese. He tried to establish close ties to the Chinese people, he fought behind enemy lines whenever possible, and he employed speed and mobility to avoid a large fixed battle. Carlson later wrote that Chu Teh, who shared the rigors of every campaign with his troops and was "loved by every man in his army," exuded the "kindliness of a Robert E. Lee, the humanity of an Abraham Lincoln, and the tenacity of a U. S. Grant,"[20] qualities Carlson had long admired.

"If a Man Has Only Legs, He Gets Tired"

To help Carlson obtain a deeper understanding about Chinese military operations, Teh arranged for him to accompany the Eighth Route Army, an elite communist force, into the field. There he could observe the fighting, talk with the soldiers, and experience their daily regimen.

Carlson explained his thinking in a Christmas Eve 1937 letter to President Roosevelt. Reading reports at headquarters might suit some military observers, "But I must *see* how these ideas and theories actually work out in practise [sic]. I must see the Partisans at work. I must see the actual work of organizing the civil populace. I must see the army on the march and in action. No knowledge can equal that which is derived from personal observation."[21]

The day after Christmas, carrying a volume of Emerson's *Essays* and guarded by a squad of Chinese soldiers armed with submachine guns, Carlson set out on what became an epic thousand-mile trek with the Eighth Route Army. An interpreter accompanied the officer, who traveled in a caravan of mules bearing medicine and other supplies for the front. Like T. E. Lawrence embarking into the deserts of the Middle East and living among Arab tribes, Carlson disappeared into the wild regions of China for his own sojourn with native forces.

Carlson fired off lengthy, perceptive missives to the White House describing his observations as he traveled with the communist military and emphasizing what made the Eighth Route Army unique. He mentioned that in the Eighth Route Army, a leader became a leader not due to rank, but because he had earned it by performing in combat. Officers shared the same discomforts as their men, wore the same quality of uniform, ate the same food, and slept in the same type of accommodations. Soldiers did not even have to salute officers when off duty.

The intellectual focus, however, most caught Carlson's attention. Officers conducted frequent meetings with their men during which they discussed the reasons for and methods of previous and future operations. Carlson wrote Roosevelt that "this army had developed a style of military tactics quite different from that employed by any other military force in China, and, indeed, new to foreign armies as well." He claimed this was so because "Leaders (officers) take the fighters (enlisted men) into their confidence and constantly explain to them what the situation is, why the army is taking certain action, etc. Before a battle the men are assembled and the military situation is explained to them so that they go into battle with their eyes open. They are told the possibilities of victory, the consequences of defeat. The result is a strong bond of understanding between leaders and fighters."[22]

He added in April 1938 that "the Chinese are constantly studying their mistakes, and improvising methods to offset the Japanese superiority in modernized equipment." He concluded that this introspection among the outnumbered Chinese forces produced a grim determination against the Japanese, a practice that Carlson lamented was not common practice in the United States. "Occasionally in our army individual leaders get close to their men, talk to them about conduct, explain the reasons for military and ethical action, but the practise [sic] is not widespread."[23]

As an example of how the Eighth Route Army's methods succeeded, Carlson pointed to a wearying march up a series of slopes and hills one wintry day. Though difficult, Carlson kept pace with the soldiers, who enjoyed few respites as they advanced. Subsisting on a handful of rice, the unit had just climbed its eighth mountain in the past twenty hours and had traveled fifty-eight miles in thirty-two hours, without one combatant dropping out along the way. When Carlson asked the soldier next to him if he were weary, the man replied, "If a man has only legs he get [sic] tired."[24]

The response gave Carlson pause. The soldier endured the marches and hardships because he understood why he fought. This spirit of ethical indoctrination infused a moral fiber in the army that could not be matched by a rule based on orders.

"It is, I believe, the most self-restrained, self-disciplined army in the world," said Carlson of the Eighth Route Army. "What I have seen is a revelation, an experience that I shall never forget."[25]

Carlson planned to implement many of the ideas should he ever command troops in battle. He confided to a friend, "If I ever have an outfit of my own, I'm going to give them ethical indoctrination. I'm going to show them how they can find the will to sacrifice, and the desire to endure. This is not a Chinese thing but a human thing. This is what makes great soldiers."[26]

Carlson navigated turbulent waters with these remarks. As far as most military and political personnel felt, for an American soldier in the 1930s to praise communist forces bordered on the insane. The communists might not be the current enemy, but they posed a significant future threat to world peace.

Besides ethical indoctrination, Carlson learned that many of the same principles of guerrilla warfare he practiced in Nicaragua also worked in China. Each time he interviewed a Chinese communist commander, one or more of three guiding tenets appeared—obtain the support of the local population, from whom would come not only soldiers but information about the enemy as well as food and shelter; maintain fluidity to avoid a fixed battle against the numerically superior Japanese; and attain unpredictability, mainly by attacking the rear and flanks of the enemy, the weakest portions, where and when they least expect it.

"But the 8th Route Army is like an eel," Carlson wrote the president, "it squirms in and out between the Japanese units. Perhaps it would be better to compare it to a swarm of hornets harassing an elephant; they strike and disappear, cut lines of communication, attack repeatedly during the night so that the opponents cannot sleep. I can well believe the Japanese officer who remarked in his diary, 'The 8th Route Army gives me a headache.'"[27]

At the same time Carlson concluded that the Japanese lacked initiative. He admired their courage in battle, but once senior commanders had formulated a plan, officers blindly executed it, no matter what unexpected developments occurred in the swirl of combat. He informed Roosevelt that "the Japanese continue to fight by rote. . . . They must fight and maneuver according to the model in the book, and cannot adapt themselves to new and unusual situations."[28]

He held no doubts as to the ultimate intentions of those in power in Tokyo. The defeat of China would merely be the initial step in its inexorable march toward world domination. "That thesis is a religion with the Japanese military-naval clique," Carlson wrote Roosevelt in November 1938. "That clique is a mad dog which can only be checked by a military defeat."[29]

"The Heart of a Soldier and Soul of a Saint"

Did Carlson's passionate conclusions influence Roosevelt? It appears that the president at least entertained some of his findings. On March 4, 1938, he discussed one of Carlson's letters with his secretary of the interior, Harold Ickes, who agreed that much of what Carlson stated supported what he had received from his sources. If the president had not heard from Carlson in some time, Roosevelt asked Missy LeHand to find out why. "My Chief loves your letters," she wrote Carlson in December 1937. "Thank you ever so much for taking the trouble to write as you do." Five months later, Roosevelt instructed LeHand to contact the Marine. "Please write him a very nice letter telling him how much we appreciate his letters, etc."[30]

A flattered Carlson returned the compliment. "I am devoted to him not only as our President, but also (and primarily) because of the things he stands for as a man."[31]

The correspondence made Carlson feel more willing to do what he could to help his commander in chief, but the relationship came with a price. Word of the communication leaked to Navy and Marine superiors. They wondered why a junior officer enjoyed such a close relationship with the president and why he left the normal chain of command to send letters directly to Roosevelt rather than to his superior officer.

Other associations harmed Carlson as well. In mid-December 1937, he met Agnes Smedley, an American author who traveled to China to study the communists and saw Carlson as that rare combination of warrior and philosopher. "Carlson is one of those dangerous men of lean and hungry look. He's a throwback from our own distant revolutionary past—a mixture of Tom Paine, John Brown—with a touch of Lincoln. But all of him is New England—craggy and grim in appearance, yet kindly and philosophical."[32]

Since Smedley worked and lived among the communists and wrote of them with compassion, conservative U.S. officials and military personnel stationed in China distrusted her. Carlson's association with her gave critics one more reason to suspect Carlson, who already had raised eyebrows with the flattering reports about the Eighth Route Army that he submitted through proper channels.

Carlson added to the enmity by criticizing his own government for providing vast amounts of steel, oil, and other crucial supplies to the Japanese, which helped sustain that nation's military adventure in China. He claimed that Japanese dreams of Pacific conquest would one day lead to war with the United States, and that aiding them now only put Japan in a stronger position while endangering the United States.

When a Carlson-authored 1938 report on Chinese military operations appeared in an Associated Press story, the Navy reprimanded Carlson. The Japanese government, upset with Carlson's views, applied pressure on the United States government to stifle him. On September 17, 1938, Carlson's superior, Comdr. Harry Overesch, cautioned Carlson that should he again appear in the press, severe repercussions would follow.

Carlson faced a dilemma. He felt compelled to alert the country to what he viewed as alarming developments in the Far East, but as an officer in the Marine Corps, he was duty-bound to obey its dictates. Consequently, on April 30, 1939, he resigned so that he could freely speak and write about subjects as a private citizen.

"I feel very deeply that I can be more useful as a civilian than as an officer," he informed Roosevelt. He stated that he would write a book about his experiences and give speeches to civic groups about the country. "As a civilian I can help to interpret to the American people the significance of events in the Far East. As an officer I cannot do so without embarrassing the government. This sounds altruistic, but I am very sincere about it, and I feel that I must follow the 'inner urge.' "[33] Roosevelt replied that he was sorry Carlson was resigning, but wished him well.

Carlson later wrote in his diary, "I am tired of attempting to adjust my action to the arbitrary whims of a superior officer. Self-preservation seems to be the first thought of an officer of the U.S. Army or Navy. His whole training tends to accentuate that inclination. As a result he inevitably takes the short view of things, considering each problem in terms of his personal economic security. He will take no action which may jeopardize his career."[34]

Part of the problem was that the Marine Corps, in existence since 1775, had little room for a man like Carlson, a reformer who challenged the chain of command. A radical laboring in an autocratic organization, Carlson was doomed before he started. Don Quixotes, he would learn, work better alone.

Two observations illustrate this dichotomy in Carlson. One Chinese official wrote that "Carlson had the tough health of a trapper, the staunch heart of a soldier, and the pure sweet soul of a saint. Add to this a deep love for mankind, freedom and democracy, and a well-tempered sense of humor, and you will have a more or less complete picture of the man."[35]

Agnes Smedley most accurately summed up the man, however. In a letter to a group of fellow authors, Smedley attempted to describe how she would cast a play in which the lead characters would be the individuals with whom she worked in China. The protagonist and the heartthrob would fall to others, for Carlson had his role locked up.

"Then there is Evans—where is he? Long and lanky and lovable, he shall be the man unconsciously reaching for the stars—but never touching them I fear. Yet that striving, alone, makes life worthwhile. He shall be the element of tragedy in my play."[36]

"I Have a Hunch"

Once his resignation took effect, Carlson wasted little time back in the United States trying to convince Americans that the United States had to halt the flow of supplies to the Japanese. He embarked on a nationwide speaking tour from 1939 to 1940, appeared on radio programs, and urged Congress to support an embargo on products to Japan, accusing the Japanese of "sword rattling" in the Far East.

During this interlude in the United States, Carlson organized the material he had gathered in China to produce two 1940 books. Both *Twin Stars of China* and *The Chinese Army* further promoted his views on the Far Eastern situation.

He twice visited Roosevelt at the White House. After his second meeting, a delighted Carlson was convinced that he had Roosevelt's blessing for his speeches and books. He wrote Missy LeHand that "I felt that he approved of what I have been doing, and that was particularly encouraging for I have tried to develop a line of argument in connection with my talks on the Far Eastern situation which I felt would lead to action which he desired, though he could not so commit himself."[37]

This letter exemplifies an attitude that had been slowly emerging in Carlson. He relished being part of the president's coterie, no matter how insignificant a one, and hoped never to disappoint him. Carlson moved in lofty circles for a high school dropout.

Bolstered by the support he received at home, at his own expense Carlson returned to China in the autumn of 1940. He traveled four thousand miles visiting Chinese factories and talking to top Chinese officials. A military observer, Marine Lt. Col. David D. Barrett, on station in the office of the military attaché in China, wrote his superiors that communist officials had met with Carlson, "formerly a major in the United States Marine Corps, whom they consider their staunch friend."[38] The more deeply Carlson became embroiled in China affairs, the more likely he was to be labeled a communist by other Marine officers.

During this visit Carlson interpreted statements from Japanese prisoners of war as meaning that the Japanese would strike U.S. Pacific holdings somewhere in 1941. He decided that he could no longer remain in China when he was needed somewhere else.

"I cut short my trip because of a hunch," he wrote home. "I feel that events in the international field are moving rapidly towards a point where it will be necessary for America to participate actively in the war. With such a prospect it behooves me to return before the break comes so that I may place my information before the authorities. I must also be in a position to offer my services for active duty."[39]

On his return trip in January, Carlson visited Douglas MacArthur in Manila; MacArthur was then a military adviser to the Filipino government. Carlson warned the noted military commander that the Japanese would attack the Philippines sometime that year, and urged that MacArthur establish a base in the mountains near Manila and train his forces to wage a guerrilla campaign against the invaders. MacArthur politely listened as a former major attempted to tell him how to run his department, then ignored every word.

With events rapidly spiraling out of control in the Pacific, Carlson reapplied for a commission in the Marines, a move that outraged fellow officers. He had already left the Corps once—a traitorous act to some—and he returned tainted by communist poison. How, they wondered, could he be an asset to the Marines?

Lt. Col. Merritt A. Edson, commander of the First Battalion, Fifth Marines, raised the most strenuous objections. Like Carlson, Edson had served in Nicaragua and studied guerrilla operations, but he detested Carlson's association with the Chinese communist military forces. Edson, a blunt, brilliant officer, had little use for what he saw as Carlson's idealist, simplistic views of society. The Marines needed energetic, vibrant commanders, not philosophers.

Despite the opposition, in April 1941 Carlson rejoined the Marines as a major. As the Marines geared up for a possible war, Carlson's talents outweighed his controversial statements.

Carlson was again with the Marines, this time fortified by a guiding philosophy that he hoped to implement. Fashioned by a New England childhood and influenced by events in Nicaragua and China, Carlson now needed a vehicle with which he could test his theories. He soon found it in an amazing group of young Marines. Carlson's Raiders were about to take the stage.

2

Specially Trained Troops of the Hunter Class

The day started peacefully for Maj. Evans Carlson that December 7, 1941. He drove to Camp Elliott from his La Jolla, California, home to check on routine matters, but the staff duty officer told him that all was in order. Assured that this Sunday, December 7, would wind up like all other uneventful Sundays in San Diego, Carlson hopped back into his car to return home.

As he drove up to the camp gates, a sentry in crisp uniform announced, "All leaves canceled, sir. The Japs attacked Pearl Harbor."[1] Carlson turned the automobile around and headed back to his offices. War, it seemed, was upon him.

In an office on the other side of the country, like thousands of sons around the United States, James Roosevelt listened with his father to the stunning developments unfolding at Pearl Harbor. A train of assistants rushed in with the latest bulletins, and James noticed that his parent, normally a vibrant core of energy, appeared more exhausted than he could ever remember.

The next day James accompanied his father to a nearby building where his father was to deliver a speech. The opening words not only riveted the young man's attention but quickly reverberated about the nation. "Yesterday, December 7, 1941—a date which will live in infamy—the United States of America was suddenly and deliberately attacked by naval and air forces of the Empire of Japan."

With those words President Franklin Delano Roosevelt asked for war, a war that affected not only his son James, who stood behind him, but millions of men and women across the land. Some, like the studious, professorial Richard Washburn of Connecticut; Jack Miller from Texas, the dashing athlete who broke every female's heart; and Chicago's Victor Maghakian, the second-generation Albanian-American whose courage gained admirers everywhere, would join James Roosevelt, the president's son, in the same unit. The outfit, the Second Marine Raider Battalion of Evans Carlson, would gain fame and notoriety.

December 7, 1941, provided the catalyst that propelled Carlson and his Raiders to success—as Marines and as individuals.

"A Dash of Elizabethan Pirate"

With the ashes of Pearl Harbor still smoldering and with many in the nation worried about a possible Japanese assault against the West Coast, the president held a late-December meeting in Washington with his secretary of the Navy, Frank Knox, and with British prime minister Winston Churchill. Among the items on the agenda was a memo written by Col. William J. Donovan, the head of the fledgling intelligence organization the Office of the Coordinator of Information, recommending the formation of an independent guerrilla-style unit, free from the Army and Navy, which could harass the Japanese.

Roosevelt loved the idea of a special forces unit that could swiftly sneak into enemy-controlled territory, take out a target, and then as quickly disappear. With much of his Navy resting on Pearl Harbor's bottom, and with the other military forces needing time to organize, it at least handed him the option to strike back at an enemy that held the upper hand. In the war's opening month Roosevelt, and the American public with him, watched helplessly as Japan devoured other nations' Pacific possessions. Guam and Wake Island had fallen; Singapore, the Dutch East Indies, Hong Kong, and the Philippines appeared doomed. In a few short weeks the United States had gone from scorning Oriental nations like Japan to absorbing a string of crushing defeats at the hands of that Oriental nation.

Worse still, especially for people on the home front, was that their military remained silent. The ominous feeling spread that the United States, at least for the moment, stood helpless to respond. "You got the impression that whatever the inventory of damage, the United States wasn't going to hit back because the United States couldn't hit back,"[2] wrote the veteran news correspondent Robert J. Casey of the weeks after Pearl Harbor.

Roosevelt could do little for the time being, especially in the Pacific. He had to wait for the nation's factories and shipyards to produce a stream of aircraft, guns, tanks, and ships before mounting a major campaign, and he had to divert most of his attention and his meager military resources to Europe and the task of defeating Adolf Hitler. Still, he and the American people longed for something to soothe their shattered morale, and President Roosevelt wanted the Japanese to realize that while they may have shorn the country's main weapons at Pearl Harbor, the United States still possessed the capability to retaliate.

Maybe a group of commandos could step in and deliver such a punch. He just needed to find the right man and the right unit.

The idea for a commando force was certainly not new to history. The word "commando" had first been used by the British to describe guerrilla units fighting during the Boer War in South Africa in the late nineteenth and early twentieth centuries.

Forerunners to Carlson's Raiders in U.S. history appeared during the Seven Years' War, when in the 1750s that same Robert Rogers a young Carlson admired guided his Rangers into combat against the French and their Native American allies in that decisive conflict. Rogers instilled in his frontiersmen an offensive spirit, the employment of surprise, and speed and mobility—all trademarks of what would become Carlson's Raiders. Continental Marines also conducted an amphibious raid in March 1776 during the American Revolution against British installations at New Providence, Bahamas.

In May 1940, the Germans had executed an audacious strike against the seemingly impregnable Belgian bastion Fort Eben-Emael, sitting atop a promontory above the Albert Canal. Reinforced bunkers cradled mammoth guns inside the fort. A rocky cliff protected one side while dense minefields and miles of barbed wire shielded the others.

Despite the hazards, gliders deposited a group of elite German soldiers directly on the fort, and after a quick battle, the Germans grabbed Fort Eben-

Emael. The soldiers, all volunteers and considered among the best the Army could offer, received specialized training for the daring mission.

With the heady success of the Germans at Fort Eben-Emael and throughout Europe, Winston Churchill asked his chiefs of staff a question: "If it is so easy for the Germans to invade us . . . why should it be . . . impossible for us to do anything of the same kind to him?"[3]

In response, Lt. Col. Dudley Clarke, a staff officer at the War Office, assembled notes about mounting similar missions. He studied past campaigns, such as the Spanish hit-and-run raids against the French in 1808–14 and what the Boers had done to halt the British.

An elated Churchill relayed Clarke's memo to the War Cabinet. "Enterprises must be prepared with specially trained troops of the hunter class who can develop a reign of terror down the enemy coast," he wrote with typical Churchillian flair. He added that he wanted "a ceaseless offensive against the whole German-occupied coastline, leaving a trail of German corpses behind."[4]

Clarke received orders to organize and train a group of commandos to carry out Churchill's desire. Clarke culled top soldiers from existing units—a move that angered many commanders—and warned them that they would endure harsher training than regular forces, would be expected to do more, and would learn to subsist with less food and fight with less sleep than regular soldiers. Clarke told associates he wanted men with "a dash of Elizabethan pirate, the Chicago gangster and the frontier tribesman, allied to a professional efficiency and standard of discipline of the best regular soldier."[5]

In June, Clarke led his commandos in their first raid, a series of four landings along the French coast. Though the mission accomplished little and proved that the men required further training, British citizens rejoiced over the event.

The Marines had studied the concept of an amphibious, raider-type force throughout the 1930s, but considered such a unit one segment of a regular Marine division rather than as a separate unit. An amphibious role became one of the missions handed to the Fleet Marine Force upon its establishment in December 1933. Two years later a landing manual included a section on raider-type forces, and in subsequent exercises Marines debarked from high-speed transports and destroyers and headed ashore in rubber boats. In more recent years a provisional rubber boat company had been included in the Navy's fleet exercises, massive mock training battles in which the Navy tested its European and Pacific strategy and tactics.

"Painfully Anxious . . . to Win His Approval"

Just as the impetus for a special raider force gathered, Carlson reunited with a man he had first met during his time with the presidential guard detail at Warm Springs. James Roosevelt, the president's oldest son, admired Carlson and joined the Marines, in part, because of his association with Carlson. Carlson was everything Roosevelt hoped to be—an adventurer, world traveler, intellectual, athlete, and ardent supporter of an idea that fueled many in the Roosevelt clan: that each person had dignity and value.

He enjoyed a lifestyle the others could never conceive. James Roosevelt's father was, after all, the president, but the two shared the same issues and emotions faced by every father and son in the country. They loved and fought, played and worked, cried and laughed.

In the end, the issue came to a son yearning to gain the respect of his father. In his autobiography, *Affectionately, F.D.R.*, James does not begin by declaring his pride in Franklin Roosevelt's many feats, but by stating how much he missed his father and how, while Franklin was loving and caring, he was often an absentee father.

"To me, he was great—a wonderful father, the most loyal and understanding parent a son or daughter could want." Then, in almost the next breath, the pain is evident. "Sometimes in looking back, it seems as if there were periods when I had no father at all." James stated that his father was a deeply caring man, but "detached and overpowering. Sometimes we felt we didn't have him at all." That, in turn, led to a desire to please the father and to make him proud. "He gave us love; in our own headstrong, often rebellious, thoughtless ways, every one of us adored him. We *wanted* [italics Roosevelt's] his love and respect . . ."[6]

Though blessed with fame, fortune, and a family name that already included two presidents, James battled early maladies. Pneumonia and a heart murmur so weakened the youth that his father carried him up and down the steps, and because of a nervous condition, James had to lie flat on the floor for a certain period each day.

James consequently feared disappointing Franklin and losing his father's trust. He struggled to match the high standard for the Roosevelt males set by Franklin and his presidential predecessor, Theodore. His undistinguished school record caused Eleanor Roosevelt to write of her ten-year-old son's record at St. Albans School in Washington, D.C., "James stands 13th in a class of 19 with a dreadful mark in arithmetic. . . . I think James is much ashamed but it is all his careless way of working & liking to have a good time so much that he neglects his work."[7]

James carried that mediocrity to Groton, a Massachusetts school for boys founded by the Rev. Endicott Peabody that Franklin had attended. James, who unlike his father failed his initial attempt at the school's entrance exam, amassed a forgettable record.

The split between James's desires and his father's expectations became evident in the choice of a university. James hoped to attend Williams College, but Franklin, a Harvard graduate, wanted his son to attend his alma mater.

"At this point, perceiving how obvious it was that Father really had his heart set on having his oldest son follow in his footsteps at the old college," James wrote, "I gave in and said I would go to Harvard." He added that he did so because "I loved Pa deeply and was almost painfully anxious to please him and win his approval in all respects."

James continued the pattern at Harvard, where he joined many of the same clubs his father had and took part in similar activities. "At Harvard," he explained, "I tried to do too many of the things which he [Franklin] did, and, consequently, was not my own man."

Later, when Franklin urged James to enter law school, "I tried once more to go along with what he wanted."[8] He lasted only a year at Boston University's Law School, after which he left to enter the business world.

James longed to please his father, yet chafed at the restrictions imposed by being Franklin's son. He searched for that perfect solution, one that would bring self-satisfaction while gaining his father's approval.

Ironically, an illness both threatened James's world and drew him more into that of his father's. In August 1921, with Franklin Roosevelt at the beginning of a promising political career, polio struck. For days the man who attacked every activity with vigor lay helpless as physicians attempted to determine a remedy.

The sight of his robust father in bed, unable to fend for himself, unnerved the thirteen-year-old James. "I shall never forget that day—September 13, 1921—when four men from the island came to the house with a homemade stretcher to carry Father down to the dock to start the trip back to New York," he later related. "We kids watched it solemnly, and that day, though I was going on fourteen, I was as young and scared as little Johnny."

Franklin tried to ease his children's fears with a cheerful smile and hearty remarks, but Jimmy could not be comforted. The father he relied upon now had to rely on others for the simple acts of sitting up in bed or donning a pair of pants. To avoid crying, James bit his lip so hard that it hurt.

Because of that illness, the teenage boy had to grow up without the companionship of his father, who was busy searching for a cure or reconstructing a political career. "These were the lonely years; for a long while during this time of illness and recovery we had no tangible father, no father-in-being, whom we could touch and talk to at will—only an abstract symbol, a cheery letter writer, off somewhere on a houseboat or at Warm Springs, fighting by himself to do what had to be done." He added, "Only now do I realize how sorely we missed him during that period."[9]

As his father's outlook improved, James enjoyed a new role with Franklin. As oldest son, he assisted his father with some of the things he could no longer do himself.

The apex occurred when he helped walk Franklin to the podium at the 1924 Democratic National Convention at Madison Square Garden in New York City. Roosevelt was to nominate New York governor Al Smith as the party's candidate, but the speech held added significance for Franklin, as this marked his first major appearance since polio struck. The audience, packed with powerful political figures, would be scrutinizing Franklin to see if he could endure the rigors of addressing such a vast crowd.

"I was Father's page and 'prop' at that convention," James wrote proudly years later of the event. "I was sixteen, tall and strong, and I was excited and elated beyond description when Father one day asked me: 'Jimmy, would you care to come along and lend me your arm?'"

His father, wearing the cumbersome steel braces that had become as much a part of him as his shoes, could walk a few steps, "painfully and awkwardly," with a crutch under one arm and grasping James's hand with his left hand. "I had learned to match my stride to his slow movements and had taught myself not to look anxious but to smile just as he did when he forced himself forward."

Slowly, in measured paces, father and son shuffled onstage. A few feet from the podium Franklin let go of James's arm, grasped a second crutch, and completed the final few steps to a thundering ovation from an appreciative audience.

Perspiration covered James's face, both from assisting his father and from the emotions of such a moving scene. "At that moment, I was so damned proud of him that it was with difficulty that I kept myself from bursting into tears."[10]

"Jimmy! What a Problem He Is"

Franklin used the momentum from that stirring speech as a launching pad to the White House. It was a time when, as James described, "we did lose a good part of that personal Pa of ours" and "when we had to begin sharing him with the world."[11]

James hoped to make his mark in the insurance world. Franklin warned his son that people would try to use the Roosevelt name for their own purposes and would seek opportunities to take advantage of him, but the words missed their mark. James became the subject of vicious attacks, made simpler for his accusers by his lack of business acumen and a sense of naïveté. His actions so frustrated his father that once, after learning from a government official that James had tried to influence him in favor of a client, Roosevelt broke down in tears. "Jimmy! What a problem he is,"[12] said a disconsolate father.

The Saturday Evening Post, then one of the nation's leading magazines, focused more attention on James when, on July 2, 1938, it ran a story about James's dealings. Titled "Jimmy's Got It," the article stated that, largely based on his connections with government, the president's son amassed large sums of money from insurance sales.

"Jimmy is a specialist in everything—life, fire, marine, air and group insurance. He mastered it all in practically no time," the writer Alva Johnston reported. "The insurance fraternity is as startled by this young meteor as the medical fraternity would be if a youngster who had never attended a medical school suddenly turned out to be America's greatest specialist in the eye, ear, nose and throat, in abdominal and pulmonary surgery, in obstetrics, pediatrics and chiropody."

Johnston stated that many of James's sales were to companies with preexisting connections with the federal government. "Some corporations which have given Jimmy insurance have been lucky [in renewing or winning government contracts]; some corporations which have denied him insurance have been unlucky."[13]

Other publications added their criticisms. The *St. Louis Post-Dispatch's*

July 1 editorial handed out free advice on how to get ahead. "To make a sure-fire success in the insurance business, and thereby gain a competence on which to enter public life and serve your fellow men, get your father elected President of the United States."[14]

From his bed at the Mayo Clinic, where he had gone for surgery to correct severe stomach problems, James fired back with a rebuttal that was printed in *Collier's* magazine. "Sure, I got into places I never would have if I wasn't the son of the President. . . . But, son or no son, I got tossed out a lot too." He said that "prospects don't wilt just because you're the son of the President. Try it sometime," and added, "Tell me if I'm screwy for having the idea that, being the President's son, they'd have called me a crook no matter what business I'd entered."[15]

Try as hard as he might to create his own identity, James was viewed by people through the filter of Franklin Roosevelt. Being the president's son carried many benefits, but it also brought its perils.

In November 1936, President Roosevelt asked James to accompany him on a trip to Argentina as personal aide. The president felt that a commission as a Marine lieutenant colonel was appropriate for James's duties and, although he was uncomfortable with the sudden jump to the military hierarchy, James accepted.

Detractors mocked James's sudden military prominence. Even Eleanor Roosevelt doubted the wisdom of such a move and facetiously asked her husband if James was a second lieutenant or a lieutenant colonel.

"He wore a very beautiful white uniform" during that trip, said James's widow, Mary Roosevelt, in 2007, "and his father joked that he sat him in the front seat so he would get shot before he did. I think when James came back from there, he was a little embarrassed by the fact that this had been given to him, because after all, these were Armed Services."[16]

The insults mounted in early 1938 when, after the death of his closest confidant and political adviser, Louis Howe, Roosevelt asked his son to work as his administrative assistant. James loved serving his father for the almost two years he labored in the White House, but it left him vulnerable to more caustic remarks in the press.

Still, the opportunity gave him the chance to work with his father, whom he hoped not to disappoint. On Christmas 1937, James wrote his father that "I often fear so greatly of doing something big or small which will bring some hurt to you, and I pray so hard that somehow it may never happen."[17]

Although he performed capably, the appointment brought more abuse.

The press labeled James the "Crown Prince" and the "Assistant President," and *Time* magazine received venomous letters when it placed James on its February 28, 1938, cover. James claimed that he was "like one of those heads in county fairs that people throw baseballs at whenever they pop up." Franklin moaned to aide James Rowe that "One of the worst things in the world is being the child of a president! It's a terrible life they lead!"[18]

Illness ended James's tenure in the White House. In September 1938, James entered the Mayo Clinic, where physicians inserted a series of rubber tubes through his stomach to repair bleeding ulcers. Physicians told James the pressures of working in the White House increased the severity of his stomach problems and recommended that he resign.

James resented the ridicule that turned his jobs into sideshows. It only fueled his determination to succeed and prove his critics wrong. He found it with the Marines.

"I Felt I Had to Fight"

Still a lieutenant colonel in the Marine Reserve, James performed various duties at different posts, including the testing of antiaircraft batteries, but the high rank bothered him. In October 1939, he resigned his commission, then rejoined the next month as a captain. He participated in the same programs as every reserve officer to learn the nuances of his rank. "I did join an artillery reserve battalion. I was a company commander in the reserves of battalion," James explained in 1979. "We did train, and I really did know my job pretty well by the time we were called to active duty in 1940."[19]

As was true with everyone else in the nation, the events of December 7 affected James. Finally, in the early morning hours of December 8, after the frantic first hours of war had abated and the president could finally catch a few hours of sleep, James helped his father into bed.

Before leaving he told his father that he wanted a combat assignment. "I felt I had to fight," he later wrote of the discussion. "I was being no braver than millions of other Americans at the time. We were swept up in a surge of patriotism such as we in this country may never know again. Although I did not say it to him, I felt that as the son of the president I had to seek combat. I'd had only the slightest taste of it. I did not yet know what it was to feel fear."[20]

Franklin interjected a few lackluster reasons opposing the move, but knew his son was right. On the eve of his asking Congress to declare war and send millions of other boys into battle, how could he object to his own son's request?

Eleanor Roosevelt assented, even though she dreaded the possible outcome. Her other three sons had also requested service, and it was likely that at least one of the four would be killed or maimed.

James headed to war. When Carlson asked him to be the executive officer for his new Raider Battalion, James readily agreed. He could think of nothing better than to work for his father's old friend.

"James joined because he felt a sense of duty, which he certainly inherited from his parents, and because he wanted to see Carlson's philosophy utilized," explained James's widow, Mary Roosevelt, in 2007. "He wanted to be a Carlson Raider. All four of the Roosevelt sons wanted to be in active service. I do not think any of them thought it was right that young men should be going into war while they were having cushy jobs at home. Technically, James was not fit to serve. He had been very ill."

Mary Roosevelt then added that another reason existed. "He also felt, absolutely, that he wanted to live up to his parents' high standards."[21]

In the war's opening months, as the Japanese pounded their way to victory after victory over outmatched U.S. forces, Carlson, with Roosevelt's assistance, assembled a unit that provided one of the nation's first responses to Japan, boosted home-front morale, and helped begin the long, arduous march to victory that ended in Tokyo Bay almost four years later.

"I Felt You Had the Key"

In the dark days after Pearl Harbor, Carlson and Roosevelt teamed up to promote Carlson's idea of a guerrilla-style unit that could swiftly carry out unconventional missions. Carlson had the expertise, and Roosevelt the powerful connections that in the convoluted ways of Washington could push an idea from conception through to completion. He provided the political muscle not only to complement Carlson's military theories and experiences but to override the opposition in military circles Carlson's unorthodox ideas were certain to create. The men formed a potent duo that, throughout much of 1942, oversaw the creation of their Raider Battalion and led them to some of the most thrilling military missions in the early stages of the Pacific War.

Roosevelt later wrote that he wanted to help Carlson sell his theories because he was convinced of their validity. He explained that the officer had "developed an idea for a special kind of outfit that would be trained to make swift, surprise attacks on these islands in order to weaken their defenses before our massed might moved in,"[22] and that he wanted to be a part of it.

James put Carlson's notions into written form, which he submitted to influential people. His name on the memo guaranteed it would be given consideration by the highest level of command. On January 13, 1942, he authored a memo to the Major General Commandant of the Marine Corps, Thomas Holcomb (his title would soon be shortened to Commandant), a personal favorite of President Roosevelt.

Titled "Development Within the Marine Corps of a Unit for Purposes Similar to the British Commandos and the Chinese Guerrillas," James Roosevelt's memo promulgated every idea Carlson had absorbed from the Chinese. Roosevelt urged the formation of an American commando unit, but unlike ordinary military organizations, one that had "a closer relationship between leaders and fighters than is customary in orthodox military organizations."

Roosevelt stated that the battalion-sized unit would not have typical ranks, such as captains or lieutenants, but would feature "leaders" and "fighters," much as the Eighth Route Army had employed. He wrote, "Leaders must be men of recognized ability who lead by virtue of merit and who share without reservation all material conditions to which the group may be subjected, arrogating to themselves no privileges or perquisites."

Roosevelt added, "Discipline should be based on reason and designed to create and foster individual volition," and that all men should be ready to "subordinate self to harmonious team-work,"[23] and be able to hike thirty to fifty miles in twenty-four hours.

The die had been cast. Roosevelt's memo placed the idea for a separate commando unit front and center. With the approval of his father already a given, Roosevelt and Carlson assumed they possessed enough ammunition to weather even the strongest objections. They failed to realize how intense that opposition would be.

The advocacy by Carlson and James Roosevelt of a separate Raider unit, even though it had the support of James's father, encountered antagonism within the Marine Corps from officers who either wanted to command their own version of a commando force or objected to the existence of such a unit.

Carlson, though, held the trump card—President Roosevelt wanted a commando unit, thus one would exist.

The only question was who would command the elite unit. Carlson stood as a prime contender, but other proponents believed they were better qualified than a man who learned much of his military doctrine from the Chinese communists. Two rose above the rest—Merritt Edson and William J. Donovan.

Edson brought impeccable credentials to the table. One military correspondent called Edson "the bravest, the most effective killing machine I met in fifteen years as a war correspondent."[24] Every Marine knew of Edson's skill with a rifle and of his gallant command during the famous 1928–29 Coco Patrol in Nicaragua's wilderness.

Edson wound up being the East Coast counterpart to Carlson and Roosevelt, but with his own variation. Edson intended to construct a battalion that could be used both as a raiding force as well as part of a conventional Marine division. His would not be purely a special forces operation, such as Carlson envisioned, but one capable of taking its place within the normal command setup. Edson, the poster-perfect Marine officer, detested Carlson's unorthodox views and considered the man at best a leftist-leaning "intellectual" who could not be trusted, and at worst an outright communist.

Carlson's other major rival in forming a commando unit inhabited a murkier world. William J. Donovan, the man for whom James Roosevelt had recently worked at the Office of the Coordinator of Information (which morphed into the Office of Strategic Services, which in turn became the Central Intelligence Agency), promoted units that penetrated enemy territory, then rather than quickly pull out remained to aid local guerrilla forces combat the enemy. Donovan alarmed top Marine commanders, however, by urging that his unit be independent of both the Army and the Navy, thereby placing it outside the Marines' realm.

Major General Holcomb felt assaulted on all sides. He not only had to contend with Donovan but with Carlson and his ally, James Roosevelt, who certainly had the ear of the president. If President Roosevelt sided with Donovan, Holcomb could lose control over a portion of his forces. If the president agreed with Carlson, might it fuel a drive to transform the entire Marine Corps into a commando-style outfit? Commandos needed neither artillery nor aviation, both of which the Marine Corps currently possessed, but as commando units without such assets, Holcomb feared the Army would eventually absorb the Corps.

This was precisely what Holcomb needed least. The Japanese had tossed Washington into a frenzy of activity, with each branch of the military seeking men and machines and weapons. Not only did Holcomb have to worry about obtaining material for his Marines, but he had to ensure the Corps had a mission after the war ended.

Though Holcomb could see the handwriting on the wall, he detected an opening. Since Donovan seemed to be focused primarily on the European area of operations, and since Roosevelt wanted a commando unit, Holcomb would give him one—in the Pacific, where the Navy and Marines played the dominant role and he could more readily retain control over the commandos. Let Donovan have Europe; Holcomb would take the Pacific. Adm. Ernest J. King, Commander in Chief, U.S. Fleet, agreed with Holcomb, and issued a January 23 order to Nimitz to develop two commando-style units capable of carrying out raids against Japanese-held islands.

Holcomb gave Edson command of the battalion forming out east. Carlson, then on the West Coast, became the likely selection in San Diego. In light of President Roosevelt's advocacy of a commando unit, Holcomb put in charge the two men who had been most ardent in promoting such a unit—Evans Carlson, with whom President Roosevelt had a close association, and the president's son, James. Not only would the battalion benefit from such personal proximity to the center of governmental power, but should the battalion not perform as expected, blame would be cast on Carlson and James Roosevelt, not on Holcomb.

On February 16, Holcomb redesignated Edson's East Coast outfit the First Marine Raider Battalion and Carlson's new unit the Second Marine Raider Battalion. Holcomb handed Edson and Carlson three responsibilities—their battalions were to spearhead amphibious landings, conduct raids that relied on speed and surprise, and coordinate guerrilla operations behind Japanese lines. President Roosevelt finally had his commandos.

In a secret personal message to Roosevelt, an ecstatic Churchill wrote, "The enemy are becoming ever more widely spread and we know this is causing anxiety in Tokyo. Nothing can be done on a large scale except by long preparation of the technical and tactical apparatus. When you told me about your intention to form commando forces on a large scale on the California shore I felt that you had the key. Once several good outfits are prepared, any one can attack a Japanese-held base or island and beat the life out of the garrison, all their islands will become hostages to fortune. Even this year,

1942, some severe examples might be made causing perturbation and draw-ing further upon Japanese resources to strengthen other points."[25]

"Some Guy Was Organizing a Hot-Shot Group"

On the other side of the world the small force of Japanese military must have been a disappointed lot. While fellow airmen executed the spectacular feat at Pearl Harbor and smashed Allied installations at Wake, Guam, the Philip-pines, and elsewhere, they had been sent to occupy a sleepy, nondescript is-land hugging the equator in the middle of the Pacific. Glory would not be theirs this December 10 morning, as only a handful of native Gilbertese watched them pull into Butaritari, the island in the Makin Atoll where they intended to establish a seaplane base. They took small comfort in knowing that however minuscule their post was at this early stage, it stood as the Japanese empire's easternmost station.

They doubted that they would ever see action during the war. Pearl Harbor had sent America reeling, and with a little good fortune, Japan would shortly force the United States to the peace table. While comrades returned to adu-lation, they could claim to have done nothing but languish in one of the war's nether regions.

A Marine officer back in the United States would change that. The foe would come to Butaritari, not in the form of a massive seaborne assault but in one of those audacious raids that stir men's hearts. Carlson's Raiders were on their way.

Disappointment to a handful of Japanese was opportunity to Evans Carl-son. Desperately seeking a military answer to the Japanese, whose triumphant army and navy spread across the Pacific and Far East in a destructive tidal wave, the president and Marine commandant handed him a dictate—forge a unit of men who could rush to the Pacific and mount an offensive strike against the Japanese.

Carlson's men would be the tip of an American sword aimed straight at Tokyo. After years of observation and thought, Carlson was about to put his vision to the test.

"At last I have received a break," the excited officer wrote his father.

"Today I was placed in command of a special unit with cart blanche to organize, train and indoctrinate it as I see fit. There is nothing like it in existence in the country. Naturally, I'm delighted. I will hand pick my personnel. Jimmy Roosevelt is to be my executive officer. . . .

"Things seem to be moving in a direction I have so long urged and had almost despaired of seeing materialize. But now I have been afforded the opportunity to practice some of the precepts I have been preaching these past years."[26]

The label "special forces" conveys a certain inaccurate image to some people. According to this notion special forces personnel are somehow different from the rest of society, men with slashed faces and crazed eyes, barbarians in modern garb waiting for a reason to revert to style.

While a handful may fit that profile, they represent a fraction of those who served with special forces units. The vast majority approximate the individual who, in his later years, is the man next door mowing his yard, walking his dog, hugging his grandchildren, or reading his newspaper.

Carlson's Raiders fit that mold; he made certain through a careful screening process. Fierce battlers they were, but like most veterans, they fought not because they were kindred spirits with seventeenth-century pirates. They fought that way because they had a job to do.

Duty summoned. The only question was whether they had what it took to answer the call, a call that went to rich and poor, educated and illiterate alike.

Men with spirit, a sense of adventure, able to improvise and think outside the box, accustomed to the outdoors—those were the men Carlson sought. He "wanted guys with different attitudes"[27] from those of the usual conscript, stated Pfc. Ray Bauml, men who could serve in a unique battalion run by an unorthodox officer who certainly did not fit the usual image of a Marine commander.

Carlson explained his ideas in a memo to one of his superiors. He stated that to fulfill its threefold mission, a Raider unit must "be flexible, mobile, possess the maximum fire power commensurate with great mobility and be composed of men physically capable and mentally conditioned to endure the hardships and overcome the obstacles necessary to accomplish the mission.

It follows, therefore, that the personnel must be volunteers for this type of work and that they must be trained, conditioned and indoctrinated for this particular type of work."[28]

In a subsequent letter he explained of the Raiders, "Their specialty is offensive operations which require top physical condition, fortitude, daring, initiative, resourcefulness, wile, a sound working knowledge of woodcraft including the ability to sustain themselves in the jungle for protracted periods, and mastery of the mechanics and technique of the means by which to place themselves in positions to surprise the enemy in amphibious operations."[29]

Word quickly spread throughout Marine bases near San Diego of an oddball officer seeking volunteers for a new unit, one shrouded in secrecy but offering a chance at early action against the Japanese.

"After a few weeks the word got out that some guy in San Diego was organizing a hot shot group," said Second Lt. Joseph Griffith. "They were looking for men, so five of us got in my car and drove down to volunteer."[30]

Carlson harshly separated the wheat from the chaff during the interview process. He had his share from outdoor states, as the San Diego recruiting station drew from locales west of the Mississippi, but Chicago's Victor Maghakian and other easterners snuck in. The Raiders came from large cities, like Dick Washburn's West Haven, Connecticut, and Joe Griffith and Jack Miller from Dallas, but also tiny habitats like Kenny McCullough's Findley, Oklahoma, Darrell Loveland's Greenview, Utah, and Ben Carson's Laseur, Minnesota. They even siphoned a Raider from a Ho Chunk enclave in Jackson County, Wisconsin, when Mitchell Red Cloud volunteered. The Native American boasted ancestry from a French nobleman and a Ho Chunk princess.

"The Raiders didn't empty the brigs of San Diego," stated Sgt. Ken McCullough of the young volunteers. "These guys were as average as you can get, not rebels or anything. They only took a very small percentage of the men who volunteered, so they weeded out the troublemakers. The Raiders were as calm a bunch of people as you would ever want to know."[31]

While Pfc. Ervin Kaplan spent hours among the bookcases of his town's library and later headed to university to study medicine, and Lt. Joseph Griffith graduated from the University of Texas, Pvt. Darrell Loveland and Sergeant McCullough dropped out of high school. Seventeen-year-old Pfc. Ken "Mudhole" Merrill had to promise his father he would finish high school after the war to gain his assent for enlisting in the Marines.

The Raiders featured men as diverse as Lt. Jack Miller, whose family later catapulted to the top reaches of Dallas's real estate industry, while Loveland had joined President Roosevelt's Civilian Construction Corps, a New Deal program to battle poverty and unemployment during the Great Depression. The Raiders were as polar as Jimmy Roosevelt and Mitchell Red Cloud, a Raider from the nation's first family and another from the nation's original inhabitants.

They included a Brooklyn, New York, orphan, Cpl. Daniel Gaston, and a fresh-faced Pvt. Franklin M. Nodland, a skinny teenager who quaffed bottles of milk so he would meet the Marine minimum weight requirement. Their ranks contained one man whose ancestry included British knights and another who, anxious to leave the country to avoid the Army military police, who sought him as a deserter, joined under a false name.

Nineteen-year-old Pvt. Silvio Costa from the Bronx, who barely weighed more than one hundred pounds, had uncles and cousins in Italy serving in Benito Mussolini's armies. He wanted to prove that the Costas were as American as any family. Pvt. William McCall, who had spent many years as a youth in the Philippines with his parents, only sought one goal—to battle his way back to those islands and free his parents, who had been incarcerated at Santo Tomas camp by the invading Japanese.

The men volunteered for Carlson's Raiders for glamour, excitement, the chance to head overseas and get the war over with, and to avoid more unpleasant tasks.

"I was doing guard duty, what I hated the most," explained Pvt. Ben Carson. "I'm marching around four empty garbage cans and I figured the hell with it. I'm never going to win a war this way. Well, the word came out that some major was going to put together an outfit and take on the Japs as fast as he could. The word was he had experience fighting the Japanese with the Chinese. They said he'd try any kind of nutty thing to get us into combat. When I got off of guard duty I started to look into it a little more. I hated that damned guard duty! That's the only reason."[32]

Simple motives—family, country, adventure, excitement, boredom—the themes that stirred writers since the epic days of ancient Greek theater moved the Raiders.

"Long or Short, I'll Accomplish My Task"

Jack Miller from Dallas, Texas, proved that. The youth had everything—great family, comfortable home, promising future. Known as a clean-cut, handsome individual, Miller's finely sculpted physique came straight from the pages of Charles Atlas. He combined the athletic traits of Jack Armstrong with the sensual appeal of a Saturday matinee film hero. Miller attacked his goals with equal parts ferocity and good nature, whether they came in the classroom or in the sports arena.

"Jack was always happy go lucky," said Henry S. Miller, Jr., Jack's older brother. "I was always very serious, but he was so likeable. He knew how to make me laugh."[33]

Like many Jewish families in those days, the Millers lived in a predominantly Jewish neighborhood in South Dallas. Their three-bedroom house was small but comfortable. Jack shared one bedroom with his older brother.

Others envied his seemingly perfect world, and his baby sister, Carmen, adored an older brother who taught her at age ten to play poker and who impressed her with his love of jazz and the big-band sound.

"I remember Jack would let me tag along with him and his friends," Carmen recalls. "When they played cards, they'd let me play poker with them."[34]

As much as Carmen adored Jack, Jack loved sports. If the family needed to find Jack, they knew where to look—the nearest vacant lot, where he and his friends so often headed to toss around a football or smash hard ground balls at each other.

If Jack could not get up a game or find anyone to play catch, he was just as content to stay home and lift weights. "He was a good athlete and had a great physique," said Carmen. "He had a set of barbells and worked out at home. Not everybody worked out back then, like they do today."[35]

Jack was more than just an athlete. He navigated his way through school halls with the aplomb of a politician, and among females with the suavity of Cary Grant. Supremely self-confident, Jack Miller enjoyed every aspect of his promising life, a facet that his always impeccable attire reinforced.

"He was a very handsome young boy," said Carmen. "Everybody was crazy about Jack. I think a lot of my friends probably had a crush on him. All the girls loved him. But he had a serious side, too, and very high principles."[36]

Those principles motivated Jack at Forest Avenue High School, where he was active in the school's Reserve Officers' Training Corp (ROTC). After graduation in 1938, he attended Southern Methodist University, where he continued to amass a stellar academic and athletic record. In his senior year, Miller was named captain of the university's swim team. People inside and outside of the Miller family marked Jack as one to watch in the future.

That is, if war did not intrude first. With Adolf Hitler disrupting the calm in Europe and the Japanese rattling their sabers in the Pacific, war loomed as a possibility. Miller leaped to the challenge. He abandoned a promising career, as well as the hearts of infatuated females, to join the Marines.

"The war was coming up, and people were deciding what they wanted to do based on what was happening with the war," Carmen said. "Jack was very patriotic. He signed up for officer's training school before he finished SMU. Then after he graduated, he went into active duty"[37]

Sensing that his country might soon be at war, Miller enlisted in the Marines on May 19, 1941. His mother, with whom Jack was very close, had serious reservations about her son leaving for service, but she shoved her objections aside in light of his determination to serve the country.

On June 3, 1941, Miller received his bachelor of science degree from Southern Methodist. After spending a final three weeks with family and friends, much of it spent consoling his tearful mother, Jack reported for active duty on June 24, 1941.

"Everybody was joining the service to fight for our country back then," Carmen explained. "And while Mother didn't like it, I remember she cried, I think my mother and my father were proud of both of their boys."[38]

Miller attended officers' training school in California, where he heard of a new unit being formed by Evans Carlson. The elite nature of Carlson's Raiders, plus the prospect of seeing combat, appealed to his competitive nature. "Jack decided he wanted to be one of them and volunteered," Carmen said. "They were very selective and choosy, and the assignments they would do would be dangerous, but Jack wanted to be a part of that."[39]

As it did to the rest of the nation, the Japanese attack on December 7 stunned Miller. On the same day he wrote Carmen, "I suppose all of you heard the news about the Japs. We were all pretty shocked about the situation, but had been told about the condition in the Pacific before." In a separate letter to his mother, Miller tried to reassure her that all would be well. "There is no need for worry—the Marines will take care of the situation in just a short time. You know we are the best fighters in the world. If there is anything the men in this outfit hate it's the Japs. . . . There is no fear or hysteria around here."[40]

On the day Miller was due to leave Texas for Raider training, he took his father aside for a private conversation. He reassured his father he would take care of himself, then explained his eagerness to serve his country and do something to help his fellow man. As James Jones, a close friend of Miller's, recalled, Jack told his father that "whether his life was long or short, he would accomplish his task by faithful service."[41]

Training camp brought together Lieutenant Miller and Pl. Sgt. Victor Maghakian, two men who, while opposite in many ways, shared similar core values. They came from different social, educational, and economic backgrounds, yet they shared a profound sense of duty and the desire to help others. The unlikeliest of comrades, they developed a lasting friendship that made each devoted to the other.

Born in Chicago, Illinois, on December 5, 1915, Maghakian was the oldest of seven children, the products of an Armenian-American family proud of its heritage. Maghakian's great-grandfather, who guided caravans throughout the Middle East, gained adulation for his military prowess. He supposedly killed 112 of their hated enemy, the Turks.

Like most first-generation immigrants residing near Chicago, Maghakian's father scraped out a meager living for his wife, four sons, and three daughters working in one of the vast steel mills. As the oldest child, Victor accepted personal responsibility for his siblings' well-being. "Victor was a quiet, dedicated man," said his sister, Virginia, in 2008. "He was always very calm, except for war. He was such a giving man."[42]

Adventure, not school, appealed to Maghakian, who thought the military would be the easiest way to escape a menial living and travel the world. He joined the Marines in 1936 almost by accident. After his father relocated the family to California, Maghakian headed to the Navy recruiting office in San Diego, intending to enlist in that branch. On the way to the recruiter, however, Maghakian ducked into a theater to watch the current film, *Pride of the Marines*, starring Charles Bickford as a tough leatherneck rushing to the aid of an orphan. The glimpse of Marine life impressed Maghakian, a feeling that solidified a few hours later when he watched a Marine band perform. "Outside, I saw the snappy Marine band marching briskly, playing the 'Marine Corps Hymn,'" Maghakian explained in 1971. "That settled it. I joined the Marines."[43]

From 1936 to 1939 Maghakian served alternating duties in the Philippines and China. He earned the nickname "Transport" for his unparalleled ability to materialize a car or a truck whenever he or his buddies needed a ride. "I never liked to walk too much," Maghakian explained after the war. "I'd scrounge around the area until I saw a vehicle I liked, then I'd steal it. Jeeps were my specialty, although I would take a truck or bicycle if that's all that was available."[44]

As Carlson had first come into contact with the Japanese during his China days, so, too, did Maghakian encounter his future enemy in that country. Like most Marines, Maghakian frequented the many bars catering to the military. "There was a fight almost every night. Marines would fight anybody—the British, the Japanese, the Russians, even the Chinese."[45]

In January 1939, he and a Marine corporal downed beer and shots at T. T. Wong's Cabaret in Chin Wong Too, China, as five Japanese officers strutted in. When a major halted at Maghakian's table and spat in the corporal's face, Maghakian jumped out of his chair and knocked the Japanese officer to the floor. One of the major's compatriots smacked Maghakian from behind with his scabbard-encased sword, drawing blood, but joined the major when Maghakian turned and dropped him with one punch. Maghakian grabbed the major's pistol from his gun belt to cover the other three Japanese as he and his buddy backed out of the door.

The next day Maghakian, fearing a court-martial, appeared before his commanding officer. Fortunately a British officer had witnessed the incident and spoke in Maghakian's behalf. Maghakian and his superior stomped over to Japanese headquarters, where they received a formal apology. Maghakian, already scornful of the Japanese because of their barbaric treatment of Chinese civilians in Nanking and elsewhere, walked away with a deeper distrust for the Oriental nation.

Carlson and Maghakian met briefly in China before he returned to the United States. When Transport heard in 1942 that Carlson was forming a suicide unit consisting of only the toughest Marines, he speedily volunteered. Carlson, familiar with Maghakian's feisty spirit, readily accepted him. Along with Lieutenant Miller, Maghakian was posted to A Company.

Far to Jack Miller's and Victor Maghakian's northeast, First Lt. Richard Washburn knew on December 7 he had to hustle back to his Marine post at Quantico, Virginia, as soon as he could. He had been visiting his girlfriend in Connecticut when the news of Pearl Harbor broke, so he quickly purchased a train ticket to Virginia. As he sat in his seat, wearing his Marine uniform, Washburn tried to imagine the challenges that awaited him in the coming months. He suddenly noticed that passengers in nearby seats or walking the aisle stared at him. He at first could not fathom their reaction, but then realized that they looked to him for reassurance, as if a solitary man in uniform could make the peril go away.

"I was in uniform and their glances were really asking me if I was up to what lay ahead," Washburn recalled years later. "Some of the civilians even came over and asked me if I felt we could do the job that was needed."[46] Others walked over, shook his hand, and wished him well.

Washburn appreciated the support, but wondered, too, when the time came if he would be equal to the task. Would he fulfill his duty and serve with distinction, or would he crack under the rigors of combat? Washburn, Miller, Maghakian, and the others would have to answer that question.

We Could Have Taken on John Dillinger

In the patriotic days following the war's start, Carlson doubted he would have any trouble gathering five hundred volunteers to man the four companies with which he would start training. To increase his chances of finding the right men, Carlson or his executive officer, James Roosevelt, interviewed each volunteer.

"Can You Cut a Jap's Throat?"

Carlson explained his motives for the interviews. He told Roosevelt that he wanted to learn why the men had volunteered for the Raiders, what opinion each had on why the war was being fought, and what motivated them that they would be willing to die on its behalf. "I won't take a man who doesn't give a damn about anything," he said to his second in command before they started the interview process. "But if he has a deep feeling about wanting to fight, even for the wrong reasons, take him. I know I can shape him into wanting to fight for the right reasons."[1] He searched for men who thought, not men who wanted to kill.

Before the interview process started, Carlson assembled the first group of volunteers for a brief introduction. He explained that the life of a Raider would not be easy. He told them to expect sacrifices and rigorous training. Those who survived would be quickly dispatched to the combat zone.

Sitting in the crowd, Pfc. Brian Quirk liked what he observed. "Colonel

Carlson stood tall and straight, hands moving with quick gestures to emphasize his speech; and his eyes, steel-blue and piercing, seemed to find each man in the audience."[2]

Carlson selected a nondescript room on the south side of the parade ground at Camp Elliott to conduct the interviews. Two card tables twenty feet apart rested in the middle—one for him and one for Roosevelt—toward which the line of volunteers approached one by one to answer the questions.

A cold exterior masked Carlson's inquisitive interior. He purposely kept them on edge to see how each Marine reacted. "Carlson's eyes were stern," said Pvt. Al Flores. "They made me feel like my preacher was looking at me. And yet he looked tough and hard-boiled like a typical, by-the-book Marine officer."[3]

Carlson plunged into a series of blunt questions. "Can you cut a Jap's throat without flinching?" he asked. "Can you choke him to death without puking?" He wanted speedy replies, not only because of the long line behind each Marine but because he wanted his boys to be able to react under pressure, as they would one day have to do under fire.

"Are you willing to starve and suffer and go without food and sleep?" Hesitation meant indecision; indecision, Carlson knew, meant death on the battlefield.

Carlson's grim gaze fixed each Marine where he stood. "I promise you nothing but hardship and danger," he stated with a calmness that unnerved many. "When we get into battle, we ask no mercy, we give none."

Thinking of his epic march with the Eighth Route Army, Carlson asked, "Can you walk fifty miles a day?"[4] That led to queries asking the Marine why he fought or about the war's origins.

"He was asking all sorts of questions—were you raised on a farm, can you walk fifty miles a day," said Sgt. Kenneth McCullough. "I told him if anybody else could, I could. He asked if I could cut a man's throat. I had to think a little. I just knew if it was them or me, I'd do it."[5]

A few volunteers passed muster right away. When Second Lt. Joseph Griffith stepped to the table, Carlson asked, "What makes you think you can be a Raider?"

"Well, I went through Jim Crowe's scout-sniper school."

"You're in."[6] Anyone who successfully completed the legendary Marine sharpshooter's demanding course was fine with him.

Pvt. Silvio Costa offered a contrast to Griffith. Carlson doubted that the 105-pound Costa could stand up to the rigors of Raider training, but Costa argued that he was as good as any man. All he asked was the opportunity to prove it. Carlson, who above all loved a man with heart, accepted Costa, who had heart in abundance.

Twenty feet away Roosevelt conducted his interviews, but with an affable, easygoing manner absent in Carlson. Roosevelt's conduct surprised the volunteers, as they expected something far different from a president's son.

Instead of trumpeting his family background or his education, Roosevelt came across as a man with whom they could share a beer and a ribald joke. "He was an extraordinary man because he was one of the guys," said Mary Roosevelt of her husband's rapport with the enlisted Marines. "He had a feel for human beings."[7]

From his Dallas, Texas, retirement community, Lieutenant Griffith agreed. "Franklin Roosevelt's son, James, was one of the finest people I've ever known," claimed Griffith. "He had every reason to be a first-class jackass, but he was nothing but a great guy."[8]

Roosevelt rejected the men who boasted they wanted to kill Japs or that they hated the enemy. They could become loose cannons that disrupted the battalion. He preferred more somber men, Marines who joined from a sense of duty.

Carlson conducted the interviews under the assumption that he enjoyed a free hand in forming his battalion, but Admiral King had other ideas. In February he ordered Holcomb to transfer men from Merritt Edson's First Raider Battalion in Virginia to San Diego.

Edson reluctantly parted with his own A Company, a group of seven officers and 190 men, including Washburn, supported by a machine-gun platoon and a mortar section. Edson hated losing trained Marines to another officer, especially to Carlson.

An equally livid Carlson decided that, as he had been forced to accept the men, he would put them through the same rigorous screening he used to trim his volunteers. Despite Edson's reputation for training top-notch battalions, to the men's surprise and Edson's consternation, Carlson rejected half of the officers and most of the enlisted that Edson had sent.

Second Lt. John Apergis still bristled at the injustice years later. "This was a hell of a mess and most of us tried to 'qualify' for such military duty," he wrote in 1991. "We were proud. The war was just started, and [we] just could not stand rejection by the West Coast mob (not meaning to insult our brothers-in-arms)."[9]

Carlson accepted a handful of the most promising men, including Washburn and Apergis, who received command of D Company, but in the process dismantled Edson's company.

Edson never forgave Carlson for what he considered demeaning and insulting treatment to his men. In a February 20 letter to Carlson's superior, Maj. Gen. Charles F. B. Price, commander of the Second Marine Division stationed on the West Coast, Edson wrote, "I had already heard rumors of Carlson's reception of these men and I was pretty sore about it. The implications contained in your letter tended only to increase my anger and disgust at what I consider to be an unjust and prejudicial attitude that has no foundation in fact."

Edson harshly condemned his fellow commander. "Whatever Carlson's so-called standards may be, his refusal to accept three out of four of these men only confirmed my opinion that the Marine Corps had lost nothing by his resignation a few years ago and has gained nothing by his return to active duty as a reserve major."

Edson brushed aside Roosevelt as an inexperienced officer who had yet to prove his worth in the military. "It is true that Jimmie Roosevelt has connections with high officials in this country. It is also true that he is a reserve captain with very limited military experience as an officer in the Marine Corps. I have already stated my opinion of Major Carlson."[10]

Now that he had chosen the men for his first four companies, Carlson transported them to Jacques Farm, a secluded location that he had selected for their training. Carlson's promise to test them as they had never before been tested was no empty threat. "We were told to get our gear and go to Jacques Farm," said Pvt. Ben Carson. "Everyone wondered where the hell was Jacques Farm? We went down to the supply depot and found a truck going out there. About eight of us helped load up bunks and mattresses and things, and then we rode on the truck. We got there and there was nothing. Carlson and Roosevelt were there, and we had to erect tents." Carson wanted to gripe, but checked his impulse. Any Marine who chose to moan received the same response from Carlson or Roosevelt, "You weren't promised a rose garden."[11]

"A Very Rugged Life, but We All Love It"

At Jacques Farm, a fallow parcel of rocky, cactus-filled land several miles south of Camp Elliott, Carlson promptly conducted a *gung ho* meeting, the first in a series of gatherings giving Carlson a platform from which he could explain his views and hand the men an opportunity to air their grievances. These unique meetings alerted the volunteers that they were, indeed, involved with something innovative.

After leading the men in singing the national anthem, Carlson launched into his discourse. He explained the path of world events over the past few years, starting with China and working his way toward Pearl Harbor, so that his Raiders would know not only how to fight but why they fought. "Carlson spent a lot of time explaining why we were going to fight," mentioned Pvt. Ben Carson. "He gave us a good accounting from Manchuria through the Chinese operations, the rape of Nanking, the whole works."[12]

Carlson explained that their training would focus on three areas—physical conditioning, ethical indoctrination, and use of the fire team. They would become jacks-of-all-trades, adaptable to any situation. "The Jap is a wily and rugged enemy, experienced in hardships," Carlson related. "And so I can promise you nothing but the toughest life while we're in the States and the toughest battles when we're overseas."[13]

After completing his explanation, Carlson divulged their new rallying cry—*Gung Ho!* He ended by offering to give everything he had for the battalion, and promised them nothing but "rice, raisins, and Japanese" as well as "danger, despair and death."[14]

The talk had an equal impact on the officers, who would have to forgo some of the normal amenities, and on the enlisted, who liked what they heard. "I didn't know anything about Carlson before," said Pvt. Darrell Loveland. "I'd never heard about the man. After listening to him talking and found out he'd spent eight years in China, I figured this is a damn good man to follow. He should know what he's doing."[15]

A chore awaited the men after their first meeting. Since only a solitary building stood on the grounds at Jacques Farm—an ancient chicken house—they had to erect barracks and a headquarters building. Until better facilities could be installed the Raiders had to live and eat outdoors, something Carlson planned as a way to toss a challenge at them on their first day.

"We spent about two weeks organizing the camp," explained Private Carson. "The mess hall had to be cleaned—about sixteen inches of chicken manure. We hauled out wheelbarrow after wheelbarrow of that stuff. Then we started getting a tad better meals."[16]

At Jacques Farm, "we started the real Raider training," said First Lt. Richard Washburn. Coming from Edson's battalion, rigorous schedules were nothing to Washburn, but Carlson's system was a different matter. His fellow officer from Edson's battalion, Lieutenant Apergis, labeled Jacques Farm the "Concentration Camp," and explained in a letter to Edson they would train for six weeks at the farm from February until April, followed by two weeks training with rubber boat landings at San Clemente, an island off the coast.[17]

Activities occupied every minute of the day. Calisthenics, swimming, running, hiking, jungle tactics, map reading, camouflaging, jungle hygiene, demolitions, sharpshooting, street fighting, cliff scaling, and sniping were just a few of the topics covered in the six weeks. Second Lt. Oscar Peatross wrote that "Gradually individuals were converted into units and an *esprit* was born; Marines became Raiders—Carlson's Raiders."[18]

The days invariably started early—around four thirty a.m.—and ended well after dark. Carlson often assembled his Raiders in a dry creek bed or a sandy location, where, working in pairs, the Raiders jogged in the sand for half an hour, then ran 150 feet carrying their buddy on their backs. That workout preceded the near daily hikes through California's countryside, treks over parched terrain, through streams, and up hills. Carlson pushed his men until they could travel seven miles in one hour with a full load, half the time running and half walking. "We marched, I think, probably more than any other infantry type of training that was in vogue at that time,"[19] wrote James Roosevelt. Twenty-mile hikes became commonplace.

"Carlson would get us all together early in the morning and say to us, 'See that mountain peak over there? We'll be there by evening,'" stated Pvt. Dean Voight. "And, off we'd go. He would do anything we could do, plus some. He was a gutsy old man. I think he could walk forever."[20]

Carlson loved to taunt the Raiders into giving their best effort, boasting that even though he was twice their age, he would beat them to the peak. Sergeant McCullough said Carlson's words had their desired effect. "We were all these young guys, and he looked old. We weren't going to let him outdo us. Roosevelt was right out there with him."[21]

The Raiders hiked fifty minutes each hour, usually carrying their twenty-five-pound packs on their backs. "We had one canteen of water, and you better have water left when you came back," said Private Loveland. "Carlson was up in front so he couldn't always see us, and if we walked by somebody watering their lawn, we'd have our canteen ready. We'd walk right through little towns up there back of Jacques Farm."[22]

Lieutenant Miller loved being with such a high-caliber outfit. In March he wrote his mother, "It is a crack outfit—each man is hand picked. They have the most marvelous spirit I have ever seen. It is purely voluntary on their part and are told before they are signed up that they are not going to get anything except work—and they are not kidding. The first night I was here we went on a long hike up the side of a small mountain—in about a foot of mud. The next morning we went on a 12 mile hike and averaged a little better than 4 miles per hour. Ordinarily 2½ mph is considered average for the rest of the service. It might be called a guerilla (I know that's spelled wrong) outfit that works on a hit and run principle."

He boasted in a subsequent letter that he and his men had hiked twenty-five miles the previous Saturday, "and it really was a killer—no casualties but a lot of sore feet." He added that at one stretch they covered eight miles in one hour and forty-three minutes. He informed his mother that he lived out of a pup tent, ate from mess gear, washed his clothes in a bucket, slept on the ground, and bathed and shaved in cold water, but would have it no other way. He added, "all in all it's a very rugged life—but we all love it."[23]

Lieutenant Peatross claimed Carlson, to weed out the physically incapable, attempted to reenact an updated, though shorter, version of the long march he endured in China. If they could handle the exhaustion, searing sun, thirst, and blisters in California, they could more readily tolerate the rigors of combat. Carlson figured that one day his Raiders would be tested in a way that he could not hope to simulate in training, tested beyond what they thought were their abilities. Like that Chinese soldier who kept marching, he intended to have his Raiders ready for that moment.

The Raiders lived in pup tents for much of their training, and little good could be said about the food, what they had of it. During long-distance hikes Carlson restricted their intake to whatever they could forage from the land or could carry with them.

"We were always hungry," stated Private Carson. "Carlson had us on a minimum diet." Though he at times wondered why Carlson placed such a harsh regimen on the Raiders, he better understood after emerging from

Guadalcanal's jungles at the end of 1942. "I think there was some wisdom in that for Carlson because when we got behind the lines on Guadalcanal, hunger was something beyond comprehension."[24]

Hardened bodies rose from peacetime flab and softness. Grim determination replaced lack of focus. Pushed and prodded by the unrelenting Carlson, the Raiders were molded into the men they were meant to be.

"As training proceeded self-confidence grew," wrote Carlson. "There was little cockiness. These men were bent on whipping an enemy who sought to destroy the democratic way of life they hold dear."[25]

One of his officers, First Lt. Wilfred Le Francois, agreed. "Only the most rugged of us had survived the weeding-out process," he stated. "Graduates of the course were rightfully considered men among men by other marines, and were very proud boys." Carlson and other officers repeatedly told the Raiders, "You are a fighter who will kill the Japs. You will be given equipment and training to enable you to win the battle. . . . You will strike hard and fast. You are raiders. You will win."[26] Le Francois claimed that after the training, the Raiders possessed a confidence some lacked when they started.

Carlson pushed to see how much his men could endure. "We're bivouacked out in the mountains away from anywhere," Sgt. Clyde Thomason wrote to friends back in Atlanta, Georgia. "There's been nothing but manual labor—marching five, eight, ten miles and calisthenics to get into shape. Twice a week . . . a thirty-five-mile hike, and once a week a seventy-mile overnight hike. We never ride. Every man will be a walking arsenal, including . . . a knife which we are learning to throw. Hope I haven't bitten off more than I can chew. We all have crew haircuts. O, my beautiful waves!"[27]

Few Raiders dropped out, as Carlson and Roosevelt had done their initial screening jobs well. Most stumbled through the first weeks, found their bearings and then, bolstered with confidence and enthusiasm, sailed through the final stages. Only a handful of men asked to be sent to other units.

Lt. Jack Miller was one of the happiest. Accustomed to pushing himself, whether with his set of barbells, in the swimming pool, or in the classroom, Miller took to the training with relative ease. Lt. Stephen Stigler said, "He was always smiling and cheerful. Even when things were at their worst, he never complained." Navy corpsman David J. Henry added, "When Jack laughed it was so spontaneous and infectious that everyone who heard him had to join with him."[28]

Miller quickly became one of the most popular members of Carlson's Raiders, a young officer everyone expected would excel in combat. He, in turn, respected Carlson as much as Miller's men did him. "This Major Carlson is one of the finest men I have ever known," he wrote his mother, "a real leader with plenty of modern experience in the far east."[29] Miller expected that with a veteran such as Carlson at the helm, he would not have to wait long for his chance at combat.

Even Edson's transferred men gradually warmed to their new commander. Lieutenant Apergis liked that the battalion, with its connections to the president, always seemed to have priority in obtaining needed supplies and new equipment. He wrote Edson that despite his initial reservations about being banned to the West Coast, "All in all this is a smart outfit and no one interferes with us. No red tape."[30]

Lieutenant Washburn readily readjusted to his new battalion. The men he commanded in California recognized his leadership talent in the first few days they were together, for here was a man who treated everyone with dignity and shared every hardship.

"Oh boy! What can I say about him?" mentioned Pvt. Lathrop Gay. "During our training at Jacques Farm, he was our platoon leader, and where we went he went, what we ate, he ate, where we slept, he slept. He was quite a guy. We had great respect for the man. You couldn't find anyone better."[31]

Training entered a more sober phase when Carlson drilled the men in hand-to-hand combat, the most personal form of fighting. The use of knives, clubs, and other small weapons required a Raider to get close to the enemy, see the face of the man he wanted to kill and who wanted to kill him, and lock in a form of combat whose result left only one survivor.

"The training given the Raiders is extensive and rigorous," depicted a 1942 Marine Corps press release. "They learn every technique of hand-to-hand fighting because war is not a noble thing and the enemy practices no code of ethics. Gouging, strangling, knifing, bayoneting and any other means of putting an enemy out of action are sometimes necessary for the success of a raiding mission."[32]

Corps veterans, like Platoon Sergeant Maghakian, already possessed some of the skills, but Raider training added to it. Carlson brought in experts, including Col. Anthony J. Drexel Biddle, a legend known throughout the Marine Corps for his talents in close-in combat. British commandos explained what weapons the enemy was likely to use, such as the sixteen-inch bayonet and sharpened samurai swords that could handily slice a man in half.

The training had its desired effect, as most Raiders came away with a deeper understanding of what they might face. "Hand-to-hand combat training made you think about what you were getting into," explained Private Loveland. "I'd better know what the hell I'm doing or I might not make it. We had pros teaching us. Carlson brought in seasoned veterans, tough people. Loveland related the time when Colonel Biddle attached a bayonet to his rifle, dropped to his knees, and bellowed, "Pull your scabbards off your bayonets, and anybody that can draw blood on me will get a three-day pass."

Each man took his turn trying to best Biddle, but none succeeded. When Loveland approached, the colonel handily knocked him three feet aside, where Loveland landed on his butt with a resounding thud. "Not a damn soul got a pass. He knew what he was doing. It was sort of like in the movie, *The Dirty Dozen*."[33]

"The street fighting was hard for me, killing with your bare hands," said Pharmacist's Mate Third Class Richard Favinger. "I was a quiet, calm kid. If you failed any of these things, you were sent back to your former outfit."

Favinger also worried about how these lethal talents, ingrained in training until they became instinct, might affect him after the war. Would a neighborhood kid yelling "Boo!" cause him to do something he might regret? "How would I react?"[34] he wondered.

At the firing range the Raiders learned to shoot weapons from all positions—standing, squatting, lying prone, or any other stance in which he might find himself during an attack. They practiced not just with the Raiders' weapons of choice—the M1 rifle, the .45 pistol, the Thompson submachine gun, and the Browning Automatic Rifle—but with the Reising .45 automatic submachine gun, the Johnson rifle, and the Johnson light machine gun. Carlson wanted them proficient with every weapon so that if theirs was damaged in combat, they could retrieve that of a dead Raider.

"Work in Harmony"

Platoon Sergeant Maghakian, Lt. Jack Miller, and the other Raiders knew that the physical training would be demanding, but Carlson's emphasis on the ideas he had learned while observing the Chinese Eighth Route Army took them by surprise. He explained to his Raiders that what made the epic march extraordinary was not that the Chinese soldier did it but how he accomplished it. The Chinese peasant struggling in the line endured not from fear of discipline but from a desire to do what was right. An inner spirit propelled him.

"But, when the going gets toughest," Carlson told a correspondent, "when it takes a little bit more drive to keep sane and to keep going, and a man is hungry and tired, then he needs more than *esprit de corps*. It takes conviction."[35]

"Carlson said that Chiang Kai-shek will take a coolie and put him in the army, keep him there for four or five years and turn him loose as a coolie," said Private Carson. "Chu Teh will take a coolie and train him so that when he gets out of the army he can get a better job. This was some of the things he talked about."[36] In Carlson's view, it was just as important that his men knew why they had to kill an enemy as it was how to kill that individual.

Carlson explained the gung ho concept during a 1945 Columbia Broadcasting System radio program. When asked what the phrase meant, he replied that in Chinese the word *gung* meant "work," and *ho* meant "harmony." Thus, the phrase "Work in harmony" guided his operations. "Fundamentally, *Gung Ho* is an ideal, the ideal of complete cooperation and mutual trust and respect between men. *Gung Ho* is tolerance, cooperation and equality. It is democracy at work."

Carlson told the radio audience that knowledge constituted the foundation of his system. "But I do believe it is your right and duty to know what you're doing, why you're doing it, and if you die, why you died." Carlson explained that in training he told his men they were soon to head into battle, a world comprising death, hunger, deprivation, and the toughest experiences they would ever meet. "What I'm trying to do is give every man in the outfit something to think about *then* [emphasis Carlson's], the knowledge and understanding that will sustain him then, for if he knows why he's there, and what good will come of his being there, he'll be stronger, a better Marine, doing a better job."[37]

Carlson mentioned that, as part of this ethical indoctrination, he abolished many of the strictures that normally separated officers and enlisted. Discipline still existed and orders were followed, but they were based on reason rather than authority. How could the Raiders fight for a democratic nation, Carlson wondered, and not exist in a democratically run battalion?

The quixotic nature of Carlson blinded him to the difficulties. He planned to democratize an organization that, by its very nature, relied on autocracy.

"My first step was to abolish all social distinctions between officers and men," he explained. "There must be obedience, of course. That was the cornerstone of everything. But I told my officers they must command by virtue of ability. Their rank meant nothing until they had proved their right to it."[38] He would select leaders by virtue of their proven talent to command, not solely on the basis of rank.

If enlisted slept on the ground, their officers slept beside them. He established a single chow line for enlisted and officers that served on a first-come, first-served basis, rather than officers in the front and enlisted to the rear. Saluting was reduced to a minimum. Officers enjoyed no benefit simply because they were officers, and they commanded because they had proven their worth. "We'll live as you live; work as you work; eat as you eat; fight as you fight," Carlson told his men. "We give up all privileges cheerfully and willingly."[39]

One day Lieutenant Griffith asked if a clerk could type a set of notes he had taken, but Carlson told Griffith that he had to type his own report, and added that he wanted it on his desk within twenty-four hours. On another occasion a young lieutenant asked a man in his platoon to clean his rifle, but Carlson made him clean his own weapon.

"We'd line up to eat chow, and Roosevelt would line up right with everybody else," said Sergeant McCullough. "He was friendly with everyone. Carlson did the same thing and got in line with the boys. I know there were some second lieutenants that didn't like it. I don't think they resented it all the way through, but at the first they wondered what he was trying to do. The enlisted liked it."[40]

All the men knew that in the field the Raiders could not halt operations to conduct a meeting. Orders were orders. But Carlson, as Lieutenant Peatross explained in a 1979 letter, wanted the men to speak up before an operation, not during it. "Carlson said that when a fire team is to scale a cliff, attack a pill box, or cross a river, if anybody had an idea how to do it, to speak up before it was done." Some of Carlson's compatriots, who believed an officer ordered and the enlisted obeyed, erroneously assumed he attempted to make every Raider, officer and enlisted, equals. What he sought was to give his Raiders the opportunity to contribute. "Carlson believed that you obtained input for the decision-making process from any rank including the lowest ranking private. Carlson thought that this process made all hands think about the best way to do things and thus in itself created initiative, resourcefulness, willingness and similar things."[41]

"Carlson was very democratic about how a military organization should work," said Pfc. Ervin Kaplan. "Officers and enlisted had the same privileges. It worked for Carlson, but the Marine Corps didn't see it as anything they wanted."[42]

Most of Carlson's men did, though. "I liked the idea I didn't have to salute anybody or kowtow to anybody, and I would be my own man," said Pvt. Dean Voight. "We never had to salute. We did show respect, but we didn't have to salute. If we wanted to we did. We knew who the officers were and we weren't going to be disrespectful."[43]

Carlson wanted discipline based on reason. He had little time for courts-martial, as they required additional headquarters personnel, a factor that would hamper his mobility in the field. Lt. Robert Burnette claimed that as each man had volunteered for the Raiders, he and other officers had few disciplinary problems. If a man's behavior concerned Burnette, he told the offender that he would be removed from the battalion if his behavior did not change. He never had to transfer a man.

When a few Raiders left camp without permission and headed to San Diego's bars and brothels, Carlson handled the issue by ordering three a.m. assemblies for his men. Within days the number of violations plunged, allowing Carlson to cancel the early-morning gatherings as well as quietly assert his authority.

Ethical indoctrination was thus more of a lifestyle than a radical makeover of the Marine command system. It focused on the men living together properly, helping each other, and respecting each other's belongings.

In another step Carlson deemphasized the role of staff and headquarters personnel in favor of handing greater responsibility to each squad and platoon. As Michael Zak has observed, Carlson wanted more input and responsibility from the men below, rather than from above. Knowing that career officers might be more resistant to these changes, Carlson favored reserve officers, men who had not been exposed to ingrained Marine customs.

Carlson so detested favoritism that when his son, Lt. Evans C. Carlson, asked to be assigned to the battalion as a lieutenant, Carlson declined. He felt his son would be subject to the harshest scrutiny, and Carlson doubted he could be impartial to his son.

Carlson's father, the Rev. Thomas A. Carlson, in mentioning his son's quandary to a 1943 newspaper reporter, added another reason. "Evans pointed out that where they were going they would be sure to get into the thick of the fighting sooner or later and while he knew he would treat his son as just another soldier it would be bound to add a complication for him when it became necessary to order his son on a mission that would probably lead to death. Even if his son accomplished some difficult mission, did an outstanding piece of work, he would have to be the last to recognize it, all because the soldier was his son. Under another commander, Evans felt, the boy might even be better off."[44]

On four separate occasions his son sought admission, only to be sent away. Finally, shortly before the battalion was scheduled to leave for Hawaii, Carlson's battalion officers convinced their commander to relent. The young man had shown his grit by applying a fifth time, and the officers were confident Carlson could deal with his son fairly. Carlson assented, but told his son to expect no favors and that the father would probably be tougher on him than on any other man.

Carlson succeeded partly due to his immense appeal—his Raiders willingly dropped their reservations to attempt what he promoted. Lieutenant Peatross stated that "there is no doubt in my mind that the rank and file of the 2d Raider Battalion would have followed Carlson to hell and back on his command, 'Follow me!'"[45]

"I Like Men Who Think"

Carlson's weekly gung ho meeting gave the officer a chance to listen on a routine basis to what the enlisted men had to say. Many meetings opened with Carlson playing the harmonica and leading the Raiders in a song, usually the "Marine Hymn." "Ahoy, Raiders!" he shouted as he faced his men, to which the Raiders replied, "Hi, Raider!" or "Gung Ho!" After discussing relevant issues and enjoying some entertainment, Carlson ended the meeting with a rousing rendition of the national anthem.

Any man, officer or enlisted, had the right to speak his mind without fear of reprisal. "It meant a lot because you were being heard by the guy who could do something about it," said Pvt. Lathrop Gay. "One guy said he had been trying to get a pair of boots for two weeks, and the next day he got the boots."[46]

Discussions then ensued, and while they covered a wide range of topics, two most often appeared—why the United States fought the war, and why the men should be involved in the democratic process. Carlson explained to *Time* magazine's top Pacific war correspondent, Robert Sherrod, "We used to hold discussions. We would tell these men the implications of the war. We would show the connection between the war in Europe and the war in the Pacific."

Without promoting his personal beliefs as to which political leader was best, Carlson hoped to show what his men could accomplish if they took their citizenship responsibilities more seriously. "I think they knew what they were fighting for," he told Sherrod. "Anyway, I tried to teach them. We tried to educate them politically—by that I don't mean we told them whom to vote for, but what to believe in. That's harder than teaching them how to shoot a gun."[47]

Carlson challenged the Raiders to think. "We'd have meetings and you could say what you wanted," said Sergeant McCullough. "He wanted his privates to know what was going on as well as the captains. That didn't occur in other Marine units. Carlson delivered lectures, and he had guests in, including Eleanor Roosevelt."[48]

Carlson chatted about political and social issues but never endorsed the Democratic or Republican point of view. Rather than organize political brainwash sessions, he wanted his men to think about issues. Thinking in training camp led to thinking under duress. With Carlson, preparing his men for the battlefield was everything.

The correspondent Jim Lucas attended some of the gung ho meetings and watched in fascination when a corporal disagreed with his captain over the maneuvers they had practiced earlier. Carlson listened intently, complimented the corporal on his suggestions, and then asked the corporal how his ideas might work in a different scenario. "I like men who think,"[49] Carlson explained to Lucas.

Lucas listened as Raiders discussed the topic of whether after the war annual incomes should be limited to $25,000. Carlson thought the notion might make it easier for poorer classes to attain improved lives, but his Raiders overwhelmingly scorned the idea. When they returned from combat, they wanted the opportunity to be wealthy themselves.

Raiders also talked about what social order should exist, or whether the South received unfair treatment after the Civil War. After listening to four privates debate the issue, "The Kind of Social Order We Want After the War," Lucas was sold on Carlson. "And I decided that here was an officer with a social conscience, a man who was interested not only in fighting but also in the things for which we fight."[50]

More than politics, Carlson conveyed a religious bent. He hoped that his Raiders would be more aware of the world in which they lived, and that by understanding why they fought, not only would they fight harder but be improved individuals guided by a social conscience. Pl. Sgt. Victor Maghakian said of Carlson, "He spoke about religion a lot—not just going to church, but living it. He was the most religious man I ever knew."[51]

When a reporter asked Carlson how he balanced his spiritual beliefs with war's brutality, he never hesitated. "I'm an out-and-out pacifist, but when an aggressor strikes I do not believe in calmly permitting his steam roller to run over me. It is necessary to resist, to whip the aggressor with one hand, while with the other we work even harder to build a social order in which war will not be necessary as an instrument for adjusting human differences."[52]

Carlson invited diverse speakers to address his men at these meetings. Besides military instructors, Secretary of the Navy Frank Knox and James's mother, Eleanor Roosevelt, spoke. The First Lady was as impressed with Carlson as Jim Lucas was, and better understood why her husband maintained such an active correspondence with the Marine officer.

"He believes in the China cooperatives," Eleanor Roosevelt wrote in a March 1942 letter after spending time with Carlson. "Those *not* government controlled, he thinks the profit motive must be eliminated & he's teaching his men that they must make all people their friends, they are fighting the system that forced all people to war, but they must not hate the people! His men are farm boys, many Southerners, C.C.C. boys but he talks to them. James gives them a 'news review' on Sundays & answers questions afterwards. He preaches race equality & has taught them a Chinese rallying cry meaning 'we cooperate'—He does everything they are asked to do & so does every officer. The Marine Corps thinks it is horrifying but the men think he & they are the finest things on earth."[53]

Carlson injected a light touch into the meetings as well. Battalion "comedians," especially B Company's Pfc. Jack Barnes, entertained the Raiders with skits and jokes. The Raiders booed one man, claiming to be an Eskimo, off the stage after an inept performance of what he claimed was an Eskimo dance. James Roosevelt even once dressed as a woman for one skit.

Poetry recitations always received high marks. Seemingly at odds with the violence and barbarity in which they were soon to be involved, Marines employed poetry as an outlet for laughter, sadness, testimonials, and pride.

The poem titled "Carlson's Raiders," set to the tune of "Ivan Skavinsky Skivar," was sung lustily by the group. The song went, in part:

> They were gathered from near and were gathered
>   from far
> They were picked from the best in the land
> A hell-raising crew that sailed the blue
> Was Carlson's raider band.
>
> They carry machine guns like pistols, they say
> And a knife that was tempered in hell
> And the Raiders all claim no mortal by name
> Could use them one quarter so well.[54]

Raiders knew well the words and sentiments behind another poemlike collection. Called the "Doctrine of the Raider Battalion," the men chanted a litany of dogma expressing the Raider outlook. The points stated:

> 1. We are Raiders of the Land and Sea.
> 2. We work together for Democracy.
> 3. Gung Ho! Gung Ho! Gung Ho! Ho!
> 4. We are tough; we are just;
>   We fight when e'er we must
>   For the right to be free.
> 5. We want to do our duty—
>   Because it's right;
>   And our duty will give those Japs a fright.
> 6. We execute all orders with a promptitude
>   That will shatter the Mikado's latitude.
> 7. We are unbeatable—because we're right;
>   Those Japs can't lick us—for we've got
>   might.
> 8. We're Raiders—for Democracy.
>   We work together; that's why we're free.
>   GUNG HO! GUNG HO! GUNG HO! HO![55]

The rhyme and cadence lacked that found in epic poems, but the words imparted everything Carlson believed important.

"A Model for Later Organizations"

Once Carlson instilled the basic concepts in his Raider Battalion, he added a unique twist that after the war became a staple of Marine organization—the fire team. As was true with so many other parts of his program, the fire team came from what he had observed in Nicaragua and China.

Carlson sought flexibility and mobility, while at the same time packing more firepower than the standard Marine nine-man squad. He saw that in South Pacific jungles, like in Nicaragua, flanking tactics would be crucial against the Japanese, but he also needed the ability to outshoot them. His solution was to create ten-man squads consisting of three three-man fire teams led by a corporal or private first class.

In reorganizing squads into three teams and a leader, rather than nine individual Marines, Carlson freed the squad and platoon leaders to focus on the larger picture rather than worry about each Marine. In the heat of a fire-fight, instead of directing the entire squad he only had to issue orders to the three fire team leaders, who in turn supervised the men in their fire teams. This provided better coordination and speed—vital attributes when under attack—than did an officer shouting orders to eight or nine men. Fire teams tightened unit control and made it simpler to coordinate movement.

To create cohesion, Carlson kept the fire teams together throughout training. The three men hiked as a team, served mess duty together, quartered together, and ate together. They learned each other's tendencies and identified how to better coordinate their movements.

Maj. Samuel Griffith, an Edson officer who had studied British commando techniques, observed Carlson's training and was astonished with how much the Raiders did together. Carlson assigned tasks by platoon, rather than to individuals—the platoon worked in the kitchen or policed the area. Griffith was impressed with a system "which I thought was very valuable, because they literally did live together, work together, eat together, sleep together, train together, and I thought that was a very valuable concept. . . ."[56]

Fire teams became a fertile proving ground for future leaders. By handing responsibility to fire team leaders, Carlson could more readily observe how the men performed. His corporals and privates first class formed a pool that spawned sergeants and lieutenants, a crucial factor once the battalion entered jungle combat and began suffering losses. At the same time, replacement Marines enjoyed a smoother transition when placed in a fire team, as they benefited from working with two veteran Raiders.

Firepower previously unseen in a small Marine tactical unit earmarked Carlson's fire teams. Normally, a nine-man squad carried one Browning Automatic Rifle (BAR) and eight M1 rifles, but Carlson upgraded the destructiveness by arming each team with one M1 rifle, a BAR, whose greater accuracy at distances of up to five hundred yards brought the enemy more quickly within range, and one Thompson submachine gun (Tommy gun), whose larger-caliber bullet and higher rate of fire—four hundred rounds per minute—could shred jungle foliage and blunt enemy charges. Carlson's squads thus met the enemy with three Thompsons, three BARs, and four M1 rifles (the squad leader usually selected the rifle), rather than the one BAR and nine M1 rifles of a standard squad.

Carlson had little trouble obtaining such weapons because of Roosevelt, whose requests raced through channels. The Raiders enjoyed the newest and best of most equipment. They had specially designed boots for their long hikes, the best walkie-talkies in the Corps, special stiletto-type knives and large Jim Bowie–type knives, riot shotguns, collapsible bicycles, chain saws, Bangalore torpedoes, and plenty of Thompson submachine guns.

"I think this created, unquestionably, a lot of unhappiness" among rival battalions, stated James Roosevelt in 1979. He added that "one of the jobs that he [Carlson] gave me was to go back and see if I could not get some better equipment. I went back and got it, and I said that Father never wrote out any orders to give us anything, but I guess now being realistic, the fact that I, as the son of the president, would walk into the quartermaster's office and say I gotta have this, and I gotta have that, maybe was part of the reason at least that we got it."[57]

At a time of high demand, when the nation's military geared for war, most officers had difficulty obtaining the additional weaponry, but Carlson only had to turn to his executive officer. Lieutenant Griffith recalled the time Carlson wanted the M1 rifle. "We were the first group in the entire Armed Services to get the Garand rifle." Griffith explained that when Carlson heard of the M1, he asked Roosevelt, "Do you think you can do something about this?"

Roosevelt called his mother and informed her how badly the Raiders needed the weapon. "Would you talk to Dad about this?" Two weeks later a shipment of the new rifles arrived.[58]

With his version of the fire team, Carlson created miniature jungle arsenals. His fire teams brought frightening firepower upon the Japanese. "That group could really put the bullets out," gushed Lieutenant Griffith. Carlson had assembled a unit capable of outshooting any comparable size group in the Army or Marines. Private Carson went even further. "We could have taken on John Dillinger and ten like him with just one squad."[59]

Carlson's revolutionary fire team proved so promising that other Marine officers followed suit. Maj. Samuel B. Griffith advised Gen. Holland M. Smith, Commanding General, Amphibious Corps, Atlantic Fleet, that every raider battalion should implement Carlson's fire team concept. In a May 1942 letter he called Carlson's Raiders the "model for later organizations." Griffith added in a later interview that "the fire team concept, which was Carlson's concept, despite claims to the contrary—was a wonderful thing from a tactical and morale point of view, from a psychological point of view and a tactical point of view."

In January 1943, when Griffith reorganized the First Raider Battalion, he followed Carlson's practices, even though he had been Merritt Edson's executive officer. Later that year an instruction manual offering material on Carlson's fire teams was issued at Camp Pendleton, and following the war the Marine Corps adopted fire teams throughout its organization. "And as far as I know," Griffith stated after the war, "the fire team concept is still in effect in the Marine Corps, the fire team organization, the squad organization of three by threes."[60]

"Twenty-one Guns in His Hip Pocket"

A mystique eventually enveloped Carlson and his Raiders. Subsequent Navy Department and Marine Corps press releases described Raider training as four months of hardship "for fighting in the tropics, for beach landings at night, for thrusts over mountains, down ravines, through swamp and jungle." The writer stated that Carlson's men jumped over double layers of barbed wire, "And all this time their bodies were hardened by long, rapid, fatiguing marches, and the men drilled for hand-to-hand combat with boxing, rough-and-tumble, knife-fighting, and bayonet fighting."

The release went on to say that Carlson's rigorous drilling prepared the Raiders for anything. "They trained—and became neither supermen, nor arch-killers, nor glamour boys, but a team with the skill to lick the Japs at their own 'game.'" The story added that at a time when the United States public wearied of reading about defeat, "Just as a conditioned thorough-bred anticipates its test on the track, so do the Raiders anticipate action on the field, confident that in jungle craft and sheer fighting ability they can whip the Japs."[61]

Along with the adulation came criticism. Too radical for an organization that is by nature autocratic and conservative, Carlson expected opposition. Some officers argued that Carlson digressed from Marine orthodoxy in favor of Chinese army doctrine. Others scorned his supposed democratic system and bellowed that while it might work during training camp, it would never succeed on the battlefield. "There could be no discipline and no morale in such an organization,"[62] claimed Maj. Gen. Omar T. Pfeiffer at the time.

Commanders who lost troops to Raider battalions griped about the inequity of losing Marines they had trained. Brig. Gen. Alexander Vandegrift, commander of the First Marine Division, wrote, "Neither General Holcomb nor I favored forming elite units from units already elite. But Secretary of the Navy Colonel Frank Knox and President Roosevelt, both of whom fancied the British commandos, directed us to come up with a similar organization." He added that losing valued men "annoyed the devil out of me, but there wasn't one earthly thing I could do about it."[63]

Carlson's friendship with President Roosevelt had the contrary effect of keeping his Raiders intact while engendering harsh censure. Officers quietly slammed Carlson for his ties to Roosevelt, but claimed that the "Second Raiders will never need any artillery support. Carlson's always got twenty-one guns [a reference to the president] in his hip pocket."[64]

A few officers rushed to Carlson's defense. One of the most astute was Maj. Samuel Griffith. Griffith claimed that Carlson's distinctive trait was his profound belief in people. "He was kind of like a prophet out of the Old Testament, strong and righteous." Rather than being a communist, "I think he was just an extremely brave and intelligent man who didn't like to bend on principle."[65]

Griffith realized that taking such an unorthodox position earned both the enmity and the jealousy of fellow officers, but "No, I don't think he was a communist. He's always reminded me of a tough New England type, craggy face, as you remember, a very simple man, I believe, very honest. I've always had great admiration for Carlson." Some brushed aside Carlson as a maverick, but not Griffith. "Well, he was a maverick, but I think we need a few mavericks."[66]

His men thought the Marines needed more Carlsons. He may not have convinced his contemporaries, but Carlson's impact on his Raiders was undeniable.

Pfc. Brian Quirk remains impressed with Carlson's loyalty, courage, and unselfishness. In a 2007 interview he called Carlson a "Christian at heart with a militarist's outlook" who always made time for his men. "It was not at all uncommon to see him temporarily set aside his personal affairs in order to chat with 'one of the boys,' as he called us. He knew by name, past experience, and capabilities every individual in the battalion." Quirk explained that "Carlson was a wonderful man. I was just a private, but he knew me all the same. That was the type of guy he was."[67]

Sgt. Adrian E. Schofield stated that Carlson would "dispose of himself as readily as he would of anyone else under his command" and that the officer "is the only man I know, except myself, with whom I would entirely trust the disposition of my own life."[68]

The pace quickened near the end of March when superiors called Carlson to Hawaii to consult about the potential deployment of his Raiders. In his absence, Roosevelt took command for the final phase of training—three weeks of landing practices off San Clemente Island and the California coast. The four Raider companies—A, B, C, and D—debarked from World War I destroyers called APDs, then headed to shore in rubber boats to simulate surprise attacks, one of the Raiders' prime missions. Roosevelt, hoping to better prepare the men for combat, pushed the Raiders harder, with companies vying with each other to set the highest standard.

In mid-April the Raiders returned to Camp Elliott, where the 250 new volunteers that formed E and F Companies joined them. Carlson now had six complete companies, plus headquarters, for a total of about eight hundred men. Carlson, again with his men, and knowing they were about to head overseas, granted the battalion a final liberty in San Diego.

Many headed to San Diego, primed for beer and women. Wearing dungarees and carrying their gung ho knives, they made a spectacle. Military police arrested groups of Raiders but Carlson, foreseeing that he might encounter such problems, posted Lieutenant Miller, Lieutenant Washburn, and other officers at different jails to immediately post bail for the men.

Training, especially in hand-to-hand combat, had brought the reality of war a bit closer. A series of war scares along the California coast magnified that reality. During one December week, with many of the Marines already at boot camp in San Diego, nine Japanese submarines attacked eight American merchant ships, sinking two and damaging two while killing six seamen. One submarine, *I-10*, had taken station off San Diego not far from Camp Elliott.

The scares escalated in February, with the Raiders deep in training. On February 23, the Japanese submarine *I-17* surfaced near Los Angeles and fired twenty shells at California oil fields. Though the forty-five-minute attack inflicted little damage, the assault rattled nerves already shaken by ominous war developments following Pearl Harbor.

Two days later antiaircraft batteries near Los Angeles fired fourteen hundred rounds at reported Japanese aircraft. The *Los Angeles Times* stated that enemy aircraft had been spotted above many Southern California locations, and that the antiaircraft rounds were the first such shots fired at an enemy invader over United States soil. In San Diego, a red-alert warning sounded air alarms and sent hundreds of air-raid wardens and auxiliary police scurrying to their posts.

The scares made Raider training more relevant. "To us Raiders, the very idea of enemy shells exploding in our country was the last straw," wrote Lieutenant Peatross. Orders directed Raiders to hunt the coastline for secret Japanese radio stations and Japanese spies. "None was found, but the search added a degree of realism to our training."[69]

A series of events helped restore a semblance of security to these worried residents. A group of pilots flying over Tokyo chipped in, and the Raider presence at Midway during that epic sea battle, followed by their stunning raid against a tiny Japanese-held atoll in the central Pacific, lifted spirits on the home front as well.

"The Eve of the Great Adventure"

In a series of lengthy letters from Jacques Farm, Carlson fed information to the president on a variety of topics, including Raider training and his son James's contributions.

On March 2, 1942, Carlson wrote Roosevelt of his pleasure with the president's son "and the fine way he has taken hold of his assigned tasks out here." Carlson stated that when James arrived in San Diego in January, he was first assigned to Carlson's intelligence section at Force Headquarters, where the two men immediately hit it off. Carlson praised Roosevelt's written estimations of world events, and "I discovered to my great delight that he saw pretty much eye to eye with me on matters social, economic, political and military."

A pleasant collaboration ensued, making it natural for Carlson to ask James to be his executive officer. "Incidentally, it is hardly necessary for me to assure you that he was selected for this post entirely on his merit and without regard to his relationship to you. I believe you are sufficiently familiar with my intellectual honesty to realize that I would show no favoritism in the choice of officers where the lives of men were concerned."[70]

James vindicated Carlson's trust by sharing every challenge of training camp, despite his fragile health. "Jimmy Roosevelt was tops," said Private Voight in sentiments that reflected how most of the Raiders felt. "He had stomach problems, but it didn't slow him down. He never acted superior. He was a regular guy. That had to be tough to do."[71]

In the same March 2 letter, Carlson discussed the progress he had made with his Raider Battalion. He said he "designed the organization and equipment with a view to providing a battalion capable of high mobility and possessing the maximum fire power compatible with such mobility." He did this, in part, by cutting unnecessary administrative overhead to the minimum and assigning multiple functions to his men. "The emphasis is on speed of movement on foot, endurance, self-sufficiency and great fire power," he reported to the president.

But more than tactics was required. His men had to be tougher than the enemy. "In order to lick the Japanese we must out-hike, out-smart and out-shoot him." Carlson added, "Our minds must be kept open to the reception of new ideas." Carlson informed Roosevelt that he had selected only 10 percent of the six thousand men who volunteered to be Raiders, which provided Carlson with a talented battalion.

"Every man is a volunteer. Each *wants* to do 40 to 50 miles a day on foot. What a man *wants* to do he can do if he is willing to make the effort. These men possess conviction. With their morale, armament and coordination I am convinced that this outfit could run rings around and cut to pieces any Japanese command five times its size."

Carlson admitted that his battalion was, as many detractors charged, "unorthodox, in the military sense, but it will do the job." For instance, he mentioned their pack, which was designed from a hunting jacket for easier mobility. Carlson agreed that it did not look very appealing, but the lighter pack allowed his men to carry their essentials while retaining speed and maneuverability.

"Of course, we are meeting with opposition from the orthodox brass hats," he stated, but he believed his men would prove their critics wrong. "I feel now that those months of experience with the Chinese guerrilla armies were not in vain."

Carlson ended the letter by promising to do whatever he could to safeguard the president's son. "Please feel no apprehension for Jim. He has already won a high place in the hearts of the men of this command. He can take it. And in the final analysis you can trust me to see that he holds himself within bounds."[72] Carlson had, in effect, established himself as James Roosevelt's caretaker.

President Roosevelt responded ten days later. He complimented Carlson on the battalion's progress and guessed that "surely there will be a chance to use it." He then added a cautionary remark that underscored Carlson's remark about watching out for James.

"I am, of course, glad that Jimmy is working with you—but don't forget that he had part of his stomach taken out and that a diet of condensed cubes would probably lay him low in forty-eight hours. For Heaven's sake don't let him know I mentioned this or he would slay me."[73]

Those sentiments would one day place Carlson in the midst of the most heated quandary of his career.

On April 23, Admiral Nimitz notified Admiral King that the Raiders had completed training five days earlier and were now ready for tougher challenges. Nimitz warned King that unless the unit embarked on active operations or a different sort of training, its high morale might suffer. Nimitz, who described Carlson's battalion as "a striking force with strength out of proportion to its numbers,"[74] announced that he was sending the Raiders to Hawaii around May 1 to practice rubber boat landings over coral reefs.

With the prospect of combat drawing near, a jubilant Carlson wrote President Roosevelt on April 29, "We are in the eve of the Great Adventure." He referred to the immense responsibilities that lay with taking men into battle, but declared everyone ready. "However, Jim and I both have put our best thought and effort into the preparation of this organization and I am satisfied that it represents just about the best America has to offer."

Carlson cautioned that no matter how optimistic they might now feel, the true test awaited in the Pacific. "The proof of the pudding will be in the eating, of course, and so I withhold the final word of conviction until this gang has demonstrated its prowess in battle. I am confident, though, that our concepts are sound. Mobility, condition, tactical knowledge, and individual initiative, volition, resolution and resourcefulness: these are the rocks on which we have built our house. Each man is conscious of their meaning and value, and each believes in them."

Carlson claimed that the Japanese, stretched to every corner of the Pacific with their initial conquests, could not possibly be strong everywhere, and that "Pure raids would keep him guessing, confuse him and cause him to alter his plans. . . ." These raids could also yield valuable information that the Army could use in planning large-scale assaults, while simultaneously disrupting Japanese lines of communication. "The situation is not dissimilar to that which has obtained in China for the past four and a half years, substituting water for land."[75] Carlson thus imagined the Pacific as a theater for guerrilla operations, hitting the enemy where they least expected, employing speedy raids or embarking on longer missions behind enemy lines, just as he had observed in Nicaragua and China.

Another motive prodded the battalion to leave California as quickly as possible—to beat Edson's men into combat. Merritt Edson's First Raider Battalion had already received orders for the Pacific.

"Our eagerness to be off increased greatly when we heard that the first echelon of Edson's Raiders had arrived in San Diego and shipped out for an unspecified destination in the Pacific," wrote Lieutenant Peatross. "Surely our turn would soon come."[76]

4

We Were Itching
for a Fight

T heir time came sooner than expected. As the ship *J. Franklin Bell* left San
Diego and charted a course toward Hawaii, the Japanese and U.S. fleets
maneuvered into position for two epic sea battles. The May clash in the
Coral Sea northeast of Australia ended in a draw. The second, centering on
the American-held Midway Island, would pull two of Carlson's companies
into the fray and help turn the tide in the Pacific.

"A Whole Different Ball of Wax"

Combat lay in the future as Carlson, now a lieutenant colonel, led his Raiders
and the newly promoted Maj. James Roosevelt aboard the troop transport,
which steamed out of San Diego on May 8. Once the ship reached open
waters, the public-address system blared with a message from Carlson. Titled
"The Task That Lies Ahead," the order announced to the Raiders the news for
which they had been waiting, that they were bound for Hawaii and on to an
early encounter with the enemy. "We become the first of our land forces of
our nation to carry the war to the enemy," boasted Carlson, who then cautioned his men against overconfidence, a mistake he believed the Japanese
had already made. "The enemy . . . is fully aware of the softness of Americans
and on this factor alone he banks to give him 75 per cent of his victories."
But, continued Carlson, the Raiders held the key to victory. "By our faith, our
energy, our courage and our intelligence—perhaps most of all by our willing-

ness to sacrifice comfort and convenience—we shall march on to victory. Even more important, we will set the pace and blaze the trail for those behind, inspiring them with confidence and showing them that we Americans have what it takes to win battles. It means work and sacrifice, Raiders, but let's go."[1]

For most Raiders, the voyage marked the first time they had left the continental United States. As the California coastline receded from view and the ocean engulfed the *J. Franklin Bell*, a distant war had suddenly become real. Each mile from San Diego brought them closer to facing their ultimate test—combat.

"Yeah, it was on everybody's mind. We were getting down to business," said Pfc. Jesse Vanlandingham. "The training was over, and it was serious now. We had a $10,000 life insurance policy. I increased it in San Diego. That brought the seriousness, too. Most of the guys didn't expect to survive at all. They told us that when we volunteered. Carlson said at a battalion meeting we probably wouldn't survive."[2]

Pvt. Darrell Loveland claimed that the departure made an impression on the younger Raiders. "There were some who were kind of uneasy about it and wondering, 'What have I really gotten into?' There were a few second thoughts. Heading to war is a whole different ball of wax than being in training."[3]

Only weeks before, Japanese submarines imperiled the West Coast. Now this ship plowed directly into submarine domain. The ship adopted a zigzag course, but without escort the defenseless vessel splashed westward at the mercy of the Japanese.

A more sober group of Raiders docked in Hawaii. As the *J. Franklin Bell* inched into Pearl Harbor on May 18 and steamed by the still-smoldering wrecks that once had been the Pacific Fleet, muted Raiders stared at Battleship Row, where the *Oklahoma* rested on its side and its compatriot, the *Arizona*, lay upside down. Reality dwarfed the tame images they had seen in home-front newspapers, making some wonder if the situation in the Pacific was worse than what they had been told. Lieutenant Peatross thought that "as our transport steamed slowly past battleship row, it occurred to me that 'battleship death row' might now be a more fitting name. On all sides we could see the almost unbelievable results of the Japanese attack: the pitiful wreckage of once proud warships, some on their sides, some bow up, others stern up, but all looking irretrievably lost."[4]

Private Loveland battled a wave of emotions as the devastation of Pearl Harbor unfolded before him. "There were a lot of ships laying on their side and the whole bay was quite oily. That's when it really started to sink in to me. I thought, 'I know what I've got to do, and here's a sudden example right here.' That will get your head out of your butt. Looking at Pearl Harbor brought it all into perspective. No anger, no surprise, just determination. It just got to me."[5]

"Cheese in the Trap"

Top military officials in Washington, D.C., and Hawaii knew that the Japanese, embarrassed over Lt. Col. James Doolittle's daring April bombing raid against Tokyo, planned to launch a reprisal, but the date and location remained a mystery. Hawaii, Alaska, the Panama Canal, and even the West Coast loomed as possibilities. Heroic efforts by American code breakers cracked key components of the Japanese naval code and concluded that the Japanese intended to hit Midway. By the end of May Nimitz knew the date, target, and composition of forces headed toward Midway.

Situated 1,137 miles northwest of Hawaii, the six-mile-wide Midway Atoll formed a strategic piece of the fragile American defense line. The atoll consists of two islands—the two-mile-long Sand Island and its smaller neighbor, Eastern Island. A 1938 government report listed Midway second in strategic importance only to Pearl Harbor. Losing the possession to the Japanese would place Hawaii within easy striking range as well as cause a possible relocation of the Pacific Fleet to the West Coast.

While elated over his forces' victory at Pearl Harbor, the commander in chief of the Japanese fleet, Admiral Isoroku Yamamoto, considered the attack incomplete since his dive-bombers and torpedo planes had missed the American aircraft carriers. As long as those floating airfields roamed the Pacific, Yamamoto remained vulnerable. To remedy this, he hoped to draw out the remnants of the American fleet and destroy it in a gigantic sea clash—the "decisive encounter" for which Japanese strategists had long planned.

If Yamamoto succeeded, the entire Pacific would lay open for his taking. A major defeat might cause his enemy to sign a truce giving Japan a free hand in the western Pacific.

Earlier in his career Yamamoto had visited the United States and observed her mighty industrial capabilities. He understood that if the war dragged on for more than six months, American factories would begin pouring out an unstoppable stream of ships, aircraft, and weapons that could spell eventual defeat for Japan. He thus devised an operation to knock his adversary out of the war before that industrial might delivered the tools of war. A threat to Midway served as the perfect bait to draw out the American carriers and whatever else remained of the American Navy.

Following an early June air strike on Midway by four Japanese aircraft carriers led by Vice Admiral Chuichi Nagumo, an invasion convoy of five thousand men protected by two battleships, six heavy cruisers, and numerous destroyers would seize Midway Island. Lying three hundred miles behind with a potent battleship flotilla, Yamamoto lurked in ambush for the American Navy.

The Japanese assembled an equally powerful punch for the American defense forces on Midway. Fifteen hundred Special Naval Landing Forces—called Japanese marines—would hit Sand Island, while a detachment of one thousand army personnel struck Eastern Island.

A confident Japanese fleet headed to battle. Their intelligence predicted that the Americans had lost the will to fight, and Japanese sailors boasted that they would "beat the enemy hands down."[6]

They would not have been so optimistic if they had known that Nimitz held their operational plans, but even such an advantage did not guarantee an American victory. The United States Navy had suffered alarming losses at Pearl Harbor, meaning that victory or defeat for the outnumbered American Navy would depend upon individual courage, instinct, and decision-making ability.

Events dropped Carlson's Raiders directly into the storm. Soon after they arrived in Hawaii, Carlson and Roosevelt, accompanied by the commanders of C and D companies, Capt. Donald H. Hastie and Lt. John Apergis, were summoned to headquarters for a briefing with Admiral Nimitz.

With an abundance of brass at the table, James Roosevelt must have felt as if he were again inside the Oval Office. Nimitz wasted little time getting to his point. He ordered Carlson to send two Raider companies to Midway, armed with as much ammunition as they could carry, "so as to sell out dearly and make the Japanese landing costly to the enemy." The phrasing of Nimitz's request bothered Lieutenant Apergis, who thought it sounded as if Nimitz were sending the Raider companies to Midway as sacrificial lambs. Being the junior officer present at the meeting, Apergis hesitated to speak, but he overcame his concerns and asked Nimitz how long the Navy expected the Raiders to hold out at Midway.

"The answer was to the last man and bullet—but if the U.S. Navy's plan, called simply the 'cheese in the trap,' worked and the enemy was enticed to go for the cheese (us on Midway) and the Jap carriers were sunk than [sic] our chances of survival increased."[7]

Nimitz told Apergis and Hastie to be prepared to fight to the death if necessary. Their companies were to be part of the cheese that Nimitz dangled in front of the Japanese. If the ruse failed, C and D companies would be stranded in the mid-Pacific and face either death or capitulation.

Carlson and Roosevelt remained in Hawaii. The Marines could not afford to lose either man, especially the son of the president, in such a desperate mission. They would stay behind and supervise training exercises for a different assignment.

"Our Purpose Was to Kill and Die"

"We were itching for a fight," explained Pfc. Jesse Vanlandingham of the Raiders in C and D companies. "The training was over and we were ready. We were the best and we felt that anybody that we ran up against, their days were numbered."[8]

Vanlandingham and his cohorts boarded one of three ships—the cruiser *St. Louis* or the destroyers *Case* or *Guinn*. Because speed was of the essence and fellow Marines—the Sixth Defense Battalion at Midway—needed help, none of the ships zigzagged as they barreled through the Pacific toward their destination more than one thousand miles away.

The Raiders reached the atoll less than three days later, looking more like a cargo of thugs than a razor-sharp combat unit. As they barely had time to settle in after the arduous California training and the long ocean trip to Hawaii before embarking for Midway, the unshaven, grimy Raiders created quite a spectacle.

Their rugged appearance was part circumstance, part design—they wanted others to walk cautiously when near a Raider. The strutting arsenals, sporting knives dangling at their sides, bandoliers sloping across their shoulders, and hand grenades bulging from their pockets, wanted people to fear them on sight.

"We were a fairly wild-looking lot," said Pvt. Virgil Leeman of C Company. "Carlson was not a traditional type of officer, and we wore green dungarees, not the camouflage uniforms we had later in the war. We had no way of having a bath or laundering our clothes, so we got pretty scrubby looking. We prided ourselves on being different from other units. Carlson tolerated a lot of stuff—Mohawk haircuts, quite a few of those, and he put up with that. We took pride in looking like that. We were a rough-and-ready outfit. We were special, tough training, pride in what we were doing. Carlson encouraged that sort of thing."[9]

The arrival of more than two hundred ferocious-looking Raiders made the desired impression. Midway personnel kept their distance, and rumors cautioned against approaching a Raider post at night or risk a knife to the throat.

Scuttlebutt stated that thousands of enemy soldiers headed their way, but the Raiders were still uncertain why they had been sent to Midway. How could a few companies halt such a potent assault force? Were they at Midway to record a heroic defense or to die?

"It was always my thought that Midway was going to be another Wake Island," said Pfc. Thomas Tobin of C Company, referring to the site where a group of Marines fought valiantly before surrendering to a vastly superior Japanese force. "Some men didn't think that C and D were coming back."[10]

"We found out our purpose there was to shoot and kill and die," said Private Loveland. "We found out when we got back that they really didn't expect us back. If the Japanese had landed, there was nothing we could do except slow them down as much as we could."[11]

In Washington, D.C., Eleanor Roosevelt fretted over the well-being of her son, whose precise whereabouts were unknown. She wrote a friend that "perhaps we have to learn that life was not meant to be lived in security but with adventurous courage."[12]

On May 2, Chester Nimitz had conducted a personal tour of Midway with its two commanders, Navy Comdr. Cyril T. Simard, in overall charge of the military forces stationed there, and Marine Lt. Col. Harold Shannon, who oversaw the island's defenses. Nimitz asked the pair what they needed to withstand an attack, then returned to Pearl Harbor to open the spigots. Fighters, bombers, barbed wire, additional men, and tanks poured to the island, especially after May 20, when Nimitz informed Simard and Shannon the Japanese might attack as soon as May 28.

Though willing to divert whatever he could toward Midway, Nimitz made clear that the island took a second seat to his most crucial weapon—the Navy's aircraft carriers. He could not afford to lose those assets, or at least lose them without inflicting graver damage on the enemy, so he informed Simard that if the choice came down to preserving his carriers or saving Midway, the island was gone. He could retake Midway later, but once the aircraft carriers, which stood as the most potent deterrent to Japanese aggression at that stage of the war, were gone, he could not soon replace them. The path to Hawaii and the West Coast would be open for Japan to strike at their leisure. The Marines, not the carriers, were expendable.

Once the two Raider companies arrived at Midway, they fell under Shannon's jurisdiction. The World War I veteran believed he could stop the Japanese at the reef. He had seen barbed wire halt the Germans during World War I, and he now so exhorted his men to string the material everywhere that they started calling him "Barbed Wire Bob." One Marine moaned, "Barbed wire, barbed wire! Cripes, the Old Man thinks we can stop planes with barbed wire."[13]

The defensive preparations intensified after C and D companies arrived. Leeman and Vanlandingham, along with the rest of C Company, took positions along the beaches on Sand Island facing the ocean or in a clump of pine trees a bit inland. Since they could not dig far down into the hard coral surface, the Raiders filled bags with sand and built upward instead. The installations they were to protect—a radar tower and shack, some fuel tanks, and a seaplane base—rested behind.

Lieutenant Apergis led the men of D Company to their stations on Eastern Island, a twenty-minute boat ride across the lagoon from their Raider buddies on Sand. Gooney birds fluttered and stumbled about, amusing the Raiders with their fumbling ways, but unlike on Sand Island, Eastern offered tempting targets for the Japanese. The triangular-shaped airstrip dominated the middle, while a main hangar, powerhouse, mess hall, water distillation plant, post exchange, and underground command post rested along the sides.

During breaks the Raiders bathed in the ocean. The water's stunning colors, a fascinating blend of turquoise, jade, sapphire, and blue, vied for attention with the star-clustered night skies. Pvt. Ralph Shawlee of D Company thought he had never seen a more stunning sight than the millions of sparkling stars that seemed to rise from the ocean and blanket the skies.

They had little time to admire nature, however. The Raiders helped the Marines of the Sixth Defense Battalion emplace light tanks in the forest, dig trenches and dugouts, clear fields of fire, and set antiboat obstacles in the water. On Eastern Island's beach, Private Shawlee stopped digging before reaching an adequate depth due to the water table. He explained that he "dug in down to only a foot and a half where we struck salt water. Not much of a foxhole—18 inches."[14]

They littered thousands of mines along the beaches and strung hundreds of miles of barbed wire, in the water and on land. "We walked out about chest high in the water and set barbed wire all around," said Private Loveland. "All the way up to the beach. Then we put some land mines and other booby traps."[15]

Raider improvisation produced tools of war from seemingly innocuous material. They shoved blasting gelatin into lengths of sewer piping, sealed the ends with hot tar, clustered them in groups of six, and planted them offshore, ready to be detonated electronically when the Japanese approached. Empty whiskey bottles became Molotov cocktails. Marines emplaced fifteen hundred of Capt. Harold Throneson's makeshift mines made from dynamite, a flashlight battery, and forty pounds of pressure, and sprinkled the beaches with hundreds of cigar-shaped boxes jammed with nails, spikes, pieces of metal, and glass. The devices could be exploded either electrically or by a Raider sharpshooter hitting a bull's-eye painted on the box's side.

As the Raiders helped strengthen Midway's defenses, additional material poured in. On May 26, an aircraft tender dropped off guns, tanks, and aircraft, while eighteen dive-bombers and seven fighters flew in to bolster the island's aging air force of sixteen Vindicator dive-bombers and twenty-one Buffalo fighters. Three days later another four Army B-26s arrived, along with twelve Navy PBYs.

Raiders marveled at the sight of one of the country's newest weapons, the B-17 bomber, as the graceful aircraft descended for landings. The addition of the plane eased fears some Raiders had that they had been sent to Midway to die.

"A B-17 bomber flew over," explained Private Leeman. "It was one of the new planes, and we went absolutely nuts when we saw it. Men were hugging each other. It revealed how we were carrying on inside. These were the savior aircraft."[16] The string of fighters and bombers that arrived in late May and early June caused one officer to joke that soon the gooney birds would have no place to land.

The additional material could not have been timelier, as it appeared the Japanese would soon strike. On May 27, Admiral Nimitz, based on information delivered by his code breakers, divulged to another admiral that the Japanese had already named the officer who was to take command of the Midway facilities.

The Raiders experienced mixed emotions as the first days of June ended. While eager for a fight, they knew that Midway was not the ideal situation for a highly trained group of commandos to showcase its talents. If the Japanese fleet appeared on the horizon, the Raiders had little choice but to remain in their foxholes and dugouts and fight to the death. It was hardly what Carlson had promised in training camp, but it was the task they had been given.

At least they had taken all precautions. Capt. Robert C. McGlashan, the operations officer for the Sixth Defense Battalion, recalled of the eve of battle, "Of course, there were a thousand things more that could have been done; but all the essential things had been done—and not a day to spare. As I turned in that night knowing that the Japs would arrive by morning, I felt that, come what may, we had done all we could."[17]

The Raiders left behind in Hawaii wondered if they might be in the thick of things as well. Rumors had the Japanese fleet returning to complete the task it started on December 7. Physicians discharged the less serious patients from Army hospitals to free beds for expected casualties, and Lt. Gen. Delos C. Emmons, the military governor of Hawaii, recommended that all women and children living in downtown Honolulu leave for inland areas. Concern spread to the mainland, where military officials canceled leaves on the West Coast and stationed a picket line of patrol boats and yachts four hundred miles off California's coast.

"My First Taste of War"

On June 3, Ens. Jack Reid, piloting a PBY on early-morning patrol, located Japanese ships seven hundred miles out. The news spread to every Marine that in less than twenty-four hours, Midway would be within range of Japanese carrier aircraft.

The famed Hollywood film director John Ford, the maker of legendary Western movies such as *Stagecoach*, starring John Wayne, hiked to the top of the powerhouse on Sand Island, not far from where Private Leeman and Private First Class Vanlandingham waited in their bunkers, to set up his cameras. He had crafted a career filming shootouts, but none could match the reality of his next project. The Navy Department had asked him to film the coming battle and, during the fray, to relay to Commander Simard what he observed.

At 4:45 a.m. on June 4, 108 aircraft launched from the four Japanese carriers. Thirty-six level bombers rose from the *Hiryu* and the *Soryu*, while thirty-six dive-bombers joined ranks from the *Akagi* and the *Kaga*. Another thirty-six fighters—nine from each carrier—escorted the bombers. The level bombers, tasked with destroying the island's aircraft batteries, would arrive over Midway first, thus clearing the way for the dive-bombers and fighters to strike against installations and oil tanks. Aircraft from the *Hiryu* and the *Kaga* would strike Sand Island, while the other two carriers pounded Eastern Island.

Fifty-five minutes later Lt. William Chase spotted the aircraft speeding toward Midway and radioed from his PBY Catalina flying boat, "MANY PLANES HEADING MIDWAY. BEARING 320, DISTANCE 150."[18] Sirens on Sand and Eastern islands sent men scurrying to their posts and aviators to their aircraft. Within twenty minutes twenty-six fighters had risen to intercept the enemy, while the scout bombers rendezvoused twenty miles east of Midway to await further instructions.

American fighter pilots met the Japanese thirty miles from Midway, where the faster and more maneuverable Zeros pounced on the lumbering American planes to keep them from the bombers. The Marine aviators bravely charged at Japanese bombers, but attracted Zeros like a magnet as they shortened the distance. Instead of attacking the bombers, the outnumbered American pilots had to spend most of their time evading the slippery Zeros.

On Midway a welcome silence replaced the awesome noise of takeoff, leaving each man alone with his thoughts. A Marine manning the radar station near Shannon's command post called out the range as the Japanese planes brought the aerial combat within sight of the Raiders ashore.

The Raiders could hardly have been comforted by what they witnessed. The American fighters, outdated F2A-3 Brewster Buffalos, had no chance against the swifter Zeros, who seemed to toy with the slower Brewsters. It appeared to some as if strings bound the Brewsters, later dubbed "Flying Coffins," to the Zeros.

Any Raider doubt about the savage nature of the war they were about to fight ended when they observed the Japanese attack Maj. Floyd B. "Red" Parks, who had parachuted from his burning Brewster and fluttered defenseless toward the ground in his harness. "As soon as his shoot opened the Japs were at him and didn't let up even when he landed on the reef," stated the official Marine report of Parks's demise. Not content to fire at him as he dangled in his parachute, the Japanese strafed the water where Parks landed to make sure they had completed their task. John Ford bristled at the lack of chivalry, and the official report added, in words with which every Raider who witnessed the attack could agree, "This enemy is cold blooded in every respect of the word. . . ."[19]

The Zeros swept aside the American fighters with ease, leaving the defense of Midway in the hands of the Marines manning the guns and guarding the beaches. Midway was naked before the Japanese.

Lieutenant Apergis gazed upward and noticed "the sky above was full of Rising Sun red ball marked Zeros." On Sand Island, John Ford observed the events through his binoculars, and was most impressed not with the Japanese but with the men around him. "Everybody was very calm. I was amazed, sort of, at the lackadaisical air everybody took. You know everybody sort of took to the line of duty as though they had been living through this sort of thing all their lives."[20]

Private Leeman might have disagreed. As the Japanese aircraft drew closer, he wondered if those hastily assembled bunkers were a match for enemy bombs and bullets. "It was scary. When the Japanese arrived we got into our bunkers and hoped they worked OK."[21]

The baptism of fire for Carlson's Raiders occurred at 6:31 when Midway's batteries, with Apergis and other Raiders in support, belched their initial salvos. The guns on Sand Island downed one Japanese plane, bringing loud cheers from Marines, but a quick succession of bombs ended the celebration. Explosions rocked both Eastern and Sand islands as bombs smashed into oil tanks, barracks, antiaircraft batteries, and other installations.

"It was the most terrifying experience of my life," claimed Pvt. James Van Winkle of C Company at Sand Island. "I imagined the whole Jap Army making a landing on my beach."[22] Private Loveland's squad leader gruffly reminded the men that as their main task was to repulse the expected land invasion, they had better not get hit.

"We were there barely forty-eight hours when the attack came, and that was my first taste of war," stated Pharmacist's Mate Third Class Richard J. Favinger of the bombings at Eastern Island. "They bombed and strafed, and there was nothing I could do except make myself invisible in that enclosure of sandbags. The bombing vibrations and the noise of the strafing aircraft was deafening. They lasted several hours, probably six different waves. They pretty much destroyed everything but the airstrip."[23]

Japanese accuracy impressed John Ford, who saw bombs tear into sheds and hangars while leaving the airstrip intact. One bomb hit an ammunition dump, sending thousands of pieces of deadly shrapnel whistling through the air, killing four maintenance men. Another demolished the command post on Eastern Island, killing the sector commander, Maj. William W. Benson.

With the onslaught heating up—"The noise during the attack was the loudest I had ever heard in my life,"[24] recalled Private Leeman—some of the Raiders rushed to antiaircraft batteries to assist the crews. Lieutenant Apergis manned a .50-caliber antiaircraft gun, part of a Sixth Defense Battalion post near his station. Despite being in the midst of an attack, Apergis could not help but laugh at the name of the Marine he assisted—Sergeant Seargent— who proceeded to add more humor to a deadly morning.

As Apergis and Sergeant Seargent waited at the gun for the first Zero "to come down on us on a strafing run," Apergis told Seargent to take cover behind the sandbag parapet. When the Zero completed its run, both men rose to "start shooting at the tail of the Jap Zero as he pulled out of his dive," but when Seargent pulled his trigger all they heard was a "click" and no firing. Seargent had stripped and oiled the gun before the attack, but in doing so he reinserted the follower bolt mechanism upside down.

"He was so frustrated that he picked up his Springfield '03 rifle—bolt action—and started firing at the Jap plane—notwithstanding I did the same with my .45 automatic pistol," recalled Apergis. "The Jap plane had fun with us—he circled around and came back at us with his guns blazing—down we go behind the sandbag emplacement. The Jap pilot came so very low this time that we thought we might get him as he pulled out of his strafing run. I don't think he was more than 20 feet high—he grinned at us, because we missed again, and thumbed his nose at us—and left for better prey."[25]

The most astounding sight had to be the Japanese pilot who brazenly flew his Zero upside down as he buzzed the airstrip. Marines stared incredulously at the vision, for a moment forgetting their guns to observe the unlikely spectacle. The pilot dropped to one hundred feet, flipped the aircraft on its back, and sped barely above the surface as he taunted his Marine foes. "Everybody was amazed," recalled John Ford, "nobody fired at him, until suddenly some Marine said, 'What the Hell,' let go at him and then shot him down. He slid off into the sea."[26]

"Those Kids Were Really Remarkable"

Within thirty minutes the Japanese had disappeared. The all-clear sounded at seven fifteen, bringing men out of their shelters to check on damage and await further instructions. They then took up their defensive positions at the beach to disrupt a possible enemy landing.

While American aviators put the finishing touches on Nagumo's carriers, the Raiders and other Marines took inventory. The fighter squadron stationed at Midway, VMF-221, was no more. Twenty-three of twenty-five aircraft had either been lost or so badly damaged they could no longer be used. Thick black smoke billowed from oil tanks, the seaplane hangar, the dispensary, the mess hall, and the post exchange. Eleven men—none from Carlson's Raiders—had been killed and eighteen wounded.

The Midway defenders left their mark on the Japanese, however. Antiaircraft batteries and fighters downed eight enemy bombers and three Zeros. As Lieutenant Apergis wrote, Nimitz's plan to offer Midway as a tempting target for Nagumo's aircraft while his own chased after the Japanese carriers worked to perfection, "and the greatest victory in U.S. naval warfare was ours . . ." Apergis added with more than a touch of gratefulness, "and it also saved our skins."[27]

The Raiders kept busy throughout the long day and night. Pharmacist's Mate Favinger helped identify the deceased Marines, resorting to fingerprinting or tattoos in the most severely burned cases. They helped clear debris, and once nightfall diminished the likelihood of an assault, loaded forty-five thousand gallons of aviation gasoline into fifty-five-gallon drums and transferred them by hand pumps to waiting B-17 bombers.

Private Leeman joined a group of Raiders to inspect a downed Japanese aircraft that had crashed near his bunker, hoping, like many American soldiers, to unearth a souvenir. One Marine ripped the silk scarf off the deceased pilot's neck, while other Raiders yanked the body out of the wreckage. Leeman sat down for a moment before he realized that, rather than resting on a chunk of the aircraft, he had plopped down atop the charred body of the Japanese pilot.

Though the Raiders at Midway had a ringside seat to one of the war's most decisive moments, they played second fiddle to the courageous Army, Navy, and Marine fliers who attacked Nagumo's aircraft carriers. American carrier planes, aided by aircraft based out of Midway, swooped down in an attack that cost the Japanese four valuable carriers, thousands of lives, and victory.

John Ford was thankful for another reason. The astute Hollywood director had observed young Americans under fire, and had been reassured that, in the Marines of the Sixth Defense Battalion and in the Raiders, the nation's future lay in stellar hands.

"The Marines with me—I took one look at them and I said, 'Well this war was won.' They were kids, oh, I would say from 18 to 22, none of them were older. They were the calmest people I have ever seen. They were up there popping away with rifles, having a swell time and none of them were alarmed. I mean the thing [a Japanese bomb] would drop through, they would laugh and say 'My God that one was close.' I have never seen a greater exhibition of courage and coolness under fire in my life and I have seen some in my day. Those kids were really remarkable."[28] Ford's documentary about the battle, narrated by Henry Fonda, won the 1942 Academy Award for Best Documentary Short Subject.

A few days after the battle the Marines sent Major Roosevelt to the island for a post-action assessment. During his tour an officer handed Roosevelt a folder containing critical evaluations of the antiquated Brewster Buffalo fighter, and asked that Roosevelt hand the folder to his father. One, Capt. Philip White, stated in his action report, "It is my belief that any commander that orders pilots out for combat in F2A-3 (Brewster Buffalo) should consider the pilot as lost before leaving the ground."[29]

Roosevelt agreed to do so, and when he subsequently traveled to Washington to make his report in person, he made a point to hand it to his father. "I believe that it resulted in considerable improvement in the situation shortly thereafter,"[30] James Roosevelt wrote *Time* magazine's chief Pacific war correspondent, Robert Sherrod, in 1948.

The Raiders cannot claim to have affected the outcome of what occurred in the waters about Midway. That honor goes to brave aviators, to code breakers, and to sailors who manned American carriers. Orders sent the Raiders to Midway, and as such they played a role in what, after the war, Admiral Nimitz called the "attack that in minutes changed the whole course of the war."[31]

Had Japan won the Battle of Midway, she could have moved about the ocean at will, even as far as the western coast of the United States. The reporter Robert Casey, who traveled with the naval forces involved in the battle, wrote that had that occurred, "We might well have been moving our bases to a more suitable place—such as the bottom of the Grand Canyon."[32]

The climactic results shifted momentum to the United States, which after Pearl Harbor had been perilously holding on while Japanese forces over-ran much of the Pacific. Those war scares that tossed the West Coast into a panic each time a supposed sighting occurred had now been eliminated. With the once-powerful Japanese navy retreating, the likelihood of California or Oregon again being threatened all but disappeared.

But it had been close. Eager to talk to men who had been under fire, Washburn chatted with friends in C and D companies. What most struck the officer was not the accounts of the bombing, but the sense of relief his friends shared. One Raider said to him, "For Christ's sake, if those Nips had been able to land, we would have been faced with thousands of them. What could two companies have done? We were just sacrificial lambs, that's all. Thank God the Navy saw they didn't get ashore!"[33]

"There's Something Big Coming Up"

While C and D companies faced the enemy at Midway, Evans Carlson es-tablished the rest of the battalion at Camp Catlin, a makeshift camp sur-rounded by pineapple fields off the main road connecting Honolulu and Pearl Harbor. Carlson was not at all pleased with the restrictive confines of Camp Catlin, so he utilized his persuasive powers, and an appeal to their sense of patriotism, to convince the owners of nearby pineapple plantations to make some of their fields available. The owners agreed on two conditions—that the Raiders did not damage any of the property and that they left the ripening pineapples alone.

After Carlson settled the administrative details, the training schedule in-tensified. Carlson gave his junior officers prominent roles in this phase. Lieu-tenant Miller hiked his men over hills to the B Company area at such a fast pace on July 23 that some of the men collapsed in the heat. Lt. Wilfred Le Francois illustrated the proper techniques for entering and securing a town.

In between training exercises, the Raiders took advantage of the one tempting item at their fingertips—the luscious pineapples. Despite Carlson's lectures on the impropriety of stealing, the delectable fruit proved too appe-tizing. Carlson eventually had to assemble and search his Raiders after field exercises, which slowed the thefts, but the men found ingenious ways to pilfer a pineapple or two. As Lieutenant Peatross humorously wrote, the Raid-ers were simply applying their training, "which had stressed living off the enemy's land, and now that we were in the field the Raiders wanted to practice what had been preached as gospel."[34]

The quickened pace of training and the rapid arrival of supplies, most likely aided by Jimmy Roosevelt, delighted Lieutenant Miller. When his parents asked in a letter whether he had any netting as protection against mosquitoes, Miller answered that "we all have plenty of it. As long as Jimmy is with us we will never want for many things."[35] He concluded that a mission could not be far off.

In mid-July President Roosevelt, anxious to embark upon another raid following the successful Doolittle bombing of Tokyo, ordered his military to execute a similar mission, one that, even if it gained little in the military arena, would boost home-front morale. Nimitz considered hitting Wake, Tinian, Attu, a steel mill on Hokkaido, and railroad tunnels on Honshu in the Home Islands, but concluded those would be too difficult. Instead he selected Makin. Nimitz's senior Marine officer, Col. Omar T. Pfeiffer, wrote, "So it was decided to pick an easy task on which to cut the raiders' teeth."[36] Whereas the Army Air Corps carried out the attack on Tokyo, Carlson's Raiders would have the honor of striking Makin.

Many reasons favored Makin as a target. The atoll stood closer to Hawaii, which meant that Carlson would not have to be transported deep into enemy-controlled waters, and a raid against the lightly held atoll would serve as an adequate test of Raider hit-and-run capabilities.

Carlson would have to prepare without sufficient intelligence. "We don't know much about what the Japs have there," Nimitz confided to Carlson. "Tarawa, near Makin, doesn't seem like much—yet. From reports Makin is their headquarters in the Gilberts. They've got a seaplane base and a great deal of supplies. As to how strong a force defends the place—we haven't much definite dope. You'll have to make your own estimate. We're allowing you two subs. That'll mean a force of about 200 men."[37]

Carlson chose A and B companies to make the raid. Those units had trained longer than the other four companies, and he wanted to see how his most experienced troops reacted under fire. Carlson assembled the officers from A and B companies and, with Roosevelt's assistance, briefed them about the coming raid and about the specialized training in landing from rubber boats they would soon commence.

In mid-July trucks transported the Raiders to Barbers Point, a stretch of beach on Hawaii's coast due west of Pearl Harbor that had been selected because its terrain and surf closely matched that of Makin. The Navy constructed replicas of Makin's radio station, barracks, and other installations so that the Raiders could rehearse their assignments.

With the rest of the battalion back at Camp Catlin, the Raiders of A and B companies embarked on daily landings from rubber boats, battling the challenging surf at Barbers Point to land at beaches strewn with lava rocks. They approached in ten-man rubber boats, each equipped with an outboard motor to help advance through the surf. Sometimes the engines worked smoothly, but more often than not the exposed motors sputtered to a standstill after being doused by ocean water.

Despite the crafts' difficulties, the Raiders became deft at maneuvering the awkward rubber boats. Each man not only trained for his precise role on the boat but learned others' as well in case they became incapacitated. Raiders drilled as boat captains, outboard motor mechanics, coxswains, fuel men, boat inflators, or paddle men. The taller men occupied positions in the bow while shorter men took spots midboat and in the stern to make it easier in walking the boats out to deeper water. While the taller men splashed into the surf first and helped carry the boat out to deeper water, the shorter men hopped in and started paddling.

Since neither of the two submarines designated for the mission, the *Nautilus* nor the *Argonaut*, could be released from duty until shortly before departure, Carlson fixed two buoys at set distances from the beach to represent the two submarines. Each day and night the Raiders paddled out to the buoys, then at a signal from Carlson commenced the return trip to the beach. Rarely did things go right.

In a foreshadowing of events, the exposed motors often sputtered and quit during landing exercises. "They would never start & out come the paddles & the boat crew had to paddle like hell to get anywhere, especially against the ocean drift,"[38] wrote Pfc. Ray Bauml in his diary on July 30 of the frequent mishaps.

"Sometimes the motors would run," recalled Private Carson, "but many times they wouldn't. The buoys were quite a ways beyond the surf line. We practiced, practiced, practiced—during the day and at night, when there was a pretty good wind blowing."[39] Without cowlings to shield the motors from being drenched, the Raiders often had to disassemble the engines after each practice run and wash the salt water out of them.

The Raiders trained for every contingency. They practiced landings in heavy and mild swells, during rain and sunshine, by day and at night. To simulate a near disaster and test their adaptability skills, Carlson scheduled one practice where the men made do without clothing, workable motors, or paddles.

Once his men were accustomed to maneuvering the rubber boats, Carlson expanded the drills from individual boat training to platoon-sized training, then company-sized drills, and eventually landings including both companies together. He at first allowed the men to paddle without equipment. When they had mastered that technique, he added cartridge belts, ammunition, helmets, and packs.

Pfc. Ray Bauml wrote to Lieutenant Miller's father that he, Jack, and the others "had quite a few happy moments practicing our rubber boat landings. You see, the ocean at this point had tremendous breakers that would come crashing upon the beach with terrific force. We had a gay time paddling our rubber boat out into the surf, fighting the breakers, and when we were a sufficient distance from shore—we would turn around and then try to ride the breaker in—using our clumsy rubber boat as a surfboard. Your boy would be right in amongst us enlisted men, laughing, having a whale of a time, enjoying himself to the fullest."[40]

After repeated rehearsals with the rubber boats, Carlson shifted to the land phase. Based upon photographic reconnaissance of Makin conducted by the Navy during its February raids against the Gilbert Islands, Carlson reproduced Makin's objectives by outlining a replica of each one a short distance inland with long strips of white cloth. The Raiders, in full equipment, then practiced landing, camouflaging the boats, and rushing inland toward their objectives. Hampered by inadequate reconnaissance, Carlson realized the outlines bore little actual resemblance to what his men would encounter on Makin, but he wanted to make them aware of where each objective rested in relation to the whole scheme, as well as to time them in their practices.

He added a sense of urgency by hinting that soon the training would end. "There's something big coming up," Bauml wrote in his diary on July 30. "We were given an explanation concerning some island which we might raid."[41] The next day they learned for certain that a raid had been planned, but were not given the name or location of their target.

Lieutenant Miller, who had so eagerly awaited his chance to command men in combat, could not share in the enthusiasm. During one of the landing exercises a crushing wave hurled Miller against the gunwale and fractured the index finger of his right hand. The accident, though not serious enough to send Miller home, prevented him from participating in the Makin Raid. The frustrated officer had to remain in Hawaii while his men, including Sergeant Maghakian, steamed to war. He consoled himself with the fact that Carlson was certain to involve the battalion in other operations, by which time the hand would have healed.

After three weeks of practice, including several night landings from submarines, Carlson set a dress rehearsal for dawn of August 6. With Admiral Nimitz and Adm. Raymond A. Spruance, the victor of Midway, observing from ashore at Barbers Point, the Raiders, in blackface and full battle gear, disembarked from the *Nautilus*, headed toward land, and drew within fifty feet before either Nimitz or Spruance detected them.

Carlson critiqued the operation afterward with Roosevelt and other officers and concluded that the session was a success save for one aspect. Stuck in the confines of a submarine for the first time, his Raiders wearied in the wilting heat caused by an additional 130 men taxing the vessel's ventilating system. In twenty minutes the temperature inside the boat soared fifteen degrees, to the mid-nineties. To remedy the effects, a five-ton air conditioner was hastily installed aboard each submarine. "Living conditions will be worse than the standards set by the canned sardines," Bauml ruefully scribbled in his diary on August 4. "The sardines at least have oil."[42]

The trial run before Nimitz and Spruance heralded the end to Carlson's preparation for Makin. The Raiders from A and B companies had proven their versatility during the many practices off Barbers Point, justifying Carlson's confidence that his men would perform as expected.

"We had no doubts as to our readiness to handle anything that might await us at the objective," wrote Lieutenant Peatross, "and it was with feelings of great self-confidence and no little self-satisfaction that we broke camp and boarded trucks for the move back to Camp Catlin."[43]

"Stood the Test of Making It"

In the immediate hours before departure, Carlson issued final instructions to his Raiders. He again reviewed the plans and objectives, and reminded the men to head ashore on Makin with bolts closed on empty chambers to reduce the possibility of an accidental firing. The last thing he wanted was for one of his men to alert the enemy to their presence before the Raiders were ready. Finally, he urged the men to write letters home and cautioned them to maintain silence about the raid.

Carlson had reason to worry. Shortly before the Raiders left Hawaii, Lieutenant Peatross and Lt. William B. MacCracken headed to the officers' club for a final round of drinks. During the evening, Carlson's officers overheard a disturbing conversation between two submarine officers. One man said, "At best, it's going to be a risky trip. Those two old, pig-iron, minelaying boats are just too big, too slow, too difficult to maneuver, and unbelievably slow in diving."

The other officer added, "Besides all that, you just can't navigate accurately enough to pop up next to one another after making a two-thousand-mile trip, and to make it more difficult, they have to arrive after dark."

As they left the club, Lt. MacCracken said to Peatross, "Peat, those bastards were talking about us."[44]

Supposedly only a handful of American officers outside the battalion knew of the coming raid. If more than that had details, what might the Japanese know?

What might that also mean for the safety of James Roosevelt, the president's son? Carlson had had serious misgivings earlier in training about Roosevelt's inclusion on such a dangerous mission and had even contacted Admiral Nimitz about Roosevelt's removal. Though he admired his executive officer, he wondered if the added risk was worth the anxiety. Carlson was like any other officer who commanded the offspring of a head of state—in addition to the many responsibilities of orchestrating a battalion in combat, he had to worry about the president's son. What might happen should the enemy kill or capture Roosevelt? Would carrying the reputation of being the officer who lost the president's son irreparably harm Carlson's career? Could he adequately supervise the actions of his men under fire with those concerns on his shoulders? Might that apprehension subconsciously alter his style of command?

Maj. Samuel Griffith, the Edson officer who had observed the British commandos and written a report on their practices, claimed that Carlson "didn't want young Roosevelt along. His thinking had nothing to do with Jimmy as a Marine. The raid was a hit-and-run operation from a submarine. Carlson just didn't want to be worrying about the President's son during an in-and-out raid like that one. Just think what hay the Nips could make if

Jimmy were captured."[45] The Japanese would display him to the world and use James as a propaganda device.

In his March 12, 1942, letter President Roosevelt had all but asked Carlson to take care of his son. Carlson hoped that Admiral Nimitz could help find a way out of the dilemma, but James Roosevelt reacted to what he saw as unfair interference. He had joined the Raiders from a sense of duty, and now, just as they were about to engage in their first mission, Carlson considered removing him.

To James's credit, he could easily have remained silent and been left behind when the Raiders left for Makin, but he wanted none of that. In the 1930s his detractors reveled in claiming James landed lucrative business contracts because of his connections. He was not about to give them more ammunition for their barbs. This raid could prove his worth to his doubters, to say nothing of gaining his father's admiration. As he wrote to his mother on July 29, he had long pondered the issue of favoritism, "and when this next job is done at least inside I'll feel I have stood the test of making it no matter what the odds."[46]

When James contacted his father, the president told Adm. Ernest King that if his son, one of the battalion officers, did not go on the raid, no one would go. While that ended the discussion, it did nothing to resolve Carlson's predicament.

Pvt. Ben Carson discussed the matter with other Raiders. These men, not easily impressed, had scrutinized Roosevelt during training and judged him worthy. However, on the eve of battle, concerns existed. "We all knew that taking Roosevelt along was a hell of a risk," explained Carson in 2007. "The story among us privates was if he gets caught by the Japanese, he'd be pretty badly beat up. Once it was settled, though, nothing was said anymore."[47]

Carlson hoped to show that his Raider Battalion, fashioned and trained after his unique notions of ethical indoctrination and the gung ho spirit, could emulate the moral fiber and fortitude exhibited by the Chinese soldiers he observed marching for hundreds of miles in the 1930s. Midway had been a minor aberration for his battalion. Makin, a surprise raid against the enemy, would pose the first test—for Carlson, for his system, for Roosevelt, and for the Raiders.

It Seemed That Confusion Reigned Supreme

O f the many Pacific locations the Japanese seized in the war's opening stage, Makin Atoll, occupied on December 10, 1941, represented her easternmost possession. As the deepest Japanese penetration toward the United States, Makin thus became a likely choice for a raid.

"To Create a Diversion"

One reason dwarfed the others for organizing the Makin Raid—to boost home-front morale shattered by early Pacific developments. The list of enemy victories galled Americans—Guam, Wake Island, Singapore, Hong Kong, the Netherlands East Indies, and the Philippines had succumbed to Tokyo's surgical strikes. President Roosevelt needed to put a dent in Japan's armor, a diversion that reassured American civilians that their military stood ready in the Pacific.

The United States would benefit in other ways. Carlson's Raiders were to destroy enemy installations at Makin, seize prisoners and documents for the intelligence sector, discourage the Japanese from advancing toward Samoa or to attempt to interdict the crucial United States–Australia communications lines, and, according to one of Nimitz's official reports titled the "Makin Diversion," "to create a diversion confusing Japanese plans and diverting forces from the stronger concentrations being assembled to attack Guadalcanal in late August."[1]

Nothing extraordinary appeared about Carlson's island objective. Other than serving as the stage for the August drama about to be played, Makin would handily have slipped into the backwaters of history, known only to its inhabitants and a few hardy adventurers that passed its way. One thousand miles northeast of Guadalcanal, Butaritari Island, which forms the southeastern anchor of the Makin Atoll, stretches eight miles from tip to tip and one-half mile wide. Clumps of mangrove dot the lagoon shore. Inland, patches of breadfruit trees, coconut palms, and scrub bush sprout from the sandy terrain making up the island's interior, resting between the handfuls of swampy marshes.

Through the years the natives added to Butaritari's features. A lagoon-side dirt road connected Ukiangong Village in the southwest with Tanimaiaki Village eight miles to the northeast, running by in succession Butaritari Village, a church, the local hospital, and Government House. Along the way three wharves extend beyond the reef to the lagoon—On Chong's Wharf to the southwest, and in succession King's Wharf and Government Wharf to its northeast. The smaller dock called Stone Pier stood halfway between King's and Government wharves.

Since December 10 the Japanese had stamped their militaristic imprint on the island, which they intended to turn into a weather station and seaplane base. In close proximity to the church resting near Stone Pier, they constructed barracks, a rifle range, and a headquarters building.

Neither the natives nor the Japanese expected their tiny island to be the scene for anything beyond a few harmless carrier air raids. A somnolent pace set in, which seemed appropriate for the slumbering Pacific isle.

The plan called for Carlson's two companies to disembark from the *Nautilus* and the *Argonaut* on August 17 and paddle toward the beaches as separate units. Based on information provided by aerial photographs taken by carrier aircraft in early February, American intelligence estimated that the Japanese would focus their defenses along the lagoon side between On Chong's and Government wharves. Thus Carlson would bring his Raiders in on the more sparsely defended ocean side. First Lieutenant Plumley's A Company would land on the left at Beach Y opposite On Chong's Wharf, while Capt. Ralph Coyte's B Company stormed ashore on the right at Beach Z opposite Government Wharf. The two companies would dash across the island, hit the Japanese from behind, then veer toward the island's center and meet in the proximity of the church.

After killing the Japanese, the Raiders were to scour the island for prisoners and documents and destroy whatever Japanese installations and supplies existed. The plan called for Carlson to bring his Raiders back to the submarines no later than nine p.m. Should they fail to appear by that time, the task force commander, Comdr. John Haines, had the authority to decide whether to remain off Makin or to depart and leave the Raiders to their fates. Should the raid proceed as expected, Carlson would lead his Raiders in a second raid the next morning at nearby Little Makin Island to the northeast.

Though all appeared to be in order, two parts of the plan bothered Carlson and Roosevelt. Rather than an unsuspecting Sergeant Major Kanemitsu, the Japanese would be on alert, not just at Makin but everywhere in the Pacific, following the August 7 Marine landings in the Solomons. Kanemitsu's men would thus be more prepared when the Raiders came ashore. Hopefully, they could still surprise the enemy from the ocean side while Kanemitsu's men faced the lagoon, but the possibility that they might be landing into heavy enemy fire seemed all too real.

Kanemitsu had, in fact, added extra precautions in light of the alert. Soldiers manned their machine-gun posts around the clock, and Kanemitsu placed snipers in the tops of palm trees. He lacked a sizeable garrison, but with their magnificent December 1941 defense the American Marines at Wake Island had already proven that an outnumbered force could inflict large casualties on an invading enemy.

Carlson bristled at the instruction to capture a few enemy soldiers. How was he to get the prisoners back to the submarines and transport them to Hawaii? The weary Raiders would be at the limit of their endurance paddling back to the submarines after fighting all day on the island, and surplus space would be at a premium on the congested boats. How could they handle extra personnel?

Some Raiders wondered if they even should. Private Carson's squad leader told his men that, because of space concerns in the submarines, they were to dispose of any Japanese soldier they captured. When a Marine asked if they could simply turn the Japanese loose after the operation, the squad leader replied, "No, that ain't disposing."[2]

"A Very Hostile Environment"

The Raiders spent the final hours in Hawaii in diverse ways. Most checked and double-checked their equipment and weapons. Some, like Private First

Class Bauml, headed to the USO center at Koailu Beach, where he washed down egg sandwiches and cake with beer. Others wrote letters home, wondering as they did if this might be their final communication with loved ones.

Platoon Sergeant Maghakian plotted to sneak Lieutenant Miller aboard the *Argonaut* so his friend could participate in the raid, but, as Maghakian later wrote, "Colonel Carlson got wind of it" and nixed the notion. Miller remained behind, but purchased a quart of top-grade whiskey for Maghakian "in case I got wounded."[3]

Late on August 7, the Raiders received the word to head out. Each man silently donned the regular issue khaki shirts and pants, now dyed black for the raid. They placed their helmets, packs, and cartridge belts in gunnysacks, then filtered to the waiting trucks for transport to the submarines.

Due to a lack of space in the submarines, fifty-five Raiders, twenty-five from A Company and thirty from B Company, had to be left behind. The *Argonaut* squeezed in a mixture of 134 Raiders from A and B companies, which the captain described as "a record for people on a submarine on an offensive mission,"[4] while the *Nautilus* took another eighty-seven Raiders from B Company. Carlson and his staff boarded the *Nautilus*, while James Roosevelt steamed out in the *Argonaut*. The two would reunite in rubber boats off Makin, then lead the Raiders toward shore.

To make room for the additional personnel and provide a place for extra bunks, the submarine crews had removed surplus torpedoes from the torpedo storage room. For the duration of the trip, both submarines would have use of only the six torpedoes resting in the tubes. Hopefully, neither submarine would have to utilize those six.

To maintain secrecy, trucks waited until after nightfall on August 7 to ferry the Raiders to the harbor, where the *Nautilus* and the *Argonaut* waited to take them aboard. Plunging into the bowels of a submarine was like entering an alien world for the Raiders, rough Marines more accustomed to outdoor rigors than the metallic confines of a cramped boat. Raiders stored their gear wherever they could in the restricted areas, then settled in for the nine-day voyage across the Pacific.

The submarines exited Pearl Harbor at nine a.m. on August 8, carrying orders to refrain from attacking enemy vessels "unless a favorable opportunity is presented for attack on a carrier or other capital ship."[5] The pair steamed out under escort until nightfall, at which time their protectors peeled off. Until the tiny force returned to Hawaii, the submarines and their complement of two Raider companies, including the president's son, were at the mercy of radar, lookouts, and good fortune. Each mile took them deeper into uncharted waters, farther from friendly forces and closer to an enemy who, for all they knew, could be lurking at any point along the 2,029-mile distance from Pearl Harbor to Makin. Unlike later expeditions against the Japanese, Carlson and his men headed across the Pacific without the comfort of knowing that a vast armada steamed with them.

"There's something about being on a submarine, and you're not a part of a big flotilla," said B Company's Private First Class Quirk. "You know it's you and this ship against the world. It's different than being on a troop transport and you can go on deck and see an armada. Here you know you are it. We had no idea what was waiting for us. You're in a very hostile environment because there were a lot of things that can cause you to become a victim."[6]

With nightfall, the faster *Nautilus* raced on ahead alone so it could arrive at Makin first and conduct a periscope reconnaissance of Makin. Men hoped the submarine navigators knew what they were doing and could locate their objective, which to some Raiders seemed akin to jumping into a lake and finding a particular pebble at the bottom.

The Raiders did not learn the name or location of their target until after the submarines left Hawaiian waters. Until that time, men engaged in a guessing game. Some swore they headed toward Wake Island as retribution for the Marine surrender of December 1941, while others suggested the Marshall or Mariana islands.

Carlson ended the guessing with his "Operations Order 1-42," issued aboard the submarines in the early moments of their voyage. The commander told his men that estimates determined there should be no more than 250 Japanese officers and men on Makin, possibly supported by seaplanes and one or two surface craft. He added that while the nearest enemy land-based aircraft was 170 miles north, and that some Japanese might be stationed on two islands seventy miles south of Makin, "No friendly forces are within supporting distance."

He reiterated the raid's main strategic purposes—to destroy enemy troops and vital installations, to seize documents and other information, to capture prisoners, and to serve as a diversion to draw Japanese reinforcements away from the American forces currently engaged in the Solomons.

He mentioned that once the submarines arrived off Makin, the men of A Company aboard the *Argonaut* would paddle over to the *Nautilus* in their rubber boats, and from there the entire force would motor in for a four a.m.

landing. Once ashore at its destination at Beach Y, situated directly opposite On Chong's Wharf, A Company was to advance northwest across the island to a road paralleling the lagoon side, secure the Raider left flank between On Chong's Wharf and King's Wharf, then veer west to eliminate Japanese troops and seize anything of value, including the Burns Philip Store, Japanese documents, and Japanese prisoners. Upon reaching the Burns Philip Store to the west, A Company was to establish contact with B Company, which should by that time be approaching from the northeast.

In the meantime, B Company would be accomplishing similar objectives in its sector. After landing at Beach Z opposite Government Wharf, the company was to move slightly northwest to the lagoon road, secure the Raider right flank, then eliminate opposition in Butaritari's eastern section and grab documents and prisoners. After securing its sector, B Company was to swing southwest to meet A Company.

Carlson instructed his Raiders that they were to place a priority on destroying the two radio stations that existed near Stone Pier and On Chong's Wharf and any seaplanes that might be floating in the lagoon. The countersigns were typically Carlson. If a man needed to challenge someone to determine his identity, he was to shout, "Hi, Raider." If he did not receive the reply of "Gung Ho," the Raider was to open fire. Carlson added that aid stations would be established in each company sector, near the left and right flanks, and in "Operations Order 2-42," he informed B Company that it was to land one squad at Beach X to the west to help secure its left flank.[7]

"Only Supposed to Raise a Little Hell"

Fortunately, neither submarine made contact with Japanese surface vessels, which meant that most of the time the submarines could steam on the surface at faster speeds. While fresh air might make conditions in the tower more bearable, the Raiders below sweltered and steamed in ghastly conditions. Despite the additional air conditioners, temperatures soon soared to over ninety degrees. Raiders could do little but remain near their bunks, which kept them out of the way of the busy submariners but also gave them more time to dwell on the sights, sounds, and, mostly, the smells.

"You feel like you're in a tomb," said Private First Class Quirk of his time in the *Nautilus*. Raiders had difficulty breathing in the intolerable conditions. Most stripped to their shorts and passed the time listening to phonograph records—Harry James, Benny Goodman, Glenn Miller, and Dinah Shore were favorites—reading books, and playing cards. Some became so bored they made a game of "liberating" cans of fruit and vegetables from the submarines' supply.

Submariners, as well, weakened in the withering heat. They later voted this trip as rougher than earlier missions that took them farther into Japanese waters. Looking for something to break the monotony, Raiders helped the pared-down crews by assuming some of their duties, but all sweated and squirmed alike.

With bathing facilities nonexistent during the voyage, Raiders joked, "We're not dirty. We're Raiders."[8] Within a few days the putrid odors of unwashed men further added to the miseries of a large group of adult men packed into a tiny space.

Meals gave little respite. With limited galley capacity, Raiders had to wait in line for breakfast and dinner. A lunch of soup and crackers went more speedily, but the submarine cooks required three and a half hours to feed all hands at breakfast and dinner.

The only time the grimy Raiders headed topside and enjoyed fresh air was during their daily exercise period. Once a day—half the complement in the morning and half in the evening—Marines stretched their muscles for twenty minutes before again descending to the ovens below. "After spending hours packed in the troop compartments like sardines in a can," wrote Lieutenant Peatross of B Company, "the few minutes spent on the open deck were spiritually as well as physically rejuvenating."[9]

The exercise had to be refreshing, for the bunks offered little comfort. Tiers of temporary bunks, stacked four high and no more than twelve inches apart, stood in every available corner and along the bulkheads. The forward and after torpedo rooms housed Raiders instead of torpedoes. Men with inside bunks had to climb over two or three Raiders to reach their destination, and during the night a Raider who twisted and turned disrupted his entire row.

"Raiders were sleeping all over *Nautilus*," stated Lieutenant Peatross. "Their gear was stowed in any available space. Rubber boats were lashed on the outside, fuel cans were stowed in the torpedo tubes, and medical and other valuable equipment were stowed inside. Places to sleep were at a premium and many 'hot bedded.' I slept on the transom (sofa) in the small, small wardroom."[10]

Many Raiders had to bend their bodies three different ways to fit into their bunks aboard the *Argonaut*. The packed quarters aboard the same boat reminded Private Carson of the family root cellar back home in Minnesota, where the clan gathered during inclement weather. "I had to crawl over four other guys to get to my bunk—it was four tiers back and if you had to get out you had to crawl over four guys sleeping, and you can imagine the animosity that created. Mine was against the bulkhead."[11]

During the first portion of the voyage to Makin, the Raiders idled the time in mundane ways, with talking, laughing, and relaxation prevalent. That mood altered five days out when the submarines passed the International Date Line. Not only did the Raiders lose a day—August 12 passed seamlessly into August 14—but they now had drawn within five hundred miles of Makin. Soon they would be within range of Japanese land-based aircraft, thereby increasing the likelihood of discovery.

A more somber mood replaced the joviality as the Raiders began preparing for what would become their country's first long-range offensive raid of the Pacific War. As if to mark the seriousness, the submarine commanders halted morning exercises for the Raiders to give more time for preparation, and at 9:29 a.m. the *Nautilus* embarked on an emergency dive when radar detected an aircraft. She remained under the surface for much of the day.

Throughout the submarines Raiders met with officers to review details of the raid. Jimmy Roosevelt orchestrated the talks on the *Argonaut*, while Carlson supervised similar discussions on the *Nautilus*.

According to Lt. Wilfred Le Francois aboard the *Argonaut*, the Raiders now focused on three items—"Live, stand watch and study our problem of raiding Makin Island."[12] He and other officers, like Lt. Joe Griffith, gathered their men together to remind them of the mission's objectives. In studying aerial photographs of Makin's beaches and surf, Lieutenant Le Francois and his men noticed white streaks of foam breaking close to each other off Makin's reef, but did not know what to make of it. In a few days, those tiny streaks would, in the form of violent waves, encompass the Raiders in a watery nightmare.

Two days before reaching Makin the men staged a nighttime rehearsal of debarking from the boat. The Raiders gathered into their assigned boat teams, numbered 1 to 8 aboard the *Nautilus* and 1 to 12 aboard the *Argonaut*, moved to their billeting areas in the submarine, then climbed a ladder and gathered in groups—even-numbered boat teams to the starboard and odd- to port.

They then moved through a hatch onto the weather deck, pulled their boats out of storage, and inflated and carried them to the debarkation stations, numbered sequentially from bow to stern. Using ropes, the Raiders hoisted the outboard motors, medical supplies, and other equipment up ladders and carried them to debarkation stations.

The only portion they could not practice was leaving the submarines. Off Makin, the plan called for the submarines to submerge beneath the rubber boats and allow them to float away.

One part of the rehearsal raised alarms—once the Raiders left the confines of the submarines and stepped into the dark onto the slippery, wet decks, they had difficulty moving around. Should uncooperative weather and harsh surf greet them off Makin, the operation could experience a rocky start. They could only hope that the gods granted smooth seas.

As the submarines neared their destination, Raiders grappled with a wide range of emotions. Some wondered if they would perform under pressure. Others debated whether they would attain surprise, or placed wagers on the likelihood of surviving. Most were eager for a fight. They had endured rigorous training since February, when Carlson gathered them and promised the men "rice, raisins, wet blankets, and glory." Now, finally, they had their chance to come to blows with an enemy who had started it with a surprise assault on December 7. "I liked the idea that we would get out to the war first and I'd have a chance to kill some Japs,"[13] said Private First Class Quirk.

Pvt. Dean Voight briefly pondered why the president's son had been allowed to accompany the group, but quickly dismissed the subject. "He went with us on most of the stuff we were doing. You'd think he had special favors, and I'm sure the Japanese would have made something had they captured him. But it was only supposed to be a one-night mission, raise a little hell, to draw attention, and get the hell off."[14]

Neither Evans Carlson, James Roosevelt, Brian Quirk, nor any Raider had much to worry about, it appeared.

"If I Miss the Jump, I'm Gone"

As expected the *Nautilus*, with Carlson aboard, arrived off Butaritari before the *Argonaut* and Jimmy Roosevelt. At 3:09 a.m. on August 16, Lt. Comdr. William E. Brockman, the *Nautilus*'s skipper, sighted Little Makin Island off the starboard bow and turned toward Makin one and a half miles astern. At 5:38 he dove and attempted to round Ukiangong Point to their south, where he took periscope photographs of the island. Rain squalls—an ominous portent for the landing—hampered his visibility, and when Brockman had trouble locating Makin landmarks, he and Carlson wondered if they had arrived at the wrong island.

Brockman remained submerged until 7:24 p.m., when he surfaced and headed to the arranged meeting point with the *Argonaut*. At 8:27 Brockman spotted what he assumed was the *Argonaut*, glistening seven thousand yards away in a moonbeam, but before he could verify the sighting another rain squall dropped his visibility to zero and blocked Brockman's view of the object. Ten minutes later Brockman arrived at the rendezvous and circled, alternately scanning the horizon and worrying about his missing companion. Could the submarine carrying Roosevelt have missed the island? One slight navigational error could shift the boat one hundred miles off course.

Thirty-nine minutes later, with better visibility, a relieved Brockman spotted the *Argonaut* on schedule. His mates in the *Argonaut*, including Jimmy Roosevelt, shared Brockman's apprehension over missing the island. Roosevelt later recalled how delighted he was when, after such a long ocean voyage, he peered through the *Argonaut*'s periscope at his objective a few miles in the distance. Brockman maneuvered closer so he could pass messages relating to the operation, then began steering to the disembarkation point with the *Argonaut* following.

Now near their goal, the Raiders started to prepare for battle. They first had an evening meal on August 15, which many joked was either their Last Supper or that they were being fattened for the kill, then headed to their uncomfortable bunks to catch whatever rest they could. Some slept soundly, but most Raiders remained awake, alone with their thoughts as the impending battle loomed.

James Roosevelt looked forward to his first taste of combat, not only because he wanted to see how he performed but also to finally exit the submarine. "I had never been in a submarine before," he stated in a 1979 interview, "and none of my men had ever been in a submarine before. Here we were sleeping in the torpedo tubes, and two chow lines a day, and twenty minutes on the surface at night to exercise. Ten days of that, we were happy that the raid was going to take place so we could get out."[15]

———

Back in Hawaii nursing his broken hand, Lt. Jack Miller lied, which, to his consternation, was his sole contribution to the Makin Raid. On August 17, the day his platoon landed at Butaritari, Miller wrote a letter to his mother stating that he should be fit for combat in a few weeks, then asked her to do a favor for his friend in B Company, Dallas native Lt. Joe Griffith. He wondered if she might telephone Griffith's wife "and tell her not to worry about not hearing from him for a few weeks. He went out for a few weeks intensive training."[16] Miller lied to maintain the raid's secrecy and to avoid alarming Griffith's wife, but he could not hide his disappointment at missing the Raiders' first offensive action. When would he get a chance to lead men in battle?

Even for the Raiders, who were accustomed to waking at the first hint of light, morning on August 17 came early. Shortly before two a.m. they rose from their bunks and gathered for a meager breakfast. After choking down a few morsels and swallowing some coffee, the Raiders donned their black-dyed uniforms, put on their boots or black tennis shoes, and assembled their gear without much chatter. They sharpened their knives, cleaned their weapons, and checked their gear. They double-checked that they had not put in a clip, as ordered, to guard against an accidental firing inside the submarine or during the approach. Men spoke in muted voices about what they expected the fighting to be like.

In the *Nautilus*, Carlson placed a copy of the New Testament in one pocket and Emerson's *Essays* in another. He moved up the planned landing of five thirty by thirty minutes when he learned that daylight would actually commence at five twenty-five. He wanted all the Raiders ashore before daylight favored the Japanese.

Raiders in both submarines followed the same procedure. At four thirty they gathered near ladders ascending to the deck and waited for a member of the crew to open the hatch. As the boats surfaced and the hatches opened, a welcome gush of fresh air wafted through the dank atmosphere, momentarily raising spirits. Once out on deck, though, a howling wind and driving rain peppered their faces, camouflaged with burned cork.

"When the word came for the Second Platoon to go up, I grabbed my sack and crawled up on deck," said Private Carson. "God, it was a mess up there. The wind was blowing, and the sub was bobbing up and down about fifteen to eighteen feet."[17]

Carlson only needed one look at the churning waters and large breakers to understand why the Japanese did not expect an assault from the ocean side of Butaritari. Who would be so crazy as to attempt such a move? On the *Nautilus* Lieutenant Peatross headed on deck and thought that the weather was so poor that "the adjective 'atrocious' seems wholly inadequate. Rain was coming down in torrents, a strong onshore wind was whipping up whitecaps all around, seas were running high with a strong onshore set, and the submarine was rolling and pitching heavily."[18] Storm clouds blocked all view of the stars, and the submarine commanders had to cautiously maneuver their boats to guard against crashing into the coral reef.

Before his men had stepped into their rubber boats, Carlson faced two decisions that changed the assault's timetable. He had already advanced the time of landing, and he now had to decide whether to abandon the rehearsed method of leaving by floating away as the submarines submerged. Hampered by the blustery conditions, Carlson had little choice but to order the men to drop their boats in the water and leap into the bobbing craft. "Now we would have to do it the hard way," wrote Peatross, "over the side, but without benefit of previous practice." Private First Class Quirk had not even stepped into his boat, and already "it seemed that confusion reigned supreme."[19]

With turbulent seas tossing the rubber boats up and down, the Raiders started the excruciating task of leaping from the submarine deck into their boats. "The submarine was supposed to submerge and leave us in the water," said Sergeant McCullough about leaving the *Nautilus*, "but we had to go over the side because of the swells. They'd raise four to five feet and then drop about ten feet."[20]

Raiders had to guard against losing their balance as the submarines rose and plunged in precipitous fashion. Carefully assembling in their boat teams, the Raiders pulled their rubber boats out of storage, lifted them onto the deck, and used pneumatic hoses to inflate them to proper size. When Pfc. William Gallagher, who shared the same boat with Private Carson, failed to properly connect the hose to the boat, an earsplitting sound pierced the darkness.

"We had a red rope—there were different colors for different units—and we pulled the boat out of the tube, then wrestled it on the deck," explained Carson. "Bill Gallagher was in charge of getting it inflated. They had a pneumatic hose up to the deck hole, and Bill got ahold of that but didn't quite get it hooked up right, and he let her go and it squealed like he had stepped on a banshee. I figured we woke every Jap within a hundred miles, but it was so damn windy and noisy, that I don't think anyone heard anything."[21]

Pfc. Brian Quirk wondered how the Raiders could safely exit the submarines without losing a man. "The rain was coming down in sheets. The swells were so high that they brought the rubber boats up, and then they would drop down fifteen or twenty feet, so you had to make the jump from the submarine into the boat when it was at its zenith. . . . I remember when it came my turn to jump, and I thought, 'If I miss that son of a bitch, I'm going down like a rock.' Luckily, I made it into the boat. The water would go up, and when it would hit the top of the submarine, it would come down like you were under a waterfall."[22]

Routine procedures that in practice took seconds, such as pulling the boats on deck, now took minutes in the arduous conditions, throwing the timetable off schedule even before every Raider had exited his submarine. Men peered into the dark waters at the bobbing boats, concerned what the sixty-five pounds of equipment might mean in even a slight misstep. Standing on the *Argonaut's* deck, Lt. Joseph Griffith described the waters off Butaritari as "unbelievable. We all got wet," and thought before he jumped, "If I miss the jump into the boat, I'm gone. Barbers Point was nothing compared to this." Private Voight came to the same conclusion on the *Nautilus*, realizing that burdened with the extra weight, "If I miss the boat I'm going straight down."[23]

Lieutenant Le Francois thought that the rubber boats "bounced around like toys and looked very frail" in the water. So much water had already spilled into the boats that to the men yet on deck, waiting to jump, it appeared boat and ocean had become one, and "you wondered if you were going to hit anything at all when you jumped for one."[24]

The Raiders realized that, as tough as they thought the surf had been off Barbers Point, it bore little resemblance to what they now encountered. Lieutenant Griffith cautioned his men that should they miss their boat, they were to think of themselves first and their accoutrements second.

The Raiders waited for the rubber boats to rise before leaping. "When it came back almost level with the deck, someone would jump in," said Private Carson. "I jumped when it was on its way down. We had over sixty pounds of gear, and Lieutenant Griffith said if you go over the side, chuck that gear right away. I was amazed that nobody was drowned."[25]

Private First Class Quirk approached the submarine's edge with caution. "We were accustomed to the waves. We had been training for it. The idea of a bullet was more frightening than the water, although when you looked over the side at the sea, you knew you'd better not slip."[26]

Cpl. Julius W. Cotten almost became the raid's first casualty when he attempted to leave the *Argonaut*. As he started to jump into the rubber boat, clutching the tripod of a .30-caliber machine gun, his foot slipped and sent him tumbling upside down into the boat. He held on to the tripod with one hand and his pack with the other, and "landed upside down looking straight up to the skies with the rain falling in my face. It was a real chore getting in."[27]

A steady series of strong waves hampered attempts to pour fuel into outboard motors without mixing in salt water. The waves pinned some rubber boats against the submarines, directly underneath the streams of water that cascaded down from the limber holes. Water levels in the rubber boats rose to dangerous levels, and waves and water from the submarines doused most of the outboard motors, putting them quickly out of commission. The Raiders had to paddle their boats just to reach the rendezvous point off the *Nautilus*.

By three thirty all boats from the *Argonaut* had successfully left the submarine and moved to the rendezvous point near the *Nautilus*. In the haphazard departure, few boats left in an organized landing formation, instead separating from the submarines whenever and wherever they could. One boat from the *Argonaut* was to pick up Colonel Carlson from the *Nautilus*, but it failed to appear. Commodore Haines impatiently paced the deck of the *Nautilus*, waiting for the tardy boat, but after twenty futile minutes he shouted to Peatross to take Carlson aboard his boat.

Peatross drew alongside. In the leap from the submarine to the rubber boat, Carlson banged his right cheekbone against a Raider's rifle butt with such force that his face immediately swelled. Though the injury bothered him the next two days, no one heard him complain about it. Peatross ferried Carlson and his runner to the rendezvous point, where Carlson hopped into another boat.

Carlson faced decisions that came as rapidly as did the waves. Rather than an organized unit of two groups, one of A Company boats and the other comprising B Company, his twenty boats had arrived piecemeal. High seas and stormy weather not only hampered communications and knocked out many of the outboard motors but made efficient reorganization impossible. Rather than sending the two companies to their own beaches as planned, Carlson decided to take the entire complement of twenty boats in as a unit to Beach Z opposite Government Wharf, the original landing point for B Company. He preferred to avoid intermingling A and B companies in this manner, but he felt that reaching shore and establishing control of his men before daylight was more crucial. He wrote in his action report that he had to act quickly in the "resulting confusion in the darkness of the night" and had word passed "as best I could for all boats to follow me."[28] The Raiders had yet to touch land on Butaritari, and already Carlson had made three changes in the schedule.

At four twenty-two Carlson started toward shore half a mile away. He signaled by waving his arms, and shouted for the other boats to align behind him. Those nearby followed, but Raiders in the boats bobbing at a distance could neither hear Carlson's shouts in the noisy surf and wind nor see his signal. Taking the initiative, they headed to shore either alone or in small bunches.

In such a haphazard fashion did the initial raid launched from a submarine in United States history begin. The series of plan changes, coming on top of the horrible weather and unexpectedly harsh surf, disrupted Carlson's timetable and tossed uncertainty into the operation.

And they had not yet reached shore.

"Badly Intermingled on Landing"

After receiving a signal to head in, the twenty rubber boats churned to the surf line and its powerful series of breakers. The few whose motors still worked had little difficulty moving through the waves and traversing the final half mile to shore, but most, their motors doused by the heavy swells, had to paddle in. Waves lifted and dropped the craft in wild rides. Raiders strained to keep the frail vessels on course, realizing that if they could not reach the beach and move toward their objectives before daylight, the advantage of surprise would be lost.

"It was raining like hell and the sea was rough," said Private First Class Bauml. "Unlike Barbers Point, these were short and choppy waves, worse than Barbers Point to get off. We couldn't see our hand in front of our face when we landed. A lot of the training kind of goes out the window. You never know when you'll get a machine gun burst or a boat will tip. So many intangibles, so many things to mess up! And the waves kept slapping at the boats. Getting on and off Makin was more dangerous than combat. If something happened, you were a goner."[29]

Private Carson faced the same obstacles in his boat. Lacking the power of a motor, he struggled to advance the craft a few yards against the resisting surf. "[Private] Bill Gallagher couldn't get the paddle in the water while the motor was on there, so we were going in circles in the surf. Finally we con-

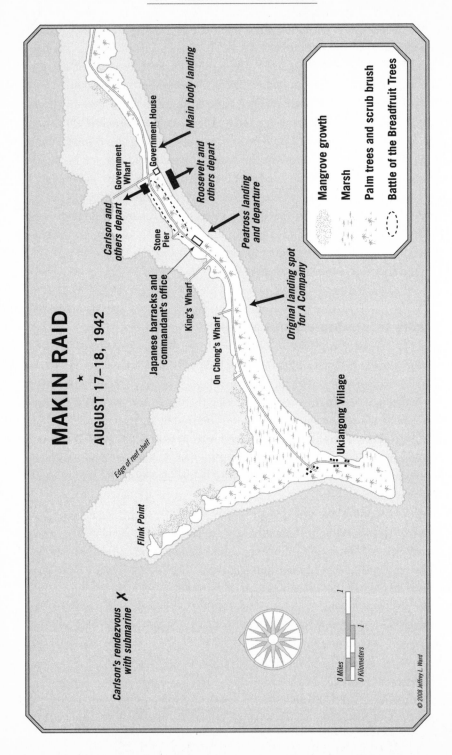

MAKIN RAID
★
AUGUST 17–18, 1942

Main body landing

Government House

Government Wharf

Carlson and others depart

Roosevelt and others depart

Peatross landing and departure

Stone Pier

Japanese barracks and commandant's office

King's Wharf

On Chong's Wharf

Original landing spot for A Company

Ukiangong Village

Edge of reef shelf

Flink Point

Carlson's rendezvous with submarine

Mangrove growth

Marsh

Palm trees and scrub brush

Battle of the Breadfruit Trees

0 Miles

0 Kilometers

© 2008 Jeffrey L. Ward

vinced Bill to undo the clamp and throw the motor over the side. When he got that done we started heading for shore."[30]

Removing the engine did not solve all their problems, however. As the boats rose to the crests, the turbulent surf bent them in half. When the boats skidded down the wave's opposite side, they snapped back, forcing the occupants to hold on for dear life. One wave tossed Private Carson out of his rear seat into the water, but fortunately he was close enough to shore that he could stand in the shallow water.

"I got into the boat OK, but it was the fifteen-foot waves at the breakers that were so rough," said Private Voight. "We didn't get tipped over until we got close to shore. I shucked all my stuff, and when I landed I had nothing but my clothes on. The water was quite deep when we tipped over. I was just about to gulp in water when I came up and the next wave took me in."[31]

As Jimmy Roosevelt's boat neared the beach, thinking it was all right to leave he shouted to the Raider in front, Pfc. Harold E. Ryan, to leap over the side. Ryan disappeared in the swirling waters, still too deep for him to stand. Ryan discarded his helmet, weapons, and web belt for buoyancy as a second wave knocked him forward. Finally, his buddies in the boat moved close enough to grab on to Ryan's hair and pull him aboard.

The violent conditions forced Peatross to return to the *Nautilus* for directions. After dropping off Carlson at the rendezvous point, Peatross headed away at a right angle from the *Nautilus* in what he thought was the correct direction, but he failed to realize that the submarine had in the interval moved from its original launching point to avoid hitting the reef. The course took him farther from shore, so he reversed directions back to the *Nautilus*, where Commander Brockman pointed him in the proper direction. Off Peatross went, badly lagging behind the other nineteen boats, toward what he thought was his original point of landing.

By five twenty, after a harrowing twenty-minute trip to shore, the twenty Raider boats had landed. Carlson and seventeen boats came ashore along a two-hundred-yard stretch of sand at Beach Z opposite Government Wharf. The boat of A Company's Cpl. Harris Johnson pulled up two hundred yards to the southwest, while the boat containing B Company's Sgt. William Yount and his Raiders landed one mile northeast of Carlson. Both groups soon joined Carlson, who now commanded nineteen of the twenty boats. Only Lieutenant Peatross remained missing.

One mile to the southwest Peatross and his men dragged their boat across the beach, camouflaged it, and then scouted the area to determine their location. They found two rubber boats containing medical supplies, machine guns, and ammunition about one hundred yards to their left, but a lack of footprints in the sand indicated that the boats must have floated in on their own. He learned later that these two boats had broken away from the submarines in the blustery weather before any Raiders jumped in.

By landing one mile southwest of Carlson, Peatross unknowingly positioned his eleven men in what would soon become the Japanese rear. During the morning's fighting Peatross would prove to be a major headache to Kanemitsu, but unfortunately Carlson failed to learn the whereabouts of Peatross's group until later in the afternoon. He might have discovered Peatross by dispatching a small scouting patrol along the island's beaches, but he opted against it and missed an opportunity to orchestrate a coordinated two-pronged assault against the defenders.

Fortunately, the sodden Raiders landed along undefended beaches. They dragged their boats across the twenty-yard stretch of sand and camouflaged them in the bushes, then awaited Carlson's orders. Later describing his companies as "badly intermingled on landing,"[32] Carlson posted security along the bushes and, with Major Roosevelt's assistance, turned to the task of restoring order.

Though he had to alter the tactics, Carlson had trained his men to think for themselves and believed he would have little difficulty achieving his objectives. "This was a good example of Colonel Carlson's leadership," emphasized Private First Class Quirk. "It was part of the training that he had put his officers and noncommissioned officers and these privates through so that they could handle any adversity."[33]

The situation improved at five thirteen, when communications with the *Nautilus* was established. The Raiders' main concern was to keep warm and dry in the miserable weather. Many had been tossed into the surf, and all had been doused with ocean water and rain. As the Raiders tramped around the beach, their footwear emitted squishing sounds that might have been humorous had the situation not been so serious. They huddled on the beach for warmth and waited for Carlson's orders to begin moving out.

"Everything Lousy"

A force as large as Carlson's cannot land on an island as tiny as Butaritari without being discovered. Shortly after five o'clock a native police officer pedaled his bicycle along the lagoon road, cautioning the natives that the Americans had landed. The Gilbertese native A. George Noran, who kept a diary of the events, and his wife headed to Ukiangong Village in the island's western portion, hoping that would take them out of harm's way.

Any doubt whether the Japanese were aware of Carlson's presence ended at five thirty when Pfc. Vern Mitchell accidentally discharged his rifle, an incident that, added to the other mishaps already plaguing the operation, led some to believe that Murphy's Law—if anything can go wrong it certainly will—hexed the Raiders. "They might as well just blow the bugle that says we're here, come find us," lamented Corporal Cotten. The gunshot caused Private First Class Quirk to worry that "we're supposed to already be killing these guys while they're sleeping in their bunks. Now we haven't even left the beach yet and we told them we're here!"[34]

Although Roosevelt later stated that Carlson's chief concern at that moment was not whether the enemy had been alerted but whether any Raider had been harmed, the commander could not hide his displeasure at the mishap. For the only time in his military career, Carlson swore at one of his men.

As dawn broke, Carlson shook off his anger and ordered his Raiders to rush across the island toward their objectives. With his men standing in the landing area designated for B Company, and with B Company's objectives looming ahead, Carlson instead ordered First Lt. Merwyn C. Plumley to take A Company across while holding back Captain Coyte's B Company in reserve. Carlson told Plumley to seize the road skirting the lagoon side, quickly survey the surrounding area, and report the force's location in respect to the wharves.

Carlson's switch added to the confusion. While B Company had extensively trained in Hawaii to occupy the terrain ahead and were familiar with the buildings and landmarks in the area, Carlson rushed A Company in instead. Complicating matters was the fact that some B Company Raiders had already started advancing into the zone as soon as they hit the beach. With Peatross's whereabouts unknown, the chances that different units of Raiders would stumble into each other rose precipitously.

To the southwest Lieutenant Peatross was just as confused. According to orders, he was not to break radio silence until after the shooting started, so he could not contact Carlson to coordinate their movements. Not until Peatross spotted the Japanese rifle range shortly after heading inland could he fix his location. The church stood three hundred yards ahead, and Peatross was planning his next move when he heard Private Mitchell's accidental discharge to the northeast. Peatross concluded that the gunfire would cause the Japanese to rush toward it, which would place Peatross to the enemy's rear. The officer took advantage of the situation to move his eleven men closer to the Japanese, whose attention would be riveted in the other direction. He sent three men to reconnoiter the land behind to make sure no enemy forces threatened his rear, and with their report that the area to the southwest was clear, Peatross determined that the only Japanese on the island rested between him and Carlson's main body to the northeast.

Since fighting had now erupted, Peatross ordered his radioman to alert Carlson to his presence behind the Japanese, but the radio, waterlogged from the trip in, failed to operate. Peatross ordered Pfc. Alexander J. Donovan and Pvt. Raymond D. Jansen to head out by different routes, locate Carlson's command post, and alert him to Peatross's location. He cautioned the two Raiders, though, that if they received heavy enemy fire, they were to return. Heavy fire forced Jansen back after three hundred yards, but Donovan failed to return. Peatross concluded that Donovan successfully reached Carlson, who would most likely alter his battle plans based on the new information and order an assault on two sides against the enemy.

Until he heard from Carlson, Peatross decided to clear his area. As he moved toward the church and a Japanese barracks, a Japanese soldier rushed out of the barracks, but fell dead when three Raiders opened fire. "These were the first shots that any of us had fired in the war; this was our first face-to-face encounter with the enemy,"[35] Peatross later wrote.

While Carlson waited at the beach, Lieutenant Plumley selected Lt. Wilfred S. Le Francois's First Platoon to cross Makin's half-mile width. Le Francois posted Sgt. Clyde Thomason in the vanguard and followed with his platoon, dropping a man off every fifty yards to serve as a guide for the following Raiders. In less than ten minutes Thomason's lead group reached the road without incident and watched as surprised natives, barely awake, stumbled out of their huts to see American Marines.

Fifteen minutes after crossing Makin, Plumley sent Le Francois back to Carlson's command post, which was at that time set up in a clump of bushes just off the beach. Le Francois informed his commander that Plumley had occupied both Government House and Government Wharf against no opposition and that he had yet to see any Japanese soldiers. Carlson sent instructions with Le Francois for Plumley to veer to the southwest and begin advancing along both sides of the lagoon road. He informed the A Company leader that B Company would be in reserve and would protect his left flank.

The native inhabitants greeted the Raiders with information on the Japanese. They informed Le Francois and Lamb that the Japanese had been preparing for three days—most likely placed on alert following the August 7 American assault in the Solomons—and that they expected an attack on the lagoon side somewhere between On Chong's Wharf and Government Wharf. Since then the Japanese had practiced defensive measures, placed snipers in the tops of palm trees, and posted guards along the expected invasion beaches. The natives could not agree on how many soldiers defended the island, but most guessed that Kanemitsu commanded between eighty and two hundred Japanese, with the majority favoring the higher number. They also reported that a concentration of Japanese stood at Ukiangong Point in the island's southwest portion.

Carlson adopted the dictum that when in doubt, one should assume the worst. Throughout the day he acted as if the Japanese commander had two hundred or more men at his disposal, more than he actually possessed. Though judicious, it caused Carlson to proceed more cautiously than he might have done.

Carlson had experienced a rough first hour. A difficult landing disrupted the boats, he had accidentally lost the advantage of surprise, his men had not arrived where they should have, and he faced a potentially larger, more potent defense than expected. Somewhat flustered, at 5:43 Carlson sent a message to the *Nautilus*, "Everything lousy."[36] Four minutes later, having learned of Plumley's occupation of Government House, Carlson sent a second message stating that the situation ashore appeared to be in hand.

To support Plumley's drive southwest and to prevent reinforcements from reaching Kanemitsu's main group, Carlson radioed the submarines to target the reported Japanese enclave at Ukiangong Point. The *Nautilus* opened fire for six minutes at 7:03, but the *Argonaut*, lacking precise coordinates and fearing they might accidentally shell the Marines, remained silent.

Meanwhile, Kanemitsu informed headquarters of his situation. "We are now all dying in battle,"[37] the commander radioed.

"Loose Cannons"

Along the lagoon Le Francois, now back from reporting to Carlson, deployed his platoon in a wedge-shaped formation. He posted a fire team on each flank and at the point, then led his platoon forward through thick brush broken by marshy areas. Raiders had to check each cluster of bushes, as well as the handful of native huts, to make sure no enemy forces hid inside, then moved farther down the road. Once they had passed the native settlement the terrain opened and enabled Le Francois to advance more quickly.

At the same time, random-size groups from B Company had been moving ahead, as well as a machine-gun section under Corporal Cotten of A Company and Sgt. Walter D. Carroll's antitank rifle section. Corporal Cotten carefully crossed the island, largely comprising at that point open land broken by palm trees and underbrush, to position the machine guns in his weapons platoon. He set up a machine gun and a mortar section just beyond Government House and laid down a field of fire to cover the other men as they moved up.

Lieutenant Le Francois and Sergeant Thomason were almost shot when they inspected one hut. Thomason approached the structure, kicked open the door, and killed an enemy sniper with his shotgun before the Japanese could turn toward him. Upon leaving, the pair came under fire when Lt. Charles Lamb and other Raiders, assuming they were Japanese, opened up. Le Francois shouted the Raider call sign, "Hi, Raider," and relaxed when he received "Gung Ho" in reply.

The errant shots showed that with different Raider units prowling about the island, unaware of each other, accidents could easily occur. Peatross later wrote, "'Loose cannons' suggests itself as a not inappropriate metaphor for such largely uncontrolled activity, and that they did not collide is amazing."[38]

The Raiders moved a thousand feet to the native hospital, where an enemy machine gun forced them to take cover. Twenty Japanese soldiers leaped from a truck three hundred yards down the road, planted the Rising Sun flag in the ground along the road, and then melted into the brush to begin their defense. "By 0630 our center and left were heavily engaged,"[39] Carlson wrote in his report after the raid.

Le Francois set a trap for the Japanese. At six a.m. he sent Thomason forward to establish a line near the road, then took a position on an elevated plot of ground so he could observe the Japanese as they slowly crept through the brush along a hundred-yard strip of land between the road and the lagoon. The officer moved the Raiders on the left flank closer to Thomason's men on the point to create a cul-de-sac. With any luck, the enemy would advance straight into the trap and be subject to fire from the flank and front.

The sun at his back worked in Le Francois's favor. It glared in the eyes of the enemy and conveniently outlined Kanemitsu's men. As the Japanese drew closer, Thomason strutted along his line, encouraging the men and reminding them to hold their fire until directed. "Thomason chuckled with glee and patted his shotgun,"[40] Le Francois later recalled of his robust sergeant.

Thomason reminded his men to hold their fire until the enemy drew within twenty yards. Suddenly, as Raiders clenched their weapons and squirmed slightly in their positions, Thomason bellowed, "Let 'em have it!"[41] and emptied his twelve-gauge shotgun.

The Japanese were caught unawares by the devastating firepower. Carlson's insistence on arming his fire teams with M1 rifles, BARs, and Thompson submachine guns paid off as Le Francois's men cut into the Japanese.

"A shot rang out . . . and all hell broke loose," recalled Cpl. Howard Young. "We had Japs in front of us, above us, alongside of us to our left, and behind us also to our left. Two machine guns were sweeping the area above our heads; slugs were chunking into the bases of the palm trees. Snipers were coming very close, but no hits."[42]

A Japanese heavy machine gun near the flag mounted a serious challenge. Bullets hit at Le Francois's feet, and nine Raiders from the First Platoon died in the next thirty minutes. "We got into a real hot firefight right off the bat, near the radio station and headquarters,"[43] said Corporal Cotten.

Sergeant Howard E. Stidham moved toward a native hut near Stone Pier to eliminate a machine gun when a burst of fire scattered the dirt at his feet. He took shelter behind a concrete block supporting the shack that, to his amazement, protected him from at least one hundred rounds from that machine gun. One bullet scraped the left heel of his boot and a piece of shrapnel ricocheted into his left arm, but he emerged unscathed from the incident.

At almost the same moment Lt. Gerald Holtom, a Japanese-speaking officer, drifted too far from the Raider line and was cut down. Le Francois heard someone yell, "Lieutenant Holtom has been shot and is dying! He needs medical attention!" A few seconds later the same voice said, "Never mind."[44]

Sergeant Stidham waited for a lull in the firing before checking on Holtom. He gazed at the body for a few seconds, "and for the first time I realized how serious this was."[45]

Not far away, Pvt. Howard Craven and Cpl. Harris Johnson dodged bullets from a Japanese sniper as they ran into a clearing. When Johnson stumbled, Craven asked if the corporal were all right. Johnson said that he was fine, started to rise, then collapsed and died.

With his BAR, Pvt. Franklin Nodland blasted the sniper out of a coconut tree not far away. The seventeen-year-old Nodland, who everyone called "Chicken" because of his boyish looks and small frame, gained every Raider's respect by carrying one of the heaviest weapons, but a few minutes after killing the sniper, he, too, was felled by an enemy bullet.

The withering fire in the fight's opening minutes took its toll on other Raider heroes. Sergeant Thomason alternately shouted encouragement to his Raiders and fired at the enemy, despite the pleas of his men to seek shelter from snipers who were no more than fifty yards distant. He ignored their appeals, but a Japanese sniper soon ended his stand.

Le Francois inched over and unsuccessfully felt for a pulse. For his deeds at Makin, Thomason received a posthumous Medal of Honor, the first such granted to a Marine in the Pacific.

In the midst of the melee, Transport Maghakian found himself in his element. The bearded, cigar-chewing Raider—every veteran Marine knew that the cigar was his trademark—waved directions to his men, when a bullet smacked into his right arm.

Maghakian later explained that "one sniper picked me out and his shot caught me in the right arm. My arm went dead almost immediately but I still had the full use of my left as I dropped to the 'deck' and played dead for fifteen minutes until another shot by him revealed his location. When he showed himself I silenced him with my automatic rifle."[46]

Instead of seeking aid, Maghakian wrapped a tourniquet around his arm, shifted his Thompson to his left, and continued to battle despite the wound. When asked how he could so calmly face death, he said that simple anger prodded him to action. "It seems to get you mad. Good and mad. Furious. You make up your mind you are going to get that so and so if it costs you a slug in the belly."[47]

Near Carlson's command post Dr. Stephen Stigler learned that a casualty required help at the front line. He and his corpsman, Pharmacist's Mate Second Class Walter Elterman, headed to the sector to locate the man.

"Due to my inexperience in combat, I led us into a field of fire of a Japanese machine gun," explained Stigler, who found cover in a cluster of palm trees. Machine-gun bullets nipped the ground near Stigler and Elterman, who could not reach the stricken Raider until the weapon was out of commission.

As the two wondered how much longer they could evade the enemy machine gun, firing erupted from the side. Suddenly, the machine gun stopped clattering. "We then saw Victor approaching us with a big smile on his face. While the Japanese had been busy with us, he had flanked them and wiped out the whole machine gun nest. He was the wounded Marine that we were seeking. He had been shot through the right wrist but had transferred his Tommy gun to his left arm and fired it from that position."

Stigler and Elterman hurriedly patched his wounds and advised Maghakian, who received a Navy Cross for his exploits, to retreat to the aid station, but the sergeant declined and returned to the fighting. "There is no doubt in my mind that had Victor not wiped out that machine gun nest, Elterman and I would have been killed or badly wounded. He saved our lives."[48]

While Le Francois's men battled along the lagoon, in the Japanese rear to the southwest Peatross deployed his men in a skirmish line near the road. They saw a Japanese soldier rush out of a building, hop on a bicycle, and pedal directly toward them. Peatross ordered his men to hold their fire until the Japanese had passed the center of their line, but in the excitement of battle the man on the right end, Pfc. Ernest R. July, opened with his BAR before the signal was given. The Japanese managed to flee a short distance, but other Raiders killed him before he retreated too far.

When a second cyclist appeared a few minutes later, the men reacted with more discipline. They waited until the enemy soldier reached the line's midpoint, then opened fire in what Peatross called "a classic example of overkill."[49] A third Japanese soldier met a similar fate.

Peatross waited a few more minutes, but when no additional Japanese appeared, he turned his men east toward the sound of battle. They crossed the road and approached what was supposedly Kanemitsu's headquarters, but found the building abandoned. As they spread out to search other structures, a man in a white shirt, khaki shorts, and pith helmet emerged from a house and waved as if signaling. Cpl. Sam Brown shot and killed the man, whom Peatross learned later was Kanemitsu. The enemy had lost its commanding officer, a fortunate turn of events for Carlson, as it forced the defenders to fight the ensuing battle without proper direction.

Peatross's men advanced to the barracks, which they also found empty. Though he could see the fighting four hundred yards down the road, he still had heard nothing from Carlson. Had Donovan reached the command post to inform the colonel of Peatross's whereabouts, or had he been killed, leaving Carlson unaware that he had a group of Raiders conveniently placed in the Japanese rear?

Carlson faced difficulties of his own. Concerned about the battle's progress, he committed part of his reserve from B Company. He turned to Lieutenant Griffith near him and said, "Joe, get those boys on the skirmish line."

Griffith, worried that his men would merge with other platoons once on the line, replied, "But I'll lose control." He believed B Company should be deployed in an enveloping maneuver against the Japanese right flank.

Carlson curtly cut off the objection. "I don't give a damn. Put them in the skirmish line. Did you hear me?"

Griffith followed the instructions, but "I never regained control of my platoon. The fighting that day was pretty much a bunch of individuals."[50]

Carlson believed he had to commit Griffith's men in such a manner to stymie the Japanese advance. A flanking attack required more time to execute, and he wanted those men on the line immediately.

With Griffith's men added to the action, the fighting now devolved into a series of thrusts and counterthrusts that occupied much of the morning. The Battle of the Breadfruit Trees had begun.

"A Shootout at the O.K. Corral"

By seven a.m. the fighting along the lagoon road had bogged down. The Japanese anchored their defense on four machine guns, two grenade throwers, automatic rifles, a flamethrower, and according to Carlson's report, "with infantry supporting the automatic weapons and with a corps of snipers operating from the tops of cocoanut [sic] trees." Carlson stated that the snipers and machine guns provided the toughest resistance. "Snipers were cleverly camouflaged and their fire was extremely effective."[51]

Until eleven thirty Carlson and the Japanese traded blows in a series of sporadic actions. Though the fighting included a pair of what could loosely be described as banzai charges by the small Japanese force, the morning unfolded mostly in individual, uncoordinated charges by Raiders against the Japanese and a few fierce thrusts against the Raider line. All, however, were sideshows to the bitter contest against Japanese snipers, who hampered Raider activity far out of proportion to their numbers.

Carlson did not help matters by keeping his men in a skirmish line. He could have ordered a rapid advance by both companies, but lacking clear intelligence about the size of the defending force, he opted to place his Raiders in a set line, thereby stalling their advance across Makin and handing the initiative to the enemy. He could have ordered a flanking attack, as Griffith wished and as he would so successfully employ on Guadalcanal in a few months, but he declined. In the early hours, the Raider commander had substituted caution for aggression, timidity for audacity.

Day one at Makin would not prove to be Carlson's shining moment.

What Raiders call the Battle of the Breadfruit Trees, so named because of the two large breadfruit trees that dominated the scene of battle, started with the first of two Japanese charges. Though sporadic breaks occurred in the fighting throughout the morning, during certain periods bullets and mortars so filled the air that one Raider called it "a shootout at the O.K. Corral."[52]

After Le Francois's men grappled with the enemy along the lagoon road, the Japanese reorganized and mounted successive charges against the Raider line, some five hundred yards from the command post where Carlson and Roosevelt directed the efforts. A bugle sound sliced the morning air, following which a wave of Japanese soldiers rushed out of the brush in the middle of the island one hundred yards distant toward the Raiders, firing and shouting insults as they ran. Le Francois stated that the Japanese "charged down the center of the island, running at full stride, holding their rifles over their heads with bayonets fixed, and shooting from that position without aiming. They came shouting, *'Banzai.'"*

Raiders held their fire until they were, as Le Francois put it, "uncomfortably close,"[53] then directed a withering blast of automatic weaponry that ripped apart the enemy ranks. Japanese stumbled and fell before a deadly staccato of gunfire, most maimed or killed, while a handful crawled along the ground toward the Raiders. Two appeared only twenty feet from Le Francois, who dropped them with twenty shots from his automatic. Behind the Japanese infantry, four light machine guns well camouflaged in the foliage and a flamethrower lent their support. Raiders quickly eliminated the flamethrower, not wanting that ghastly weapon anywhere near them, but the machine guns plagued the Raider line all morning.

"The machine guns were going off, mortars. Everything was letting loose," explained B Company's Pvt. Neal F. Milligan. "Ever hear of the 4th of July? That's what it was. We were in fields with a lot of brush, and the bullets were cutting the leaves off the trees."[54]

Raiders brushed off sweat and dirt as the Japanese tried to push them off the island. Enemy bullets pierced both ankles and the side of Pfc. Donald D. Daniels, who refused to let any Raider leave the firing line to help him reach the aid station. The injured B Company Raider crawled all the way back to the beach for first aid.

A Japanese bullet glanced off the grenade jacket that Pvt. Joseph J. Woodford, also of B Company, wore, setting the jacket on fire. Facing the ironic fate of being killed in an explosion of his own grenades, Woodford frantically "tore at that jacket like a mad man" and tossed it as far away as he could. In the heat of the moment he lost his helmet and risked injury to rush out and retrieve the valuable piece of gear. "The fellows told me afterward that the bullets of Jap snipers could be seen kicking up the sand right behind me as I ran,"[55] Woodford later said.

When a sniper bullet bloodied Cpl. I. B. Earles's mouth, the Raider jumped up and shouted, "I'll get those heathens by myself! Show me where they are!"[56] Despite the cries from fellow Raiders to take cover, Earles rushed through the brush, shooting at any Japanese he saw. Earles charged and wiped out a machine-gun nest, then slumped dead from eleven bullet wounds.

Earles's A Company buddy, Cpl. Daniel A. Gaston, became so enraged at witnessing his friend's death that he, too, leaped to the attack. Platoon Sergeant Maghakian observed the heroics and later wrote Gaston's family that "nothing could hold Danny back. On the left, another Jap machine gun opened up. Disregarding his own safety, Danny stood straight up and charged squarely into that nest, his Tommy-gun blazing full automatic. He undoubtedly killed four or five Japs in that charge before he went down fighting." Maghakian added, "Please believe me, every man in the Second Marine Raider Battalion loved Danny Gaston and he will always live in our memories, fighting in spirit side by side with us until we drive every enemy of freedom and democracy off the face of this good earth."[57]

Other Raiders fell. A bullet into the forehead of Sgt. Norman Lenz of A

Company paralyzed the Marine veteran for life, while Lieutenant Le Francois had to be removed when five machine-gun bullets mangled his right arm and shoulder as he directed efforts along the line near where Thomason had been killed.

After a brief lull in the fighting, the Japanese regrouped and launched a second furious attack on the Raider line. Again preceded by a bugle call, the Japanese, their numbers badly reduced by the previous assault, rushed the Marines, who fought with a reassurance inspired by repulsing the first attack. When they beat back this second attempt, organized Japanese resistance on Makin ended.

"The Fighting Had Become a Free for All"

Centered in the area of the breadfruit trees and bushes broken by open stretches of land in Makin's midsection, south of the lagoon road between Stone Pier and the native hospital, the Japanese abandoned frontal assaults in favor of their masterful use of camouflage and the skill of snipers to keep the Raider line bogged down. The Japanese, dressed in green camouflage uniforms that blended perfectly into the background, attached leafy twigs to their helmets for better concealment. Snipers posted in trees fastened coconuts to their bodies to better hide their positions.

Only once in the next two hours did Pl. Sgt. Melvin Spotts fire at a visible target, shooting where he thought the enemy was, but during that time snipers accounted for most of the casualties suffered in his sector. "The fighting had become more or less a free for all," said Spotts, who added that "the Japanese were near perfect at concealment and camouflage."[58] Only when the Raiders abandoned fire discipline and blasted away the tops of palm trees instead of trying to locate each sniper did they make any progress.

Rather than an organized counterattack, the Raider line dissolved into individuals or small teams attempting to eliminate single targets. "One spot would start up, and another eased down," said Sergeant McCullough. "Every man dropped down and hugged the ground," added Private Milligan. "In that brush, we didn't know where everybody was at, who was getting hit, or who was hitting who. Everybody was alone at their spot."[59]

Corporal Cotten grabbed whomever was close by, regardless of their company, to form an attack group centered on his machine gun. The fighting had narrowed to the three-yard plot of earth at their feet.

"We were kind of on an individual mission there," said Private Carson. "It was like that for most of the guys. There was very little integrity of organization. Whatever you could see to shoot at, you shot, as long as it wasn't a Marine. I shot about three clips, sixty rounds. I'm not sure if I hit anything, but we hosed down a lot of areas."[60]

Lieutenant Griffith, who led his unit into the left flank as Carlson ordered, claimed the morning action at Makin was an unorganized movement across the island's midsection. "It worked out individually," he stated in a 2008 interview. "Peatross was one of the few units to act as a unit. Le Francois also, but it had degenerated to a man-to-man, fire-team-to-fire-team advance against the Japanese."[61]

Carlson depicted the action in similar terms. He explained in an interview after the raid that the fighting now had become "a case of taking out the individual machine-gun nests by flanking operations, followed by direct and bloody action."[62]

Platoon Sergeant Maghakian epitomized such valor. Already wounded in the arm, for the first time in his Marine career Maghakian disobeyed orders by refusing to remain at the first aid station, claiming that the Raiders needed his help against the stubborn snipers. Rather than order someone else into the fighting, Maghakian accepted the risks himself, explaining, "A lot of them were young kids. You couldn't send a green kid against a pillbox."[63] Since so many noncoms had been wounded or killed, he felt an even greater urgency to reach the front.

Cpl. Leon R. Chapman from B Company and his ammunition carrier, Pvt. Kenneth M. "Mudhole" Merrill, fired more than four hundred rounds from their light machine gun at an enemy machine gun. While Chapman and Merrill kept the enemy pinned down, Corporal Wygal crept toward the gun from another direction, hurled in a grenade, then leapt in and killed the surviving soldiers with his knife and pistol, an action that earned Wygal a Navy Cross and praise in *Time* magazine.

Raiders found the bodies of a dozen Japanese soldiers strewn about the gun. Sergeant Stidham paused from battle long enough to check the bodies for souvenirs, when suddenly one of the supposed Japanese dead groaned and rose to his knees. Stidham dispatched the soldier with a knife thrust into his chest and learned a valuable lesson about assuming the demise of a foe.

Raiders often wiped out entire machine-gun nests, only to find more Japanese soldiers rush up and take over for their fallen comrades. Corporal Young had to attack one gun position three or four times because of such tactics.

The snipers proved as resolute. Corporal Cotten approached one tree, ready to lob a grenade to the top, when the sniper's bullet hit a grenade attached to a web strap on his chest. The grenade split apart, but fortunately failed to explode. Cotten pulled the pin, counted to three, and heaved his grenade as far up as he could. Besides two Japanese soldiers, Cotten's grenade killed a monkey that had taken refuge in the tree.

Sgt. James Faulkner found himself trapped in the field of fire from three snipers. He spotted one hiding behind a tree one hundred feet away, but his shotgun shells failed to pierce the foliage. "Damn, I'm hit," Faulkner cried when a bullet hit him in the hand. When a few moments later a second bullet struck the sergeant's head, he cursed, "Damn it! They got me." Faulkner, who refused evacuation, cursed again when a third bullet struck, this time piercing his side and leg. "Goddammit! They got me again!"[64] Now weakened from blood loss, Faulkner finally agreed to be taken to the aid station, where a Raider handed him a canteen full of Scotch to soothe the pain.

As a communications man near Carlson at the command post, Sergeant McCullough stood behind the front lines, yet he at times felt like a walking bull's-eye. "I survived because of luck, and then I was back a bit [at the command post with Carlson]. Those little antennas on the walkie-talkies were chrome, and they reflected sunlight, and the Japanese were very good at recognition. The chrome thing came straight up by your ear. I think because of Makin, they designed them different after that."[65] Of the five communications men who landed, only McCullough avoided injury.

At no time did the Raiders feel they were losing the fight. Their only concern was whether they could silence the opposition in time to carry out their objectives and return to the submarines. If they failed to wipe out the Japanese before exhausting their limited supply of ammunition, they faced the unappetizing prospect of leaving the island under fire.

They did not realize that they had already killed most of Kanemitsu's defenders.

It Will Forever Remain a Ghastly Nightmare

"Composure Is Contagious, Too"

During the morning fighting, Carlson's presence in fighting areas was evident while Roosevelt, following his boss's orders, remained at the command post to coordinate communications with the submarines and with other Raider units. Numerous Raiders commented on Carlson's apparent obliviousness to enemy bullets during visits to the front areas, which he believed crucial in instilling confidence in his men. He strolled out in the open as Raiders in concealment held their breath for fear he would be hit, calmly chatting with Raiders or inspecting the progress, then returned to the command post to consult with Roosevelt.

Raiders never knew when they might find Carlson at their side, pipe in mouth, to check on the progress. One man recalled, "I'd turn around and there was the Colonel, calm as hell, smoking that stinkin' pipe of his." Carlson would greet them warmly and ask how they were doing. "It helped you feel not so scared, his being right up front with you."[1]

"Carlson seemingly had no fear of dying," said Private First Class Quirk. "In combat he was the calmest, like he was delivering an English lecture. He was so calm that he calmed you down. He talked to you like he was giving you an English assignment for the next day. Fear is contagious, and composure is contagious, too."[2]

While Carlson was free to come and go, Jimmy Roosevelt, as executive officer, took care of the nuts-and-bolts tasks of the battalion at the command post four hundred yards behind the fighting. He read messages, chatted with Carlson when he was there, and discussed matters with any officers that stopped by. Situated in a small shack that reminded Sergeant McCullough of a hog pen, the command post became the hub of activity coordinating the raid. Trees and underbrush lent partial concealment, but the post was subject to fire from snipers and from Japanese aircraft later in the day. Wounded Raiders filtered in to the adjoining aid station, set up in a building with a cathedral roof, where Dr. Stigler and corpsmen labored to keep them alive or patch them up so they could return to battle.

In his role as a communications specialist, Sergeant McCullough held a front-row seat to battalion activity. He observed Roosevelt's actions and listened as Carlson discussed the course of battle with his executive officer. "He was pretty businesslike," McCullough stated of Roosevelt, whose bald head glistening in the sun humored some of the Raiders. "He did a good job."[3]

Though Roosevelt was comparatively safe with the action occurring a few hundred yards away, no point on the island was immune to attack. Snipers shot a walkie-talkie out of his hands, and twice the president's son discharged his weapon at enemy soldiers. Raiders killed two snipers lurking in proximity to Roosevelt's post, and a post-raid photograph of Roosevelt chatting with reporters showed a bandaged right middle finger. When reporters asked him of it, Roosevelt declined to explain, instead talking of the Raiders as "the finest group of men in the world."[4]

In the thickest part of the fighting, Carlson checked that his executive officer, the president's son, was safe. Carlson liked the way Roosevelt ran his command post, but had to continually remind his executive to stay in the rear areas. In the battle's aftermath he wrote President Roosevelt that his son "was as cool as the proverbial cucumber and kept the loose ends tied together without a hitch," even though sniper bullets were a constant threat to him during the morning of August 17. "Time and again I had to tell him to get into a sump hole and stay there so that I could be assured that my communications would continue to function," added Carlson, "because he insisted on sticking his neck out to see how things were going."[5]

By eleven a.m. the fighting was mired in the middle of Makin Island, snatching crucial time from the destruction of key installations, the seizure of documents and information, and other objectives. Killing enemy soldiers in a morning-long set battle was not an apt substitute for accomplishing the mission's objectives. "Instead of maintaining the mobility necessary for a raid of this type, the Marines had allowed themselves to get bogged down in a fruitless fire fight that had dragged out all day,"[6] concluded a Marine document. Carlson had handed the momentum to a smaller force of Japanese defenders.

After closely observing Japanese tactics in China, which Carlson thought too rigid, he concluded that "an aggressive opponent had a tremendous advantage. Here was an obvious weakness waiting to be exploited."[7] At Makin, however, he failed to take his own advice and allowed his men to become stalemated rather than aggressively dispatching flanking attacks. The man who had been more comfortable fighting guerrilla style, employing forces in speedy hit-and-run jabs while avoiding the enemy's main body, as evidenced by his service in Nicaragua and China, had opted for a set-piece attack at Makin. Had Carlson faced a larger enemy force, the Japanese might have successfully driven him into the sea.

Luck smiled on Carlson in the form of Peatross's unit. While the Raiders eliminated the snipers to their front, Peatross's eleven men created a diversionary attack by hitting the Japanese from the west. In all, Peatross's group killed eight Japanese along the road while losing three men. They harassed the enemy rear, destroyed a radio station, shot and killed the driver of a Japanese car as it sped down the road, and created havoc that helped deflect forces from Carlson's line.

In his report on the raid Carlson credited Peatross, an officer who was under fire for the first time, as an example of the Raider initiative he had tried to inculcate during training. The officer earned a Navy Cross for so completely harassing enemy forces to the rear.

"It's Wise to Assume the Worst"

While the Raiders battled on land, the two submarines passed the morning a mile out at sea. They carefully scanned the skies for approaching enemy aircraft, as the last thing a submarine wanted to face was an air attack while on the surface.

The *Nautilus* had already shelled the Ukiangong Village area to eliminate supposed Japanese reinforcements. Roosevelt radioed a second request at seven ten, this time to shell two vessels in Makin's lagoon—a thirty-three-hundred-ton transport and a thousand-ton gunboat. The ships, which one

Raider feared was the advance element of the potent Japanese Combined Fleet, produced great apprehension. No one knew how many reinforcements the boats might carry. "This caused me much consternation," said one of Peatross's men, Pfc. James C. Green, "because I knew that if the Japanese landed reinforcements our small group would have very little chance to escape."[8]

Roosevelt, perched amidst a clump of bushes, bullets whistling about, relayed his messages via a walkie-talkie to the submarines. "I was about five yards from Roosevelt," stated Pvt. Denton E. Hudman of B Company, "and he was on the radio giving instructions to the sub which way to shoot. Roosevelt was in the middle of the island, too. He was calm, did a good job."[9]

The *Nautilus* opened fire at 7:16, constantly altering the range and deflection to cover the entire lagoon in the absence of a precise target location. At 7:23 the *Nautilus* ceased firing. Sixty-five rounds sank both ships with what Commodore Haines called "the sheerest good luck."[10] Raiders offered silent prayers of thanks with the boats' disappearance, as it meant their lifeline to the submarines, their sole manner of leaving Makin Island, remained intact.

Though the *Nautilus* destroyed the two Japanese boats, Carlson had no idea whether any Japanese reinforcements had debarked from the ships before they were sunk. If a substantial number had landed, he faced larger numbers than ever. His Raiders had already been depleted, in numbers and ammunition, by the morning's fighting, and now the defenders' strength had possibly increased.

Natives informed Carlson that as many as sixty Japanese marines had been aboard the patrol craft. Though lacking verification, Carlson could not dismiss the thought. As commander he had to assume the worst and plan his tactics as if the Japanese had, indeed, received the reinforcements. Peatross claimed that the issue "seems to have heightened Carlson's apprehension."[11]

As the morning unfolded, little had gone right for Carlson. Starting with the rocky departure from the submarines, a series of unfortunate incidents plagued the operation. While each on its own may have been minor, the aggregate produced a combination of blows that temporarily perplexed the commander. His frustration intensified in late morning when a series of air attacks pummeled his line.

The first aerial attack occurred at 11:30 when two Navy Type 95 reconnaissance aircraft arrived. Both submarines quickly dove, and Raiders held their fire while the pilots scouted Makin from above. After fifteen minutes, the aircraft dropped two bombs, neither of which struck inside Raider lines, then headed north.

A more destructive raid followed in the early afternoon. At 12:55 the *Nautilus* surfaced, but radar picked up twelve contacts twelve and fourteen miles out. Faulty radio communications prevented the submarine from notifying Carlson, so the *Nautilus* dove and alerted via underwater sound the still-submerged *Argonaut* to remain where she was. Expecting enemy aircraft to be a problem until two hours before sundown, by which time the planes would have to leave to return to their home bases before dark, the pair stayed underwater for the remainder of the afternoon. They had, in effect, been put out of action for the day.

The twelve aircraft, which included two Kawanishi flying boats, four Zero fighters, four Type 94 reconnaissance bombers, and two Type 95 seaplanes, struck the island at 1:20. For the next seventy-five minutes they bombed and strafed Raider lines, causing few casualties but rattling Raider nerves.

"I got caught out in the open beach. All we had to hide under was a big palm leaf, and that really doesn't give you a lot of security," said Corporal Cotten. "At least the camouflage was there. The guy made a pass and came close enough the dirt piled up."[12]

Cpl. Howard Young waited out the bombings by pressing his body as close to the ground as possible. He stated that he was petrified until he realized the aircraft were shooting blindly rather than focusing their efforts on him. In an effort to avoid the bombs and shrapnel, Private Milligan jumped into a shallow taro pit and alternately huddled close to one side or the other, depending upon the direction of the incoming aircraft.

After seventy-five minutes, ten planes left while two others, a Kawanishi bomber and a Type 95 aircraft, landed in the lagoon off King's Wharf about two miles out. Sergeant Stidham and another Raider set up their Boys antitank rifles close to the lagoon and, accompanied by Marines manning three machine guns, opened fire when the first aircraft drew within a thousand yards. The Type 95 aircraft burst into flames and sank, while the Kawanishi executed a speedy turn in an attempt to evade the gunfire.

Platoon Sergeant Maghakian directed the shooting at the Kawanishi by observing bullet splashes through a pair of binoculars. When Maghakian informed Stidham his first shot came up short of the target, Stidham raised his sight, took aim, and directed a steady stream of gunfire at the Kawanishi. Tracers and incendiary rounds from all five guns zeroed in on the bomber, which managed to slowly rise into the air a short distance before crashing in flames into the lagoon.

The Raiders had destroyed both aircraft, but as with the two vessels earlier, did any reinforcements leave the planes beforehand? Natives told Carlson that thirty-five Japanese soldiers poured out of the large seaplane, but the figure could not be confirmed. As he had with earlier estimates, Carlson assumed that reinforcements had strengthened his opposition.

Some have questioned Carlson's assumptions relating to the size of his Japanese opponent. Peatross, for one, hits his commander's quick acceptance of native reports. Peatross states that because of his service in Nicaragua and China, Carlson, like any combat veteran, should have developed a feel for how a fight unfolded, how the sights and sounds indicated the battle's progress. "As he walked along the battle line and talked with his Raiders," Peatross wrote, "saw with his own eyes the enemy dead strewn about the battlefield, and heard with his own ears the marked diminution in the volume and variety of enemy fire until all that remained was intermittent sniper fire, Carlson should have realized long since that the prize was his for the taking. But he didn't." This produced an exaggeration of Japanese strength and caused what Peatross labeled "Carlson's seeming operational timidity."[13]

Others counter with the argument that Carlson had little choice but to accept the larger figures. Information from native residents who had intermingled with the Japanese since the previous December could not lightly be dismissed. "The natives told us there were about 180 Japanese on the island," mentioned Sergeant McCullough. "We had some intelligence that there were about 100, but naturally you pay attention to what the natives say because they're on the island. Carlson was faulted for thinking there was 180 on there, but he had firsthand information, not something intelligence told us. It's wise when you're in a situation like that to assume the worst."[14]

Another point of contention centers on Private First Class Donovan, whom Peatross had sent to locate Carlson. Donovan reached Carlson around two, informing him that no Japanese existed in the southwest section of the island, and that Peatross's men could attack the Japanese rear. Peatross claimed that after the raid, when he and Carlson sat aboard the *Nautilus* on the way back to Pearl Harbor, Carlson told Peatross that Donovan's arrival was one of the high points in the day. Despite the good news, Carlson declined to act, a fact that perplexed Peatross.

"But high point notwithstanding, he seems to have discounted or completely ignored Donovan's information on the enemy situation. Instead, he chose to remain in a defensive posture and made no attempt to link up with my group, thereby leaving the initiative in the hands of a few snipers." Peatross added, "Given all of the objective evidence available to him—that of his own direct observations, that of his Raiders who had been in contact with the enemy for several hours, and that provided by Donovan—it is difficult to understand why Carlson, a seasoned combat commander and an experienced intelligence officer, was not more aggressive in carrying out his mission and persisted in overestimating the enemy's strength or, even worse, underrating his own."[15]

It appeared that Carlson, who had proven his courage in Nicaragua, in China, and even on this first day with his complete disdain for enemy bullets, at Makin had become indecisive.

"The Effect of Resolute Men"

With a lull in the air attacks, Carlson now began a two-phase withdrawal to the submarines. With Japanese snipers in thick foliage holding up the Raider advance, and with the specter of Japanese reinforcements strengthening their hand, Carlson pulled back the line to an open area in hopes of luring the snipers onto more accessible ground.

At four p.m. he held the left flank in place, then withdrew the center and right flank two hundred yards. If the Japanese followed they would come under enfilading fire from straight ahead as well as from the Raiders remaining on the left flank, or at least be bombed by their own aircraft that thought they were hitting American positions.

Some of the Raiders could not understand the reason for the withdrawal. "We thought he was crazy for a minute," said Platoon Sergeant Maghakian, "but just for a minute."[16]

Shortly after executing the withdrawal, at four thirty Japanese aircraft arrived for the third air attack of the day. As Carlson hoped, for thirty minutes bombs fell on Japanese soldiers who had crept forward in light of the Raider pullback. Shrapnel cut through the palm trees and foliage, taking a toll on the snipers who had blocked Carlson's advance.

When the final plane departed for the day, Carlson faced another decision. Roosevelt suggested they immediately begin pulling back to the beaches for their rendezvous with the submarines rather than use up precious time by staying in place. Carlson could either remain in line, wipe out the defenders, attain some of the mission's objectives, then pull back to the beaches for the departure to the submarines, thereby delaying the withdrawal, or he could begin a more orderly extraction now.

Carlson visited the front lines to assess the situation, asked other officers for their advice, and then opted for Roosevelt's suggestion. The submarines were crucial to the war effort in the Pacific, and he did not want to endanger them by making them wait off the island while the Raiders completed their missions. Besides, as he stated in his report, "The enemy still appeared to be strong in our front, and he was in a position to receive reinforcements."[17] At five p.m. Carlson sent a handful of men back to the beaches to begin preparing the rubber boats for evacuation and ordered the rest of the Raiders to begin extricating themselves from the line.

One Marine historian concluded that at this crucial moment, Carlson "seemed to vacillate"[18] between his options before finally choosing to pull back immediately. In a surprisingly harsh report on the raid, in October 1942 Admiral Nimitz censured Carlson for too readily abandoning the mission.

"Although the mission of destruction of enemy forces and installations had not been completed, after the last bombing the raider commander decided to withdraw according to plan." A more critical statement pertaining to the strength of Carlson's opposition followed this relatively mild rebuke. "It appears that there were only a few Japanese soldiers left alive, yet such is the effect of boldness in a few resolute men that it seemed to the raider commander at this time that he was still opposed by a large force."[19]

While this took place in Makin's midsection, to the west Peatross faced his own decision. In the absence of hearing from Carlson, Peatross concluded that he should pull back to the beach at the appointed time and head out to the submarine, where he hopefully would be reunited with the rest of the Raiders. Around three p.m. Peatross and his men destroyed anything of value to the Japanese, then turned toward the beach.

Though Carlson and the Raiders had spent a trying first day at Makin, they were about to face what one Raider called "the most harrowing [five hours] in my life."[20]

"A Life-or-Death Struggle"

At six forty the Raiders began pulling out from the front line and withdrawing to the beaches, where boat crews had already prepared the rubber boats for the departure. By seven a covering force stood guard above the beaches in case the Japanese attempted to disrupt the proceedings, with orders to remain until the other Raiders had entered the water before taking the final boat out.

The Raiders gathered in small groups, with most of the force assembling by seven p.m. To improve the chances of the wounded making it back to the submarines, Dr. Stigler and Dr. MacCracken placed them into different boats according to the severity of injury.

An unanticipated incident with Major Roosevelt tested Private First Class Bauml's nerves as he waited on the beach. An accidental discharge of his rifle, which Bauml cradled with the barrel pointing to the sky, sent nearby men, including the president's son, scattering for cover. The mortified Bauml sheepishly explained to Roosevelt what had happened, all the while petrified at how close he had come to injuring Roosevelt. No one wanted to be the man responsible for harming the president's son.

Strategists had selected seven thirty to leave Makin Island so that darkness would hinder Japanese observation and to take advantage of a high tide, which would make it easier for the boats to traverse the reef. However, they had not foreseen the dangerous combination of the speed of the waves and the rapidity with which they followed each other.

By seven fifteen the boats had lined up along the southern beaches, where doctors and corpsmen carefully lifted the wounded into different boats. Due to the severity of Sergeant Lenz's wounds, which left him paralyzed, they placed him into the first along with Dr. Stigler in the hopes of transferring him as quickly as possible to the submarine, where Dr. Stigler could operate on him. Lieutenant Le Francois lay in the second, tended by a corpsman, while the twice-wounded Lamb occupied the third boat to leave. The rest of the Raiders spread out to walk the boats out to chest-high water, at which point they intended to hop in and begin paddling toward the reef. A daunting task tested each Raider at the end of an exhausting day.

The boats at each end of the line started leaving at seven thirty, followed by the next in order as the string of boats worked its way toward the center of the line, where Carlson orchestrated the effort. Since the units had been intermingled since early morning, Raiders walked to the nearest boat in line, without regard to whom they joined. "We just sort of got ten guys and got into a boat," said Sergeant McCullough. "We didn't go out by fire teams or platoons. It was pretty much you got in with other guys. Carlson was right there overseeing everything."[21]

Carlson remained, with the covering force posted behind as a rear guard, until every boat had entered the water. When he was confident that every Raider, including the covering force, had departed, Carlson splashed into the surf at seven thirty to join the Raiders manning the final boat.

Carlson assumed the covering force had already left, but in fact the unit still guarded the high ground above the beach, protecting the Raider rear until they were positive every other man had departed. They assumed someone would retrieve them when the force dwindled to two boats—one for Carlson and one for them. However, at the other end Carlson made his own incorrect assumption. As overall commander, it was Carlson's responsibility to make sure he was the last Raider to leave the island.

Pvt. Ben Carson blamed a sergeant who directed Carson and the covering group to their post. "Carlson got in the last boat," said Carson, "and there wasn't a boat for us to leave in. We didn't know this at the time. We didn't feel at that time that we were being abandoned. The Sarge should have let Carlson know he left us as a covering force. There was a lack of communication."[22]

As it turned out, Private Carson and the rest of the covering force had box seats to the drama in the surf that was now to unfold as the weary, hungry Raiders dragged their boats into the water. Each man advanced "into a life-or-death struggle to beat through the heavy waves to safety," declared Le Francois. Colonel Carlson stated it more bluntly by labeling the time spent in the water "a struggle so intense and so futile that it will forever remain a ghastly nightmare to those who participated."[23]

Each boat followed the same routine. The Raiders with Lieutenant Griffith grabbed the rubber handles on the boat's side and walked the boat out as far as they could. The swirling surf battered their legs in the shallower water, buckling some of the men's knees and serving as an ominous harbinger to the coming ordeal. When the water had risen to their chests, Raiders hopped into the boat and began paddling toward the reef and its angry breakers.

Most boats made it through the initial rollers, but faltered as a series of waves drenched them with salt water and buffeted the tiny craft. Roosevelt's boat made it over one roller only to be immediately smacked backward by a second, more violent set of waves, requiring Roosevelt and the men in his boat to paddle more furiously simply to return to where they had been. Those wounded who could, plus other Raiders, bailed out the water that had risen to the gunwales to prevent the boat from sinking, but the unrelenting ocean tossed back twice the amount of water they dumped overboard.

"Them damn waves seemed like they were eighteen feet high," said Private Milligan. "It was kind of like being in a football game. You don't know when or who's going to hit you, but you know you're going to get hit."[24]

The Raiders in Private Hudman's boat paddled as furiously as they could, yet when Hudman looked shoreward after fifteen minutes, they had moved a mere fifteen yards. Sergeant McCullough described the time in the water as "the toughest thing I'd ever done," while Private First Class Bauml said, "We paddled and paddled and paddled. My muscles were aching. You could see them almost popping out because they were so strained."[25]

The first wave that crashed into Lieutenant Griffith's boat knocked it sideways. Before they turned the boat back onto its correct course a second roller smashed into it, followed almost immediately by a third that flipped the boat and tossed equipment and Raiders, wounded and unharmed alike, into the water. Waves towered above the boats, hanging momentarily suspended in a watery taunt before crashing down on the exhausted men and knocking out the few motors that had coughed to life. Other boats drifted upward into the curls, teetered on the brink of the wave for a few seconds, and then tipped over backward, tossing occupants and weapons into the raging surf. Overturned boats dashed and darted in different directions as drenched Raiders, gasping for air, struggled to reach the surface. Sergeant McCullough and the Raiders with him tried in vain for three hours to make it through the breakers, but each time the waves hurled them back to the beach, where the drained men rested before embarking on what proved to be yet another futile attempt.

In his post-raid report, Admiral Nimitz stated that several Raiders probably drowned trying to leave Makin. According to *Time* magazine, Roosevelt saved three Raiders from drowning. Three times the surf tossed the paralyzed Sergeant Lenz into the water. Each time other Raiders quickly came to his aid.

Pvt. Dean Winters struggled in the surf when he heard a man near him shout, "Shark!" then disappear under the surface. Winters never saw the man again. Corporal Cotten heard the Marine warn other Raiders from coming close to him as a shark had already bitten him.

At different spots along the beach, clusters of Raiders regrouped, headed into the surf to retrieve a boat, and repeated their efforts to puncture through the breakers, sometimes four or five times before their weakened muscles quit from the strain. Le Francois lay on the beach after his fifth attempt, worried about his fate should the Japanese capture him, for he had heard horror stories of what the Japanese did to the wounded. Sergeant Stidham lost his rifle, pistol, and knife to the surf, and could not remember how many times he tried to paddle beyond the reef before collapsing on Makin's sand and falling asleep.

"We got overturned, overturned, overturned," said Private First Class Quirk. "It was frustrating. You started to get a hopeless feeling about getting off the island, and we knew if we didn't get off, the Japs would be coming back the next day or the day after. We had no ammunition now. I had thrown over my gear."[26]

From his perch above the beach, Private Carson witnessed the struggle unfold a few hundred yards from shore. "As we looked toward the surf we could see boats being turned over backwards by the onrushing waves, dumping the wounded into the surf," Carson recalled of his beleaguered buddies. "Raiders would stick with the wounded and drag them out of the surf back up on the beach. Nowhere could we see a boat drilling its way through that surf and time after time the boats would wash up on the shore only to be righted by the dumped-out crews, and the struggle through the surf would begin again."

One thought bothered Carson as he watched the battle. Those Raiders who made it back to the beach were weaponless, and many lay in the sand stripped of all but their underclothes. What could those Raiders do to repel a possible Japanese attack? "We rear guard Raiders were wondering just how long this thing could go on before [we] represented the remaining firepower."[27]

"Where the Hell Have You Been?"

Somehow, eighty men succeeded in reaching one of the submarines. Sergeant McCullough claimed that it all depended on the vagaries of the waves at the location a boat entered the water. His crew battled in vain to leave Makin, while boats one hundred yards to his side passed beyond the reef and out to the submarine. A boat close by Corporal I's glided through the surf with relative ease, despite having wounded aboard.

"They were right alongside of us and they paddled out through that surf. It looked like the sea just calmed down and parted, and they picked their way through it, and four people paddled where twelve of us couldn't even contain a rubber boat. It's uncanny. The hand of the Lord was taking care of them. They were only three to five yards from us. The current was the same, the swells and frequency, and yet they paddled straight through."[28]

No one cared which submarine they paddled toward. As long as it was American, they were going straight at the nearest vessel. Private Hudman traveled to Makin on the *Nautilus* but returned to the *Argonaut*. Cpl. Dell Grant of B Company was so relieved at safely battling through the waves to the *Argonaut* that he kissed the submarine's rail when he finally arrived.

A mile away Lieutenant Peatross fruitlessly waited at the beach in the dark in case Carlson appeared, then led his men into the water. They uncovered their boat, inflated it, and dragged the boat to the beach. Before leaving, Peatross carefully studied the surf for fifteen minutes to determine a pattern, and noticed that every fifth wave seemed to be smaller than the previous four. Waiting for a fifth wave, Peatross and his men jumped in and began paddling. Good fortune blessed the group when the engine kicked to life.

"That way, Sam," Peatross told Cpl. Sam Brown as he pointed toward the open sea, hoping that one of the submarines actually lay in that direction. "But if you can't find a submarine, just get me as close as possible to North Carolina."[29]

Around seven forty-five they spotted the flashing green light from the *Nautilus* (the *Argonaut* flashed a red light), and twenty minutes later Peatross and his grateful Raiders climbed aboard. Peatross gave a quick report to Commodore Haines on what had occurred ashore, and reacted disbelievingly to the news that his was the only boat so far to reach the submarine. Within fifteen minutes, aided by the brandy Commodore Haines gave him, Peatross was sound asleep.

More arrivals soon awakened Peatross. The scenes he witnessed topside as exhausted Raiders struggled aboard stunned Peatross. "They all looked like pale shadows of the men I had last seen early that morning, and I knew that they had been through a terrible ordeal."

The men in subsequent boats, who had spent more time fighting Makin's currents, looked "like nothing less than zombies." At least some of the men in the first boat retained a few weapons, but those who followed came alongside without rifles, packs, helmets, even clothes.

"Standing on deck and watching the last boat approach, I could scarcely believe my eyes. This was no longer a team, but a group of humanoids held together only by the boat they rode and their individual wills to survive. Some had their eyes fixed in a thousand-yard stare and seemed almost catatonic, paddling like automatons. Not a paddle, however, was to be seen; instead, the boat was being propelled by palm fronds and hands."[30]

When he glanced at Lieutenant Griffith, he barely recognized the Texan, a tough officer who "looked like he had aged twenty years."

"Where the hell have you been?"[31] Griffith asked Peatross upon seeing the supposedly lost officer. The two caught up on the day's events as the submarine crew brought food and liquid to the Raiders.

Four boats reached the *Nautilus* and another three the *Argonaut*, safely conveying eighty men. Besides Peatross's and Griffith's groups, Dr. Stigler and his patient, Sergeant Lenz, reached the *Argonaut*, while Private First Class Quirk found safe haven with the *Nautilus*.

The whereabouts of another 120 remained in doubt.

Those men lay on the beach, wet, exhausted, and hungry. Carlson saw the futility in expecting weakened men to succeed against a surf that had tossed back stronger men like twigs, and abandoned the attempt to rendezvous with the submarines. He hoped to reorganize the men ashore and figure out his next step.

Carlson surveyed his Raiders and concluded "that all men were in a state of extreme exhaustion." Most had lost their gear, and the wounded lay helpless as other Raiders gasped for breath. More than half the boats were scattered about the sand. Carlson set up a defense line above the beach, comprising the covering force and other able Raiders, then sat down to determine his next moves.

According to his report, he and the other 120 Raiders gathered on the beach with little equipment, "and waited miserably in the rain for dawn and another attempt to pass the surf."[32]

"We went to the beach and flopped down," said Sergeant McCullough. "We began to wonder if we were ever going to get off the island."[33]

"Is There Anyone Who Thinks We Ought to Surrender?"

As day one at Makin wound to a close, Evans Carlson faced the worst dilemma of his military career. An exacting landing ended with an accidental discharge, sending his Raiders into a set battle and planting confusion in the ranks. Those were mere foreshadowings to a traumatic evacuation that left his two companies drained, perplexed, and uneasy. He somehow had to restore order from the chaos and find a way to remove the remainder of his men from the island before Japanese reinforcements cut off his retreat route. He had no idea who had successfully reached the two submarines, how many Raiders currently lay on Makin's beach, or the strength of the Japanese still on the island.

At eleven p.m. gunshots from the security detail posted above the shore interrupted his thoughts. Pfc. Jess Hawkins of B Company opened fire when a patrol of eight Japanese soldiers approached the perimeter. Before falling wounded from two shots to the chest, Hawkins killed three enemy soldiers and forced the others to flee, but the event added to Carlson's predicament. "This incident showed that enemy resistance was by no means ended,"[34] he wrote in his report of the raid. The near certainty that the next morning would bring additional Japanese reinforcements and renewed air attacks compounded his quandary. Other than his covering force, few Raiders possessed weapons with which to defend themselves.

Carlson's next step sparked a controversy that exists to this day. Did the Raider commander consider surrendering? If so, who first broached the subject? Though some Raiders contend that Carlson advocated a capitulation, others either vehemently deny the allegation or claim to know nothing.

Most accounts agree that around midnight, Carlson gathered his officers and a few other men for a meeting, at which time the subject arose. Discussions then spread to the Marines scattered along the beach. "In our regular gung ho meetings, there was little protocol," stated Corporal Cotten. "Everybody's opinion counted. That night, the little groups got together and followed the same procedure. There were about ten of us together."[35]

According to this version, three points of view arose among the Raiders—some wanted to ignore the hazards and continue to fight, others favored making another attempt to reach the submarines, and a third suggested surrendering. Debates flared into heated arguments, with no side gaining domi nance. This version has Carlson meandering from group to group as an impartial observer, trying to ascertain the prevailing mood.

James Roosevelt later called this night at the beach one of the most dramatic moments of his wartime career. He stated in postwar writings that Carlson collected his men on a small rise above the beach, asked what they felt the Raiders should do, then took a vote. "Carlson ran a democratic show," Roosevelt wrote. "This night we voted on survival—whether to surrender or try to survive the night and escape when the tide went out in the morning. We voted to stay and try to escape."[36]

Doubt exists as to which meeting he refers. Some Raiders assert that Carlson purposely met with selected officers, without Roosevelt's inclusion, to keep the president's son at arm's distance from such a distasteful topic. If so, Roosevelt most likely sat in on one of the smaller group discussions while Carlson contemplated the issue with his officers.

That a man could be present on the beach that night and know nothing about the surrender until long after the raid, as some state, strains credibility. Either they did not know or, most likely, due to the sensitive nature of the subject, they cared not to discuss the matter. One of the most astute observers, Lieutenant Griffith, claims he only learned of the matter when he read Peatross's 1995 book, *Bless 'Em All: The Raider Marines of World War II*, and neither Private Milligan nor Private First Class Nugent heard of the surrender issue until back in Hawaii after the raid.

"We didn't know anything about surrendering," stated Milligan. "I didn't learn about it until I came back. We didn't know what the officers were planning. They got in a group, and we were down there on the beach. Carlson didn't consult the whole bunch." Private First Class Nugent added, "As far as I know, talking about surrendering never happened. I don't know where that came from. There must have been something, but the group I was in, we never heard about it until a lot later."[37]

There is little doubt the topic arose. However, the matters of who first brought up the notion and how seriously Carlson pondered the matter are open to debate. The historians Jon T. Hoffman and George W. Smith assert that, with little input from other officers, Carlson chose to surrender, with Smith even claiming that the decision was so abhorrent to Carlson it "was intentionally hidden from the public for almost half a century."[38] How that can be possible, in light of the fact that Michael Blankfort included the matter in his 1947 biography of Carlson, is mystifying, but it shows the depth and bitterness caused by the controversy.

Other historians, like Tripp Wiles, claim that Carlson never ordered his Raiders to surrender, but offered it as an option that each man might consider, much as some Raiders contemplated fighting while others deliberated over another attempt to leave the island.

"Carlson was thinking about surrender," said Private First Class Bauml, "but he didn't make up his mind to do it. He was just discussing it with his officers or whomever the hell he was talking with." Sergeant McCullough, one of Carlson's most avid supporters, claims the commander was rarely more than ten yards from him, and he never heard Carlson tell his men to surrender. "Carlson might have considered it, but I don't know that it was ever brought up out loud. I was pretty close to him the whole time, and I never heard any discussion at all."[39]

James Roosevelt claimed the suggestion to surrender came from a Raider "whose name I will never reveal as long as I live." Roosevelt added that Carlson told the man if he left the beach and found any Japanese to whom the men might surrender, "then you have the right to come back here to tell me and the men will have the opportunity to express their views." When the individual supposedly returned without locating any Japanese, Carlson asked, "Is there anyone else who thinks we ought to surrender?" When no one did, the matter was settled.

Roosevelt explained that Carlson resorted to his long-standing belief in a democratically run outfit whenever possible, even on the sands of Makin. "Carlson never suggested that we surrender," stated Roosevelt. "It came from an entirely different person. But Carlson handled it in the way he believed in, which was not ever to overrun anybody—give them a chance to express their views. He was pretty certain that he was right, that no one wanted to surrender. And the idea was thrown away."[40]

Then there is Blankfort's 1947 version, which has Carlson walking along the beach when he overheard a group of Raiders heatedly arguing. When one man mentioned surrendering, Platoon Sergeant Maghakian bellowed, "Shut up!"

The Raider, obviously frightened, countered that the submarines had abandoned the Raiders to their fate and that since they stood thousands of miles from help, the men ought to consider surrendering.

"Shut up!" Maghakian said again.

When the Raider shouted that he was going to find Carlson and convey his thoughts, Maghakian slapped him. "I told you to shut up. I warned you," said the irate sergeant. Another man vowed that he would never surrender, to which Maghakian added, "And don't worry. Carlson and Roosevelt aren't either."[41]

"The Spiritual Low Point"

It appears certain that Carlson, at a minimum, contemplated the surrender issue. As commander he had a duty to examine every eventuality, and compelling reasons made capitulation a viable, if distasteful, option. His men had inflicted heavy casualties on the Japanese throughout the day, but he neither knew how many they killed nor how many Japanese survived. The seaplane may have brought additional reinforcements, and the eleven p.m. skirmish with the Japanese patrol indicated the enemy had fight left. As a responsible commander, he had to assume the Japanese would be preparing for a dawn attack against his meagerly armed Raiders. Should they somehow repulse that charge, Carlson assumed he would later face a more potent attack by the Japanese reinforcements certain to pour into Makin in the next day or two.

A daylight evacuation to the submarines carried too great a risk. The same Japanese aircraft that had harassed them that first day would return, most likely in larger numbers, on day two. The submarines would have to remain underwater throughout the day to avoid being caught on the surface. The earliest he could hope to reach the submarines, the Raiders' sole lifeline to safety and a return to Pearl Harbor, would thus not be until after dark of the second day, but this exposed his men to piecemeal attacks by Japanese land forces or, worse, being trapped on Makin by Japanese surface vessels interdicting their path to the submarines.

If Carlson, who Captain Coyte claimed was disturbed over his inability to extricate the Raiders from the island, concluded that additional fighting would only result in more casualties, he may have seen the step as reasonable. Lieutenant Griffith thinks it is possible that Carlson considered surrendering. "He had the wounded, and there was no place to go. He realized he couldn't fight. All the weapons were gone."[42]

Carlson must have felt as if he stared into a bottomless chasm. If so, he was far from alone. "I had only a knife and one hand grenade," explained Pfc. Kenneth J. Seaton of B Company. "Someone else had a rifle and another Tommy gun but most were cold, wet, exhausted and weaponless." Seaton added, "We were miserable and scared. There were no personal heroics, just an effort to hang on until the next day. We wondered if we would be captured or killed by the expected Jap reinforcements." Sergeant Stidham stated that the Raiders went through a "roller coaster ride" of emotions and experiences and that they "bottomed out in the absolute depths of despair on the beach that night."[43]

Though Carlson joked with some of the men, "Don't say I didn't warn you, boys. I told you it would be tough in the Raiders,"[44] his surface calm masked a turbulent interior. He stated as much in his report.

"The situation at this point was extremely grave," he reported to Admiral Nimitz. The battle in the water "had disorganized us and stripped us of our fighting power." He gazed about him, at the 120 wet, shivering men who faced a new day without weapons or hope of aid, and empathized with their agony. "Rain and the fact that most of the men had even stripped themselves of their clothes in the surf added to the general misery. This was the spiritual low point of the expedition."[45]

Of course, there was also the matter of the thousand-pound gorilla in the room, the issue everyone knew existed but hoped to avoid—the presence of Jimmy Roosevelt. Carlson had pledged to his commander in chief, at least by implication, to look out for his son. Carlson had checked on his executive officer during the day, and had even inspected the beach area that night, after the boats returned, to verify that Roosevelt had safely escaped the treacheries of the surf. He was visibly relieved when he located the president's son.[46]

"He implied that he felt personally responsible for the safety and well being of the President's son," Peatross wrote of Carlson, "and indicated that he felt the death of Jimmy Roosevelt might seriously hamper the war effort and was ready to go to any extreme to save him."[47]

Carlson and his officers conferred about what to do with Roosevelt. The two alternatives to safely leaving Makin were Roosevelt's death or capture. Capitulation might avoid Roosevelt's death, but in captivity he was certain to be used as a propaganda ploy, possibly being paraded about Tokyo in restraints for the world to see. "James's life was probably more in danger than anyone's," said his widow, Mary Roosevelt. "If the Japanese had captured him, it would have been a real problem."[48]

Carlson knew Roosevelt enough to realize that his executive officer would spurn a surrender simply to save his own life. They somehow had to get Roosevelt off the island alive.

"Carlson Would Never Have Surrendered"

Then there is the issue of the surrender note. Most Raiders, including the private who helped deliver a surrender note to a Japanese soldier, accept the version written by Lieutenant Peatross in his 1995 book. According to that account, around three thirty a.m. of the second day Captain Coyte and Pvt. William McCall, both unarmed and acting supposedly on Carlson's orders, left the beach to find a Japanese officer to whom they might surrender.

When Coyte located a Japanese soldier inside a native hut, he composed the document. Addressed to the commanding officer, the letter read:

> *Dear Sir:*
>
> *I am a member of the American forces now on Makin.*
>
> *We have suffered severe casualties and wish to make an end of the bloodshed and bombings.*
>
> *We wish to surrender according to the rules of military law and be treated as prisoners of war. We would also like to bury our dead and care for our wounded.*
>
> *There are approximately 60 of us left. We have all voted to surrender.*
>
> *I would like to see you personally as soon as possible to prevent future bloodshed and bombing.*

The signature on the note is strangely illegible.

Coyte told the enemy soldier he and McCall would wait at the hut for him to return with a response. Shortly after the Japanese soldier left, a gunshot brought Coyte outside. Two Raiders approached from the road, one armed with a pistol, who explained that they had just shot an enemy soldier. Assuming the men had killed the messenger, Coyte returned to the beach and told Carlson he had been unsuccessful. That supposedly ended the matter with the note.[49]

Private McCall later endorsed the above-stated version. "Carlson came and told me to accompany Coyte and look for some live Jap soldiers and give them a note," he stated after the war. "I did not read the note. I don't know who wrote it, but Coyte had it. I don't know if it was signed. My job was to go with Coyte. As far as I know, Peatross's account of the surrender was accurate."[50] McCall declined to comment further, as if wishing the entire matter would somehow disappear.

Questions surround the incident. The unusual note contains information one would assume would not be found in such a document. Why, for instance, would the writer divulge how many Raiders remained on Makin? Why is the signature on the note, which Japanese reinforcements supposedly found later and sent to Tokyo for use in propaganda broadcasts by the infamous Tokyo Rose, impossible to discern? Why have so many Raiders remained silent on the issue, even many years later? Why did Private McCall agree with Peatross's version, then lapse into silence on the issue?

Raiders still cannot agree on what happened. As with the entire surrender controversy, one group accepts Peatross's version, another rejects it, while the largest group remains silent.

"The word started around here that we would surrender in the morning [and] this didn't set so very good with anyone," Pl. Sgt. Mel Spotts wrote in his diary after the raid. He added, however, that "there appeared no choice. Most of the weapons had been lost in our attempts at getting off."[51]

Private First Class Quirk agreed with Spotts. He stated that Peatross, a highly respected officer who retired a general, relating the issue lends it credibility. Quirk explained in 2007 that while he found unpalatable the idea of yielding, "I think it's possible Carlson considered it because he was a very compassionate man. You got to figure his position. He didn't have any weapons. My guess is there were very few guys who had weapons. I lost mine. What are you going to do, say, 'Hell, we're going to fight the sons-of-bitches with our hands!'? No. You don't have an alternative. Are you going to bite them? What was he going to do without weapons? He had no alternative." Quirk admitted he had difficulty accepting the issue earlier in his career, but "I never saw it as clearly as I do now."[52]

Another faction argues as fervently on the other side. "That wouldn't have happened," states Sergeant McCullough of the surrender note. "Roosevelt was still on the island. Carlson would have fought till he was dead before he'd do something to jeopardize Roosevelt. Why would he surrender if the president's son was right there? He was nervous about it."[53]

Pvt. Dean Voight agrees, claiming, "No, Carlson would never think of that. Some of the guys thought of it, but I wouldn't surrender. I didn't think he would, either. As far as I was concerned, he said he was going to stay and for us to get off. I think the surrender idea came from some one person, but I don't think Carlson would ever have surrendered. I was ready to go down fighting, not surrender."[54]

Years after the event Mary Roosevelt expressed her husband's belief. "I think if Jim was sitting where I am talking to you," she told the author in 2007, "he would say Carlson would never have surrendered."[55]

Despite the contrary reminiscences and opinions, it is obvious that something occurred that first night at Makin. Carlson's biggest quandary rested with James Roosevelt. If he surrendered, the president's son became a propaganda tool of the enemy. If Carlson and the Raiders fought to the death, he was the officer who, despite written assurances to the president, had lost the president's son.

The latter alternative would seem more logical. A last-ditch fight to the death, in which James Roosevelt became a casualty, would have been more palatable with people back home than a surrender. The American public could have accepted, even found noble, the death in battle of a president's son, but allowing him to fall into enemy hands alive was a different matter.

Removing Roosevelt would resolve the dilemma.

"Everybody's Been Having a Helluva Time"

The men spent a fitful, miserable night on Makin. Lieutenant Le Francois, himself badly wounded and in need of medical assistance, described the men near him as "the most disheartened, forlorn, bloody, ragged, disarmed group of men it had ever been my experience to look upon. Their heads hung low, and despair frayed their spirits."[56] Platoon Sergeant Maghakian passed around Miller's bottle of aged whiskey to wounded men so they could dull their pain.

Aboard the *Nautilus*, Lieutenant Peatross asked Commodore Haines for permission to lead ten men ashore to aid the Raiders at the beach. Haines turned him down, stating that the best course was to wait until daylight and assess the situation.

"For remainder of night maneuvered to remain as close to the beach as possible within a mile," stated the *Nautilus*'s War Diary. "Stories of Marines received on board indicated that all boats had apparently tried to leave but experienced great difficulty in riding over the surf and that the Colonel was considering surrender."[57]

Few men enjoyed any sleep back at the beach. They gathered in clusters and huddled near brush one hundred feet from the water and hoped that daylight, should they last until then, would somehow bring newfound optimism.

As dawn approached Carlson announced that he intended to remain on Makin that day with the wounded, move across the island to the lagoon, and take his men to the submarines in native outrigger canoes at night. He added, however, that any man who felt strong enough to challenge the surf that morning had his permission to make another attempt. Groups of Raiders coalesced along the beach, grabbed a rubber boat, and braved the surf. Among them, following Carlson's order to leave, was Jimmy Roosevelt.

A mile offshore observers on the *Nautilus* spotted the activity, prompting Brockman to risk his submarine by moving dangerously close to the reef to shorten the distance. To avoid being trapped in shallow waters by a Japanese air attack, Brockman backed the *Nautilus* toward the reef so the submarine pointed toward open sea and deeper depths.

Taking advantage of a benevolent surf, the first Raider boat arrived at the *Nautilus* at 7:19, followed eighteen minutes later by a second boat carrying the seven men in Private Carson's boat. Lieutenant Peatross, who had yet to see or make contact with Carlson or the main force of Raiders since early the previous morning, raced over to one of the occupants of the newly arrived boats, Sgt. Frank J. Lawson, and asked for an update of events onshore.

"Sergeant Lawson, what's going on back there?" Peatross asked.

"Lieutenant, everybody's been having a helluva time getting off the beach, and when we left the Colonel was getting ready to surrender."

Peatross replied incredulously, "What are you talking about? Surrender?"

Lawson explained that the exhausted Raiders ashore possessed few weapons and little ammunition. He said that Carlson worried about his wounded and that a surrender might be the only humane course of action.

Lawson then expressed his concern about Roosevelt and pointedly asked Peatross the question that had concerned Carlson before leaving Pearl Harbor. "If Roosevelt's death would be so bad, why in hell's he on the raid in the first place? Besides, wouldn't it be better for the President's son to be killed than captured and used for propaganda?"

Peatross relayed this information to Commodore Haines and Captain Brockman, and recommended that they try to send a rescue party ashore.

"Peat, that crusty old boss of yours isn't going to surrender; he's just too tough for that," Haines emphasized. "But I do believe he could use some help, so here's what I want you to do."

He told Peatross to choose five volunteers, strong swimmers all, who would take one of the boats that just arrived and return to shore to relay a message to Carlson. Peatross briefed the volunteers—Sgt. Robert V. Allard,

Sgt. Dallas H. Cook, Pfc. Richard N. Olbert, Pvt. Donald R. Robertson, and Pvt. John I. Kerns, all from B Company—and instructed them to tell Carlson that the submarines would submerge during the day to avoid air attacks, but would return at 7:30 p.m. for the final evacuation. Peatross then relayed Haines's words, a stirring promise to come to the aid of the Marines.

"We are going to stay here until we get every living Raider off that island and, if we have to, we'll send every able-bodied man ashore, sailors included."[58]

The volunteers left the *Nautilus* at seven forty. They paddled to a point just outside the reef, where they shot a line shoreward to help their tired comrades depart. One then swam in to convey Haines's message to Carlson.

While the volunteers risked the waters to help the Raiders ashore, two other rubber boats, filled with fatigued men, bounced through the surf toward the *Argonaut.* One carried a reluctant James Roosevelt, ordered off the island by Carlson, who wanted his executive officer aboard a submarine while he remained on Makin until the last Raider was safely off. Carlson cut short Roosevelt's objections, and later wrote President Roosevelt, "I had to lay the law down in order to get him to go back to the sub so as to assure that at least one of us would be in position to carry on with the battalion."[59]

Raiders in Roosevelt's boat not only filled the inside but clung to the boat's side as the waves tossed them from side to side. Roosevelt, who unsuccessfully battled the surf only a handful of hours earlier, now found himself again drenched by more waves. Watching from shore, Lieutenant Le Francois held his breath as the boat carrying Roosevelt and Lamb tipped over and tossed its occupants into the water, nearly drowning Lamb in the process. The men returned to shallower water, uprighted the craft, and embarked on their second attempt minus Lieutenant Lamb, who concluded his chances for survival were better ashore with Carlson than in Roosevelt's tiny boat. Lamb helped shove the boat toward deeper water, waved good-bye to Roosevelt, then followed the group's progress as it headed toward the breakers.

Roosevelt battled surf and sea creatures. An enormous manta ray, which Sergeant Stidham compared in size to a barn door, flipped out of the water two or three times not more than twenty yards from the occupants. "I don't recall anyone uttering a single word," recalled Stidham, sitting in the boat beside Roosevelt, "but I couldn't help but notice that the rhythm of the paddles picked up a beat or two."[60]

Stidham also noticed that Roosevelt, a man he knew could have avoided combat due to his poor physical condition, paddled with the best of them to help his group smash beyond the breakers and reach open sea. "He was just a good egg," Stidham said of the president's son. "He was a first-class guy. He was 4F material with bad eyes, bad feet, and a bad stomach, but he never complained. He pitched right in and pulled his own weight, helping to get us back to the sub."[61]

According to another occupant with Roosevelt, Private First Class Bauml, water filled the boat to the gunwales, adding weight to the craft and slowing the Raiders' progress. The men strained against the extra burden but, assisted by good fortune and their own extraordinary efforts, finally arrived at eight a.m. alongside the *Argonaut*, only moments before Japanese aircraft appeared overhead.

Crew members scurried on deck to assist Roosevelt and the others out of the boat before the enemy planes targeted the submarine. "It was getting harder and harder," said Bauml, "and then I heard guys in the conning tower shout, 'Hey, Marine, get your ass up here!' I was the only guy left in the boat. I was holding the boat next to the sub and the prow, the front, was starting to pull away. The sub was starting to go down because a plane was coming. I could see it in the distance. I jumped on the sub and got to the top of the conning tower and just dove down. You could see the red flashes of the plane's machine guns as the sub went down."[62]

By the slimmest of margins Roosevelt and the men with him escaped harm. The *Argonaut* slipped beneath the surface as explosions rocked the surface. Another fifty Raiders had reached the submarines, leaving Carlson on the island with seventy Raiders.

Luck did not favor the five volunteers, though. In coming to the aid of the men ashore, they exposed themselves to danger in the open waters between the beach and the submarine two hundred yards away. When enemy aircraft arrived, the five were caught defenseless. Roosevelt asked the *Argonaut*'s skipper, Lt. Comdr. J. R. Pierce, to remain on the surface until the boat had drawn alongside, but Pierce could not place the fates of five Marines over that of his crew, the Raiders aboard, and his boat, to say nothing of the president's son. "We went under," Roosevelt recalled after the war. "And we never saw the men from that raft again."[63]

The five Raiders in Sergeant Allard's group disappeared amidst a shower of enemy bullets. Sergeant McCullough observed the struggle from shore and waited without success to see his friends again appear on the surface.

Lieutenant Le Francois watched the aircraft race across from the lagoon side, swoop low as they neared their targets, then strafe the helpless men and bomb the submarine. An explosion engulfed the *Argonaut* as she dove for safety, making the men onshore think the submarine had been hit. "Poor gobs," muttered a Raider near Le Francois. "There goes our transportation too."[64] The tired men faced the grim prospect that their sole ticket home, the submarines, had been destroyed.

Fortunately, the Japanese antipersonnel bomb exploded upon impact with the water and caused little damage to the *Argonaut*. Had the missile been a depth bomb instead, Roosevelt and more than one hundred men would have wound up at the bottom of the ocean.

While the air attack missed the two submarines, it ended what Admiral Nimitz later described as the "piecemeal evacuation."[65] The submarines remained under the surface for the rest of the day, leaving Carlson on land to figure out how to extricate his men from a tricky predicament. "I was over two thousand miles away from America and felt helpless,"[66] stated Pvt. Dean Winters.

A Poor Fit with the Map

"A Child's Version of Pirates"

The previous twenty-four hours had seen little but hardship, unexpected developments, and tenuous leadership from Carlson, but the dawn of day two brought startling changes. Coyte and McCall had reported seeing few Japanese soldiers about the island, leading Carlson to wonder if he and his seventy men might, instead, actually hold the advantage rather than facing a superior enemy. Revitalized by both the news and a new day, an invigorated Carlson issued a series of orders to energize his men and to put the raid back on schedule. It appeared that while waiting for evacuation later in the day he might, after all, successfully complete the missions assigned him in the operations plan.

According to Sergeant McCullough, a more assured Carlson gathered his Raiders in an impromptu gung ho meeting and informed them of his intentions. He explained that they would cross the island and relocate near Government House, closer to possible food and water supplies, that he was sending patrols to both ends of the island to determine the exact nature of their opposition, and that they would wait on Makin throughout the day until dark, when the submarines could once again surface and he could arrange a rendezvous to leave via the lagoon side.

Carlson wanted to replace the demoralizing night and talk of surrender with aggressive, optimistic actions and thoughts. According to Private Mc-

Call, with the arrival of daylight Carlson asked him to refrain from mentioning that they had considered surrendering.

"By this time I had learned that the enemy force ashore consisted of only a few men who were widely scattered,"[1] Carlson wrote in his action report. He sent patrols out to confirm the information, then led his Raiders to the lagoon side. Emboldened by their leader's optimism, a new enthusiasm swept through the Raiders, who crossed to Government House, dug in at new positions, and waited for new orders.

Once at his new location, Carlson took steps to complete his mission, which was to destroy Japanese installations and matériel and to obtain information of value. Raiders, acting more like Boy Scouts on a camping trip, destroyed the radio station near On Chong's Wharf, a thousand barrels of aviation gasoline, and anything else they thought might be useful to the enemy. Some rummaged through the Japanese commandant's office, where they seized documents and charts and removed a pistol and wristwatch from a body identified as Sergeant Major Kanemitsu. Others collected canned meats, fish, and biscuits at the trading station, where they also found blue and pink men's silk underwear. Within minutes, a handful of hardened Raiders donned the undergarments, producing such a spectacle that Le Francois said, "They looked like a child's picture-book version of a gang of pirates."[2]

Islanders greeted the Raiders with welcome drinks of water and coconut shells filled with juice. "I don't know what it was," said Pvt. Dean Winters of a proffered drink, "but it tasted pretty good. It lit me up. I hadn't eaten or drank anything since we were on the sub."[3] Private McCall walked over to the wounded Lieutenant Le Francois and handed him a bottle of Japanese beer he had taken from a pantry.

Another islander gave A Company's Capt. James Davis a sarong to replace the pants he had lost to the surf, while other Raiders scoured buildings and rooms for souvenirs. "Many of our men were trophy happy," stated Le Francois. "In years, if not in experience, they were boys and, like all boys, wanted souvenirs."[4] Compared to the previous day, the Raiders bounded about Makin with a zest that came straight from their commander.

While the men executed their orders, Carlson visited the scene of day one's fighting to collect weapons and to determine the number of killed. He and the men with him counted eighty-three enemy dead at the battlefield, and another thirty along the lagoon road. Combined with the supposed Japanese killed when the Raiders destroyed the two Japanese aircraft, estimates ranged from 100 to 150 killed. Carlson noticed that some Japanese who took refuge behind palm trees appeared to have died when Raider .50-caliber machine-gun bullets pierced directly through the soft wood. At the same time, Carlson discovered the bodies of fourteen Raiders, eleven on the battlefield and another three who had been with Lieutenant Peatross.

During the day Raiders hunted down and killed two enemy snipers. Though Carlson's orders called for seizing a prisoner, few took it seriously. In his report, Carlson shrugged off the lack of prisoners with, "We wanted to take prisoners, but we couldn't find any."[5]

As expected, between 9:20 a.m. and 5:30 p.m., Japanese aircraft bombed and strafed Makin four separate times on August 18. They focused their efforts on the lagoon side, where the Raiders dug in and waited out the attacks. The final Japanese aircraft left without harming any of Carlson's men.

"Buddies We Never Expected to See Again"

In the midst of gathering food and counting the dead, Carlson started preparations for evacuating his force. If the surf prevented him from reaching the submarines on this second night, Carlson knew that he and his men would most probably be stranded on the island, staring at a fate that offered, at best, incarceration in a Japanese prison camp for the war's duration. With enemy reinforcements certain to soon arrive, neither submarine could wait around Makin and risk being destroyed, especially at this stage of the war, when Nimitz had precious few ships with which to check the Japanese.

Carlson chose the lagoon side as his best chance to extricate his force. Natives had assured Carlson the surf was gentler there than on the ocean side and that the Japanese had not emplaced any large guns at the lagoon entrance.

Carlson again dispatched patrols to make sure every Marine had gathered at the lagoon. Though the patrols reported that everyone was accounted for, Carlson had no way of knowing for certain. The previous day's intermingling of companies, and the fact that part of the force had already reached the submarines, made an accurate count impossible.

In exchange for some weapons, ammunition, and $50, Carlson arranged with the island's chief of police, Joseph Miller, and his brother William to have the dead Raiders (now eighteen, up from fourteen) buried. Before leaving, Carlson personally turned each deceased Raider on his back and said a prayer over the man.

Carlson sent Lieutenant Lamb and two other men to inspect a forty-foot sloop anchored off Stone Pier. Gunfire greeted Lamb as he approached the sloop in a rowboat. He pulled alongside, tossed a grenade through a porthole, then boarded the boat and killed a Japanese soldier. A quick inspection found the shabby sloop taking on water, meaning Carlson would have to turn to his other alternative—rubber boats supplemented with two native outriggers.

Out at sea, the Raiders' ride back to Hawaii surfaced at 6:10 p.m. and headed toward the scheduled rendezvous point off the ocean beaches. The submarines arrived at seven thirty about three-quarters of a mile offshore, where they awaited a signal from Carlson.

In the absence of working radios, Sergeant McCullough provided communication with a flashlight. Climbing a palm tree to gain sufficient elevation, McCullough flashed out a signal informing Haines of Carlson's change in plans and asking the submarines to meet at Flink Point at the lagoon's south entrance at eleven p.m.

Carlson started the evacuation at six, when the Raiders dragged the four remaining rubber boats across the island to the lagoon side and strapped them together, with a native outrigger attached at either end. They placed two working motors—brought back to life by the mechanical skills of Corporal Cotten—to the outer rubber boat at each side, and posted the strongest Raiders with paddles on the outside of each native rigger.

Under the supervision of Captain Coyte and Lieutenant Lamb, the Raiders started into the water. Men gently lifted the wounded onto the center cross seats of the rubber boats, then hopped into one of the six sections and prepared to head out.

Once the Raiders had assembled, everyone held their breath while Cotten and another Marine tried to start the two motors. The engines coughed and gasped, then kicked to life in a welcome roar. At eight thirty the makeshift vessel, looking much like one fashioned by castaways, plunged into the water and veered toward Flink Point and, hopefully, a rendezvous with the submarines.

Progress matched the previous night's agonizingly slow pace. One of the motors needed to be refueled when it sputtered out of gas, a tricky and time-consuming procedure in the waves. Carlson somehow kept the boats, now being propelled by one motor, on proper course by aligning the raft with a bright star along the horizon. "It seemed we would never get past the point and into the open sea where the subs were waiting,"[6] Sergeant McCullough recalled in 2007.

According to Sergeant McCullough, the eight to ten men in the rubber boat on the far right side complained that the raft moved too slowly. They asked Carlson if they could cut loose and attempt to make it back to the submarines on their own. Carlson declined at first, thinking the men had a better chance if they remained with the main group, but granted permission a short time later when the improvised vessel had made little progress. The men cut loose and drifted away, but were never seen again.

It was not until after ten p.m. that they finally arrived at the lagoon entrance. A recognition signal from the submarines in the distance caused the Raiders to slap one another on the back, but they still had two miles to churn through the waves, two miles that Lieutenant Le Francois described as "packed with terror and fraught with agony." He added that the raft "pitched and tossed, and the rubber boats groaned as they beat and tore against one another. Lines snapped and were replaced. The current twisted us in the wrong direction, and the oarsmen strained and pulled us back on the right course again."[7]

The submarines, bobbing up and down in the dark, blended into the environment. "Can you imagine being in a rubber boat, with five- to six-foot seas, in the black of night, and you're two miles away and all you've got to signal was a flashlight?" asked Corporal Cotten in 2008. "The chances of locating the submarine weren't good. The conning tower rose only fifteen to twenty feet up, and them trying to locate a pinprick light was small."[8]

The Raiders found their submarine, though. As they neared the *Nautilus*, searchlights illuminated the scene and forced the Raiders to shield their eyes. Finally, at 11:08, Carlson and his tired men pulled alongside. Submariners first helped the wounded aboard, then offered a hand to the other relieved Raiders.

Sergeant Stidham and Lieutenant Peatross waited with other Raiders who had left the first night to greet "buddies we never expected to see again."[9] Peatross could hardly believe the spectacle that walked by him as once proud Raiders, now haggard, arrived.

"Never before or since have I seen such a motley looking group of humans or such an outlandish looking craft as that which came alongside the *Nautilus* that night," Peatross wrote. "In comparison, the Raiders who came out the first night would have looked healthy. As I watched Carlson come aboard, I was astounded at the change in his appearance. He had always been somewhat lanky, but now he was gaunt—a walking skeleton. In the 43 hours that had passed since I put him aboard the Company A boat for the trip to the beach, he seemed to have aged at least 10 years."[10]

Carlson and the other officers embarked upon a head count to determine if every Raider was accounted for, but as was true on land, an accurate count was all but impossible. Men from A Company mingled with their B Company companions, and no one on the *Nautilus* could determine which men had safely arrived aboard the *Argonaut*.

Peatross felt better when the Raiders told him they had patrolled every corner of Makin to make sure every living Raider reached the lagoon that night, "hence there was no reason to think that anyone had been left ashore." Peatross added that had there been any doubt about Raiders being on the island, Commodore Haines would never have reneged on his vow to stay until every Raider was back on board. "Later, after interviewing nearly all of the Raiders aboard the *Nautilus*, my best estimate was that the only men unaccounted for were the five men in the rescue party, and we had good reason to believe that they had been killed."[11]

Sergeant McCullough explained that once they arrived at the *Nautilus*, he figured the eight to ten men who had headed out on their own had made it to the *Argonaut*. Carlson agreed with both Peatross and McCullough, and reported to Haines that "he was satisfied that all surviving personnel of his command had been evacuated from the island."[12] Since the submarines had to maintain radio silence for the trip back, the only way they would know for certain was to wait until they pulled into Pearl Harbor, where an accurate muster could be taken.

"And It Was for Us"

Once every Raider was back aboard a submarine, crew members slashed the rubber boats and punctured holes in the native outriggers to send them to the bottom. At 11:53 p.m. the *Nautilus* and *Argonaut* set course for Hawaii, while Raiders made themselves as comfortable as possible in the confines that suddenly did not seem as cramped or inconvenient as they had seemed on the way out.

Some of the men needed time to calm down from the two-day ordeal. A crew member offered Corporal Cotten a cup of coffee, which he had to grab with both hands because he shook so severely. "I think I just let down after I got into the security of the submarine and felt the security of the people, the weapons," Cotten recalled. "You're living on adrenaline so long, it took both hands to get that cup up to my mouth. We had only eaten rations, so we were hungry. I found a secluded corner, sat down, put my head between my knees, said a prayer. One of my favorites—the 23rd Psalm. By the time I got to the last part, I probably dozed off or something. I had good intentions, anyway."[13]

The next day, while Dr. MacCracken operated on five men for twelve straight hours, other Raiders discussed the positives and negatives of the raid. Most concluded it had been a success as they had been able to kill most, if not all, of the garrison, and destroyed much valuable material.

While aboard the submarine, Pvt. Ben Carson supposedly overheard a conversation between Carlson and Captain Coyte during which Carlson told his officer to forget that the surrender note was written. Carlson added that "if you want to be a hero you can't talk surrender." When the pair noticed Carson and another Marine nearby, Carlson ordered Carson to leave, but before the private was out of range he heard Carlson mutter to Coyte, "Do you think he heard what we were talking about?" Carson stated, "I got the feeling they didn't want us to hear what they said."[14] Private McCall also stated that Carlson preferred to keep the surrender issue under wraps.

The implication is that Carlson intended to eradicate mention of the surrender issue. Carson has no one to corroborate his story and McCall, currently in poor health in a nursing home, declines to comment further on the issue, forcing historians to rely on his 1999 statement, "There was a tacit agreement between Carlson, Coyte, and I that nothing more be said between us about the surrender note. I do not have anything that I'd like to straighten out—what's done and said is over with. Carlson and Coyte are dead. Nothing needs straightening."[15]

What occurred among those four individuals remains unclear. That a private might accidentally overhear a conversation between a colonel and a captain about hiding details of such a controversial subject is suspect, but one cannot completely discount Carson's claim. The researcher must find an answer elsewhere, an answer Colonel Carlson himself provided when he returned to Pearl Harbor.

After traveling another 2,029 miles, on August 25 the *Nautilus* pulled into Pearl Harbor, one day ahead of the slower *Argonaut*. As they passed each vessel in port, ships' bands played "Anchors Aweigh" and "From the Halls of Montezuma" while other military units, including some of their brethren from the Raider Battalion, stood at attention. Raiders collected on the deck to witness the astonishing turnout. "All of a sudden I realized that the bands were playing and the people were cheering, and it was for us,"[16] said Jimmy Roosevelt.

Dr. Stephen Stigler noticed the contrast between the spit-and-polish Marines ashore and the men returning from action. "We were not exactly dressed to be saluted or salute back because most had lost a lot of our clothes when the surf was so heavy. Most of us had to divest ourselves of our clothing just to handle the heavy surf and swim. The Navy folks loaned us some clothes, but we were a pretty ragtag bunch." He added, "It was my most vivid memory of the war. I was so moved they were cheering us; it felt like we had really done something meaningful and good."[17]

Tears coursed down Corporal Cotten's cheeks as he stood on the *Nautilus*'s deck. "I never felt so humble in my life. We were all on deck, raggy, black outfit, jet black, all at topside lined up. We came down Battleship Row and we were all out there, and here's the battleships, heavy cruisers, destroyers, support tenders—everyone was out in dress uniform, the flags dropped to half mast. I'll tell you, you had a bunch of old men crying. Today, if I dwell on it, I still get heavy mist."[18]

Disbelieving Raiders stared at the many top-ranked officers, uniforms replete with the trappings of office, who turned out for them. Reporters and photographers captured the occasion for people back home.

When Carlson's boat pulled up, Nimitz stepped aboard and shook hands. Carlson handed him Kanemitsu's sword, which Nimitz promised would be sent to the Naval Academy's museum, then attempted to shrink into the background. Nimitz would have none of it.

"They're waiting to hear from you back in the States," he remarked to Carlson. "Makin has made you and your Raiders famous." Sergeant Stidham, a veteran Marine aware of the raid's mishaps, received affirmation that their actions benefited the country. "The realization was slowly sinking in that we had gone from the status of a courageous and fortunate bunch of dumb-dumbs to what Kipling would probably have defined 'a bloody bunch of heroes.'"[19]

Nimitz stepped aside as the wounded were carried off. He then escorted Carlson and Commodore Haines to his office for a preliminary report.

"We Mourn the Loss of Each"

The next day Carlson gathered his Raiders at Camp Catlin for two purposes—to give his men the opportunity to discuss the operation, and to honor the comrades who did not return. After listening to the remarks, which mirrored much of what he included in his official report, Carlson delivered an impassioned eulogy for their fallen comrades.

"Each had his special place among us, and that place is imperishably his," Carlson began. "Being human, we mourn the loss of each. But I believe that these gallant men who so eagerly, so willingly went forth to meet the enemy would not have us weep and bemoan their passing. They loved life, these comrades of ours. They were vital, eager, thoughtful and realistic."

Carlson next addressed the issue of sacrifice and duty. "They had convictions even to the point of sacrificing their lives. They believed that if this country of ours is to be saved, the job of saving it belongs to those who enjoy the benefits of our institutions. They didn't ask someone else to perform the task for them. They went out to do it themselves."

Rather than weep over their loss, Carlson believed each deceased Raider would ask them to rejoice over the example they set and the type of person each man was. These men, Carlson reminded the crowd, would always be with them in spirit. "Allard, with his boyish smile; Johnson, with his strange scowl; Jerry Holtom, with his lumbering stride and eager, half-embarrassed manner; and the others. You know the characteristics of each as well as I. Who will say that the spirit of all these men we know so intimately does not remain with us?"

Carlson explained that lacking the ability to render full honors to the slain on the battlefield, "I placed each on his back that he might rest more easily, and I said a silent prayer over each." He then arranged a more proper burial with the natives. "And so, they lie there today, in the soil of that delightful South Pacific isle, beneath the palms under which they won their victory."

Carlson ended with a reminder of what their sacrifice meant for the survivors. "It behooves us, who remain, to rededicate ourselves to the task that lies ahead. The convictions of these comrades are our convictions. With the memory of their sacrifice in mind, let us here dedicate ourselves to the task of bringing into reality the ideals for which they died—that their sacrifice will not have been in vain."[20]

After Carlson completed the eulogy, a Marine officer from headquarters wondered if Carlson had missed his calling. He remarked to an associate that the Raider commander "should have been a chaplain."[21]

As a reward for the Raiders' exploits, for the next week the Navy posted them at the Royal Hawaiian Hotel, a plush resort normally reserved for submariners. Superb cuisine, free-flowing alcohol, and the nearby Waikiki Beach made for a memorable time, a respite that ended with preparations for training camp.

Platoon Sergeant Maghakian, who joined the other wounded men in the hospital, missed the festivities, but idled his time with Lieutenant Miller, the first man to visit Maghakian. Transport thanked his friend for the whiskey that proved such a help at Makin, then shared details of the raid.

Lieutenant Miller, still disappointed that he missed the raid, sent a letter to his mother about the post-action celebration. "Well all the boys are back and getting along swell. You know I was supposed to go but they wouldn't let me because of my hand. Which was really a tough break for me." He informed his mother that he had fully recovered from his injury and told her she most likely knew he was in Hawaii, what with the reports of the Raiders and Makin appearing on all the front pages, and asked her not to "worry about me if you don't hear from me for some time."[22]

Lieutenant Miller had an inkling the Raider Battalion would soon again be in the mix, thereby providing him a chance to contribute to the war effort.

"We Enjoyed Basking in All the Glory"

On August 25, the Marine Corps announced that the Raiders had been involved in actions in both the Solomons, where initial elements had landed at Tulagi, as well as at Makin. This first official mention of the Raiders, combined with the news that the United States was, at long last, hitting the enemy on land as well as at sea, ignited a whirlwind of media coverage and commentary, all highly flattering to the Raiders, to Carlson, and especially to James Roosevelt. The adulation increased at an August 27 press conference that Carlson and Roosevelt conducted with the media in Hawaii.

The release could not have come at a better time for people back home.

The Doolittle Raid in April and a triumph at Midway in May had brought some good news, but people still awaited a land assault against the enemy. With his raid at Makin, combined with the action in the Solomons, Carlson handed home-front morale a huge psychological boost.

"The public was tired of hearing bad news," Carlson later told a reporter, "and our little raids gave them the sort of news they wanted to hear." He added that while he detested war, when combat became necessary it should be fought in one way. "If the Japs want a war, I'm for making it so ruthless that they will have no stomach for it!"[23]

The jubilant reaction from home surprised the Raiders. "Not until a long time later did I realize that this was part of the strategy of winning something for the sake of morale," said James Roosevelt after the war. "We were so down after Pearl Harbor that we had to sort of set the tone that the tide is going to turn and here is the evidence of the tide turning."[24]

Sergeant Stidham noticed the same phenomenon. "We had no concept of the hunger the American people had for some good war news and this operation had attracted the attention of every citizen in the country." Photographers and reporters from every esteemed publication, including *Time* magazine and the *New York Times*, inundated Camp Catlin, eager to obtain a morsel of information with which to regale home-front readers. Many of the Raiders were more than obliging, some to the point of exaggeration. "The raid consequently was blown completely out of proportion as it related to the total war effort, and we unashamedly enjoyed basking in all the glory,"[25] stated Stidham.

Publications relayed information provided by the Navy Department pertaining to the raid's accomplishments. *Time* magazine reported the destruction of radio stations, gasoline, and trucks, and the seizure of supplies whose origins hit home. "They also found many a record of pre-war U.S. policy: the trucks had been made in the U.S., the gasoline containers bore the trademark of a U.S. refiner, the Jap garrison's corned beef had a U.S. label on the cans."[26]

The press exalted Carlson's Raiders as the nation's superheroes. Flowery phrases depicted them as men led by "hard-bitten veterans" who "fought, gangster fashion, for 40 hours," while a Marine press release stated, "The lads of Carlson's Marine Raiders can give plenty of hot lead and cold steel to the Japs, and can tell them why while they are doing it."[27]

Newspapers and magazines happily reprinted the words to Raider songs, tunes supposedly sung by Carlson's men—"Lustily singing fighting men are

'Carlson's Raiders'"—not only in training but before action. One song gaining popularity was set to the tune of the University of Notre Dame's "Victory March." Accounts trumpeted a connection to the "American guerrilla fighters from pioneer times," and warned that the enemy was "sure to taste their steel technique many times before the Pacific war is over."[28]

Carlson and Roosevelt basked in the same adulation. One writer described Carlson as a character "almost out of fiction"[29] while others praised the man's enthusiasm and originality. Carlson's gung ho philosophy gained credence at the hands of reporters, who saw in the unusual system a fascinating counterpart to the ordinary military routine.

One reporter decided to hold what he uncovered. The news correspondent Samuel E. Stavisky interviewed some of the wounded Raiders, eager to learn of their stirring exploits. Instead, he listened as the men talked of confusion and despair. "I was dumfounded, then, by the startling, differing version told by the men I interviewed. I talked to six, and each individually swore he was there in the council of war that decided on surrender. The Raiders, elite of the Corps, willing to surrender rather than fight to the death! Unbelievable!"[30]

Stavisky knew that no military censor would allow the story to be released, so he put it aside until after the war.

"Our Son Acquitted Himself Well"

Like the rest of the country, Franklin and Eleanor Roosevelt learned of Makin from reading the morning newspapers. On August 22, while his son rested aboard a submarine, President Roosevelt scanned the brief accounts, then asked his White House secretary, Stephen T. Early, whether he had "seen where Jimmy was in a show."[31] As they chatted about the raid Eleanor walked in and asked her husband if he could tell her anything more about what had occurred. The president had no more details other than what he had read, but the information was enough to make both proud.

Their satisfaction increased when they perused the flattering accounts. In Massachusetts, the *Springfield News* remarked that Jimmy's critics could "now eat their words" and asserted that Jimmy's participation in such a dangerous action proves "that democracy is working in America as it is intended to work."[32]

In a direct reference to the 1938 *Saturday Evening Post* article that harshly rebuked the president's son, on August 24 Iowa's *Sioux City Journal* published another article titled "Jimmy's Got It," this time using it as a reference to his grit rather than a slam against profit-mongering. Drew Pearson, the influential Washington, D.C., columnist and a longtime critic of the Roosevelts, tossed an olive branch at the man he once had castigated as being nothing more than a self-serving individual taking advantage of his father's immense power.

"This column threw plenty of harpoons into Jimmy Roosevelt in the old Boston insurance days, so now it takes pleasure in evening up the score." Pearson called the Raiders "the most dangerous branch of the marine corps," and stated that "Men who have served with Jimmy pay him great tribute, say he has the courage of a real leader, inspires confidence. No one seeing him unshaven for days, looking gaunt and hungry on the battle front, would ever recognize him as the son of the President."[33]

Newspapers admonished Jimmy's critics to be wary about disparaging Roosevelt lest a Marine be near. In New Jersey, the *Newark Evening News* quoted Marine Sgt. James Alverson as saying, "If you are ever around and you hear it said that Jimmie Roosevelt got where he is because he is the President's son, tell 'em to say it rather softly if there are any marines around."[34]

An editorial in the *Boston American* included words from a proud Eleanor Roosevelt as well as praise for her son. "For long months past, people have written many things which were not particularly pleasant reading about various of our children," the paper quoted Mrs. Roosevelt as saying. "Now, suddenly, over the radio and in the press, they say something good has been done by one of our sons.

"I am glad, of course, that our son acquitted himself well. It would never have occurred to me that anything else would happen. I am sure that every one of the men whom I saw in that California camp, which I visited before they left, acquitted himself equally well."

The editorial then added, "We think she has good cause to be proud, for—as the country well knows—her sons have not elected to sit at mahogany desks and ornament the Washington scenery, but have freely chosen to go into the thick of things and share the risks and perils of war with the millions of other men who love the United States sufficiently to fight for it."[35]

James Roosevelt, who had taken a bloodstained Japanese flag from Makin for his father, had the chance to personally brief his parents later that month, when Carlson dispatched him to Washington. Using an aerial mosaic of the island, Jimmy summarized the operation's details as Franklin and Eleanor interjected questions. The son then handed his father a lengthy letter from Carlson, reminiscent of those China days when Carlson and the president often corresponded.

Carlson began with an admission that the president's son had caused great anguish for him as a commander. "Naturally I was apprehensive about taking him [James] along," wrote Carlson, "but he was eager to go and I finally decided that this job would provide an admirable opportunity for his initial indoctrination in the mysteries of battle. I did not anticipate that the fighting would be as tough as it turned out to be."

Carlson explained that he intended to recommend James for a commendation, then spoke of what the raid meant to his novel concepts of a Marine battalion. "It is a source of deep satisfaction to both of us to see our labors now receive general approbation. Jim and I knew we had the right formula, but it was so unorthodox that the opposition for months was both virulent and persistent."

Carlson mentioned that the raid had given his men newfound assurances in their ability to triumph over an enemy that had been seen as unbeatable. "We are far from being boastful as a result of this raid. But it is true that this experience with the enemy has filled the men of this battalion with confidence. They know that in an even fight they can lick him hands down. And they have also learned that it is possible to outwit him."[36]

Makin was Jimmy Roosevelt's triumph. After enduring enormous pressures as a younger man, growing up as he did in a household where lofty goals and success were the expected rather than the extraordinary, James compounded his problems with a series of disastrous commercial endeavors that handed ammunition to his father's political foes and humiliation to the family.

Change began when he entered the Marine Corps and worked with Evans Carlson. James flourished in his new role as an officer, gaining praise from his men and from Carlson alike. Rather than being marked by poor grades or economic miscues, James relished his part in a raid that stirred the imaginations of the nation. No one could justifiably claim he gained this adulation because of his father. He accomplished it on his own. James had convinced one of the most skeptical groups in the nation—the United States Marines—that he was worthy of their esteem.

James, later promoted to lieutenant colonel, received a Navy Cross for his actions at Makin. According to the citation, he continually risked his life by unhesitatingly working while under enemy sniper and machine-gun fire, and

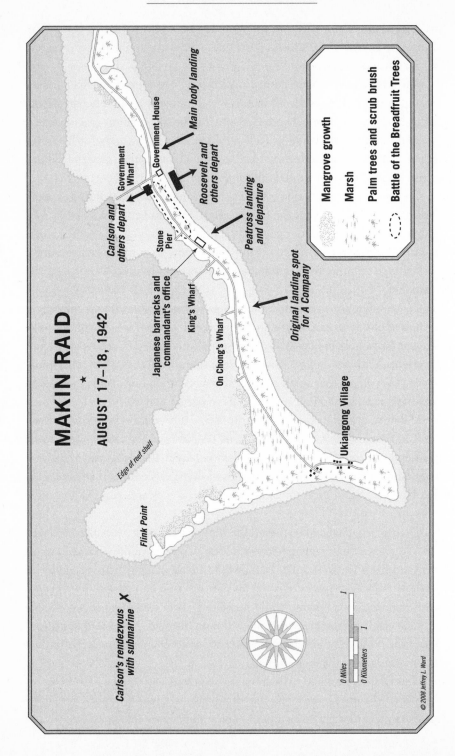

MAKIN RAID
★
AUGUST 17–18, 1942

Main body landing

Government House

Government Wharf

Carlson and others depart

Roosevelt and others depart

Peatross landing and departure

Stone Pier

Japanese barracks and commandant's office

King's Wharf

Original landing spot for A Company

On Chong's Wharf

Ukiangong Village

Edge of reef shelf

Flink Point

Carlson's rendezvous with submarine ✗

Mangrove growth

Marsh

Palm trees and scrub brush

Battle of the Breadfruit Trees

0 Miles   1

0 Kilometers   1

© 2008 Jeffrey L. Ward

he "displayed exemplary courage in personally rescuing three men from drowning in the heavy surf."[37]

Three people certainly read those words with pride and gratification—Franklin, Eleanor, and James Roosevelt.

"Everyone Didn't Love Us"

James Roosevelt and the other Makin Raid Marines could indeed be pleased with the results of their mission. They had accomplished most of the objectives, and while it was doubtful that they caused any major diversion of forces from the Solomons area, they undeniably caused great consternation in Tokyo, where Japanese military leaders fretted over which location in their far-flung Pacific empire would be next on the American hit list. "They will make surprise attacks on other islands in this way," chief of staff of the Japanese Combined Fleet Adm. Matome Ugaki wrote in his diary on August 18, "and we must never relax." The next week the admiral urged that garrisons be speedily dispatched to other island locations as "We should never let Makin's case be repeated."[38]

Carlson stated after the war that he believed the raid held great value to the military and the public. "As a military venture this raid was not of any great import; its significance lay in the fact that America had taken the offensive; that American men had out-witted, out-fought and out-maneuvered the Japanese at their own game." He claimed that while the ensuing publicity spread word of his gung ho philosophy, he also, according to Peatross, wished he had carried a backup plan into battle. "No commander ever expects to fail in an operation," Peatross quotes Carlson as supposedly saying to Sergeant McCullough, "but he should have a plan ready, just in case he does."[39]

With the nation in need of heroes, the Navy graciously awarded a large number of medals to Carlson's companies. The Medal of Honor was awarded to Sgt. Clyde Thomason, while twenty-three Raiders, including Carlson, Roosevelt, Le Francois, and Maghakian, received Navy Crosses.

Japanese wartime communiqués painted the raid in different hues. The statements claimed that a "small and numerically inferior" Japanese garrison on Makin had repelled an assault by two hundred Americans in "furious hand-to-hand combat," and that the "dismal defeat of the American landing party proved that it is virtually impossible for the Allied Navy to achieve any measure of success against the Japanese Navy."[40]

Despite the outward praise and acclaim, criticism of Carlson's command slowly gathered steam. Critics castigated the raid as a waste of manpower and money that succeeded only in utilizing a handful of Marines to destroy an isolated outpost, an action that had little positive impact on the war. Some suggested, in hindsight, that the raid actually cost more American lives in November 1943, when the Marines hit the beaches at Tarawa. Because of the Makin Raid the Japanese fortified Tarawa, another atoll in the Gilbert chain, into a near-impregnable island bastion that cost the Marines three thousand casualties in three days of brutal combat.

Gen. Holland Smith, one of the top Marine strategists of the war, contended of Carlson that his raid at Makin "was a spectacular performance by his 2nd Marine Raider Battalion but it was also a piece of folly. The raid had no useful military purpose and served only to alert the Japanese to our intentions in the Gilberts. The intensive fortification of Tarawa dates from that raid."[41]

Carlson's most acerbic critic proved to be one of the men who earned a Navy Cross at Makin, Lt. Charles Lamb. In 1956, Lamb penned a harsh rebuke of Carlson as background notes for a history to be published by the Historical Branch of the Marine Corps. Lamb freely admitted that his distaste for Carlson and his methods dated to the early 1930s, when he observed Carlson and concluded he was "a martinet, who at times enforced discipline with mass punishment methods, and that he would not tolerate inefficiency or unmilitary conduct and appearance."

Lamb's animosity deepened by the time he joined the Raiders. Lamb believed Carlson's gung ho approach negated all that was good about the Marine Corps and brought anarchy into a situation calling for discipline. Lamb wrote, "I developed an extreme personal dislike for Carlson and was very distrustful of his words and methods. He was cognizant of my attitude."

Lamb does not challenge Carlson's courage, reserving his rebukes for command tactics. At Makin, Carlson's audacity "was beyond question. He strolled around, smoking his pipe, with no apparent concern of danger." But the colonel erred by exercising "poor command and control of his organization at all times." He added later, "However, it is debatable if there was any command from the time of landing until the return of Carlson to the submarine."

Lamb does not rebuke Carlson for considering a surrender, but chastises him for not knowing enough about the enemy's situation. "Certainly a commanding officer deserves criticism if his estimate of the situation is so erroneous as to condone the writing of a surrender note and then discover that there is no opposition."

With the favorable publicity the battalion received after Makin, Lamb feels that Carlson "exploited a battalion to glorify himself in the eyes of the public."[42]

Most Raiders ignore Lamb's remarks or attribute the episode to jealousy over Carlson's public notoriety. Peatross rushed to Carlson's defense over this issue. "I daresay that had almost any other lieutenant colonel in the Marine Corps been in command at Makin, there would not have been so much as a whisper of criticism."[43] Peatross also argued that any criticism or praise for organizing the raid should go to Admiral Nimitz and his staff. As they later appeared to be satisfied, Peatross wondered what all the shouting was about.

Lt. Richard Washburn, though not involved with the raid, nevertheless made valid points in a postwar interview. He called the raid "a real gutty move, but I think its aftermath was the beginning of some real problems for the Raiders." The media made Carlson's battalion its new darling. Each story heralding the raid or Carlson's gung ho approach created more animosity toward the men, especially among Marine officers already irritated with Carlson's connection to the White House or his supposed ties to the communists. "But now the brass is really upset. These Raiders are taking the spotlight away from the thousands of other Marines struggling in that damn jungle. And what is this gung ho business anyway? Everyone didn't love us."[44]

"Examples of Extraordinary Heroism"

Carlson's official report became the subject of controversy before he had written the final draft. In the version he wrote while aboard the *Nautilus*, Carlson included an account of the surrender issue. Carlson wrote that after the calamitous attempt to leave the island that first night, his intent was to wait for daylight, move to the north side of the island, locate outrigger canoes, and leave by the lagoon side. He then added the words, "If we were attacked by a superior enemy force in the meantime I believed that the wise course would be to surrender because we had no effective means of defending ourselves."[45]

This sentence establishes three facts. It proves that Carlson considered surrendering. It shows that Carlson had not decided to surrender during that first night, only that he would consider it the next day if attacked by superior forces. When the second day produced evidence that his Raiders had all but eliminated the garrison, surrender became a moot point. Finally, it confirms that he was not trying to conceal his actions, as Private Carson and Private McCall assert. If he wanted to do so, he would not have mentioned it in this August 21 report.

Rather than Carlson, Admiral Nimitz was the man who censored all reference to a possible surrender. When Nimitz read Carlson's initial report after the Raiders had returned to Hawaii, he called his senior Marine staff officer, Col. Omar T. Pfeiffer, into his office. According to Pfeiffer's oral history, when he walked in Admiral Nimitz had the report open on his desk.

"Pfeiffer, have you read this?" asked Nimitz.

"Yes, sir, I've read it."

"I've never heard of anything like this in all my life," Nimitz snapped. "There is not as much iron in that man as I thought. You take this report back and get ahold of that young man and tell him that no report from my command will have any word, or even idea, of surrender in it!"

Pfeiffer called Carlson to his office and relayed Admiral Nimitz's wish, but the commander balked. "It's true," Carlson argued, "and it will stay in the report."

"Oh, no it won't," replied Pfeiffer. "It comes out or you come out."[46]

With that threat firmly established, Carlson agreed to alter his report and to tell his company commanders to do the same.

The remainder of Carlson's report was a lengthy examination of the two-day raid and a list of suggestions about how to improve. Carlson was quick to recommend better motors and means of communications, and added that Marines had to be better prepared to deal with snipers camouflaged in trees. "Japanese sniping was excellent and their snipers were so well concealed that it was necessary to shoot off branches of trees in order to get the snipers—a most uneconomical operation."

Carlson recommended that the Navy continue using commando-style raids, as this first mission appeared to disrupt and confuse the enemy. "I am more convinced than ever of the value of raids in the conduct of war in the Pacific, especially raids from submarines." He claimed the Japanese command in the Marshalls was surprised by the operation and that "It did not know how our force got ashore, at what points it had landed, whether it was merely a raid or an occupational force or whether it was the spearhead of a larger force which intended to drive into the Marshalls. Such raids can be used to confuse the enemy, pull him off base and open the way for the drive of a larger force against vulnerable and vital points."

Despite the fact that the raid contained miscues, Carlson praised his Raiders for performing well under duress. During the action the men were often intermingled, "yet each individual displayed initiative, resourcefulness and a willingness to work effectively in whatever team he found himself. None had been under fire before, but there was no hesitation about closing with the enemy. In fact, most of our casualties came from careless exposure to enemy fire in order to 'take out' the opposition. There were many examples of extraordinary heroism which will be made the subject of special recommendation at a later date."

Carlson concluded with a harsh self-appraisal. Without using the exact words, he hinted that he was far from pleased with his own performance the first day at Makin. "Finally, I would invite the attention of all military leaders to the illustration provided by our situation at Makin on the night of August 17th which emphasizes a truth that is as old as the military profession: no matter how bad your own situation may appear to be, there is always the possibility that the situation of the enemy is much worse."[47]

"The Importance of the Offensive"

Carlson's self-examination paled compared to what other officers wrote. Carlson could handle condemnation from his peers, but rebuke from a superior officer was another thing. In the pages of the official reports of Makin were the words of men with intimate knowledge of the raid and judgments by superior officers, especially Admiral Nimitz, that carried import to a man like Carlson. Their praise would be welcome; their censure would sting.

Commodore Haines's report contained a mixture of praise and criticism, but generally concluded that the raid succeeded. Haines contended, "This mission, the first of its kind so far as is known, in history, is considered to have successfully accomplished its primary mission, i.e. the destruction of enemy troops and installations on Makin Atoll." He added that because of a series of factors, including a lack of training and faulty communications, the success was "not as great as had been hoped," that the losses "were greater than had been anticipated," and "had not an accidental discharge of one of our firearms occurred thus alerting the enemy, a complete surprise would have been attained." He contended that similar raids would be beneficial against some of the smaller, weaker Japanese bases, and praised Carlson "for his splendid leadership and untiring efforts in organizing, training, and taking into successful action against an unexpectedly powerful enemy force, the Marine Raider Unit."[48]

Admiral Nimitz was not as kind. In a report that had to be hard for Carlson to read, Nimitz rebuked Carlson eight times in seven pages. He praised the raid's results and assessed Japanese losses at two vessels, two seaplanes, radio stations and other installations, and 100 to 150 Japanese killed. Nimitz recommended some of the same items mentioned by Carlson and Haines, such as improved tactics against snipers, then moved to the main portion of his report.

Nimitz minced few words in faulting Carlson's decision to pull back to the beach on the first day. "Although the mission of destruction of enemy forces and installations had not been completed, after the last bombing the raider commander decided to withdraw according to plan."

Nimitz dismissed Carlson's argument that he had to start pulling his men back if he were to meet the prearranged time to withdraw with a two-sided criticism—he praised Japanese resoluteness while disparaging Carlson's timidity. "It appears that there were only a few Japanese soldiers left alive, yet such is the effect of boldness in a few resolute men that it seemed to the raider commander at this time that he was still opposed by a large force."

Nimitz then evaluated Carlson's tactics that first day, where his Raiders settled into a set-piece battle with enemy snipers and machine-gun nests. "In raids of this nature which depend above all on surprise and swiftness of execution, the raiding force cannot let itself be tied down by position fighting. It must maintain mobility, striking rapidly, seeking to surprise and rout the enemy before they can recover and organize defenses. Should the force be pinned down by a 'fire fight,' it must continue offensive reconnaissance instead of retreating or remaining static. After the first part of the engagement, the raider force did not strike aggressively; for example, the platoon on the left flank suffered no casualties and made slow progress."

Nimitz's third rebuke concerned the native reports pertaining to the size of the Japanese garrison and to enemy reinforcements. Nimitz felt Carlson put too much credence in the reports, which Nimitz stated could have been exaggerated by rumors or tainted by enemy design. Nimitz wondered if trepidation over Japanese reinforcements might have been planted among the natives by the Japanese to "influence the decisions of the raider commander.

Active patrols would have given him sound information as to the location and strength of the enemy."

Nimitz reserved his harshest assessment in addressing what he saw as a lack of aggression. "The old story in war of the *importance of the offensive* [emphasis Nimitz's] was again demonstrated." Nimitz contended that had the Raiders sent reconnaissance patrols on the afternoon of August 17 and "pushed forward instead of withdrawing, they would have discovered that the apparent heavy resistance was the fire of only a handful of men fighting to the death. They could have destroyed installations on the island and re-embarked at their leisure, probably saving most of the loss of life from drowning and from strafing by planes on 18 August." In other words, aggressiveness by Carlson and his force on August 17 would have saved Raider lives on August 18, harsh words for an officer to read.

Nimitz also stated that Raider firepower was weak and their aim poor, and that faulty dispositions of troops bunched the Raiders together, making it easier for the Japanese to inflict casualties. "With equal courage, approximately equal numbers, and equal boldness of leadership, our Marines will defeat the Japanese every time."

In a backhanded compliment, Nimitz claimed that the raid succeeded due to the "courage and endurance of the Marines and cool headed cooperation of submarine personnel." The omission of Carlson's name speaks volumes.

The admiral continued by asserting that fortune both helped and hindered the operation, but that "Losses were somewhat larger than they should have been," even though the goals of the expedition were achieved. "Considerable damage was inflicted on the Japanese, and at a crucial time in the Solomon Islands operations they were forced to divert men, ships and planes to the relief of Makin Island."

Nimitz even used Carlson's own words against him. He included Carlson's statement that the enemy might be in a worse predicament, but compounded the insult by adding another sentence of his own. "To this might be added another truth that a few resolute men seem like battalions."[49]

Carlson had worked assiduously to craft the Raiders according to his gung ho philosophy, often to the derision of fellow officers, and he now had to digest Nimitz's damning words. Even worse—since the report would be sent to every top Pacific and Marine commander, including the commandant, General Holcomb, Carlson's comrades would read every caustic word.

"Not Exactly Like a Whipped Dog"

To properly judge whether Makin was a success or failure, one must examine it from three perspectives—the military, the home front, and the personal. From the military point, Makin had little impact on the enemy. The Japanese diverted a few troops from Guadalcanal, but nothing that affected their operations in the Solomons. The Japanese speedily replaced the men and supplies lost at Makin, an atoll they continued to control until late the next year. By then, in large measure due to the Makin Raid, the Japanese had so strongly fortified the Gilberts, particularly Tarawa, that the Marines paid a dear price for its November 1943 seizure. In hindsight historians can judge the raid as, at best, a helpful military experiment.

Hindsight, though, overlooks the immediacy of the raid's impact on the home front. Carlson's raid knocked the enemy on its heels and, along with the Doolittle Raid and Midway, halted the long line of Japanese successes that dominated their front pages. People's faith in their military was restored. One need only read the newspaper and magazine articles of the time to understand the raid's effect in the United States. Carlson and his Raiders registered a resounding triumph when viewed through the home-front prism.

Though Carlson must have appreciated the flattering accounts that flooded across the nation, on a personal level the commander knew he had underperformed. An introspective person inherently knows whether he or she has adequately executed the tasks at hand. A singer may receive acclaim, but knows during the concert if he has hit a sour note. A baseball pitcher may win a game, yet have turned in a subpar performance.

Sergeant Stidham stated as much when, years later, he assessed the raid. "This prideful feeling [in the home front's reaction], however, was tempered by the fact that we got ourselves in that predicament in the first place, suffered many more casualties than expected, and ended up losing a large share of our weapons and equipment. In other words, we were not exactly like a whipped dog coming home with his tail between his legs, but we were not at all boastful of how we executed our carefully laid and rehearsed plans." He added, "We were surprised to be greeted like heroes when we got back to Pearl Harbor. We thought the operation had been one big foul-up."[50]

Carlson, whose gung ho philosophy espoused the critical examination of one's performance, would be hypocritical if he did not apply the same standard to his own actions. He knew, even before reading Nimitz's harsh assessment, that Makin was not his best performance.

Why? Carlson seemed to let events dictate his reactions, rather than shaping events himself. In the jungles of Nicaragua and the vast reaches of China, Carlson witnessed the efficacy of guerrilla operations, but at Makin he found himself quickly involved in a more conventional battle involving set lines. Rather than orchestrating a freewheeling flank attack, Carlson supervised a battlefield operation, one in which he lacked expertise and confidence.

In Michael J. Zak's astute 1981 thesis, the Marine officer argued that Makin was not a suitable mission for the Raiders. Carlson had trained them for guerrilla warfare, where they needed self-sufficiency and initiative to deal with unexpected conditions. "Then came Makin," Zak wrote, "a poor fit with the map. Makin had specific objectives, known terrain, and a predictable enemy situation."

Uncomfortable with his assignment, which conflicted with his past experiences, "Evans Carlson paid the ultimate price on Makin; he watched his organization disintegrate before his eyes."[51]

Did Roosevelt's presence affect Carlson, consciously or unconsciously? In a response to a request from his commander in chief, Carlson had promised President Roosevelt, a man he had known since the mid-1930s, that he would look out for his son. Did the thought of the president's son being killed or captured so weigh on Carlson that he became a different commander than the one who had earned a Navy Cross in Nicaragua? Hesitancy marked the first day, when Carlson engaged in a time-consuming set-piece battle, stalled when confronted by enemy snipers, and became mired in the surrender issue.

Though most Raiders dismiss the notion that the presence of James Roosevelt affected Carlson, it might explain his timid direction on the first day and night. He appeared to act with more vigor after Roosevelt left the island. After the president's son was safely back aboard the submarine on the second day a bolder, more decisive Carlson returned.

As Carlson's executive officer, Roosevelt might have been more of a concern to his commander than an executive officer normally is. It is one thing to look after your executive officer. It is completely different when you receive a letter from the president asking you to take care of that officer.

Adm. William Halsey, as feisty a battler as there was, could understand. Later in the war, when Eleanor Roosevelt wished to visit the men on Guadalcanal, he objected in his role as commander of the South Pacific. The fighting had, for the most part, moved away from Guadalcanal to the northern Solomon Islands, yet Admiral Halsey worried for her safety.

In 2008, two of the few surviving officers from Carlson's battalion, Lt. Robert Burnette, who fought on Guadalcanal, and Lt. Joseph Griffith, a veteran of both the Makin Raid and the Guadalcanal fighting, said they understood Carlson's anguish. Burnette claimed that Carlson "would never have surrendered Roosevelt to the Japanese" and that as an officer the specter of having the president's son under his command was "not something I'd want."[52]

Lieutenant Griffith related an anecdote that occurred in the immediate aftermath of Makin. One night, as he and the other Raiders recuperated in the Royal Hawaiian Hotel, Griffith, Commander Brockman, and Commodore Haines relaxed with a few drinks and casual conversation. Suddenly, the topic turned more serious and someone asked Haines why he did not order the submarines to leave Makin that first night, when things looked bleak. Haines's blunt answer lends insight to the dilemma Carlson faced.

"I didn't want to go back to the United States, be taken directly to the president, and tell him why I left his son on the island," answered Haines. "So we stayed."[53]

"One of the Things That Really Burns Me"

Makin provided plenty of controversy, but none more so than when details emerged that nine Raiders had been stranded at Makin. The first indication that someone may have been inadvertently left behind came when the Raiders held muster in Hawaii, the first opportunity Carlson had to accurately record which men had returned. The muster confirmed that eighteen men had been killed on Makin and that twelve were missing and presumed drowned.

However, the native A. George Noran spotted four Raiders in a hut a few days after the raid. He gave them food and contacted a Catholic missionary, but the Americans were eventually captured. Noran does not suggest how the men happened to be in the hut while the other Raiders had departed.

Natives and a French priest witnessed the Japanese capturing nine men within a week of the raid. On August 30, a ship transported the captives to Kwajalein, where on September 2 they were imprisoned in tiny cells. The Japanese commander, Capt. Yoshio Obara, intended to convey the nine to Japan, but when shipping was not available, Vice Adm. Koso Abe, the commander of the Marshall Island bases, ordered Obara to execute the Americans.

Obara, who had relatives in the United States, reluctantly selected an execution detail and set the date for October 16, a day that recognized Japanese war heroes. The Japanese took the nine Americans to a clearing, forced them to kneel on the ground, and beheaded each man.

The story emerged after the war when a native who had witnessed the executions, Lejena Lokot, testified about the details at a war crimes trial. Corroboration came from an American prisoner, Army Air Corps officer Louis Zamperini, who stated that while a prisoner in Kwajalein, he had seen scratched on the cell wall the names of nine Makin Raiders. When he asked his captives what became of the men, they informed him they had been beheaded. In 1946, three Japanese officers were found guilty in the incident. Two, including Obara, received prison sentences, while Admiral Abe was hanged in 1947.

When James Roosevelt returned to Makin during the November 1943 assault against the Gilberts, natives took him to a common grave that supposedly held the remains of eighteen Raiders and told him another nine men had been captured. The fates of three other men were at the time unknown.

Matters worsened for Carlson in 1946 when the Associated Press ran a story about the nine missing Raiders. Carlson replied that it was possible some men may have reached a nearby island, but that if he believed that anyone was still alive, he would never have left Makin.

From where did those nine men come? Sergeant McCullough points to the boat that left Carlson on the second night. "If one of them guys or two of them on the left side of the boat was a little stronger than the right side, then they veered to the right and went right straight into Little Makin Island."[54] Others claim that either the nine made it ashore from an abortive attempt to leave Makin the first night and simply failed to return to the main body in time, or had been sent to the northern end of Makin and then forgotten.

Raiders friendly to Carlson point to the overriding confusion, the harsh surf, and the impossibility of knowing which men reached which submarine until they reached Pearl Harbor. Some absolve Carlson of guilt in the matter.

James Roosevelt stated that every man on the island knew they were going to evacuate and that they had a responsibility to return to the beaches in time.[55]

"Another thing," said Sergeant McCullough. "On the second day, they all knew we were going to the other side of the island and getting off. They all knew. One of the nine would have said something about getting to the other side. They weren't left behind, I'll tell you. We were close together, and how could they not know? That's one of the things that really burns me, where they blame Carlson."[56]

Other Carlson defenders point to the patrols the colonel dispatched to check both ends of the island before departing. Private First Class Quirk studied every record he could locate and concluded "there is no way one living Marine Raider was 'left behind' on Makin because of negligence, indifference, or incompetence."[57] He supports this by pointing to the island's small size and a lack of jungle terrain, making it easier to scout, and that each man knew the withdrawal location and should have experienced no difficulty in joining the main body. He believed that the Raiders in question came from men who had missed a submarine in one of the departures and landed on another island before returning to Makin, as well as the five men trapped by strafing Japanese aircraft the second morning.

Some historians, notably Tripp Wiles in his 2007 book, *Forgotten Raiders of '42*, censure Carlson for the mishap. They assert that despite the chain of events, a commander's prime responsibility is to know the whereabouts of every man under his command. Since nine men were left behind to suffer a gruesome fate, they lay the guilt at Carlson's feet.

A resolution occurred in 1999 when the Army's Central Identification Laboratory in Hawaii sent a team of forensic specialists to Makin, where they identified the remains of nineteen Raiders, rather than eighteen, in the common grave. In addition to the eighteen already listed as deceased by Carlson, the specialists confirmed the identity of Pvt. Carlyle O. Larson, one of the missing and assumed dead. Their efforts established the final tally at nineteen Raiders killed on Makin, nine executed, and two still missing and presumed dead, most likely by drowning in the surf.

Largely through the efforts of the United States Marine Raider Association, an active survivors' group, the thirty Raiders have not been forgotten. On August 17, 2001, on the fifty-ninth anniversary of the Makin landing, thirteen of the nineteen Raiders were laid to rest in a touching ceremony at Arlington National Cemetery. At the request of family, the remains of the other six were buried in their hometowns.

On Armistice Day 2003 twenty-two members of the association traveled to Kwajalein to dedicate a plaque in honor of the nine executed Raiders. In a sign of the volatility over the issue, an earlier plaque had to be altered when Raiders objected to the inscription as stating that the nine Marines were "mistakenly left behind." The new inscription read that they were "captured."[58]

Makin thus was a bittersweet episode for Carlson. This first chance to show that his Raiders, a unit cast in the guerrilla mode he had witnessed in Nicaragua and formed according to the gung ho practices he had seen in China, would work, went awry. A raging surf knocked him off balance, and instead of being in control, Carlson appeared to be one step behind as events rushed at him.

While he gained fame for his Raider Battalion and praise for the men's unquestioned courage, an inner voice whispered that he had underperformed. The next mission, whenever it occurred, would prove beyond question the value of his system and of his Raiders. His gung ho method could succeed if given the right opportunity.

We Rode to the Sound
of the Guns

arlson received his opportunity ten weeks later, when he and his Raiders disappeared into the dense jungles of Guadalcanal. For a month he staged a deadly game of cat and mouse with the Japanese, and when Carlson led his ragged Raiders back inside the perimeter protecting Henderson Field nearly five weeks later, he had routed the enemy forces in a spectacular mission behind enemy lines that proved to be the capstone of his military career and redemption for the Makin operation.

"That was the great adventure of my life,"[1] stated Pvt. Virgil Leeman of C Company of what has become known in Marine annals as the Long Patrol. Leeman selected Guadalcanal despite later fighting in Bougainville's jungles and battling for his life on Iwo Jima's sands.

"A Little Taste of the War"

On September 6, less than two weeks after returning to Pearl Harbor, Carlson and his battalion, now up to six companies, boarded the USS *Wharton* for the 3,500-mile voyage to Espiritu Santo in the New Hebrides, a chain of islands 550 miles southeast of Guadalcanal and 1,400 miles east of Australia. Espiritu Santo, the main staging area for troops bound for Guadalcanal, would be their home until they received their next assignment.

Platoon Sergeant Maghakian almost missed the trip. Because of his wounds, doctors at Pearl Harbor tagged Maghakian for transport back to the States, but the hard-bitten sergeant was not about to allow his buddies, particularly Lieutenant Miller, with whom he had forged a tight bond, to see action while he stayed behind.

The trip included three stops along the way—at Canton in the Phoenix Island group on September 11, the Fiji Islands five days later, and Noumea, New Caledonia, three days before their September 22 arrival at Espiritu Santo. Along the way now Captain Griffith and other officers who had fought at Makin delivered lectures on what they had learned from the August raid, as well as talked to the Raiders about the nature of jungle warfare they were likely to face in Guadalcanal. James Roosevelt conducted sessions on the ship's fantail to discuss events in the war's other theaters. Doctors cautioned the men to take the daily doses of atabrine, a medicine to counter the effects of malaria, and explained the ravages of jaundice, filariasis, dysentery, and other illnesses endemic to Guadalcanal's jungles.

Officers mostly focused on the current situation in Guadalcanal, where fellow Marines held a tenuous toehold in their efforts to seize the island from the Japanese. A pamphlet titled *Lessons Learned in the Philippines* included tips from men who had fought there about Japanese military techniques and tricks. The pamphlet was supposed to better prepare the Raiders for the coming battle, but it so graphically portrayed the enemy as a determined, ruthless, skilled fighter that it had unintended results. "The Japanese themselves could not have produced a document better designed to further their cause,"[2] stated the recently promoted Captain Peatross.

Their apprehension increased on September 22, when the *Wharton* arrived at its destination and unloaded Carlson's six companies at Espiritu Santo. For most of the Raiders, until now the war had been little more than an inconvenience in their lives, a distant specter others had fought. Now the same waters of the Coral Sea that lapped against their shores also touched Guadalcanal's beaches less than six hundred miles—one day's sailing—to the northwest.

Carlson led his men to Camp Gung Ho, the Raider quarters in a coconut grove situated on a bluff overlooking Espiritu Santo's harbor, and began implementing the measures to prepare his Raiders for combat in the jungle.

"The flies were terrible, terrible!" said Lt. Robert Burnette of E Company. "There were dropped coconuts all over the place and that drew the flies. At chow you had to wait and get the flies out of the way to take a bite." Burnette added that the Japanese also did what they could to make their stay miserable. "We got a little taste of the war because single airplanes would sometimes come over and drop bombs."[3]

As if mirroring the war that raged not far to the northwest, their training intensified. Sessions with live ammunition and hand grenades alternated with hand-to-hand combat drills. Japanese submarines twice shelled the island. While no one was harmed in the seaborne attacks, officers noticed that the men trained with more efficiency and concentration following each shelling.

"Any News from Jimmy?"

Whatever the future held for the battalion, Roosevelt would not be a part of it. In early October he received orders to San Diego to organize and train a new Raider Battalion. The Raiders felt they had lost a friend. Their initial misgivings had been swept away by Roosevelt's professionalism and willingness to share the same discomforts and hazards as the men. "Jimmy is leaving us and is going back to the States," Lieutenant Miller wrote his parents on October 10, "and he offered to mail a letter or two for me so I thought I would take advantage of the opportunity."[4]

"I loved that man," said Pl. Sgt. Rhel Cook of F Company. "He was a good man. He was just one of us. The last time I saw him he had tears running down his face because he wanted to go to Guadalcanal so bad."[5]

Carlson would miss him even more. His right-hand man had become a cohort as well as a valued assistant. Before Roosevelt had been gone two weeks Carlson wrote, "I miss you keenly. So does the outfit. We all gathered for a brief meeting the other day—most of us—and when the question period came along the first question was: Any news from Jimmy?"[6]

As much as the men quizzed Carlson about Roosevelt, Carlson pestered his superiors for another crack at the enemy. He did not want to allow his highly skilled battalion to sit idly by.

"Yeah, he didn't want to lay around," said Pvt. Darrell Loveland. "He didn't believe in when a man is trained to as high as he can be, that you don't use them. No sense sitting around. From Midway in June until now, we had been training over and over and over."[7]

Every Raider chafed at the inactivity. They followed the progress of fighting on Guadalcanal to their north and wondered when their time would come. "The entire battalion was itching to get up to Guadalcanal at once but instead we chewed our nails, fretted and strained like a bunch of thoroughbreds ready to bolt out of the starting gate,"[8] explained Pvt. Lowell Bulger.

On October 22, Carlson proposed to superiors at Guadalcanal an operation in which two or three companies landed on Guadalcanal's south coast, crossed the mountains, and hit the Japanese from the rear in a classic guerrilla operation. Though the idea had merit, Adm. Richmond Kelly Turner, commander of naval forces in the Solomons, instead ordered Carlson to land two Raider companies at Aola Bay forty miles east of the perimeter to provide security for construction units building another airfield. Though Turner's plan only called for the Raiders to be at Aola for a day or two before Army units relieved them and they returned to Espiritu Santo, it at least placed Carlson on the island. Who knew what might then happen?

"We Are Losing the War"

Since June, when intelligence first detected that the Japanese were constructing an airfield in the Solomons, Guadalcanal dominated American attention. Admiral Nimitz could not allow the enemy to retain control, as in Japanese hands aircraft from the island threatened the crucial supply lines connecting the United States and Australia and further entrenched the enemy in the southwest Pacific. Conversely, in American possession the Solomons could become the staging ground for the ocean offensive to Tokyo and, in Henderson Field, hand Nimitz an unsinkable aircraft carrier that compensated for the four American carriers already lost in the war.

Starting in August, when Marines carved out a tiny toehold on Guadalcanal, the antagonists waged a bitter six-month contest to determine mastery in the southwest Pacific. Marines were given the task of holding Henderson Field until Nimitz could scrape together sufficient forces to push the Japanese off the island.

The situation in October appeared grim. Assailed by enemy land forces on Guadalcanal and the Japanese navy offshore, the Marines mounted an inspiring, but fatiguing, defense. Their commander begged for more troops and additional supplies, but pressed by equally demanding needs from Europe, the United States had precious few to divert their way.

One officer wrote that in the besieged enclave around Henderson Field, with enemy forces moving about at will, he now "knew to a certain extent how the boys on Wake and Bataan must have felt,"[9] two locations where defenders eventually had to capitulate. The bleak outlook caused the government to release surprisingly realistic estimations as a way of preparing the public for a potential loss.

"We are losing the war,"[10] *Time* magazine quoted Army Lt. Gen. Brehon B. Somervell in its September 7, 1942, issue. The next month, in an attempt to alter the situation, President Roosevelt ordered the Joint Chiefs of Staff to send every possible weapon and soldier to Guadalcanal. Adm. William Halsey, the freshly appointed commander of forces in the South Pacific, vowed to keep his Navy in the Solomons and to rush every last weapon to the men ashore until victory had been attained.

The Japanese viewed Guadalcanal with the same urgency. General Masao Maruyama, commander of Sendai Division, spoke to his men before an October 22 attempt to take Henderson Field. "This is the decisive battle between Japan and the United States in which the rise or fall of the Japanese Empire will be decided. If we do not succeed in the occupation of these islands, no one should expect to return alive to Japan. [We] must overcome the hardship caused by the lack of material and push on unendingly by displaying invincible teamwork. Hit the proud enemy with an iron fist so he will not be able to rise again."[11]

Sturdy fingers made up that iron fist. As the historian Joseph Alexander has stated, at Guadalcanal the Japanese had displayed disciplined fighting, skill in night combat, an ability to construct elaborate sunken fortifications, and a willingness to fight to the death. In addition, they possessed an astounding talent for filtering men and supplies through Guadalcanal's jungles into a semicircular position about Henderson Field.

The Japanese scorned their opponent as weak and ineffective. A training manual stated, "Westerners—being very haughty, effeminate and cowardly—intensely dislike fighting in the rain or mist or in the dark. They cannot conceive night to be a proper time for battle—though it is excellent for dancing. In these weaknesses lie our great opportunity."[12] The American fighting man was reputedly lacking in spiritual strength, vulnerable to flanking attacks, indifferent, and petrified of hand-to-hand combat.

Americans held equally demeaning images of the Japanese. One Marine told the writer John Hersey that he wished he faced the Germans, who "are human, like us." The Marine added, "But the Japs are like animals. Against them you have to learn a whole new set of physical reactions. You have to get used to their animal stubbornness and tenacity. They take to the jungle as if

A smiling Colonel Carlson exudes confidence in this photograph taken after his service on Guadalcanal.

James Roosevelt supports his father during a train stop in the 1930s. The son offered significant help to his father at key times, but later stated that his time with the Marine Corps proved to be the most rewarding part of his career.

Capt. Richard Washburn, the professorial officer who so ably commanded the Raiders at Asamana and answered the question whether American troops were up to the challenge.

Jack Miller strikes an impressive pose as he enjoys a Texas summer day before the war.

Victor "Transport" Maghakian. Jack Miller wrote on the reverse side, "Victor Maghakian—best friend when we are out in the boon docks."

Transport Maghakian (*right*) stands with Evans Carlson and Lt. Wilfred Le Francois (*left*) on the set of the movie *Gung Ho!*

Kenneth McCullough at a Raider reunion in 2007.

Brian Quirk, here in his Illinois home in 2007, counts his time with Evans Carlson, during both the Makin Raid and the Long Patrol, as highlights in his long Marine career.

During the 2007 Raider reunion in San Diego, Ervin Kaplan enjoys a light moment.

Carlson and Roosevelt
at Camp Catlin, Hawaii,
before the Makin Raid.
FROM THE ROBERT BURNETTE COLLECTION

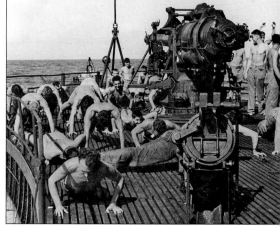

A group of Raiders enjoys a brief
exercise period on the bow of
the USS *Nautilus* on August 11,
1942, on their way to Makin.
NATIONAL ARCHIVES #34493

Raiders rehearse for the Makin
Raid while aboard the USS
Nautilus, August 12, 1942.
NATIONAL ARCHIVES #11714

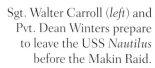

Sgt. Walter Carroll (*left*) and
Pvt. Dean Winters prepare
to leave the USS *Nautilus*
before the Makin Raid.
NATIONAL ARCHIVES #11722

A photograph of Makin Island taken through the periscope of the USS *Nautilus* shortly before the Raiders headed toward shore.

At Makin the Raiders used rubber boats like these, here shown before filming a scene for the movie *Gung Ho!*

Colonel Carlson aboard the USS *Nautilus* moments after he returned on August 18. The signs of strain are evident.

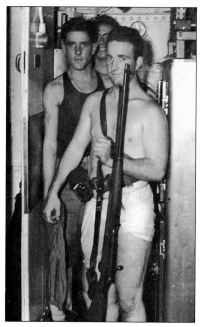

Cpl. Edward Wygal and Sgt. C. L. Golasewski show off weaponry aboard the USS *Nautilus* following the raid. NATIONAL ARCHIVES #11724

Pvt. Dean Winters holds a captured Japanese rifle following the Makin Raid, August 18, 1942.

NATIONAL ARCHIVES #11728

The USS *Argonaut* returns to a military welcome at the Pearl Harbor Submarine Base after the Makin Raid. NATIONAL ARCHIVES #11746

A jubilant Carlson and Roosevelt after their arrival in Pearl Harbor following the Makin Raid.

Carlson, James Roosevelt, and Lt. Comdr. Jack Pierce, commanding officer of the USS *Argonaut*, share a laugh aboard the boat upon its return to Pearl Harbor.

Adm. Chester W. Nimitz (*back to camera*) greets Maj. James Roosevelt aboard the USS *Argonaut* upon his return to Pearl Harbor following the raid.

Two of Carlson's commandos pose after returning to Pearl Harbor. Their youthful appearance belies the lethal talents both possess.

NATIONAL ARCHIVES #11747

Colonel Carlson and Major Roosevelt hold a flag taken from Japanese headquarters during the Makin Raid.

NATIONAL ARCHIVES #40182

A smiling Jack Miller (*second from right*) relaxes with (*from left:*) Lt. Wilfred Le Francois, Lt. Merwyn Plumley, and Lt. Charles Lamb.

FROM THE JACK MILLER COLLECTION, DeGOLYER LIBRARY, SOUTHERN METHODIST UNIVERSITY, DALLAS, TEXAS, A2004.0001

Many of Carlson's Raider officers are pictured in this group photo found in the Jack Miller Collection, including Peatross, McAuliffe, Schwerin, Coyte, and Early.

FROM THE JACK MILLER COLLECTION, DeGOLYER LIBRARY, SOUTHERN METHODIST UNIVERSITY, DALLAS, TEXAS, A2004.0001

A Raider poses for a photo near a native hut with one of Jacob Vouza's scouts. The scouts' knowledge of the terrain and jungle proved invaluable to Carlson.

FROM THE KENNETH McCULLOUGH COLLECTION

Natives and their shelters practically blend into the dense jungle. At times the Raiders could see only yards ahead.

FROM THE KENNETH McCULLOUGH COLLECTION

Happy that the fighting has ended at Asamana, a few Raiders wash in the Metapona River near the village. A few huts stand in the upper right.

Carlson (*middle, wearing glasses*) discusses tactics with other officers during a break on the Long Patrol.

Native carriers cross a kunai grass field to bring supplies to Carlson's men.

Raiders on patrol cross a kunai grass field. The knee-high grass shown here grew to four feet in other locations, making the Long Patrol an arduous trek that alternated among kunai grass fields, dense jungle, rivers and streams, and mountain ridges.

FROM THE KENNETH McCULLOUGH COLLECTION

A native scout leads a Raider patrol across one of the many streams. Thick jungle looms in the background.

FROM THE FRANK CANNISTRACI COLLECTION

Raiders, wary of what might be hiding in the dense jungle blanketing the shore, carefully advance along a river sandbar.

FROM THE FRANK CANNISTRACI COLLECTION

Raiders encountered many obstacles during the Long Patrol. Here a patrol balances its way across a wooden bridge spanning one of Guadalcanal's marshes as they leave the Aola area.

Carlson uses a break in patrolling to wash his feet and socks in one of the numerous streams that dissected the jungle. With him are Capt. John Apergis (*left*) and Australian Maj. John Mather.

During a break on the Long Patrol, Carlson (*left*) poses with Jacob Vouza and Major Mather (*right*).

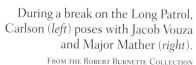

A Raider company winds along a ridge's crest during one of its patrols. FROM THE FRANK CANNISTRACI COLLECTION

Raiders often came across the decaying bodies of Shoji's forces as they pursued the Japanese away from the Marine perimeter at Henderson Field.

FROM THE KENNETH McCULLOUGH COLLECTION

Raiders set up a camp at one of their locations along the thirty-day patrol on Guadalcanal. Notice the lean-to used as a shelter. FROM THE KENNETH McCULLOUGH COLLECTION

A bearded "Wild Bill" Schwerin observes while a Raider mans his Boys gun during the Long Patrol.
FROM THE KENNETH McCULLOUGH COLLECTION

A group of Raiders climbs a steep, jungle-clad ridge during the Long Patrol. Nature's obstacles like this combined with disease to ravage the Raiders, many of whom suffered severe weight loss.

The Raiders had to scale tree-covered ridges similar to this during the final stage of their Long Patrol.

A cross similar to the one pictured was used to mark Jack Miller's grave-site. Jungle growth quickly obliterated signs of the site, making location of his remains almost impossible.

The Long Patrol complete, Carlson (*sitting, right*) poses with a group of his men for a *Life* magazine photographer. They hold a few souvenirs seized during the month behind enemy lines.   FROM THE FRANK CANNISTRACI COLLECTION

Carlson enjoys a moment with his son, Lt. Evans Carlson, after the Long Patrol.

NATIONAL ARCHIVES #2163—A

Jacob Vouza received many accolades after the war, including honors from the Queen of England. He maintained close ties with the Raiders until his death.

FROM THE HERBERT C. MERILLAT COLLECTION, MARINE CORPS RESEARCH CENTER, QUANTICO, VIRGINIA

Film actor Randolph Scott as Evans Carlson addresses his Raiders during a scene from the 1943 movie *Gung Ho!*

Marine Raider Pete Arias, a veteran of the vicious fight at Asamana, here poses with a Raider buddy, Frank Cannistraci, during the 2007 San Diego reunion.

The Marine Corps reveres the men who helped establish its reputation. Here a Marine band serenades a group of Raiders and thei families during the 2007 Raider reunion.

they had been bred there, and like some beasts you never see them until they are dead."[13]

By early November the American commander on the scene, Marine Maj. Gen. Alexander A. Vandegrift, canceled scheduled operations in western Guadalcanal to counter a growing threat east of the perimeter around Henderson. Vandegrift lacked knowledge of both the number of enemy troops to his east and of the island's interior, where jungle-shrouded terrain masked not only crocodiles and swamps but also the trails along which the Japanese moved their men and supplies. He needed someone who could push into that jungle and determine the location and strength of his foe.

Another unknown faced men at Guadalcanal, one that each Marine could only answer in his own way. The noted novelist James Jones, himself wounded at Guadalcanal, best posed it in his history of the war. "But did we have the kind of men who could stand up eyeball to eyeball and whip the Jap?" He added, "The Japanese, with their warrior code of the bushi, had been in active combat warfare for ten years," while Americans had been peacetime civilians. "Could we evolve a soldier, a *civilian* [italics Jones's] soldier, who could meet them man to man in the field? Did we have enough crazies and suicidals? Enough weird types of our own, to do that? Not everyone was sure we did."[14]

Jones posed the same question Captain Washburn (Joseph Griffith, Peatross, Apergis, and Washburn had since been promoted to captain) had faced when, traveling by rail the previous December, commuters asked if he were up to the task. Washburn, Miller, Maghakian, Carlson—each had to answer it on Guadalcanal.

"We Were Nervous Coming In"

Carlson selected Capt. Harold K. Throneson's C Company and Captain Washburn's E Company to accompany him to Guadalcanal and alerted the other four Raider companies to be prepared to move out on short notice. He hoped that once his men were in place, superiors would find a more suitable task for his battalion.

On October 31, Washburn and Throneson led the 266 men in the two companies—four officers and 129 enlisted men in each—aboard the USS *Manley* at Espiritu Santo to begin the trip north to Guadalcanal. Carlson followed with the seven officers and twenty-five enlisted men in the headquarters company.

The quiet Washburn was about to gain his first combat experience. He trusted that his men, labeled "Junior Raiders" by the original four companies because of their late start, were ready to show they were Raiders in fact as well as in name.

Washburn did not have as much faith in the *Manley*. The Navy had modified the World War I–vintage destroyer into a troop transport by placing belowdecks bunks stacked four and five tiers high. Raiders sweated heavily in the stifling, cramped conditions, and wondered if the thin hulls provided adequate security against an attack or heavy seas. Captain Washburn figured "we all knew that they would be caskets if they ever took a hit or a torpedo."[15] Later, when a storm engulfed the ship on the voyage's second day, Pvt. Lowell V. Bulger of C Company recalled that "those little tin cans were tossed about like corks. The bow dipped under twenty-five-foot waves and doused the entire ship with seawater. These thin shelled, old World War I destroyers shuddered, creaked and moaned" as they tried to avoid crashing into nearby vessels, and green Raiders lay in their bunks and vomited into their helmets. Practically every man in Captain Washburn's company succumbed to the violent conditions, which caused Private Bulger to state, "Needless to say we were all ready to storm any beach when our tiny convoy hove to in the fairly calm waters of Indispensable Strait of Aola."[16]

The November 4 landing could not arrive soon enough. At five thirty a.m. they climbed down netting into Higgins boats and settled in for the short ride to shore. Most carried only a few essentials, as they had been told they would be ashore for only a day or two.

As daylight filtered in, the men obtained their first glimpses of Guadalcanal, an island that had, by now, gained almost legendary status for the vicious combat since early August. Multiple blue hues layered the tropical waters that lapped against golden sands. Palm trees and green jungle covered the fields and hills inland, serving as sentinels for the sharp ridges and mountain peaks towering behind. Beneath the beauty, however, lurked horrors that had, until now, existed only in the Raiders' imaginations. Nature, in the guise of incessant rains, thigh-clutching mud and jungle vines, insects, spiders, crocodiles, and disease, waited with the Japanese to reduce Raider ranks.

As the Higgins boats steadily moved toward shore in a pouring rain, Capt. John Apergis, a member of Headquarters Company, wondered about their reception. Supposedly Martin Clemens, a British official who organized the

Solomon Island scouts, would be waiting ashore. For all Apergis knew, the Japanese hid just behind the beaches, waiting to deliver a counterpunch to the landing. A scheduled bonfire lit up the semidarkness as a marker for the incoming Raiders, but what lurked beyond that tiny circle of light? Some officers undoubtedly recalled the Japanese slaughter of the Goettge Patrol, a group of Marines hacked to death the previous August. Could the enemy have another atrocity waiting for them?

Pfc. Ervin Kaplan, one of Washburn's men, thought everything appeared calm as his Higgins boat neared shore. He crouched low to take advantage of cover lest any gunfire from shore greet them, and was reassured by the look of confidence exuded by the other men in his craft.

Others were not as positive. "We had no idea what to expect coming in our Higgins boats," said Washburn's close friend First Lt. Robert W. Burnette. "We didn't know if we would get opposition. I thought we might."[17]

Not far from Burnette, Pvt. Darrell A. Loveland of C Company battled nerves as well as uncertainties about what waited onshore. "We thought we would have to fight our way onto the beach. Definitely. Sure, we were nervous coming in. Sort of like going into a football game, only you're 130 pounds and the guy across the line from you was 230! That kind of fear. We really didn't know what to expect. Some guys said prayers. You could see crosses going, saying 'Hail Marys.'"[18]

They need not have worried. Clemens and Maj. John Mather, an Australian intelligence officer and, with Clemens, an organizer of the native scouts, greeted them at the beach. "I say, what kept you chaps?" Clemens asked the nearest Raider. One Marine wondered where the Japanese were, while another asked a native what disease caused the scars that covered his skin. "Bomb bomb disease,"[19] answered the scout.

Mather examined the Raiders as they rushed ashore and found much with which to be impressed. The weaponry, especially the Tommy guns and the BARs, would give them a distinct advantage in the jungle, where they could shred foliage with the heavy firepower. Their stellar physical condition and youth—even the officers, except for the leather-faced Carlson, looked young—augured well for whatever lay ahead.

As Carlson spoke with Clemens and Mather, Throneson and Washburn moved their men one mile inland to the banks of the Aola River. Washburn wondered why anyone could think of Guadalcanal as one of those romantic South Sea islands, as he and his company ran smack into "heat, sweat, mosquitoes, rain, stink—everything that makes a jungle repulsive."[20]

Private Bulger's platoon occupied a high spot along the river's east bank as part of a line that extended inland in a semicircular defensive perimeter. Impassable swamps and jungle cut between different groups of Raiders, so that Bulger and the men could barely see the Raiders next in line to them, while dense foliage reduced their fields of fire. Bulger and the others dug shallow foxholes in the mud and slime along the river, while Burnette's Weapons Platoon set up light machine guns at the flanks to cover the trails leading to the beach and mortars to guard the river crossings and trails leading to the river.

They remained at their positions into that first night on Guadalcanal, when "pitch black darkness descended" and left individual fire teams alone with their thoughts. Every Raider faced this unnerving initiation to the nighttime jungle, where noises that sounded innocent by day suddenly took on a more ferocious nature. Private Bulger, who carried an M1, passed the night with BAR man Pvt. Kenneth Meland and Pvt. Darrell Loveland and his Tommy gun. The trio waited upon a twenty-foot knoll along the river, flanked by swamps on either side, and hoped to make it to dawn. They sat in their shallow foxhole, trying to determine the natural jungle sounds from what could be man-made and attempting to adjust to the "eerie jungle noises, huge crawling land crabs, two-foot long tree lizards, crocodiles swimming in the hundreds of rivers, creeks, and slews, and millions of insects, voracious mosquitoes, carriers of a variety of jungle fevers . . ."[21]

"The Jungle Was the Enemy's"

Dawn not only brought welcome relief for the Raiders but an altered mission for Carlson. An airdropped message from General Vandegrift handed Carlson the task he wanted all along, a chore perfectly suited for the skills of his battalion and the purposes of the Jacques Farm training—an unconventional campaign in Guadalcanal's interior consisting of hit-and-run, surprise assaults. For the next month Carlson was to scout west toward the perimeter to determine the strength of enemy forces between Aola Bay and Henderson Field, as well as to interdict any of the fifteen hundred Japanese who had escaped a trap set by other Marine and Army elements to confine them along the coast at Koli Point ten miles to the west. Success on both counts would stabilize the situation near the Henderson perimeter.

Carlson had no idea how difficult or dangerous the mission might be—

Capt. John Apergis wrote that the Marines were "'blind' as to the disposition of the enemy troop formations" and that "the jungle was the enemy's"[22]—but that only heightened his anticipation. Unlike Makin, a rehearsed, staged action with predetermined objectives, at Guadalcanal Carlson enjoyed a free hand to implement the lessons of Nicaragua and of China.

Carlson "was at home in such blind tactical situations," wrote one of Captain Washburn's men, Pfc. William D. Lansford. "He'd trained our battalion precisely for unorthodox warfare, so he was confident we'd do the job when we met the enemy. Guadalcanal would be our acid test . . . [the opportunity] to test his tactics in terrain so wild that it was largely unknown, even to the coastal natives. The downside was that we'd be greatly outnumbered by the enemy."[23]

Carlson would depart on November 6, assisted by 150 native scouts and supply carriers under John Mather and Martin Clemens. When they reached Tasimboko eight miles west, scouts that were more familiar with the territory around Henderson Field would replace the original group and take the Raiders to the perimeter.

Carlson needed the native scouts. Possessing only inaccurate, outdated maps, Carlson willingly accepted valuable aid from men such as Tabasui, who guided them during the early days, and the heroic Jacob Vouza, who had already earned epic status for his work earlier in the fighting. Mather instructed Carlson that rather than money, which was meaningless on an island lacking stores, the scouts would work for food and tobacco.

Fascinating characters, such as Platoon Sergeant Maghakian, Capt. William "Wild Bill" Schwerin, and Carlson himself, abounded in the Raider Battalion, but none may have been as amazing as Vouza. Captured by the Japanese in the early stages of the fighting on Guadalcanal, Vouza survived torture when Japanese soldiers repeatedly bayoneted the islander after finding a tiny American flag in his possession. Despite the agony, Vouza refused to divulge any information, even though being questioned for hours.

Though bayonet slashes tore Vouza's throat, chest, arms, and stomach, he still refused to talk. The Japanese eventually left him for dead, but Vouza regained consciousness, chewed through the ropes that bound him to a tree, and crawled three miles back to Marine lines. Weakened from blood loss and the ordeal, Vouza looked so ghastly that Martin Clemens could barely look at him.

Carlson met with Washburn and Throneson on November 5 to map out the details. He left a rear echelon at Aola that every four days would ferry supplies by landing craft to coastal spots along his route. From there, native carriers would hike the food and ammunition to Carlson's jungle location. In the meantime the transport would return to Espiritu Santo to bring in B, D, and F companies. Much to Lieutenant Miller's chagrin, already antsy over missing the Makin Raid, A Company was to remain in the New Hebrides until further notice.

The next morning Carlson took his first steps into the jungle, followed by the 266 men of Washburn's and Throneson's companies. Driven by a desire to prove his battalion's worth, Carlson was a man intent on locating and wiping out the enemy, an officer who, according to Martin Clemens, "lost no opportunity in harassing them."[24]

"I Stink Like a Billygoat"

Carlson may not have known much about Guadalcanal's interior, but he could have taken a word of caution from the master storyteller Jack London. After the author visited the island, he wrote that if he were a king and had to banish his chief opponent, Guadalcanal would do just fine. Ninety-two miles long by thirty-three miles wide, Guadalcanal rests ten degrees below the equator. A line of volcanoes and ridges forms a spine across the island's midsection, while lower-lying areas sport lush jungles broken by wide fields of razor-sharp kunai grass. Numerous rivers and streams traverse the fields and jungle, whose canopy towers one hundred feet above the surface. Vines, swamps, ridges, and rotting vegetation house a zookeeper's cornucopia of leeches, scorpions, snakes, crocodiles, lizards, fist-sized spiders, centipedes, and three-inch-long wasps. Hot and humid when sunny, miserable during the near daily torrential rains, Guadalcanal's succulent appearance dissipates upon closer observation.

At daylight on November 6, Carlson led his two battalions and accompanying native scouts into Guadalcanal's interior. He intended to scout west toward the perimeter into areas of reported Japanese presence, halting briefly at villages along the way—first Gegende, then Reko, Kima, Tasimboko, Tina, and Binu. Carlson issued for a four-day supply of rice, raisins, bacon, and tea.

Within a few paces Washburn had already noticed the jungle's festering, dank smell. Behind a point consisting of a squad accompanied by a native scout, at three paces apart the Raiders moved along native trails so narrow they permitted only a single file. Rivers, creeks, and swamps impeded the line, which stretched to one mile in length, while the torturous heat and humidity bathed each man in sweat before they had traveled a quarter mile.

Liana vines, festooned with what Private Bulger described as "thousands of fish-hook barbs," reached out from all sides, forming irritating tentacles lying in wait to slow their progress. Men hacked bushes with their Raider knives, but one cleared foot of jungle path led to a second cluttered one. "Those vines would rip and tear your face or hands or arms right through your dungarees," stated Private Bulger. "These lacerations would quickly fester and become a running sore which remained during our entire stay on Guadalcanal."

By the end of the first day, impeded by vines and streams, the Raiders had moved only five miles through the thick jungle. Despite advancing only that short distance, Bulger stated that "we fell exhausted asleep in the rain."[25]

On the morning of November 7, Carlson chastised his men for their tardy pace of the day before. In hopes of improving the performance, Carlson traveled with the point, and despite advancing through near impassable rain forest and checking each side of the trail for Japanese, the companies picked up the pace.

The morning sun quickly heated the jungle, where steam from dampened leaves made the Raiders think they had stepped into a Turkish bath. The terrain at first unfolded in a monotonous pattern—broad jungles skirted the sides of rivers and streams before opening to fields of sharp kunai grass. Along the way the Raiders crossed and recrossed winding rivers and inspected villages. Captain Peatross, the commander of B Company, which, along with F and D companies had joined the battalion on November 10, marveled at the difficulties of traversing the island's rivers.

"It had rained fairly hard during the night, and the river was running more than five feet deep in some places; hence fording it was time-consuming and risky," Peatross wrote of crossing the Berande River, one-third of the way from Aola Bay to Henderson Field. "Although we strung a lifeline between the banks, the shorter men still had to struggle to keep their footing, and a few even had to tie their toggle ropes around their waists and toss the ends to Raiders on the bank for an assist out of the stream. The running water cooled our bodies, washed the sweat and stench from our clothes, and made fresh men of us—at least for a few minutes."[26]

Days fighting the terrain ended in nights struggling with fears, both real and imagined. Even when the Raiders spotted no enemy soldiers, the Japanese certainly waited close by. Gunshots from nervous Raiders frequently punctured those early nights.

"Although we were well trained for jungle operations," wrote Captain Peatross of his company's initial night on Guadalcanal, "we knew that we had to be particularly careful on our first night, since our men would be more easily spooked than on any night afterwards, particularly after having heard so many horror stories about the wily Japanese on Guadalcanal."[27]

Carlson's first engagement occurred at Reko, a tiny native village along the Bokokimbo River five miles west of Aola Bay. When Carlson and the point squad arrived, empty Japanese ration boxes and cigarette packages littered the otherwise deserted village. Carlson posted sentries and allowed the other men to bathe and wash their uniforms while the main body, some four hours behind, caught up to the point.

Around two p.m. the parrots and myna birds suddenly stopped their strange sounds. Within moments shots rang out on the opposite side of the Bokokimbo. Raiders grabbed their weapons and jumped into the river, slowed by the neck-deep waters that pressed against them as they headed for the other side, weapons and packs held above their heads. Though bullets kicked up splashes about them, all reached the far bank safely.

Private Loveland and a few others fanned out to search for the Japanese. In an opening not far from the river, they later came across ten Japanese skinning a dead wild pig. Raider fire killed two and scattered the rest, with the Raiders in hot pursuit. Private Bulger discovered a wounded Japanese and yanked him to the trail, with the man's intestines dragging in the dirt, and found an oilskin packet containing money and papers sewn in his uniform. Carlson sent for an interpreter, but before the man could come forward to interrogate the Japanese, the enemy soldier succumbed.

A humorous incident broke the tension of that first firefight. Upon hearing the initial gunshots, Pfc. Warren G. Alger leaped for cover but instead landed in the midst of the vicious liana vines. While the fighting raged, Alger tried to free himself from the barbs, which held him suspended three feet above the ground. After ten minutes of fruitless struggle, Alger's cries for help reached fellow Raiders, who came to his aid. Alger had to endure the ignominy of being trapped in such an ungainly place as well as the laughter from his comrades.

When the skirmish ended, Captain Apergis strolled over to where the dead Japanese lay on the ground. The image of the young soldiers, even though they belonged to the enemy, bothered him. Those boys were individuals with hopes and dreams for the future, much like him. Their ambitions had suddenly ended with a few bullets. But for fate, one of those bodies might just as easily have been his. Apergis gazed at the fallen enemy for a few moments, then walked away.

Following the first skirmish, Carlson established a base camp at Binu, a village between the Balesuna and Metapona rivers three miles from the coast. His patrols had already established that the twelve-mile area between Aola Bay and Binu sheltered few, if any, Japanese troops, and working out of Binu would allow him to move his operations west and scout the jungles between Binu and Henderson Field. As Binu was the last inhabited village between the Balesuna and Henderson, Carlson also had a ready supply of scouts for the next phase of his operation.

More important, Carlson might soon have plenty of Japanese to pursue. By November 10, Marine and Army units had moved against the fifteen hundred Japanese reinforcements in the jungle three miles to the village's northwest. Vandegrift had hoped to confine the enemy to the coastline, where the Marines and Army battalions could gradually destroy them, but a thousand Japanese eluded his trap during the night of November 10–11 and fled inland toward the Metapona River. By occupying Binu, Carlson placed his battalion in the most advantageous place to intercept these troops. Carlson briefed Washburn and the other company commanders and emphasized that on the next morning he wanted his Raiders to aggressively patrol the area west of Binu to the Metapona. He cautioned that they were likely to collide with sizeable enemy forces.

As the Raiders ate their normal meal of rice and bacon that evening, the likelihood of battle dominated talk. Men momentarily nudged aside the thought by celebrating November 10, the 167th anniversary of the Marine Corps. Plt. Sgt. Frank J. Lawson recalled that one year earlier he enjoyed a feast of turkey and dressing, ham, mashed potatoes, and ice cream. "Then I was all spit-shined and decked out in my dress blues," Lawson remarked, "but just look at me now. Tonight, I'm dirty, ragged, unshaven, stink like a billygoat, and don't have a single one of all those goodies I had a year ago. . . ."[28]

The men of Washburn's E Company, who would play a prominent part in the next day's battle, acted with an assurance bred from confidence in their commanding officer. Since training, Captain Washburn had combined insistence on doing things the right way with a deep fondness for his men.

He pushed them in training, but also gave them situations in which talented men could utilize their abilities and leadership skills. In Guadalcanal's jungles, where difficult became the norm, he shared every adversity with his men.

"We called him 'Jungle Jim,'" related Pvt. Lathrop Gay of Washburn. "Very few officers are as excellent as Washburn."[29]

His officers agreed. First Lt. Cleland E. Early, commander of the Second Platoon, claimed that Washburn "was a great unassuming man having the respect of all Marines who knew him. He was a great leader, calm under fire, tenacious and mission oriented. He was a modest person and did not seek the acclaim that he gained throughout his career." Washburn's Weapons Platoon commanding officer, Lieutenant Burnette, needed few words to describe his close friend, calling Washburn "one of God's noblemen."[30]

As corpsmen handed out the daily doses of atabrine to combat malaria and salve to ease the discomfort already being caused by jungle rot, Raiders not on sentry crawled into their half shelters for a bit of rest. They would need their strength for the next day.

"An Awesome Barrier to Our Front"

The Raiders awoke the next morning—Armistice Day—sensing a fight. They gathered their gear and swallowed some cold food—heavy overnight rains soaked fires and extinguished the possibility of warm chow—and waited for orders.

Carlson was on the move and issuing orders to the five company commanders at the crack of dawn. In an attempt to intercept the fleeing Japanese, Carlson fanned out a four-layered patrol to search the terrain between the village of Asamana along the Metapona River and Guadalcanal's northern coast four miles to the north. He ordered Captain Throneson and C Company to move west eight miles from Binu to Asamana, where native scouts reportedly spotted a group of Japanese soldiers. Washburn was to lead E Company one and a half miles north of C Company, then veer west to explore a trail along the Metapona. Capt. Charles F. McAuliffe and his D Company platoon was to scout the area one mile to Washburn's north and make contact with the Army's 164th Infantry fighting along the coast, while Capt. William "Wild Bill" Schwerin's F Company marched north to Tetere to patrol the area between that village and the Balesuna River. Captain Peatross and B Company would remain at Binu as base security and as a reserve force.

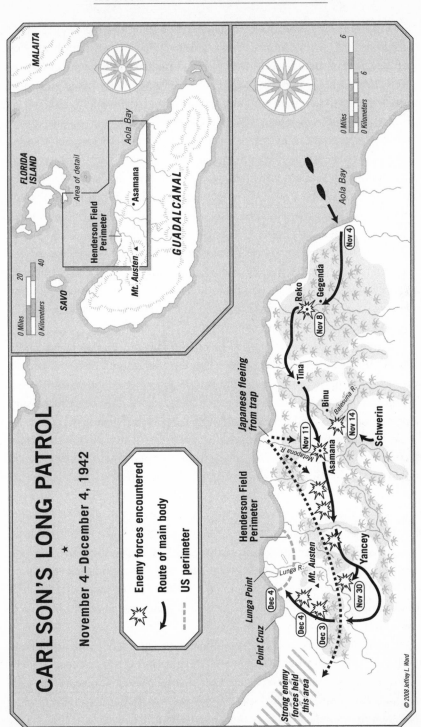

CARLSON'S LONG PATROL
★
November 4 – December 4, 1942

Enemy forces encountered

Route of main body

US perimeter

As the sun slowly rose over the horizon, heralding another sweltering day in Guadalcanal's withering heat and humidity, four lines of Raiders in single file followed their native scouts out of Binu. The men shuffled up a sharp low ridge before plunging into a broad field of kunai grass. With the jungle waiting on the field's far side, the four companies veered onto separate courses and soon lost sight of each other.

Little happened during the first few hours as the four companies spread farther apart. The lull ended at ten a.m. As Washburn's E Company crossed another kunai grass field northeast of Asamana, mortar shells crashed near the column. Washburn evaded the mortar attack by guiding his men into a nearby jungle along the Metapona River, but in the process detected mortar explosions and gunfire emerging from the C and D Company sectors.

Fellow Raiders were under fire. Captain Throneson's C Company had patrolled the eight miles from Binu to Asamana, following a native trail leading to the village. "The heat and humidity was almost overpowering and our dungarees were soaking wet with sweat,"[31] recalled Private Bulger, who occupied a spot with the point.

By nine a.m. the company had reached a coconut plantation two miles from Asamana. Abandoned Japanese ration packs littered the area, causing the Raiders to move more cautiously. Bulger and other elements of the point left the coconut grove shortly before ten and entered a three-hundred-yard-square kunai grass field enclosed on three sides by heavy jungle.

At the point Pvt. Pete Arias, a squat, muscular Mexican-American from California, smelled danger. The jungle-shrouded field provided a perfect killing arena for the Japanese, who could hide in the bushes while decimating the Raiders as they crossed in the open. The scouts that Jacob Vouza had sent to the area the night before reported that the field provided an excellent location for an ambush.

Three point squads spread out as the company approached the grass. The right and left flank points walked fifty yards behind Arias and the center point squad, with Throneson and the main body following. The men carefully scrutinized each yard of the thick kunai grass before advancing another few steps toward the jungle.

Arias's point squad entered the jungle, while the left point, comprising the fire team of Private Bulger, Private Meland, and Private Loveland, stood fifty yards farther back. The thick jungle masked the camouflaged Japanese machine-gun position, whose soldiers ignored Arias and patiently waited for the larger main body of Raiders to move closer.

As Arias neared the jungle's edge, Cpl. John D. Bennett raised his hands for the others to halt. "That's as far as he got," said Arias. "This machine gun opened up and just wiped him out, wiped out my squad." Stitched across the chest by machine-gun bullets from a nest less than twenty yards away, Bennett fell dead, while through pure chance Arias and two others dropped to the ground without being touched. Fifty yards back in the open field, Private Loveland's group spread out and charged toward the jungle before hitting the turf. Men in the main body rushed forward until heavy fire forced them to seek refuge among the grass.

"The sounds of battle increased to a deafening volume," recalled Private Bulger as Japanese rifles, machine guns, hand grenades, and mortars directed a frightening array of power their way. The enemy "presented an awesome barrier to our front."[32]

"This Was No Small Enemy Patrol"

At 10:10 a.m., only ten minutes after Washburn's report of a mortar assault, Throneson notified Carlson at Binu that he, too, was under attack. As information tumbled into headquarters, Carlson discerned a favorable situation. With the Japanese apparently focused on stopping C Company in the kunai grass field, if C Company could hold its position long enough for Washburn and McAuliffe to head south from their patrol areas, he could bring D and E companies onto the enemy rear and flank and trap the Japanese in a massive envelopment, just as he had seen the Chinese Eighth Route Army do in the 1930s.

John Mather watched as Carlson crisply issued a series of orders to catch the enemy off guard. "Carlson started to do this immediately with confidence and ability," wrote Mather. "All his previous training and preparation came to the fore and it was soon apparent to all ranks that he knew exactly what he wanted to do and how he would go about it."[33]

By eleven a.m. preparations were in place. Carlson ordered Washburn to veer south along the west bank of the Metapona River, cross at the village of Asamana, and hit the enemy attacking C Company from the rear. Meanwhile, Captain McAuliffe was to bring D Company directly south against the Japanese left flank, while Wild Bill Schwerin embarked on a forced march back to Binu and further orders. Carlson also sent a reserve platoon from B Company to reinforce Throneson in the field.

Private Arias, Private Loveland, and the other C Company Raiders knew nothing of these developments as they concentrated on staying alive in that kunai grass field. Arias hugged the ground directly in front of the machine gun, blazing from less than twenty yards away. Fortunately, in the tall grass neither Arias nor the Japanese gunner could see each other. Raiders rolled or crawled to the left or right as bullets kicked into the dirt nearby and mortar shells plowed the grass. Here and there a Raider would suddenly rise, race a zigzag course for ten steps, then disappear again into the grass. Three times Japanese bullets hit Pvt. James E. Van Winkle as he attempted to seek shelter, and Sgt. Richard Fye took a bullet in his buttocks while directing his men.

With enemy snipers and machine guns firing from less than 150 feet away, Private Loveland and Private Bulger had shuffled left toward the field's center, when they met Cpl. John Sullivan on a .30-caliber light machine gun. Sullivan, the sole unwounded survivor of his gun crew, sprayed the jungle and trees, while Pfc. Woodrow Greenlee, shot in the hip, attempted to drag himself to the rear. Bulger shouted to Meland, but when he received no reply he assumed he, Loveland, and Sullivan were stranded at the front. The rest had either retreated or been killed.

"We knew at once that this was no small enemy patrol,"[34] said Private Bulger. He and the other Raiders faced the remnants of the 228th Infantry Regiment, recently arrived from Bougainville, and Shoji's 230th Infantry, seven hundred men who had escaped the combined Marine-Army coastal trap the night before. Hopefully, aid would arrive before the enemy wiped out the entire company.

As Washburn led his men to C Company's rescue, Captain McAuliffe faced his own quandary with his platoon from D Company. His men had advanced only a short distance across a field toward Throneson two miles away when Japanese troops hidden in the jungle opened fire. Two Raiders fell dead from the initial flurry of bullets, and the other Raiders scampered for safety amidst machine-gun bullets and rifle-grenade explosions. McAuliffe's men had to crawl along the ground as they attempted to pull out of the field.

McAuliffe erred when he allowed himself to be cut off from the rest of his platoon. Instead of traveling with the main group, McAuliffe placed Pl. Sgt. Harold Schrier in charge so that he could be with the point squad. Enemy opposition quickly sliced McAuliffe and his squad from Schrier's men, in effect decapitating the commander from his platoon.

For much of the day, McAuliffe and his thirteen men remained in the field, unable to either retreat or to reach Throneson in his own field to the immediate south. The day's success now fell on the shoulders of Washburn, the officer whose quiet demeanor caused train commuters to wonder about the value of the American fighting man.

"The Guys Were Mowing Them Down"

Before deciding on his course of action, Washburn discussed matters with Lieutenants Burnette, Early, and the colonel's son, First Lt. Evans C. Carlson. They had decided to cross the Metapona, move swiftly south, and attack the enemy rear, when a messenger ran in with Carlson's orders to do the same.

"Like a Civil War outfit," recalled Lieutenant Early of Washburn's swift advance to help fellow Raiders, "we rode to the sound of the guns."[35] For a time Washburn led his company—spread out in single file—along the Metapona, a winding river whose twists and turns would become all too familiar to Raiders in the coming days. Advancing as rapidly as possible, Washburn halted his men only long enough for Jacob Vouza to send scouts ahead and report on what they observed.

When he had taken them partway to Asamana, he ordered his men to cross from the east to the west bank of the river. The waters, swollen from recent heavy rains, produced such strong currents that the men attached ropes from one to another to traverse the stream. By ten fifteen Lieutenant Carlson's First Platoon stood on the west bank, with Burnette's and Early's platoons following close behind. Not far upstream lay the tiny village of Asamana, more a collection of mud huts amidst the jungle than an organized settlement.

Washburn led his men into a kunai grass field, where he came across a section of grass that had been stomped down by men walking three to four abreast. The signs of enemy activity caused him to proceed with unusual caution. To inspect the village ahead, he dispatched Vouza's scouts, who returned with reports that, other than a few Japanese soldiers inside the village, Asamana was deserted. When the staccato sounds of gunfire from the field to Asamana's east increased in tempo and volume, Washburn ordered his company to proceed on the double.

At the point, Lieutenant Carlson's platoon reached Asamana first, which was unusually quiet considering the battle raging to the west. Carlson ordered a few men to check the native huts, then waited for Washburn's orders.

Action heated up as soon as Washburn arrived at the edge of the village. Two hundred yards to the east he saw a line of soldiers, some stripped, fording the river south of the village, holding their equipment and weapons above their heads. Not having any field glasses, he at first thought they were members of C Company, but after a second look concluded they were Japanese soldiers. "They were having a holiday, laughing and shouting among themselves," Washburn recalled. "We slipped up and let them have it with our machine guns and automatic rifles."[36]

Washburn called Lieutenants Early and Burnette to the side for a quick discussion. So the main body of Japanese could cross the Metapona and escape through the village into the jungle beyond, a strong rear guard had apparently blocked C Company two miles to the east in the field and D Company to the north. Washburn had spotted this main force with his binoculars. He believed that with the enemy's attention focused elsewhere, he could move his company closer and attack not only the enemy in the river but the Japanese rear guard from behind. Washburn sent Burnette and Early back to prepare their platoons for action, then moved his communications people, Private First Class Kaplan and Pfc. Jesse Vanlandingham, to a shielded, tree-covered spot in the jungle alongside the trail to Binu with orders to keep in touch with Colonel Carlson.

The terrain around Asamana offered benefits to both sides. A small cleared area surrounded the village, which was encased by the jungle. Beyond the jungle along the western side stood another kunai grass field, while thick jungle covered both the south side of the village as well as the land on the Metapona's east bank.

Washburn established an L-shaped defensive line, anchored at each end by Burnette's machine guns, along the riverbank to enable him to fire at the Japanese while protecting his right flank from an attack out of the jungle west of Asamana. When the men were in place Washburn gave the order to fire.

The Japanese in the river, caught without their weapons and, in most cases, their clothing, had no chance in the initial torrent of Raider fire. "It was like shooting birds," Private First Class Vanlandingham stated of the opening volleys. "The guys in the front lines were mowing them down."[37]

The Japanese on the bank reacted skillfully to the onslaught, quickly bringing Washburn's advance platoon under fire. A Nambu machine gun situated among the roots of a large banyan tree on the village side peppered the Raider line. Each time Raider fire killed the gunner, another appeared to take his place. As the Nambu rattled away, Lieutenant Early and a few Raiders crawled toward it, hoping to draw close enough to eliminate it with hand grenades.

From his position at the point, Cpl. Frank M. Kurland dropped to the ground before the Nambu hit him, but the Marine directly behind him, Pfc. Lorenzo D. Anderson, Jr., was not as fortunate. The young man had almost been sent home with malaria, but had begged Lieutenant Early to allow him to remain on the patrol. Impressed by the private's attitude, Early convinced the company's doctor that Anderson's motivation would overcome any problems caused by his illness. Anderson, who refused to allow malaria to keep him out of action, died instantly from a bullet between the eyes.

Japanese mortar shells, with their muffled "whoomp" sound, scattered pieces of deadly shrapnel and tree branches among the Raiders, who hugged lower to the ground in an effort to avoid the missiles. One hit so close to Kaplan and Vanlandingham that the concussion briefly knocked out Vanlandingham.

Early's group finally managed to destroy the pesky Nambu. When they moved up to inspect the position, they found several bodies scattered about the mangled gun. Early turned over one body and narrowly avoided death when a grenade lodged in the soldier's hand exploded. The fortunate Early escaped with shrapnel injuries to his left hand.

Pvt. Lathrop B. Gay, an ammunition carrier for a machine gun, observed the value of a veteran presence in how a sergeant handled a jittery young gunner. "One of the gunners was really cutting lose. We had this sergeant who was a tall guy who smoked a pipe, and he walked up behind the gunner and tapped him on the back. The gunner jumped about two feet off the ground. The sergeant said, 'You can't scare 'em to death. You've got to kill them. Take it easy.' The sergeant went back to a tree, lit his pipe, and started firing. Here's bullets going everywhere and he's telling the gunner to take it easy, make your shots count instead of shooting all over the place."[38]

When two Japanese companies, aided by a second enemy machine gun from across the river and an intense mortar barrage, counterattacked at eleven thirty to threaten his flank, Washburn pulled his Raiders back to the jungle to reorganize. He radioed a message to Carlson explaining that he faced at least two full-strength Japanese companies at Asamana.

Assuming they had scared off a minor Raider patrol, the Japanese resumed crossing the Metapona.

"One of the Best Field Leaders"

The Japanese had not figured on Washburn's caginess. Instead of pulling out of the area and waiting for Colonel Carlson to send reinforcements, Washburn regrouped in the jungle, then launched a second attack at noon. Burnette's and Carlson's platoons charged straight at the enemy while Early's platoon skirted north and crossed the river to envelop the enemy from the east. Washburn employed what would become Colonel Carlson's trademark tactic throughout the Long Patrol—flanking maneuvers.

If the first confrontation had been a surprise to the Japanese, the second momentarily paralyzed them, as more had gone into the water to bathe or cool off from the humidity. To the north of the river, crossing Raiders charged toward the village while a machine gun set up across the river by Early, combined with one firing on the village side, created a deadly cross fire. Bullets sliced into the water and Japanese alike, turning the Metapona red. Washburn had again caught the enemy unaware.

Though slower to react, the Japanese mounted a vigorous defense that included the use of mortars. "All this time the intensity of fire from the other side had increased," Washburn recalled later, "sweeping the bank on our side, and mortar shells started dropping in on us."[39] In response, Washburn brought Early back across the river and sent him west around the village.

The fighting lapsed into a deadly montage—one side charged and fell back, then the other staged a counterattack. Washburn, who carried a shotgun, was hit in the foot, but the thick leather of his Raider boot halted the bullet before it creased his ankle and saved him from serious injury. Lieutenant Burnette killed one Japanese thirty feet away with a blast from his shotgun. Burnette's machine guns prevented the Japanese from using the river crossing, while Early and Carlson controlled the empty village.

Washburn's men fought the larger Japanese force to a standstill throughout the afternoon, but eventually the enemy's overpowering numbers and firepower took its toll. The enemy commander sent his men farther south to cross the river, then brought them back to strike Washburn's exposed right flank.

By four thirty Washburn's men had battled for six hours in the stifling heat and humidity. Now low on ammunition and water, the exhausted Raiders had little punch left. When a mortar barrage indicated another all-out effort by the Japanese, Washburn opted to withdraw rather than remain in an exposed position against superior numbers. "As the sun set," wrote Pfc. William D. Lansford, "we could see large groups of Japanese infantrymen closing in around us. In minutes, we'd be trapped against the riverbank in the dark."[40] Washburn concluded his company had done all it could and ordered a withdrawal and started back to Binu.

Realizing that the sole avenue of escape lay through a narrow gully and trail to the north, Washburn stationed a machine gunner, twenty-year-old Pvt. Joseph Auman, at the exit to provide cover. He first withdrew one platoon as a second stood guard, then the other two in succession. Auman remained at his gun until the Japanese closed in and killed the young American.

"He knew he would die," said Private Gay of his friend, but "he kept firing. We took off because the Japanese were getting around behind us and we were certainly outnumbered."[41] Auman was awarded the Navy Cross for his actions.

Severely handicapped in weapons, men, and ammunition, Washburn chose to retract his men from danger rather than needlessly expend a company of highly trained Raiders. In the process, his men inflicted huge losses on the enemy, with the 133-man company killing 120 Japanese against a handful of losses.

Washburn's three lieutenants, Burnette, Early, and Carlson, earned Silver Stars for their roles in the fighting, which constituted the main offensive action of Asamana. So, too, did Captain Washburn, a man who shunned publicity.

"A quiet-spoken Marine Corps [officer] who headed a deadly fighting machine in the jungles of Guadalcanal was recently awarded the Silver Star Medal for 'extraordinary heroism and distinguished battle leadership,'" read a Marine Corps press release issued after the battle. "His men, all tested jungle fighters, regard him as one of the best field leaders in the Marine Corps."[42]

Washburn and his men had together answered those Connecticut train commuters.

"I Wanted to Cry, but I Could Not Produce Tears"

While Washburn battled the Japanese near Asamana village, back at his Binu command post eight miles away Carlson attempted to make sense of what was occurring. With Private First Class Kaplan transmitting a stream of messages, he knew how Washburn fared, but he had heard little from Throneson in the field or McAuliffe a few miles to C Company's north.

At least he knew where Captain Schwerin and F Company were. At one p.m. Schwerin guided his men into Binu after a wearying forced march from the coast. Carlson ordered them to rest and eat while he cemented plans to head toward Throneson and the beleaguered C Company. Carlson figured that the larger threat rested in the woods encasing Throneson, while Washburn appeared to have things under control one-half mile to the west in the village. Besides, Carlson wanted to see what had been going on in that kunai grass field with C Company and to learn what had happened with McAuliffe and his reinforced platoon from D Company.

While Carlson determined his next moves back at Binu, Throneson tried to extricate Arias and his other men from the field. They could not remain in place, as that would subject them to increased mortar barrages and most probably a counterattack, but a withdrawal required them to retire in full view of enemy machine gunners and riflemen. Throneson felt he had little choice but to execute a pullback and ordered his mortars to provide as much cover as possible.

Private Loveland and Private Bulger had remained in the kunai grass since the opening moments, hoping to catch a lull in the fighting during which they could pull back. Most men had chosen to slide sideways two hundred yards to the right, where jungle foliage provided protection, but each time Loveland and Bulger tried they came under heavy fire. "We felt naked as a jaybird and knew that any enemy sniper in a tree could spot our progress through the grass," Private Bulger wrote later.

Loveland and Bulger laboriously crawled on their bellies, keeping as low as possible in the tall grass to provide smaller targets. The pair came upon one Raider, delirious from his wounds and lack of water, and concluded the only way the injured man could reach safety was if they carried him out of the field. Loveland and Bulger rose from the grass, picked up the helpless Raider, and shuffled as quickly as they could under the burden toward the jungle. They ignored the enemy bullets, as "by that time we simply didn't give a damn,"[43] and somehow dodged enemy mortar shells and bullets to make it safely to the tree line, where other Raiders dragged them to safety.

Not far from Loveland and Bulger, Private Arias pondered his next move as mortar shells hurled clumps of dirt on him. In the confusion of the battle Arias had not received the message to pull back. "It was hotter than hell, and mortars were hitting behind me. I laid there and said the hell with these people and started crawling back. I was alone now in the grass. Before you know it I heard somebody else, and it was a guy from our platoon looking for something to eat. He didn't have his weapon. We crawled and crawled."[44]

Throughout the course of the afternoon C Company Raiders filtered across the kunai grass field to the jungle along the right flank. When Private First Class Onstad finally exited the field, the nonsmoker grabbed a couple of cigarettes from another Marine and deeply inhaled. "I did suck in two or three of those," he wrote. "I wanted to cry, but I could not. I was too dehydrated. I could not produce tears."[45]

While Throneson extracted his company from the field, Captain McAuliffe faced confusion to the north. After being pinned down with the point squad, McAuliffe led his men in one direction while Pl. Sgt. Harold Schrier took the rest of the platoon back to the coconut grove. Schrier waited until almost dark for McAuliffe to arrive, but when he failed to appear, Schrier started back to Binu.

McAuliffe did not rejoin Schrier because he had trouble navigating the field. Each path McAuliffe followed led to more enemy fire. Near exasperation, he told the native scout to take them to his home in the nearby hills, where they waited for matters to calm.

McAuliffe and nine men stumbled into Binu around three p.m., a few hours before Schrier's group, looking so exhausted that they reminded Peatross of the weary Raiders who reached the submarine that second night at Makin. Peatross headed to the command post with McAuliffe, who reported to Carlson that he had brought with him what he assumed were the sole survivors from his reinforced platoon. Schrier and the rest, McAuliffe thought, must have been killed. Upon hearing the report, Carlson's face flushed with anger, but the colonel controlled his emotions sufficiently to ask McAuliffe for the last known location of his platoon. Carlson sent Peatross and a platoon from B Company to the area to search for survivors.

John Mather, who stood near Carlson, wrote that McAuliffe was "quite hysterical and exhausted." He questioned McAuliffe about his tactics in pulling his men off the battlefield, and "I formed the opinion that this particular officer had no idea of what he should have done and that very likely he would have been successful in bringing home his whole force if he had known to move it by sections and to employ covering fire to do so. He certainly did not appreciate the enormity of his offence in abandoning a portion of his force whilst engaging with the enemy."[46]

Peatross had taken his men only a short distance before they met Platoon Sergeant Schrier guiding the remainder of D Company back to Binu. Schrier reported that after being cut off from McAuliffe and the point, he gathered the remainder of the platoon, including two dead and a handful of wounded, held muster to see who was missing, then waited for McAuliffe. In the heat of combat, while the sergeant had taken every proper step available, the company commander had allowed himself to be cut off from his men.

At three thirty, Carlson, accompanied by Schwerin's F Company and the rest of B Company, left Binu. With McAuliffe out of action and Throneson in need of help, Carlson headed to the only place he hoped he could make a difference—the battlefield.

Carlson arrived at the coconut grove in less than one hour to find a disconcerting scene. In Carlson's opinion, C Company was in disarray, with Throneson walking in a daze a mile behind the front lines. From all he could discern, Throneson's only offensive action was to employ his mortars. He apparently had not advanced anywhere. Carlson quickly moved to the kunai grass field with Throneson following at his heels.

Around four fifteen Carlson radioed Henderson Field to arrange for an air strike. To ensure accuracy he had Private Loveland and Private Bulger fashion a rude arrow out of T-shirts pointing directly at the jungle locations of the Japanese. The privates collected twenty T-shirts, carefully constructed a huge arrow, then watched as ten minutes later six aircraft bombed and strafed the indicated sectors.

Once the aircraft left, Carlson sent Schwerin and Peatross to scout the jungle. Except for the dead, no sign of the enemy existed anywhere. The Japanese had withdrawn to the south. With dark closing in, Carlson left Schwerin's F Company and one platoon of B Company at the front while he took the rest of the force back to Binu.

"It Was a Lovely Armistice Day"

Due largely to Washburn's steady hand, the Raiders registered a decisive victory at Asamana. Carlson estimated the number of enemy killed at

160—twenty-four by C Company, sixteen by McAuliffe's men, and 120 by Washburn's E Company. The Raiders lost ten killed and thirteen wounded.

Displeased with the actions of Captain Throneson and Captain McAuliffe, as well as with one of his lieutenants from C Company, Carlson relieved the officers three days after the battle. He stated in his report about his two captains that he removed them due to their "incompetency. Both had displayed total ineptitude for leadership in battle, and both were so badly shaken by their experience as to be incapable of commanding my confidence or that of their men."[47] At the same time he praised the other officers, particularly Washburn, for their stout leadership.

In his book about the Raiders, Captain Peatross stated that Carlson's dismissal of McAuliffe had destroyed a promising career before the officer had a chance to learn from his mistakes. Peatross wondered if Carlson had not acted in the heat of the moment, and mentioned that Carlson had conveniently forgotten the errors he committed at Makin.

Proper or not, Carlson evaluated a situation and took action to remedy the lapses. Some leaders overlook faults in their subordinates, either because they are unwilling to take action or, more likely, because they think the relief of an officer under their command is a poor reflection on their own leadership skills.

Carlson had the good sense to select promising men, like Washburn, and to relieve those he felt were not up to the test. When confronted with the enemy, Washburn took control of events by immediately organizing a counterattack to confound the Japanese. Throneson and McAuliffe had not, instead allowing events to control them.

On that day, Armistice Day, November 11, Captain Washburn's father wrote his son, "I was in the front lines off Verdun on November 11, 1918. I wonder what you are doing today."[48]

The father would have been proud to learn what the son had accomplished. Carlson was so impressed with Washburn that he promoted him to major. "He used his head," he confided to *Time* magazine's correspondent Robert Sherrod. "I promoted him on the spot and it was good for morale, because every man in the company knew that Washburn deserved it."[49]

Typically, Washburn wrote his father that he had no idea why he had been promoted. "I was a little lucky one day and the colonel (mistakenly) thought I had done a good job," stated Washburn. "So I move up—just the luck of the Irish, that's all."[50]

Later, when fellow officers suggested he deserved a Purple Heart for the bullet that grazed his boot, Washburn declined. According to June Washburn, the officer's wife, he preferred that his men receive the acclaim, not himself.

The nationally prominent radio commentator Raymond Swing, a friend of Carlson's, chipped in the same day by featuring the Raiders in his November 11 broadcast. Swing told his large audience that they could learn much from such a splendid battalion.

"The Marines are tough, but there is a special branch of the Marines which is especially tough. These men are called Carlson's Raiders." He added, "They are a peculiarly American brand of commandos, and I repeat that they are tougher than Marines, if there can be such a thing."

Swing explained that what gave the Raiders their uniqueness was the democratic ways Colonel Carlson tried to follow. Swing continued that while many strive for an improved world, "there is none more inspiring than these tough Raiders under Evans Carlson. They are going to whip the craftiest and sturdiest of the enemy, and do it all the more ably, by knowing why they are fighting and the kind of world they want. They are a steady invitation to all civilian Americans to think as hard and live as hard for true democracy as they are doing it in Guadalcanal. Such men will win us a genuine armistice day if the civilians back home don't lag behind in their thinking."[51]

The next month Carlson thanked Swing for the fine broadcast. He explained that on November 11 a group of five hundred Japanese had escaped a trap, but at Asamana, "By pure luck my patrols were across their path." Carlson claimed that his men fought "with satisfactory results. It was a lovely Armistice Day."[52]

He had a right to be proud. In August he had allowed his Raiders at Makin to become bogged down in what had been their only set battle to date. Asamana proved different. Because he had split his patrols into four arms, he created a perfect opportunity to execute a flanking maneuver on the enemy. When one arm fell under fire, the others could swing to its aid. He had engaged a larger force than at Makin and, due to his plan, to the leadership skills of men like Captain Washburn, and to the bravery of Private Auman and others, had forced them to withdraw.

Carlson now turned to the main portion of the Long Patrol, a rugged four-week stint in Guadalcanal's jungles that tested every tenet of Carlson's gung ho system.

The Law of the Jungle

After Asamana, Carlson entered the second of three phases in his Long Patrol, where the freewheeling Carlson, unhampered by operational plans or formal orders, orchestrated a dynamic guerrilla campaign. Flanking moves, hit-and-run attacks, speed, stealth, and surprise earmarked this stage, as Carlson disappeared into the jungles in pursuit of Colonel Shoji's retreating forces. Uncertain and hesitant at Makin, Carlson relished his independence at Guadalcanal, where he waged war the way he envisioned. Turned loose on the Japanese and guided only by his own rules, Carlson tore into the jungle with a vengeance. In the process he proved the value of his gung ho methods and helped shatter the myth of the Japanese superman.

"Kill or Be Killed, End of Story"

The day following Asamana, Carlson returned to the battlefield to mop up any Japanese forces that remained. Captain Schwerin had already determined that the bulk of the enemy had fled to the south, so Carlson spent much of the day searching for and burying dead Raiders.

Raiders scouring the site of C Company's fight with Shoji's troops came across a grisly discovery when they found the mutilated body of Pvt. Owen Barber staked to the ground. Pfc. James F. Clusker, Jr., who had spent a frightening night in the kunai grass avoiding the Japanese, related the details.

After being wounded in the fight, Clusker lapsed in and out of consciousness into the night. He awoke after dark, parched and smarting from a stomach wound, when he heard voices one hundred yards away. Managing a muted cry, the injured Raider received a chilling response. "Over here, Yankee, over here."[1]

Clusker knew that no Raider would speak in that manner, so he lay still in the grass and hoped that the enemy would pass by. At one point the Japanese closed to within five yards of the Raider, who tensed with each step, but they moved on without spotting him.

A welcome relief ended when screams pierced the nighttime stillness. The Japanese had discovered the wounded Private Owen not far from Clusker and made him the object of their barbarity. Clusker lay all night in his kunai grass sanctuary, trying to block out Barber's shrieks as the Japanese tortured him.

Private Loveland gazed at Barber's body in stoic silence as anger and hatred simmered. Knife slashes, too many to count, disfigured Barber's once youthful face, but what most disturbed Loveland and the other Raiders was not the lifeless body of a compatriot, nor the lacerations. The Japanese had castrated Barber and stuffed his testicles in his mouth.

"I remember seeing him there," recalled Private Gay of E Company in 2008. "He was a young fellow, I think only seventeen. That made us decide, OK, no prisoners. We didn't really have a chance to catch that many before, but after this . . ."[2] Gay's voice trailed off, his silence completing the thought.

The Raiders currently held two prisoners. After observing Barber's mangled body, Carlson asked a group of Raiders if any had a friend killed in the previous day's fighting. When a few raised their hands, Carlson pointed to the prisoners and told them to take care of them. The men led the prisoners into the jungle, killed them, and left their lifeless bodies to rot in Guadalcanal's heat.

For the remainder of the patrol, the Raiders showed no mercy to the enemy. Vengeance alone did not produce this desire. Practicality also entered into play. They barely carried sufficient food for themselves, let alone to feed an enemy, and Raiders would have to be taken from patrol assignments to guard the enemy. "We couldn't take care of them," explained Private First Class Kaplan. "What the hell are you going to do with them? It was just impossible." Other men, like Lieutenant Burnette, agreed. "We just couldn't do it. We couldn't be watching them all the time."[3]

Besides, the Raiders risked incurring the scouts' wrath in keeping Japanese alive. Ever since the Japanese had landed in Guadalcanal, they had abused the natives' women and killed their families. Vouza and his men sought retribution for that treatment. "Vouza," said Private Loveland of the famed scout, "he had a mean look and a sharp knife." Private Gay agreed with that assessment. "We didn't have the food to take prisoners, and if we had, the natives would have given us a hard time," said Private Gay. "The natives all had knives, and they were not peaceful fellows. One had a hatchet. They hated the Japanese and were really on our side."[4]

Every Raider had heard of the August massacre of the Goettge Patrol. Now they had their own evidence that this was to be a war without limits, one of kill or be killed. The laws of the jungle, not of man, ruled on Guadalcanal, and if the enemy wanted to fight that way, so would Carlson's men.

The Raiders took their cue from Colonel Carlson, who saw nothing contradictory in conducting a war ostensibly fought for democracy and fair play while employing brutal tactics. As long as a war had to be fought, he would wage it with the same severity and brutality as his foe. Carlson wrote Raymond Swing of a time at Guadalcanal when a reporter asked Carlson if he hated the Japanese. "He got the idea, I presume, from the thoroughness with which my men kill all Japs who appear in their path."[5]

Jim Lucas, a Marine combat correspondent who admired Carlson, wrote in a Marine Corps press release that "Colonel Carlson also teaches his men to hate, and to fight—efficiently, effectively." In a rough draft of Lucas's release that exists in the Evans Carlson Collection at Quantico, Virginia, Lucas quoted Carlson with words that a censor later removed before releasing it to the public.

"We never take a prisoner," Carlson said. "That's not our job. I tell my men to kill every Jap they meet—lame, halt and well. We've no accommodations to care for our prisoners." Carlson added of the Japanese, "They're too treacherous, for one thing. They killed most of our medical corpsmen who tried to help them, so we take no chances."[6]

Carlson did not try to suppress news of their actions with regard to prisoners and even addressed the issue in his action report, where he asserted that only one route led to victory in the Pacific. With the Japanese, "Be tenacious, persistent, aggressive, ruthless. He has no sense of honor where his opponent is concerned. We must be ruthless in exterminating him, whatever his condition may be. In similar circumstances we may expect no quarter. Moreover, destruction of the military power of the enemy is the subject of this war. This means systematic and persistent killing of the men who compose that power. The sooner it can be accomplished, the better."[7]

Some of the Raiders believed that Carlson hated the Japanese because of what he had witnessed in China. "You have to understand one thing," said Sgt. Nathan Lipscomb. "Carlson hated, I mean hated, the Japanese. I guess he had a reason when he was in China. As far as I know we sent back two, but Carlson basically wanted them all killed." As Private Loveland said, "It was kill or be killed, end of story."[8]

Pfc. Edward T. Hammer of D Company describes a time they captured a prisoner. "I took one prisoner to Colonel Carlson. He said, 'Boys, we don't have facilities to take prisoners.' Boom. He shot him. He was laying on the ground, and Carlson just shot him. I was standing right there."[9]

If the Japanese were going to utilize such brutal tactics, the Raiders would answer in kind. "We didn't take any prisoners," explained Pfc. Thomas Tobin of C Company. "Some people might say that's horrible, but hey, that's war. That's the way it is. The Japanese had no mercy to us."[10]

Private First Class Quirk attended a Chicago-area Catholic school, where he learned to recite the catechism by rote to avoid retribution from strict nuns, but he had few qualms about what he now had to do. "We couldn't take them with us. They captured and tortured a Raider. It was a brutal war." Quirk spoke of "Making that transition from being a kid going to junior college, to this," a transformation each Raider on the Long Patrol had to endure. "I didn't have hostile feelings toward anyone, that's not my nature. But you learn it's gotta be your nature. The law of the jungle—kill or be killed. It didn't bother me, because I knew that's the way the game was played."[11]

That is why one Raider—enraged over what the Japanese had done to his parents, civilians captured in the Philippines—could so readily slit the throat of two Japanese prisoners, while another could later write in his diary in a matter-of-fact manner about wading through the bodies of dead Japanese. "I found one alive but wounded and I shot him. He watched me with his eyes all the while."[12]

While the Barber incident set the tone for the Long Patrol, Carlson had first established that attitude during training at Jacques Farm. Carlson reminded his men that they had to steel themselves for whatever type of war the South Pacific offered. Guadalcanal featured its own brand of savagery. As the Raiders plunged deep into the island's jungles for the middle stage of their patrol, they were prepared to fight the enemy on his own terms.

"The Signal to Give 'Em Hell!"

From November 12 to November 24, the Raiders concentrated on clearing the area between the Metapona and Lunga rivers, eleven miles of winding rivers, kunai grass fields, tangled underbrush, and jungle canopies. Hot on Shoji's trail as the Japanese attempted to join the main force west of the perimeter, Carlson's men engaged in near-daily ambushes and firefights as they pursued their foe.

November 12 offered a taste of what was to come. Carlson assigned his companies search sectors along both sides of the Metapona River. As Captain Peatross's men scouted the banks, they spotted a native boat containing three Japanese soldiers paddling toward them. Rather than shoot them, which might alert Japanese forces lurking nearby, the Raiders allowed the boat to float closer, then leaped into the water to grab the three. In the scrap that ensued, the Raiders had to kill one of the Japanese, but captured the other two and held them for a brief interrogation before disposing of the enemy.

In the field abutting the village, Washburn located the body of Private Auman slumped over the tripod of his machine gun, but the gun was missing. Raiders later discovered the gun in the river, apparently tossed there by Auman or his gunner to keep it from enemy hands, a last noble deed performed by a man who knew he was soon to die.

"I have a picture of the three graves," Washburn wrote in 1963, "which we dug when we returned, and the date [of their deaths], of course, is November 11, 1942. I remember how ironical I thought it at the time that we were fighting, dying, & killing on that date which commemerated [sic] the end of the War to end all Wars."[13]

Later that day the first of what turned out to be a steady stream of Japanese stragglers stumbled into Asamana, unaware that the Marines controlled their bivouac. At periodic intervals throughout the night, the Raiders killed twenty-five Japanese. All they had to do was wait until another one or two enemy soldiers appeared, kill them, and then wait for more. It was so simple that Carlson later stated, "It was like shooting ducks from a blind."[14]

The next morning scouts reported large numbers of enemy forces in the jungle to their north, west, and south. Carlson radioed for artillery support and ordered C Company up from Binu to strengthen his numbers.

The artillery barrage caused the Japanese to rush from their shelter in a series of attacks against Carlson's base at Asamana. A lookout posted in a tree called in the incredulous report that a clump of brush moved toward them from the west. Carlson swung his binoculars to what appeared to be moving foliage eight hundred yards out, only to notice two companies of enemy soldiers, camouflaged from head to toe in vines and leaves, inching forward. The Japanese advanced one hundred yards, halted for a few minutes to see if the Raiders had detected their presence, then moved forward again. Carlson waited until the targets drew within one hundred yards, then poured artillery as well as machine-gun and mortar fire on the enemy. Within minutes the Japanese attack collapsed, treating the Raiders to the unusual spectacle of watching foliage-shrouded soldiers rushing away.

Carlson rebuffed five separate enemy attacks on November 13, each time drawing the Japanese closer, where his artillery-backed Raiders could be more effective. At times their own artillery shells landed so close to Raider positions that Carlson ordered his communications man, Sergeant McCullough, to radio the Tenth Artillery to readjust their fire.

"Are you scared, Mac?" Carlson asked McCullough during one particularly heavy barrage. When McCullough admitted he was, Carlson replied, "Well, don't worry. I am, too."[15]

The spectacle unnerved Pfc. William D. Lansford until he looked at his commander, Captain Washburn. While the enemy surged forward and bullets snapped nearby, Washburn stood in the open, calmly directing his men. "Our leader's bravery was most reassuring to us nervous privates,"[16] stated Lansford.

After repulsing the series of attacks, Carlson returned to Binu that afternoon before leading a patrol to Volinivu on the west side of the Metapona. In conjunction with Marine commanders from other units operating along the coast, Carlson moved his base of operations from Binu to Asamana, from where he would patrol the terrain south and west of Binu. Once having cleared the area from Binu to Asamana, Carlson could leap westward to a new sector.

The next morning scouts informed Carlson that a group of Japanese soldiers had sought shelter to the east in a jungle sanctuary five miles south of Binu along the west bank of the Balesuna River. At eleven a.m. Capt. Wild Bill Schwerin, guided as always by the scouts, led a patrol from F Company out of camp to the site.

Wild Bill, lugging a twelve-gauge shotgun and two .45 pistols, scouted the enemy position, which could only be attacked through a narrow defile guarded by a sentry. Schwerin and his men waited patiently in the jungle for three hours until the sentry turned back to the camp for his lunch, then slowly moved through the opening. Eighty feet distant two groups of enemy soldiers sat around campfires, eating rice balls, while their rifles rested against trees out of their reach.

Schwerin divided his patrol and assigned each half one of the Japanese groups. "When you hear my shotgun," Schwerin told his Raiders, "that's the signal to give 'em hell!"[17]

Schwerin crawled closer, then rose and emptied his shotgun at the enemy. With that signal his Raiders turned their automatic weapons on the Japanese, wiping them out in under one minute, while the scouts hastened in and slit the throats of any Japanese still breathing. Schwerin's men killed fifteen Japanese and recovered weapons and documents, including some of the personal effects of Japanese Major General Kiyotaki Kawaguchi, who had earlier led the charges against the Marines at Henderson Field.

This ambush encapsulated the tactics Carlson had attempted to instill during Raider training. Traveling light and living off the land, his men, while carrying heavy firepower, had surprised the enemy by ambushing the Japanese in their own stronghold.

This and other such raids over the next three weeks debilitated Shoji's forces. Already weary from evading the coastal trap and from the fight at Asamana, Shoji now had to worry that, at any moment, Carlson's Raiders would materialize from the jungle. They could never let their guard down, could never remain long in one spot for fear that Vouza's scouts would soon be on their tail. What had once been their ally—Guadalcanal's jungles—had now become their liability. Carlson had penetrated their domain and had removed one of their most valuable assets.

Knowing he had the enemy on the run, Carlson intensified the pressure. For the next two days his Raiders scoured west and south of Binu, seeking out and destroying any enemy stragglers they encountered. By November 16 they had shoved the enemy west out of the Binu-Asamana region and forced them to regroup on the Metapona's other side.

After clearing the region east of the Metapona River, Carlson organized company-size scouting expeditions that crossed the river and concentrated on the three-mile-wide stretch of jungle between the Metapona and the Nalimbiu Rivers, the second of the four major rivers running in parallel courses between Binu and Henderson Field. They engaged in daily encounters, rang-ing from a handful of men to platoon-size clashes. "We were constantly running into those little characters and having shootouts,"[18] said Captain Washburn of the fast-paced action.

"The Steel Was Underneath"

From the middle of November until the first week of December, Carlson pursued Shoji's troops in the classic guerrilla-style mission he had sought since his days in Nicaragua and China. The Raiders hounded their haggard opponents through the jungle and across streams, in kunai grass fields and along hill crests. With his tactics and leadership Carlson confused the numerically superior Japanese, corralled them to the west side of Guadalcanal, and helped gain security for the tenuous perimeter at Henderson Field.

On November 16–17, patrols picked up signs indicating that the enemy had all but abandoned the three-mile area between the Metapona and Nalimbiu rivers for the hills to the west. It appeared that if Carlson were to continue dislodging the Japanese, he would need to force them out of the five-mile stretch of jungle and kunai grass fields between the Nalimbiu and the upper Tenaru rivers, then scale the precipitous jungle-clad hills and mountains that dominated the terrain south of Henderson.

Looming above every other natural feature, standing as an ever-present reminder that victory could only be claimed when Carlson possessed it, was Mount Austen, the lofty 1,514-foot prominence that commanded a superb view of Marine movements at Henderson Field.

On November 17, General Vandegrift summoned Carlson from the jungle to discuss the next phase of the Raider operations. Vandegrift wanted Carlson to first clear the Nalimbiu-Tenaru area, then locate the main trail behind Mount Austen along which the Japanese brought in men and supplies from the west. Once complete, Carlson was to scale Mount Austen and search for enigmatic Pistol Pete, the generic name given to Japanese artillery that had rained shells on the Marines inside the perimeter. Patrols from Henderson Field had failed to locate the big guns in the dense growth blanketing Mount Austen and its adjoining summits, so Vandegrift told Carlson and his unconventional battalion to find and destroy the guns.

Carlson returned to his command post and outlined the next stages to his officers. From their base camp on the Nalimbiu, they would scout the Nalimbiu-Tenaru region. Once that had been cleared of opposition, Carlson would move his camp to the upper Tenaru River as his base for further operations into the hills.

Within a week he would stand along the upper Tenaru River two miles south of the perimeter, gazing at the slippery slopes of Mount Austen towering nearby.

Throughout the Long Patrol, whether the action involved squad-sized units or company-strength detachments, Carlson relied on the same tactics to defeat Shoji's troops. From his base camp, Carlson fanned out patrols to explore nearby trails, jungles, and fields. When one portion of his patrol encountered the enemy, they formed a defense line to hold the Japanese in place while Carlson swung his other units toward the fighting in a flanking or an enveloping maneuver. Unlike Makin, where a rigid operations plan dictated the Raider movement, at Guadalcanal Carlson was free to select his own course. He neither received nor issued an operations plan, instead relying on an improvisational, swift method of attack that guerrilla commanders most loved.

Carlson divided his six-company battalion into three teams of two companies each. While one team remained at the base camp in reserve, the other two teams headed into the jungles or the fields in pursuit of the enemy. Both teams were to contact Carlson at the base camp every two hours, or as soon as hostilities occurred. In this manner, Carlson maintained the ability to speedily shift companies from one sector to another or to order the reserve company into action as reinforcement.

"Our strategy was to send platoon and company size patrols, operating from a Raider base," wrote Captain Apergis. "The companies operated in echelon of columns to the left and apart from each other. In other words, a company operated independently and as soon as the enemy was engaged one platoon would establish a base of automatic fire, and the rest of the columns would outflank the enemy formation. Search-find-attack and outflank. With our superior fire power, we overwhelmed any Japanese unit or encampment we encountered."[19]

The chief of staff of the First Marine Division, Lt. Col. Merrill B. Twining, explained that Carlson succeeded on the Long Patrol because he performed the unexpected. The Japanese had often followed the same tactics when attacked—dig in and fight to the death. While that eventually resulted in their defeat, it forced the Marines to pay a heavy price. Most Marine officers, according to Twining, hoped to avoid such carnage by utilizing the "collar and ass" approach—deploying the main force to locate the enemy and hold them in place—hold the collar—while an enveloping unit hit the enemy's right or left flank—hit them in the ass.

Such an enveloping maneuver by a smaller force was often ineffective in the jungle, however. The Japanese simply ignored the weaker flanking unit and focused on the main body that had first contacted them.

Carlson reversed the order and used his main body as the enveloping force. While the embattled company held the Japanese in place and made them think they were the main force, other companies converged and struck at a right angle to the line of advance. In doing so, Carlson directed an unexpected attack in strength against the enemy flank or rear. "For the first time in the Guadalcanal campaign," wrote Twining of Carlson's operations, "maneuver alone operated to our advantage." Twining added that "Carlson used this maneuver several times during the course of his pursuit, always to good effect."[20]

Years later Raiders marveled at the tactics. "They would put up a front," said Sergeant McCullough, "but then there'd be a circling action. While they was keeping them busy at one place, they'd hit 'em at another."[21]

The tactics provided the script, but Carlson's fire teams supplied the punch. Carlson declared in his Long Patrol report that the fire teams, carrying their M1 rifle, Tommy gun, and BAR, "worked beautifully" and "left little to be desired."[22]

One of the Raiders, Pfc. William J. Onstad, later compared the fire teams to his high school football squad, where each individual had certain responsibilities and each man looked out for the other. He stated that their firepower gave the Raiders an advantage that the Japanese could never counter. "Imagine the surprise of the Japanese when they met up with a ten-man squad of Raiders in the dark or on a jungle trail. Within fifteen seconds the Japanese would be caught in an organized hail of 275 bullets."[23]

The increased firepower instilled confidence in the Raiders. The enemy could not hope to match their weaponry, and, armed with that knowledge, the men headed optimistically into action.

"When you're first fired at, your tendency is to stay still," explained Private First Class Quirk, "but that's when you've got to move. You've got to get fire superiority by firing back, and we had so much firepower. The Japanese had those single bolt rifles, which was like kid stuff to us. And we were not afraid, because we know from our training that the answer to survival is getting superiority in firepower. We had that drilled into us, and it gave us a lot of confidence. The fear is there, but you move. You're like a boxer. When you're hit you instinctively come back at them. The best response is aggressive, not defensive and negative."[24]

Added to the divergent patrols and the fire teams was a third element of Carlson's success—speed. As Shoji's columns retreated westward, Carlson repeatedly struck at his flanks and rear, usually in small-scale clashes that ended within thirty minutes. Like hounds nipping at a fox's feet, the Raiders crept up on the Japanese, struck swiftly, then hastily retired in guerrilla-like fashion.

Similar to those guerrillas in Nicaragua and China, Carlson's men popped up at unexpected places and retreated to unpredictable locations, rarely remaining long at one camp. "The reason I think we were more successful than our enemies," wrote Private First Class Onstad, "was because we did not spend two nights in the same place. We were on the move every day."[25]

Speed was vital in that vile terrain, where lingering in one spot was to risk being caught in a counterattack. Martin Clemens credited Jacob Vouza's scouts with helping Carlson succeed where another unit might fail because they guided the Raiders along jungle paths through uncharted wilderness and enabled the Raiders to travel lighter than a more conventional unit could. Carlson "would not have got far without scouts and carriers."[26]

He applied the lessons of the Eighth Route Army at Guadalcanal. "He tried to make Chinese out of us," explained Private Hasenberg. "He'd say that the Chinese could march fifty miles in a day on nothing but a handful of rice, so that's what we had at Guadalcanal."[27]

The training begun at Jacques Farm produced greater results in the kunai grass, jungles, ravines, and ridges of Guadalcanal than at Makin. "If we hadn't had superior training we just couldn't have stood the guff,"[28] said Pvt. Edward Grajczik after the patrol ended.

They also benefited from Carlson's presence, who not only seemed to become calmer as the situation grew riskier but who also, at his advanced age, outwalked and outhiked the younger Raiders he commanded. Private Gay recalled the time when he almost passed out because he had not taken his salt tablets. Carlson checked on Gay, then scurried ahead to be with the point. "Here was this guy who outwalked us all. It gave us the feeling that if he could do it, so can I."[29]

Men all along the patrol lines grew accustomed to seeing Carlson suddenly appear, sharing a few friendly words and then moving on. Pvt. Ashley W. Fisher of B Company claimed one reason stood above the rest for their success at Guadalcanal—Carlson. "Our success was due to our leadership, which was the result of the tone set by Lt. Col. Carlson. He was everywhere and seemed never to be tired! His style was personal. If he asked you to do something, you could bet that he was doing as much. If you didn't eat, he didn't eat."[30]

John Mather worried that Carlson needlessly exposed himself to harm by so frequently walking with the point, but he wanted to be where the greatest risks prevailed. Lieutenant Burnette claimed that Carlson dashed to the front so often for no other reason than, "He's Carlson." He wanted to be with his men and believed actions spoke more firmly than did words. Pl. Sgt. Rhel Cook of F Company stated that Carlson was a "surprisingly quiet man," but that "the steel was underneath."[31]

Carlson's impressive knowledge of the Japanese mind and tactics helped him plot counteractions for Shoji's moves. "Carlson seemed to be miles away mentally when we were near a fire fight," said Gunny Sgt. Dick Staihr. "He knew the Oriental mind, how they operated militarily, and was two or three steps ahead of them all the time."[32]

Carlson's instincts amazed Captain Washburn. "I think the operation was a great success and Col. Carlson was a fearless, inspirational leader. He seemed to have a sixth sense as to where the enemy was located and what he was going to do. The statistics speak for themselves. We did much to relieve pressure on the perimeter."[33]

Many Raiders recall times when Carlson paced along the trail with them, suddenly halted as if detecting a presence, and blended into the jungle. "He seemed to have a very good knowledge of how the Japanese behaved," said Private First Class Kaplan. "On one occasion, on a march, we stopped and he and a couple of Raiders went off into the bush. We heard some gunshots and they came back carrying a Japanese pack. How the hell he knew there was a Japanese soldier out there I'll never know."[34]

The post-Asamana period was vintage Carlson, for he now navigated a world with which he was familiar. Here he could implement the tactics he observed and utilized in his previous postings.

"I thought he did quite well at Guadalcanal," said Pvt. Ben Carson. "He seemed more firm here than at Makin. When we were at Jacques Farm, we were always taught to know more than the enemy knows,"[35] which according to Carson did not seem to be true at Makin.

Guadalcanal, though, was something different.

"This Is No Place for You"

The Raiders awakened on November 18 like they did every other day on the Long Patrol. Shortly after dawn, platoon sergeants walked among clusters of sleeping men, igniting them to life with brusque shouts to "Get off your asses!" Many Raiders, their schedules set to an internal clock, needed no prodding, and few had enjoyed a sound sleep on the hard jungle ground anyway. They arose, heated some tea over the fire if time permitted, swallowed a cracker or some rice, and gathered their gear.

Unless they enjoyed the aid of a native carrier, every enlisted Raider lugged as much as eighty pounds of equipment with him. Private First Class Onstad packed two .45 pistols, one Browning Automatic Rifle, one belt of ammunition containing five hundred rounds, a Bowie knife, two canteens of water, four hand grenades, his pack with pup tent and sleeping bag, and a shovel. Radio communications men, like Private First Class Kaplan, labored with the bulky radio, whose four parts required three men or native carriers to carry its 120 pounds.

With the command of "Saddle up!"—Raiders used that over the more conventional "Fall in!" as if forging a connection with their military predecessors in the cavalry—the companies fell into place and set off single file along the trail in search of Shoji and his men. The native scouts were posted to the front of the company line with the squad whose turn it was to be the point, while rear guards took position to keep a watch on movement behind the company's line. When in more open terrain, flank guards moved fifty yards from the main line should the enemy draw uncomfortably close, while in the denser jungle spots, where they could barely see ten yards ahead, the flanks drew within a few paces or blended altogether into the line.

"A lot of it was open, and I mean where you could see twenty-five to thirty feet in front of you," said Private Loveland. "A lot of times you're completely covered over with vines, but on the side of a hill or a riverbank it's as wide open as a sidewalk in town. We walked accordingly. If it was wide open we spaced ourselves up and either hurried across or had fire protection and got across."

While the Raiders could easily move two to three miles each hour in open terrain, the pace slowed in denser areas, where they hacked through tentacle-like webs formed by the foliage and jungle vines. "Branches grabbed at us and slowed us down," stated Loveland. "As you got into the real thick part, we had to march hand on pack, your hand on the pack of the guy in front of you. It was so dense you had to do that. That happened normally real early in the morning or as it was getting dusk. If we heard a shot we'd all fall and get into the jungle, and wait to see what happened."[36]

In marching along the trail the line often resembled a slender green snake, moving haltingly at times and rapidly at others. Because of the fits and starts, Raiders at the end of the line had difficulty keeping pace with the men ahead. The front portion moved smoothly across kunai fields and open areas, which required the tail end to step more lively to avoid falling behind, but when the point encountered obstacles, the entire column slowed.

Private Gay learned the hard way to avoid sitting during breaks. "I was in a machine gun squad, and we carried eighty pounds of ammunition, using mortar bags that had compartments in front and another in back, then a box in each hand with a strap. I'll tell you, walking through those rivers and jungles with eighty pounds of that on you, plus your personal gear, was a job. The first time we stopped for a break, I sat down. When we had to go again, I couldn't get up. Every time we'd stop for a break after that, I'd lean against a tree instead of sitting down."[37]

Few marks distinguished officer from enlisted. Neither Carlson nor any other officer wore emblems, and after a few days on Guadalcanal, everyone's uniform looked the same—ragged, torn, and dirty.

Jacob Vouza or other scouts, assisted by the Raider point platoon, led the mile-long procession of Raiders as it wound through the jungle or crossed kunai grass fields. Cognizant of the dangers inherent in being the point unit, where contact with the enemy often first occurred, Captain Washburn and other officers alternated the point platoons, but they had no control over Colonel Carlson. The commander frequently walked at the front of the long company column, ignoring Washburn's or Griffith's requests to fall back to the main group and its relative safety.

"When Carlson was with us, he and I were the point," explained Captain Griffith in patrolling with D Company. "Normally the company commander is back a little, but not Carlson. I had to go with him. There'd be one man ahead of us."[38]

Carlson gave fits to F Company's Pl. Sgt. Rhel Cook. It seemed that whenever his platoon had the point, Carlson materialized at the exposed position, but the hardened Marine veteran, whom Carlson called Cookie, handled it in his usual blustery style.

"I made him leave the point. As soon as he came up I'd stop the point. I'd tell him, 'Get out of here, Colonel. This is no place for you. I'm not moving the point until you get back to the main body." He'd say, 'Cookie, I want to see what's going on.' I'd say, 'Well, you just get back to the main body and we'll make sure you know what's going on.' He'd go mumbling off by himself."

Cook sometimes succeeded, sometimes not. Even when he did convince Carlson to leave, he soon reappeared with a query or comment. "He always seemed to know when we were going to run into trouble. He might come up and say pull the point back a little bit, or extend the front. We kept a space between the point and the main body. He was really a father figure to so many of us."[39]

As they moved west, the Raiders came across numerous signs of distress among Shoji's troops. Abandoned equipment and dead Japanese, many felled by malaria or some other tropical disease, littered the trails near the Nalimbiu River. With bodies rapidly decomposing in the oppressive humidity, Raiders often came upon little more than uniform-shrouded skeletons.

Carlson patrolled each area until he was certain the enemy had been cleared. Normally that took two or three days, at which time he advanced his battalion base west to a new location. In this manner he maneuvered through the jungle toward the Tenaru and Lunga rivers.

"The Jungle Was Jap"

Carlson selected one of the most abysmal places to wage war. Guadalcanal's natural terrain provided challenges enough, but along with the rivers and jungles and ridges came other tests—mosquitoes, leeches, blisters, and ringworm sapped their strength, while malaria-infested water, crocodiles, spiders, and a weird cacophony of nighttime sounds assaulted their nerves. The Raiders faced more adversities in their month on the island than they had tolerated in their lifetimes. As Captain Washburn pointed out, fighting in the Solomons "was grueling as hell. Believe me, that jungle could be an enemy in itself."[40]

Like the sand, heat, windstorms, and thirst that challenged T. E. Lawrence in the Arabian desert, Guadalcanal tested Carlson and his Raiders in unimaginable ways. They battled two enemies on the island—the Japanese and their ally, the jungle. As the correspondent John Hersey pointed out, while the American military possessed certain advantages, "the jungle was Jap."[41]

The Raiders entered an eerie world unlike any other they had experienced. The slimy, dense foliage emitted an ever-present putrid, dank odor that hovered over the battalion wherever it moved. John Hersey claimed the jungle "had seemed alien, almost poisonous,"[42] a statement few Raiders would dispute.

Thousands of fallen leaves covered the narrow jungle trails with a slippery blanket, making walking perilous. Here and there as they trod along, a Raider would lose his balance and crash to the ground, weighed down by the ammunition and equipment he carried. Sunlight often helped little, as the jungle canopy blocked access to much of the daylight. Scouts and the men on the point had to hack through branches and vines, especially the wicked, hook-festooned liana vines that handily ensnarled men and lacerated their skin. "It was just like removing porcupine quills,"[43] Loveland said of delicately prying loose each thorn from his skin.

Besides vines, the Raiders had to be wary of tripping over the banyan tree roots that spread out, tentacle-fashion, across the trail. During one patrol nineteen-year-old Pvt. Alton Adams stumbled as he walked, an action that dislodged the safety pin in one of his hand grenades. Rather than endanger the lives of those around him, Adams shouted that a hand grenade was about to explode. As he rushed off the trail, Adams reached for the grenade to hurl it away, but it exploded before he had the chance. The severely wounded Adams had to be evacuated, but his selfless thinking saved other men's lives.

Even worse was the shelter the twisted roots provided for hidden Japanese snipers. "The undergrowth was pretty heavy and you couldn't see far," explained Platoon Sergeant Cook. "The primary tree was the banyan tree. It kept expanding and the roots spread. You could practically get lost in it because the roots were all over. In a firefight they were great to hide in, but they could also be hiding a sniper. A Japanese might be within ten feet of me and I wouldn't see him."[44]

While the Raiders patrolled mostly in the jungle, they spent about one-third of their time trudging through kunai grass fields, which offered their own form of unpleasantness. Each step through the chest-high grass, through either heat, humidity, or drenching rain, shook lose hundreds of insects, and the Raiders had to be wary lest a Japanese sniper or machine-gun nest lay hidden in the grass.

Whether through jungle or field, rivers bisected the paths along which the Raiders advanced. Patrols often had to cross and recross the same meandering river as they searched a single sector, at times splashing through foot-deep water while at others battling torrents that reached to the armpits. "It seemed like we crossed the same one two or three times, there were so many small rivers," said Cpl. Frank M. Kurland of E Company. "At this one, the water was up to our chest, and the only way we crossed it was two men stood on the bank, one guy went into the water and grabbed his cartridge belt. Then a third would do the same until you had a human chain across. Everyone had one free hand to help the next guy coming in, and one arm on the belt of the guy ahead of him."[45] On other occasions patrols used ropes to bind the men together as they crossed swift-flowing streams.

Rude bridges, little more than logs loosely tied together, sometimes helped them traverse rivers and swamps. As the Raiders inched across, the logs became less stable and more slippery, tossing men and weapons into swamps or streams, an unappetizing prospect with crocodiles prowling about.

At least the cooling waters that swirled around their waists and feet offered temporary relief from the sweltering conditions, but it could also be a nuisance. Their footsteps stirred up the river's sand, which in turn weaseled into their boots and irritated their feet. Lieutenant Burnette's feet so bothered him that he finally removed his boots, slung them over his shoulder, and continued barefoot.

Besides the streams and rivers, Guadalcanal's daily rains added to their misery. "We were wet all the time," said Private Loveland. Uniforms felt like medieval suits of armor with the extra moisture, and rain coursed down their faces into their eyes. When the sun returned, the increased heat and humidity replaced the rain or river water with perspiration. "The sun would come out and it was stifling hot," said Lieutenant Burnette. Temperatures smashed the one-hundred-degree mark, a landmark made more excruciating in the thick humidity. "You'd pant, and you stopped and sat down, and panted. The water just dripped right off of you," added Loveland.[46]

Under those conditions it did not take long for the uniforms to rot. Platoon Sergeant Cook's trousers and dungaree jacket crumbled to pieces long before the patrol ended, but he had to make do with what he had. Within the patrol's first few days, Private Gay's socks decayed, and he tossed away his undershorts because they so badly irritated him.

This alien world belonged not only to the Japanese but also to the insects and animals that inhabited it. The Raiders listened to a stunning array of animal sounds—the mocking screech of parrots, monkeys screaming in the trees, land crabs and lizards scurrying about, and wild pigs munching on coconuts unnerved many a man during his first week in the jungle. One bird emitted a noise that sounded like a human banging two blocks of wood together, while another imitated a barking dog. A unique bird whistled three times, then received a similar answer from a second bird elsewhere in the trees. The night after the battle at Asamana, Private First Class Onstad wondered what caused the scratching and clawing he heard coming from the jungle. He investigated and found that a group of lizards had begun feasting upon some dead Japanese.

A startled Private Gay leaped up when a four-inch-wide spider crawled up his arm. Spiderwebs hung loosely from tree to tree, "and these damn spiders just sat in the middle, and you'd see them swaying in the wind. Those I didn't care for, and they were all over the damn place."[47] Those spiders bothered Gay more than the three-foot iguana he spotted once.

Private Loveland hated the centipedes that invaded him when he crossed fields, or the leeches that attached to his skin when he pushed into streams and swamps. After traversing a field, "There'd be 150 centipedes crawling up your leg. They were as long as your index finger and about as fat. It's no picnic. What bothered me more was where our belts fit. In the jungle there's these things like fleas and they got in and irritate you. Then there were the leeches when you went in the river. Them suckers would get right on you. We just pulled them off. It hurt, and we'd rub salt or iodine or whatever. That's just part of living."[48]

The worst, though, came from the millions of mosquitoes that inhabited Guadalcanal's many damp areas. Private First Class Kaplan one day counted sixty mosquitoes on his forearm alone. Men tied the bottoms of their pants to their boots and draped handkerchiefs from their helmets down over their necks to reduce exposed areas, but nothing completely succeeded.

"The mosquitoes were all over," said Private Leeman of C Company. "There was not much you could do to get away from the mosquitoes. You'd be slapping your arms."[49]

At night, men dropped netting over their faces and slept with their helmets on to protect themselves. "At night they came out in hordes," explained Private Hasenberg. "We had a mosquito netting that covered our head. You'd put it over your helmet and tie it around your collar. You'd put socks over your hands to keep the mosquitoes away and tuck your trousers in your socks. Otherwise they'd eat you alive."[50]

"We Were the Hunters"

Raider survivors claim, however, that rather than the animals or heat or vines, suspense was the worst part of the Long Patrol. They could never relax, day or night, for somewhere in that jungle or in those kunai grass fields Japanese soldiers waited to kill them. From Colonel Carlson to the lowliest private, one had to remain vigilant, for not to do so could mean death for them and for their buddies.

"Each step you're looking, always looking for the unexpected," said Corporal Kurland. "If they're waiting for you, they'll see you before you see them. Nothing you can do. If your time's up, it's up. You try to push it out of your mind."[51]

"It's not a good way to fight a war," added Sergeant Lipscomb. "You never know when you're going to run into somebody. You had to be alert all the time. At nighttime you heard sounds, and you don't know what they are. You imagine most anything."[52]

Even reporters recognized the strain Guadalcanal placed on Raiders and other American units. In 1944, a *New York Times* correspondent, Foster Hailey, wrote that "Guadalcanal was a testing ground for nerves and stamina and fighting skill. In no other theater of war were men under such continuous physical and mental strain for so long as were the marines in the Solomons."[53]

They had to be prepared, for a firefight could break out at any moment. Their purpose was to find and kill the enemy. Carlson intended to apply pressure on Shoji's forces and relentlessly pursue him until he had been chased out of the region.

"A Japanese could be hiding anywhere, but we were always chasing them, and they were always hiding out from us," said Private First Class Quirk. "We were chasing the Japs—go, go, go go."[54]

Carlson knew that if he let up, Shoji would enjoy a respite during which he could reorganize his troops into a more effective fighting unit, so he constantly prodded his men to keep on the move. Private Leeman explained, "We were such a mobile outfit, the Japanese just didn't know we were there. We were doing the ambushing." Or, as Private Gay mentioned, "We were the hunters. We weren't worried about them. We were after them, we were going to get them, they weren't going to kill me."[55]

Carlson warned his officers that, like any wounded animal, Shoji would strike whenever the Raiders drew near. As Carlson intended to stick close to Shoji, attacking his rear and flanks, the Raiders expected near-daily brawls with their opponent.

Victory or defeat in jungle firefights often came down to who fired first. Yards usually separated the antagonists, and like the Western gunslingers from an earlier century, whichever man squeezed off the first shot lived to see another day. "In the jungle," said Pfc. William D. Lansford, "you fight sometimes maybe up to ten feet apart. It's quick-draw time. The guy that levels his weapon, and fires first, wins."[56] Should they come under fire from a group of enemy snipers camouflaged in trees or bushes, the Raiders mounted an answering fire as quickly as possible to subdue the sniper fire, or simply blasted away at the foliage in hopes of killing the enemy.

The fighting changed many Raiders, at least for the duration of the patrol. Marines who had, only a year or two before, attended a college football game or escorted their favorite girl to a high school prom now battled a skilled foe in some of the worst terrain in the world. That could not help but alter an individual.

"These are all kids from Pennsylvania, New York, and so forth," said Private Gay, "and after a week out there in the jungle we were next to animals. We observed things we never would have observed before."[57]

Captain Apergis had felt compassion for the first enemy dead he saw after landing at Aola Bay. Within a week disgust had replaced compassion. He told a correspondent that "after seeing his buddies shot down and having them die in his arms he came to really hate and loathe the enemy and lusted after him. He said when he was in this condition he would pass their dead bodies and actually spit upon them in his disgust and hate."[58]

Both Carlson and his men attribute the same thing with helping them perform so magnificently during the Long Patrol—the rigorous, and informative, Raider training Carlson implemented at Jacques Farm, which both physically and mentally prepared the battalion to endure whatever difficulties awaited. Carlson not only put his men through a painful physical regimen but in his gung ho meetings he bluntly explained that in volunteering for the battalion they should expect hardship and death. He reminded them of this at Guadalcanal to forestall complaints.

Captain Washburn recalled the time at Guadalcanal when Carlson spoke to the men about the distance they would travel during the patrol in going from Aola Bay to Henderson Field. He then added, "But, gentlemen, it's only twenty-two miles as the crow flies."

When one Raider quickly replied, "Yeah, Colonel, but we ain't crows,"[59] everyone burst out laughing, but the incident was a stark reminder of the harsh conditions they would encounter.

The occasion also illustrated the high state of Raider morale. Carlson, Roosevelt, Washburn, and the other officers designed their California training so that the Raiders would conclude that they were the best outfit in the Marines. "Morale was never a problem," stated Private Leeman. "It was the special organization that we were. We were all so proud to be part of the Raider Battalion. His training methods paid off at Guadalcanal."[60]

That benefit of intense training showed up in the men's determination, especially as the patrol entered its third and fourth weeks, when the environment, disease, insufficient food, and lack of sleep had taken their tolls. "We were all run down, pretty well beat," described Pfc. Jesse Vanlandingham. "You're just hoping you make it another one hundred yards down the trail instead of worrying about long distances."[61]

The men persisted because if they did not, their fellow Raiders expressed their displeasure, not because of insensitivity but because one or two Raiders would have to take care of the demoralized man until he could be evacuated. That could not be tolerated in the jungles of Guadalcanal. Most men responded to gentle taunts, although a few fistfights flared. Private Loveland recalled more than one occasion where two Raiders squared off.

"If you get a guy down in the dumps, you kicked him in the ass. There were some nasty words. Guys got on them when it happened. Poke him in the nose, get him to bawling, to get his nose back where it belongs. Didn't happen too often. Most of our problems came after a battle. You'd get back and regroup, and two or three guys haven't shown up yet, and that's when you start to think—look what happened to me, or to Paul. That's the bad part."[62]

Some took drastic measures. When two Raiders threatened to shoot themselves in the foot so they could be evacuated, Pl. Sgt. Frank J. Lawson warned that if they did, he would shoot them in the other foot and abandon them in the jungle, where either animals or the Japanese would finish the job.

"Thinkin and Waitin Is Hell"

Patrolling occurred during the daylight hours. When the sun set, the Raiders posted a tight nighttime security arrangement. Each company bivouacked in its own area near the base camp, where Captain Washburn and the company commanders assigned security sectors to each platoon. The platoon leader in turn allocated areas to the squads in his platoon, and squad leaders appointed sectors to their fire teams. The fire teams farthest out, on what was called the listening post, made up the first line of defense.

The Raiders often stretched string lines connecting three fire teams. One or two men occupied each foxhole or position, which stood approximately twenty feet apart. One man slept while the other kept watch, then reversed after two hours. They lay awake in the jungle, eyes focused, trying to differentiate normal jungle sounds from those made by humans. Bushes cast off shadowy shapes that loomed as enemy infiltrators, and crabs scampering through the underbrush sounded like approaching Japanese.

"That's all you do, you listen," said Private Loveland. "There's not much moonlight or anything because the trees are too thick, but you do an awful lot of listening to learn the difference between somebody crawling and a hog eating a coconut. A lot of times we would string C-ration cans and put rocks in 'em. Anything cross over would jingle it. Different squads used different things."[63] If a sentry heard anything suspicious, he tugged at the string to quietly alert the men near him.

Since anything moving was considered hostile, an ironclad rule was to never leave your position. Most hunkered down with their weapons, a Raider knife or bayonet beside them, and waited for an attack or infiltrator that hopefully would never come. Rarely did the enemy approach at night, nor did the Raiders typically embark on missions after dark in the jungle, but one could take nothing for granted.

"I had fear," said B Company's Pvt. Dean Voight, as rough a Raider as any. "If you didn't, there was something wrong with you. It's scary, but you grin and bear it. You can't walk away from it."[64]

Since Guadalcanal is home to hundreds of species of wild animals, the jungle never lacked for sound. Streams and rivers masked the noises, making it more difficult for guards to determine what they heard. To Marine sentries, the click of a water canteen cover as it was being removed sounded exactly like the bolt of an enemy rifle.

"You can't imagine the noise," said Platoon Sergeant Cook. "The land crabs climbed the coconut palms and cut the coconuts down with their claws, and you'd hear the crabs rustling around and the coconuts falling. The macaw bird was really noisy—a loud screech that'd make the hair stand up on the back of your neck. There was always something like that going on, and you had to learn to separate the sounds from what a Jap would make. It was almost impossible, so you were on edge almost all the time and got little sleep."[65]

Gunshots one night caused Carlson to radio the advance security and ask if they were being attacked. "No attack. Troops trigger-happy," replied the sentry. On other occasions jittery Raiders fired at wild hogs or monkeys. "We had to get used to the sound," said Private Loveland. "When you're in the jungle grass at night, you'll fire at anything that moves."[66]

Pfc. John W. Studer of C Company so vividly recalled those long nights at Guadalcanal that he later composed a five-verse poem titled "Just Thinkin'" about the experience. Two of those verses convey his emotions.

> Layin out here in the jungle,
> Lookin ahead in the mist
> Helmet pulled over my forehead,
> And tommy-gun clutched in my fist.
> Wonder if Japs are lurkin'
> Waitin to rush with a yell,
> Close in with bayonets flashin,
> Thinking and waitin is hell!
>
> Thinkin a lot of the home folk,
> Tales they'll expect you to tell,
> Memories you've oft tried forgettin,
> Memories of buddies that fell.
> Workin and fightin is easy,
> Thinkin and waitin is hell![67]

Since they had neither the time nor the inclination to set up pup tents, the Raiders improvised. Sometimes two men draped one poncho atop a pile of leaves, lay down, then pulled the other poncho across them for cover. Mostly, they lay or sat where they were and made the best of a bad situation.

One night the Japanese attempted to infiltrate Private Loveland's sector on the listening post. Loveland tugged the string that wound to the man to his right, but when he received no response he suspected something had happened. Loveland grabbed his gung ho knife and waited silently in the dark, not knowing what to expect, when suddenly a Japanese soldier jumped into his hole. "I stabbed him right away, any damn place I could feel there was no bone," recalled Loveland. "I stabbed him a lot." Loveland felt the Japanese body go limp as blood dripped onto him.

Loveland lay the rest of the night with the dead Japanese soldier beside him, waiting in case other enemy appeared. "You're scared out of your mind. In the heat, these bodies will start moving on you. This dead Jap started making noise, and I wondered how you shut them up!"[68] Loveland later learned that the man to his right had his throat cut and had been stabbed a number of times.

Another night, in heavy rain, Captain Peatross made his usual inspection tour of his platoon areas. Finding all in order, Peatross started digging a foxhole for himself, but when he reached eight inches his tool hit something solid. Peatross scraped dirt away with his hands to discover what he had struck. "Suddenly to my great surprise and no little revulsion my fingers were tracing out the unmistakable features of a human head: chin, lips, nose, eye-sockets."

Peatross had come upon a Japanese corpse. He quickly piled dirt and mud on top of it and moved to another spot a few yards away, but he uncovered a second body there, then two more not far away. "Suppressing my feelings of revulsion and a strong urge to vomit, I dug as deeply as I could without disturbing the bodies and made my bed on top of them, thereby gaining some protection from mortar fragments and bullets that their living comrades might send our way."[69]

"You Can't Believe How Hungry You Are!"

After a wearying night the Raiders would have appreciated a decent breakfast, but instead settled for rice and raisins. "No one gained weight on the Long Patrol," stated Private First Class Kaplan. Carlson admitted in his report that "This problem of food supply was a constant worry throughout the expedition, for the men could not carry more than four days supply on their persons, compact as was the ration of rice, bacon, tea and raisins."[70] That food had to make do during the first ten days of the patrol, after which they also received a daily chocolate bar. Captain Plumley remained at Aola to supervise the assembly and delivery of rations to the Raiders as they advanced west in the jungle. When native carriers could not transport the rations to more desolate regions, Plumley arranged for air drops.

Not surprisingly, the men soon wearied of eating the same food each day, but Carlson reminded them he had warned the Raiders to expect little. Captain Griffith recalled when another Marine commander told Carlson that if he and the battalion headed down to his sector, he would have his cook prepare a sumptuous meal, but Carlson declined. "He wanted us living tough," said Griffith. In 1963, Captain Washburn claimed that "it has only been within the past few years that I have been able to abide rice."[71]

Men prepared their food by heating rice in their helmets, then tossing in a hunk of bacon, raisins, chocolate, or whatever else they might scrounge from the jungle. When conditions prevented fires, they munched on cold rations.

Their charred, blackened helmets had become the receptacles for a variety of provisions, as Raiders became more creative and less selective in what they ate. Scouts brought in vegetables and fruit, showed them how to cook bananas, and pointed out which roots were safe to eat. The general rule was that anything from the jungle that tasted bitter should be avoided.

The jungle menu offered some respite with wild potatoes, red peppers, and tasty tree lizards. After unsuccessfully chasing a bunch of chickens through one village—"those darn chickens could fly up on the roofs of the huts and we couldn't get near the things"[72]—Private Gay discovered a nest with three eggs, a treasure that he and his fire team lovingly cooked and devoured.

Captain Schwerin shot two cows, which the Raiders with him quickly butchered and cooked, but the rich meat took its toll. "They had the cows hanging from the trees," said Private Gay, "and we went wild and cut off big hunks, held it over the fire, and loaded up on that. About midnight we thought we were gonna die. Too rich. Were we sick! If the Japanese had hit us then, there was nothing we could have done. I was nauseous, vomiting."[73]

Private Arias, a Mexican-American, loved the hot red peppers that grew on bushes, but they, too, caused a problem. One night as he lay in his hole, Arias's testicles suddenly numbed. Worried that a spider or scorpion had bit him, Arias reached in with his hand to discover that juices from the peppers had been the cause. The vegetables had been crushed during the day, spreading the hot juices on Arias's midsection.

Like prisoners of war who subsist on a meager diet, the one dominating thought was of food. "You can't believe how hungry you are!" said Private Gay. "You don't think of girls. You don't think of your mother. You think of food. We were going down a trail and this one guy stopped me and said, 'Oh God! What a great place to put up a hamburger place!' You're not thinking of your wife or girlfriend. No way. You're thinking of food."[74]

Even hunger has its limits, though. Most refused to partake when the native scouts devoured skewered scorpions.

Fresh drinking water was not as severe a problem. Tablets supposedly made river water safe to drink. They learned that the moist, chewable center portion of a palm tree provided plenty of liquid, or that the bamboo plant and certain vines yielded water. If the water they obtained from the vine was clear, they felt free to imbibe.

During one patrol along the upper Lunga River, Private Carson scooped some water without dropping in his purification tablet. The company physician reprimanded him, as such a practice could lead to malaria or some other ailment. Carson continued on, and when he rounded a corner of the river and spotted the bloated bodies of dead Japanese, asked, "Doctor, does the [tablet] take care of that, too?"[75]

"I Was Wearing Rags Over My Feet"

For their monthlong patrol, a vicious circle entrapped the Raiders. The many rigors sapped their energy and made them more susceptible to disease, and the various diseases in turn made those rigors harder to endure. Ravages from Guadalcanal insects dwarfed the harm inflicted from Japanese bullets. While Carlson's report listed sixteen killed and eighteen wounded Raiders as combat casualties, another 225—six and one-half times the number of battle losses—had to be evacuated due to tropical diseases. Malaria most decimated the battalion, removing 125 men from the ranks, with ringworm (seventy-one) and dysentery (twenty-nine) following. On Guadalcanal a mosquito caused more harm than a bullet.

Pvt. Lowell Bulger recalled that "those blood-sucking demons could easily penetrate any loose woven material and drink their fill."[76] If scratched, the bites became running sores that, in the jungle's dampness, never completely healed until after the patrol.

Since the Japanese controlled the regions providing most of the world's supply of quinine, a medicine used to combat malaria, company doctors and corpsmen handed out atabrine, but they faced a continuous struggle in getting the Raiders to take their dosages. Atabrine turned the skin and eyes yellow. Others balked because of the medicine's bitter taste and the unfounded rumors claiming that atabrine caused sterility, a rumor happily repeated by Tokyo Rose in her broadcasts to the Americans. Raiders joked that the only medicine bottle the corpsmen did not have to hide from thieving hands was the atabrine bottle. Those who failed to take the medicine, however, usually contracted malaria.

Ringworm, more commonly called jungle rot, is a fungal lesion that can invade any part of a man's body. It rapidly spreads in circular patterns, producing such intense irritation that those affected in the genital area could barely walk. Days of patrolling through swamps and rivers, followed by nights sleeping in damp holes, led to a high incidence of ringworm.

"On some of the guys it was really bad," said Private Gay. "You could almost not wear the boots. Jungle rot makes a hole in you. I sat and looked at a fly crawling across my hand, and it disappeared into the jungle rot. It could be anywhere on your body. We had no way of treating it. You cut yourself, get a mosquito bite, or a scratch from a thorn. I had the rot on my back and legs the whole patrol."[77] Private Gay suffered so severely from ringworm that after the patrol a replacement Marine, after seeing his scarred back, asked if shrapnel had caused the disfigurements.

If one were fortunate to avoid contracting malaria or ringworm, dysentery, which Private First Class Kaplan called "the order of the day," was certain to strike. "My stool started crawling away. It had bugs in it,"[78] mentioned Lieutenant Burnette. Men maintained a proper distance from the Raider directly ahead of them in case he had diarrhea. The worst afflicted sliced open the seat of their pants and allowed nature to take its course, while those on the listening post at night had no recourse but to remain where they lay. Some used jungle leaves for sanitation, but as certain plants produced a toxic substance that irritated the skin, they had to be careful which plant they chose.

Fungus so horribly afflicted the men's feet that many had to cut off their shoes after the patrol to remove them. Platoon Sergeant Cook tried to wash his extra pair of socks each time they stopped near a stream to ensure clean feet, but he fought a losing battle in Guadalcanal's humidity.

To deal with a particularly irritating sore on his foot, Pvt. Eugene Hasenberg sat down, popped it open, squeezed out the puss, and continued on the patrol. "You make do,"[79] he explained of the improvisation and of the need to keep up with the patrol.

Bothered by a painful ingrown toenail, Pvt. Dean Voight cut a hole in the toe of his boot to make room for the bandaged toe. Like Hasenberg, Voight took the temporary step because he could not afford to retard the patrol's progress. "It hindered me, but what are you going to do?"[80]

"I had my feet get so damn big I couldn't wear shoes from the jungle rot," said Sergeant Lipscomb. "By the time we got into camp that last day, I was wearing rags over my feet. I couldn't get my shoes off. It took me many, many years to get rid of it."[81]

Though infrequent, baths boosted everyone's morale. Captain Peatross recalled one time he and his men collected the rations that had been carried to the patrol from Aola and found a delightful surprise—a cake of lye soap for each man. Peatross stated that his uniform "still reeked of the sickeningly sweetish odor of decaying flesh, and the opportunity to bathe was most welcome."

The men first washed their underdrawers and set of utilities in the lye soap, then wrung them out and draped them over bushes to dry. A thorough cleansing removed "from our bodies several days' accumulation of dirt and grime," a process that made them feel like new men. Peatross added that "we gained new strength and a fresh feeling that maybe we could make it through another day."[82]

Peatross's bathing was the exception, however. As the patrol wound into its second and third weeks, the number of stricken Raiders rose alarmingly. Despite their superb physical conditioning, long days in the jungle, subsisting on a meager diet and laboring in damp conditions, took their toll. Carlson had no choice but to send the sickest men back to the perimeter. He also used this as an opportunity to remove any man he considered unsuited for combat or a morale problem. He wrote James Roosevelt a few days after the patrol ended, "Attrition due to disease was high—casualties low. I pared out the weaklings ruthlessly, with the idea of keeping the combat strength lusty & rugged."[83]

Practicality guided the evacuations. Keeping one ailing Raider on the line meant that one or two other men had to take care of him and carry a part of his burden. Carlson sent back seventy men on November 19, forty on November 25, and another sixty on November 26. Some units, especially C and E companies, who had first landed, saw their strength reduced by 80 percent.

Ironically, the men feverish with malaria or felled by dysentery had to walk back to the perimeter, as only the severely wounded left on stretchers. Sergeant McCullough, who never thought he would experience anything as dreadful as his time in the surf the previous August at Makin when he almost drowned, claimed that his evacuation to the perimeter, across mountains and rivers, while he suffered from a malaria-induced temperature of 102 degrees, was just as taxing.

Private Gay, shaking from malaria so badly that he once lay in the ashes of a fire to warm himself, departed on one of the final evacuations. Private Leeman shivered as he walked all the way back to the perimeter, a trip that required crossing streams and hills, all the time maintaining their vigilance against an ambush.

"The colonel sent us down to the beach," said Leeman. "It was difficult, mainly in the river. We crossed and walked thirty feet of shoreline, crossed over and repeated the process, zigzagging our way down the Tenaru River to the perimeter. We were all feverish with malaria on the way out."[84]

By November 24, the Raiders had cleared Shoji's troops from the Metapona River to the upper Lunga, south of Henderson Field. They had been in the jungle for three weeks, pursuing the Japanese across forty miles of the harshest terrain imaginable, crossing and recrossing the same rivers and streams, living on a poor diet, simultaneously battling disease and the Japanese.

For the Raiders still on patrol, the final ten days, from November 25 until December 4, would be at least as rigorous as the first two phases. Though demanding, it became the stage for the triumph of the Raiders.

Where No Other Marines Have Ever Been

B y November 25, the Raiders had forced Shoji and his men beyond the Lunga River, thirty miles from Aola Bay, striking their rear and flanks in a series of attacks. As the Raider Battalion stood at their base camp near the Lunga, one more task remained. Soaring above neighboring ridges and mountains amidst jungle-clad ravines stood Mount Austen, a towering mass of rocks and jungle foliage. Before reaching the safety of the Marine perimeter at Henderson Field and the end of the Long Patrol, Carlson and his men would have to conquer that final obstacle.

"Today Is Thanksgiving"

At long last, Lieutenant Miller rejoined his mates. The officer had chafed at remaining in Espiritu Santo with A Company while the other five companies fought at Guadalcanal. So far he had nothing but Raider training to show for his efforts, but on November 25 he and the rest of A Company landed at Guadalcanal and marched to Carlson's base camp deep in the jungle. Almost one year after Pearl Harbor and more than three months after the Makin Raid, Miller had arrived in the combat zone.

He and the other A Company Raiders looked civilized compared to the bearded, gaunt Raiders who had existed for weeks in the wild. The men showed obvious signs of their ordeal. An item as common as a toothbrush, which Miller took for granted, was relished by these Raiders, who drew lots to determine who would receive one of the surplus new toothbrushes that arrived along with A Company. As Washburn's men, without such implements since November 4, had used mud and their fingers to remove particles from their teeth, a real toothbrush was a welcome sight. When one of the newly arrived A Company men cut the rind off his bacon and tossed it away as garbage, six veteran Raiders lunged for it, cut it into equal portions, and devoured it.

With Miller, Platoon Sergeant Maghakian, and the rest of A Company supplementing their ranks, on November 25 Carlson embarked on the third phase of his Long Patrol. Operating from his base between the Tenaru and Lunga rivers, he planned to search the region around Mount Austen for Japanese and to locate two items that had vexed the Marines at Henderson Field since September—Pistol Pete, the artillery that had subjected the airstrip to almost daily shellings yet eluded every Marine patrol sent out to find it, and the main east-west trail along which the Japanese had ferried men and supplies to the region near the field.

The Raiders, weary from three long weeks in the jungle, headed out on November 25. Patrols filtered southwest to swing behind Mount Austen, moving through dense jungle and up the first of a series of precipitous coral ridges. The jungle's stillness, broken only by the sounds of their footsteps and a handful of bizarre birdcalls, spooked some of the A Company men, who had yet to settle in to their new assignment.

Abandoned Japanese equipment littered the trail, and a squad from B Company discovered one hundred rifles, which they handed over to Vouza's scouts. On November 26, patrols destroyed thirty-six thousand machine-gun rounds, six hundred artillery shells, and eight land mines. They encountered only the occasional Japanese straggler, who, according to Pvt. Lowell Bulger, was "captured, interrogated, and dispatched."[1]

That same day, in Dallas, Lieutenant Miller's family celebrated Thanksgiving with the usual fare. Miller's brother, Henry, wrote him, "Wish you could have had chow with us today. Our thanksgiving [sic] dinner included turkey & dressing, cranberry sauce & pumpkin pie. Hope it won't be long before you can have them again."[2]

Most Raiders had forgotten the day was Thanksgiving. Pfc. John Schoch lined up for head count that morning with the other members of E Company, when to his delight each man received a chocolate bar. "Enjoy your dinner," said a bearded and grimy Captain Washburn. "Today is Thanksgiving."[3]

That night Lieutenant Miller and Platoon Sergeant Maghakian climbed into the lean-to the pair built each night for sleep. As usual, they chatted about the day's patrol, about food, or whatever struck their minds. They concluded that with Miller's business savvy and Maghakian's amiability, after the war the two should open a real estate and insurance business together. After debating an assortment of names for their enterprise, the Marine lieutenant and sergeant settled for "Jack's and Victor's, Inc."[4] The prospects of working together after the war gave both men something to look forward to.

On November 27, Carlson moved his base camp four miles up the Tenaru River in preparation to tackle the sequence of ridges shielding Mount Austen. He posted A Company with Lieutenant Miller and Schwerin's F Company in a subsidiary camp two miles upstream, Peatross's B Company and Griffith's D Company in a camp two miles downstream, while he remained in the middle at the base camp with Captain Washburn's E Company and Capt. Bernard Green's C Company.

The next day Captain Schwerin guided A and F companies up a steep trail to the top of a sharp ridge situated in a two-mile strip of terrain between the Tenaru and Lunga rivers. When they reached the crest they discovered an artillery position containing a supply of 75mm shells, but Pistol Pete was nowhere in sight. Disappointed at not finding the gun or guns that had pounded their brethren inside the perimeter, Schwerin at least knew those irritating guns could not be far away.

Meanwhile B and D companies searched for the Japanese supply trail. Along the way they came across the emaciated bodies of two Japanese. In the absence of gunshot wounds, Schwerin concluded that starvation and disease had decimated Shoji's forces, already reduced by the frequent Raider attacks of the past month. The prospect that the enemy might finally be relinquishing control of the interior east of Henderson lifted everyone's spirits.

"Only a few minutes earlier we had been so exhausted that we felt we just couldn't take another step," wrote Captain Peatross. "Now, we were on the trail again, and I thought to myself: 'What a wonderful creation man is. His mind can tell him one minute that he can't take another step and almost in the very same minute tell him he can move on again.'"[5]

The men continued patrolling between the two rivers, when the jungle suddenly opened onto a path heading to the Lunga. Thinking that he might have located that mysterious Japanese supply trail, Peatross pushed partway up Mount Austen before stopping for the night. He would have to await daylight before verifying the discovery.

"We Were a Motley-Looking Crew"

On November 29, Carlson moved his base camp farther up the Tenaru south of Mount Austen to a spot where the trail led west over ridges. He remained there for the next few days, overseeing the patrols as they searched for Pistol Pete and the main Japanese trail.

The closer they drew to Mount Austen, the more arduous became the terrain, which contrasted sharply with the kunai grass fields encountered during their first few weeks. Precipitous cliffs and sharp ridges, broken by ravines and gullies, replaced the level land. The Raiders, many of whom had been on patrol for an entire month, had to scale the features in steady downpours that impeded their progress up the slippery slopes. Though men dropped ropes to the Raiders below and pulled them upward, a few lost their footing and tumbled back down, yanking others with them. Private Bulger so labored to move even yards up the ridges—"that damn mountain," as he called it—that he stated of November 30, "I thought this is the day I might not make it. . . ."[6]

"It was extremely rough," said Private Carson. "It took us most of the day. It was slippery, it was raining. You helped the guy behind you and the guy in front of you helped you. You had ropes, but everything was so slippery and muddy."[7]

Conditions did not improve when they headed down the reverse slope. When the single-file column reached the crest separating the Tenaru from the Lunga Valley and began descending on the Lunga River side, men half ran and half slid down in the rain. Private Bulger chuckled when some Raiders "sat down and slid down the hill on our rumps, like a bunch of playful otters on a mud slide."[8]

That same day patrols found a telephone wire coursing down a narrow ravine. The Raiders followed the wire into an abandoned bivouac area on the south bank of the Lunga, where, to their delight, they found the much-sought artillery piece, accompanied by a 37mm antitank gun. The Raiders dismantled Pistol Pete and tossed the pieces down a hillside, which finally ended its long reign outside the perimeter.

Later that day Cpl. John Yancey and a squad of six men located another enemy encampment on a rocky slope. One hundred Japanese soldiers rested at the bivouac, with their weapons and machine guns neatly stacked against trees in the bivouac's center. Unfazed at the long odds, Yancey counted on his automatic weapons evening the score.

In a pouring rain, Yancey and his group charged into the middle of the bivouac, automatic weapons spraying hundreds of bullets into the unsuspecting soldiers. The swift assault and murderous fire gave the enemy no opportunity to reach their rifles. Most died where they sat, while others fled toward the jungle covering at the ridge's top or jumped into the river. Raiders scrambled up and down the slope shooting the Japanese, while scouts and Raiders bayoneted any Japanese still alive. Afterward, Raiders dumped seventy-five enemy bodies into a hole, where, according to Private Bulger, they "covered them up without remorse or ceremony."[9]

Carlson, who later called this thirty-minute firefight "the most spectacular of any of our engagements," cited Yancey for showing an initiative that caused him to react "promptly and with vigor."[10] Yancey received the Navy Cross for this encounter.

Because Carlson had thrust so deeply into enemy-held territory and into such sinister mountain terrain, native scouts could no longer bring forward the food and supplies needed to continue the patrol. On December 1, a DC-3 aircraft made several runs over Carlson's location and, in an operation John Mather labeled magnificent because of the mountains on either side of the river, dropped rations into a jungle clearing. The plane flew low toward the opening, where crew members pushed over the side hundred-pound bags of hardtack, raisins, rice, tea, and bacon in a free fall to Carlson's men. Much fell into enemy hands in the jungles or into the river, but Raiders retrieved 75 percent of the food stores. A sniper killed one Raider, Pvt. Glenn Mitchell of A Company, when Mitchell strayed too far into the jungle looking for the bundles.

The Raiders welcomed the fresh supply of food, but by the first week in December many neared the end of their endurance level. Some had been in the field since November 4, and all but Lieutenant Miller and A Company had spent at least three weeks in Guadalcanal's miserable jungles, resulting in short tempers and dwindling patience.

"Everybody was getting pretty beat," said Private First Class Vanlandingham. "It was going on nearly a month, and a lot of guys had already crapped out and been evacuated. There was an awful lot of jock itch. We had one guy in our squad almost covered with it. I don't know how he could wear any clothes it was so painful. We all had it to a certain extent. We'd had the same underwear on for thirty days. I never shaved during the thirty days. Pretty much all the guys had beards. We looked like hell. We were a motley-looking crew."

The tempers led to altercations among men who, unless on liberty and influenced by one too many beers, would normally never take a swing at their buddies. Vanlandingham and the typically stolid Private First Class Kaplan squared off one day near the end of the patrol.

"I nearly killed him," Vanlandingham said of Kaplan. They had marched through the jungle all day in the rain, and before finally coming to a halt Vanlandingham began building a fire out of wet wood. "I had to find a dead tree that I could cut through the outer part, that was wet, and get some dry wood out of the center of the tree. I had a pretty good fire going right next to a tall tree shelter." Kaplan arrived, pulled off his wet jacket, and hung it up from a branch over the fire so it could dry, but the jacket slipped down and put out the fire. "I was about at the end of my rope anyway, so I grabbed him and threw him down in a temper fit. I grabbed his hair and was fixing to bang his head on a rock when I realized what I was doing and let him up. Tempers were a bit short."[11]

On December 2, the Raiders vented their anger at the enemy instead of each other when one of Captain Peatross's patrols surprised a group of Japanese soldiers. Assuming the Americans would never venture into the heavy rain, the men sat around a fire without posting security. Peatross quietly moved his ten men within fifty yards of the enemy, where at his signal the Raiders pumped automatic weapons fire into the startled group. Nine Japanese died instantly, while a tenth stumbled a few steps before collapsing and dying.

As he examined their bodies for documents, Peatross saw additional signs that their monthlong pursuit had exhausted the enemy. "They were a pitiful sight: emaciated beyond words, pale and sickly looking; one had a crutch, and another had a crude homemade splint on his leg. Their uniforms were in rags, and although each had a rifle, not one had a full clip of ammunition. That notwithstanding, had they pooled their cartridges and placed a single marksman at the top of the gorge, he could have picked off every man in our patrol. On the other hand, perhaps none of them any longer had the physical strength to scale the steep walls of the gorge."[12]

Upon resuming the patrol, Peatross pushed through a gorge to a spot where a heavily traveled trail dissected an open field. The trail meandered southward across the Lunga, and continued along Mount Austen's slopes before veering northwest toward the Matanikau River, where the bulk of the Japanese forces stood. Peatross concluded that he had finally located the main Japanese supply route.

General Vandegrift ordered Carlson to return to the perimeter in the first week of December. However, Carlson was bothered by reports of Japanese atop Mount Austen. To check into the matter, as well as to make certain that his patrols had located the main Japanese supply route, Carlson requested and received permission to remain in the field for an extra few days.

"The Proudest Moment of Our Young Lives"

Carlson now had to sell the extended time to his fatigued men. The jungles that surrounded him that December 3, 1942, morning seemed more appropriate for paradise than for the hell he and his Raiders had endured for the last thirty days. On the surface, rivers and streams dissected luscious green foliage. Below, however, lurked a seamy underworld of danger—from nature in the guise of crocodiles and malaria-carrying mosquitoes and poisonous insects, to human predators in the form of the crack Japanese 230th Infantry Regiment, commanded by Col. Toshinari Shoji.

In the first long-term commando mission behind enemy lines of the war, for one month Carlson and his Raiders had pursued Shoji's men deep in Guadalcanal's jungles. The ordeal exhausted Carlson and his battalion. Jungle trails existed, but they were trails in name only, narrow tracks blocked and camouflaged by banyan trees, huge roots, and vines. Daily rains drenched the Raiders, who labored in suffocating humidity each day under the tropical sun.

Carlson's Raiders had fought in these deplorable conditions for most of November and the first few days of December. They engaged the enemy in three major firefights and more than twenty skirmishes along the way, while battling the usual exotic mixture of jungle diseases. Malaria, dysentery, and ringworm formed deadly allies with the Japanese to deplete their thinning ranks. They had seen friends die; they had killed those who tried to kill them. They had subsisted on worm-infested rice and tea.

The Raiders had expected the mission to end on December 1, at which time they could return to the relative safety of the U.S. perimeter surrounding

Henderson Field, but Carlson had one more assignment for them. They stood almost within view of the airfield and safety, and recognition from fellow Marines that they had triumphed in proving that a commando-style outfit could contribute to the war effort, but he was going to ask them to delay going back. They faced one more task before completing the patrol—to navigate the steep, slippery slopes of Mount Austen and eliminate newly located enemy positions atop the mountain that had plagued Henderson Field.

Carlson collected his Raiders about him, as he always had done, to explain the orders and the reasons why they should be carried out. They walked toward their commander looking every bit as poorly as he did—grimy beards masked haggard faces, and thinned, almost skeletal frames protruded from dirty uniforms. Going back to training camp in February, his Raiders had accepted every challenge that came their way. Now, despite the rigors of the last month, he was about to request they face another. This time Carlson acted not so much the role of a military commander but more a Knute Rockne rousing his football players to extra effort.

He congratulated his men and said that, as they had completed their tasks, they had been ordered to the perimeter, where better food and quarters, along with its comparative safety, awaited. However, rather than lead the entire battalion to Henderson, Carlson explained that under the command of Captain Washburn he was sending the companies that had been in the field the longest—C, D, and E companies—back to the perimeter by retracing the route along which they had come up. While Washburn took these men down the Tenaru, Carlson would lead the other three companies—A, B, and F—up and over the forbidding Mount Austen.

Carlson waited for any grumbling to dissipate. He knew the men of those latter three companies would prefer avoiding Mount Austen's challenges, and that the fatigued men longed to return to more civilized conditions, where they could catch up on missing sleep. Some complained that as they had been in the jungles for a month, could not another battalion be sent in?

Carlson replied that one more task awaited. He told them that a patrol had scouted the top of Mount Austen and reported that, while the "ascent was precipitous," they had discovered that "at the top, at the hub of a spider web of ridges, the Japanese had dug a strong position which was unoccupied."[13] Carlson explained that if they could rush to the crest and beat the Japanese to those prepared positions, they could not only spring another ambush on the enemy but further relieve the pressure on Henderson Field and shorten the fighting on Guadalcanal.

He agreed that another unit might be up to the task, but the Raiders were in place, they were capable, and furthermore, they had an obligation to fulfill. If they could regroup, if they could one more time draw on those deep wells of strength that had carried them this far, they would return to Henderson Field as conquerors, not only of the enemy but of themselves and of that tendency in human nature to take the easy way out. One more test awaited the Raiders, and Carlson along with them, to gain the vindication that had been delayed at Makin. Ever the dramatist, Carlson ended by leading his men in singing "Onward Christian Soldiers" and the "Marine Corps Hymn," perfect theater to conclude an astounding patrol, a bit of Broadway transposed to the jungles of Guadalcanal.

"With our chests bursting with pride, we sang the hymn at the tops of our voices," wrote Private Bulger, "hurling a daring challenge to any enemy soldiers within sound of our voices." He added, "To those of us who were there, it was the proudest moment of our young lives."[14]

"I Seen Red"

One of those who heard Carlson's stirring words, Lieutenant Miller, prepared to head up Mount Austen's foreboding slopes. Like the other Raiders accompanying Carlson, Miller turned his gaze toward Mount Austen, the landmark they had to cross to claim victory. "Mt. Austen was a huge, nightmare hunk of fantastic terrain," wrote Lt. Col. Merrill B. Twining. "All the navy's Seabees could never have built a road to its forward crest overlooking Lunga Point."[15] It stood there, a cautionary sentinel daring anyone to conquer it, a fixed reminder that success first requires adversity. The Raiders faced a threefold test—they had to scale the prominence, subdue any Japanese they encountered on the summit, and, in what would be the final act of a hopefully triumphant patrol, descend into the perimeter.

Pondering the height and its challenges, Miller walked to Lt. Stephen Stigler, the battalion's doctor sent to accompany Captain Washburn's group, to shake hands and wish him well.

"Take it easy, Jack," Stigler muttered to Miller.

"Sure," replied Miller. "I'll see you in a few days."[16]

Rather than a single peak, Mount Austen, also known as Mount Mombula, was a collection of perilous ridges two miles south of the airfield separated by dense jungle. Standing in the midst, as if to assert its governance as well as its independence, rested the main peak. To reach it, Carlson had to lead his men through yet more thick jungle, then climb rocky slopes made more perilous by the inundating rains.

At 1,514 feet Mount Austen dominated Guadalcanal's northern coastline, providing magnificent views of Henderson Field as well as of Ironbottom Sound, the scene of heralded naval clashes between the Japanese Imperial Fleet and the U.S. Navy. From its summit Japanese patrols directed artillery fire down on the Marines, secure that American jeeps and trucks could never traverse the inhospitable terrain and clamber toward the top. The Raiders faced a difficult task not only in scaling the obstacle, but in eliminating any Japanese at the summit before beginning an equally harsh trek back down the opposite slope to Henderson Field.

"The climb up Mombula was long and arduous,"[17] Carlson wrote in his report. Men slipped and fell attempting to climb the steep slopes, now more a quagmire due to the recent rains. Men leaned forward to grab on to a branch in hopes of pulling themselves upward, yard by yard, hampered by slippery leaves and branches and the additional equipment they carried. Some used ropes to haul up the ammunition and other supplies, but most struggled upward on their own, facing Mount Austen's impediments with an inner strength developed first at Jacques Farm.

"It was very difficult," said Private First Class Vanlandingham. "It had rained constantly, so the ground was muddy and slick. You reached to catch a branch, get ahold of it and pull yourself up. That was so difficult, especially after a long day's march. We were pretty well beaten down. The only thing that kept me going was I'd look ahead and thought, 'If I can just make it up to this next tree.' Then I'd find another one. If you stumbled, you'd slip down the hill."[18]

It seemed that, after they had conquered so many tribulations, Mount Austen posed an unfair supplementary test to Carlson and his men. With sweat breaking out on grime-covered faces and rain tapping against helmets, the Raiders headed upward, gasping in the higher elevations with its lack of oxygen, hoping that another ten feet would bring them within view of the summit. The seemingly tireless Carlson allowed them to take only one twenty-minute break during the six hours it took to reach Mount Austen's summit.

As they approached the crest, Carlson sent the point forward to inspect the vacated enemy positions discovered earlier. They arrived just in time, as once the point gained the top and surveyed the reverse slope, they spotted an enemy patrol winding toward them, unaware of the Marine presence. The Raiders silently waited for the Japanese to draw closer, but the lead soldier, who had apparently sensed trouble, suddenly halted and ordered the patrol to take cover. The point immediately opened fire on the Japanese, killing three in the initial burst.

A two-hour melee ensued. From their positions in the trees the Japanese replied with automatic weapons and machine guns, while Carlson sent squads out on each flank to envelop the enemy, the tactic that had worked so well for him during the monthlong patrol. When the Japanese countered with a flanking maneuver of their own, Carlson sent Miller's platoon to one side and a second platoon to the other to move around the Japanese flanks and hit from the side.

Eighteen-year-old Pfc. Frank F. Tassone earned a Silver Star by single-handedly crawling under heavy fire and destroying a Japanese machine-gun position. Cpl. William Orrick walked erect, blasting with his shotgun at the Japanese in what other Raiders later called one of the most gallant actions of the patrol.

With the action becoming more intense, Miller led his men into position, according to Platoon Sergeant Maghakian, "a long ways back in where no other Marines have ever been."[19] At the point Pfc. Ray Bauml walked ten feet behind a native scout, while Miller followed another ten feet behind, ready to issue orders to his men as they slowly moved forward in single file. As senior platoon leader, Miller did not have to be so far forward, but he wanted to be in the best position possible to direct the action. Besides, Miller preferred being with the men up front, sharing the same risks they faced.

At a signal from the scout, who indicated enemy soldiers directly ahead, Miller halted the column momentarily, then sent Bauml and four men into thick brush on one side of the trail while he and another group, including Platoon Sergeant Maghakian, veered into the jungle on the other side. They inched forward in the thick underbrush, with tree branches and heavy foliage masking what lay ahead. "It was so quiet—it was positively eerie," Bauml wrote after the war. "I had the feeling of strange eyes watching my every move and yet the surrounding foliage was so thick, I could not see a thing."

Bauml froze when he heard branches rustling. He turned toward the sound, prepared to open fire, when Lieutenant Miller and his runner emerged. A relieved Bauml welcomed the officer, who smiled "with that boyish grin he had"[20] and asked if Bauml had seen anything. Bauml had not.

Miller moved three paces when machine-gun bullets from a Japanese soldier camouflaged not more than twenty feet distant stitched Miller across the chest and face. "The gun almost tore his head off,"[21] recalled Bauml. He slumped to the ground, barely alive, with a mangled jaw, wounds to his throat and arms, and a nearly severed tongue. As Bauml rushed to protection amidst a cluster of thick trees, he laid down covering fire to shield his officer. Bullets peppered the tree trunk behind which Bauml took refuge, but failed to puncture through to hit the Raider.

"I don't know how those Japs slipped in behind us with our squad laying right there,"[22] wrote Bauml. It was another indication of how, in Guadalcanal's jungle, an enemy might stand feet away without divulging his existence.

Being as far forward as he was, Miller took the full brunt of the gun bursts. As soon as the firing diminished, Bauml crawled toward Miller, lying in the grass bleeding profusely from disfiguring wounds to his jaw and mouth. Miller's runner darted away to get a corpsman, who administered a shot of morphine when he arrived. After the Raiders had eliminated the Japanese, they discovered that the weapon that had wounded Miller, whom Peatross called "a pleasant, clean-cut, handsome, young Marine,"[23] was an American-made Thompson submachine gun, most likely retrieved from a dead Marine somewhere on Guadalcanal.

Platoon Sergeant Maghakian fought not far from the fallen officer, at first unaware that his friend had been hit. When one of Maghakian's men screamed for help, Maghakian rushed to his aid under heavy fire and dragged the wounded Raider to safety. When he returned and learned that Miller had also been felled, Maghakian hurried to where his friend lay. He saw the corpsman working over Miller, who had obviously been hit in four or five different spots.

"Transport," Miller muttered in near delirium before the morphine took effect. Maghakian huddled as close to Miller as he could to comfort him, but Miller could barely speak. The sight of his bloodied friend, lying helpless in the jungle, enraged Maghakian. "I seen red," he later wrote. "I got sore and went after the machine gun nest because we were having lots of trouble from it and there was a sniper up in the tree and we could not tell where he was. . . ."

Maghakian told two of his men to cover him while he headed down the ravine, "to get this machine gun nest with a grenade." Maghakian knew the sniper would have a clear shot at him, but he figured the only way to eliminate the enemy was if Maghakian exposed himself to fire. Besides, he had a debt to settle for Lieutenant Miller. "I knew the sniper was going to get me but that was the only way to expose him so I went down zig zagging. . . ."

Maghakian, driven by rage and guts, knocked out the enemy gun. The sniper wounded Maghakian in the wrist, but in the process divulged his position to other Raiders, who quickly put him out of commission with gun blasts.

"I made a human target out of myself but I did the job," Maghakian later wrote, "and I did not care if I never came out of it because I knew I could save lots of lives if I knock it out and besides I seen everything in the world I have been to China and Philippines so I did not care as long as I revenged Jack."[24]

Maghakian had his vengeance, as well as a broken wrist. The bullet's impact shattered Maghakian's wristwatch and so imbedded it into his skin that for years after the war, pieces kept working their way through. Ten years later a doctor removed some of the metal and found that the watch's main spring had wrapped around an artery. Once the doctor removed the offending spring, the numbness Maghakian had felt since the wound disappeared.

Despite entreaties from the corpsman to go back for treatment, Maghakian remained in the fighting. He continued to direct the men atop Mount Austen until blood loss so weakened the sergeant that he could no longer contribute.

Carlson brought forward the remainder of his forces. Individual Raiders rushed into a draw to eliminate a group of snipers, embarking on a grand shootout reminiscent of Wyatt Earp and the old Wild West. When the fighting ended, twenty-five Japanese dead littered the area.

Captain Peatross was inspecting the bodies for useful information when one Japanese leaped to his feet. "Shoot the bastard!"[25] shouted Carlson from a few yards away. Peatross leveled his shotgun and killed the enemy soldier as he raised his rifle.

Later that night Lieutenant Miller regained consciousness long enough to carry on a brief conversation with a few officers. Two company physicians, Lt. William B. MacCracken and Lt. Charles G. Robinson, agreed to take turns watching over the stricken officer during the night so he would always have a physician at hand.

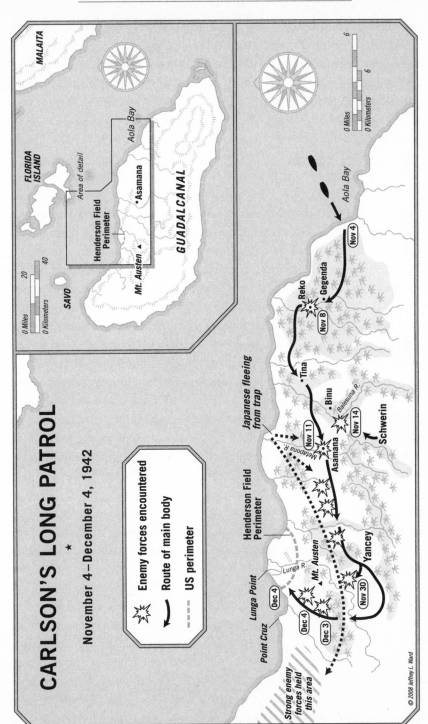

CARLSON'S LONG PATROL
★
November 4–December 4, 1942

Enemy forces encountered
Route of main body
US perimeter

© 2008 Jeffrey L. Ward

"I Cried Like a Baby"

Lieutenant Miller was able to joke a bit the next morning. When Captain Apergis asked Miller what he most wanted once they reached Henderson Field, he mentioned beer.

"I'll try to find you a bottle," laughed Apergis.

"A bottle, hell," mumbled Miller, "I want a case."[26]

A sense of urgency drove Carlson that morning. In eliminating the Japanese positions on Mount Austen, he had attained his final objective, but Miller needed surgery quickly if he was to survive. The two-mile descent to Marine lines at Henderson would be no simple task. A narrow trail offered the speediest route, but as always it meandered through thick jungle. He could traverse the distance in a few hours, unless an enemy attack stalled his advance. Even though jungle rot so infected some of the Raiders' feet that they had to halt every once in a while to empty the blood from their shoes, Carlson counted that they would, as they had throughout the patrol, summon the required strength to move Miller and the other wounded to Henderson.

Carlson had his men on the move by daylight, with Cpl. Orin Croft's squad from B Company taking the point. Five hundred yards down the summit, the winding trail straightened out, providing a perfect spot for the Japanese to set an ambush. Cpl. Albert L. Hermiston of the lead fire team stepped forward cautiously, eyes scrutinizing each bush and tree along the path. At almost the same moment that Hermiston gave the signal for those behind to hit the deck, a Japanese machine gun opened fire, killing Hermiston and the man next to him.

The second fire team in line moved up to envelop the Japanese. Pfc. Cyrill Matelski spotted a soldier wearing an American helmet rise from the undergrowth, but when he shouted the recognition signal, "Ahoy, Raider," the man shot him between the eyes. Matelski had come upon a Japanese soldier using an American helmet as a subterfuge.

Corporal Croft's third fire team wiped out a machine-gun nest, but Carlson ordered a second envelopment when Japanese forces outflanked his first attempt. After two hours of fighting, the countermove forced the enemy to flee and Carlson could continue toward the perimeter.

Miller's condition deteriorated during the delay. Lieutenant MacCracken and Lieutenant Robinson walked beside Miller's stretcher, doing what they could to make him comfortable. Platoon Sergeant Maghakian, who lay in a stretcher behind Miller's, slowly rose when he heard Miller feebly call his name, but he could not reach his friend in time. "By the time I got my native boys to put me down and I almost got to him," Maghakian wrote Miller's father, "he died in the doctors [sic] arm."[27]

Word of Miller's death filtered back to Carlson, who came forward to conduct a brief burial service. As Raiders gathered around, helmets respectfully in hand, Carlson removed a flag from Miller's pack and said a few words about what the officer's death meant to the Raiders and to his family. Raiders then placed Miller in a shallow grave off the trail and marked the spot with a rude wooden cross. Graves registration personnel would supposedly pass through after the fighting had ended and remove the body for proper burial.

"We gave him a decent burial on the side of the trail," wrote Maghakian to Miller's family, "and I am not ashamed to admit I cried like a baby which I have never done in my life I am supposed to be pretty tough."[28]

Lieutenant Miller died halfway down Mount Austen's northern slope. Although they still had a few hours before reaching Henderson Field, Maghakian and the others could see the airfield below from where they buried Miller. Miller succumbed "within sight of the division perimeter—the Promised Land, as it were," wrote Captain Peatross of the somber moment, a fact that sickened Miller's frustrated men, who so badly wanted to get their officer to division medical care. "It hurt when I heard Miller had died before they could get him to aid,"[29] said Captain Griffith, like Miller a native of Dallas.

Colonel Carlson agonized over Miller's death, as he had done with the passing of each Raider. Men knew that when reports arrived of a Raider death, Carlson was beset with grief. One Raider said, "You couldn't talk to the Old Man when we lost someone. You were afraid to, because you expected to burst into tears just looking at him."[30]

Miller's death so affected other Raiders that two men crafted poems about the incident. Pfc. Robert N. Herriott of B Company wrote "Beside the Trail" so soon after the event that *Leatherneck* magazine printed it in its March 1943 issue only four months later. Herriott wrote:

> That rugged cross, native made, may it be
> A token of remembrance, our ever humble fee.
> There it stands in this faraway tropic land
> A monument placed within God's helping hand.
>
> To you, pal, a prayer from my now weary heart—
> How true I know the best of men must part.

Each passing pair of eyes now lowered in sorrow,
Plans vengeance as evening gives promise of tomorrow.

You, Mother of a Raider, wipe away every tear.
Not once did your son betray a sign of fear.
We know you will face your loss, serene,
In knowing that your son was a real Marine.[31]

Another Raider took time to write in his diary for December 4 that "Lt. Miller died today." He added a poem for Miller that included the words:

Into the fetid jungle mud,
Rank with death and stained with blood,
Marines move through the gloomy space
To seek those hiding in this place.
The noise comes bursting from the trees,
Machine guns searching for our knees.
From mortal man to lump of clay . . .
Lt. Miller died today.[32]

For his valor in leading his men on December 3, Lieutenant Miller was awarded the Navy Cross, the second-highest honor that can be bestowed on a Marine after the Medal of Honor. Its citation's stark words best describe his sacrifice: "He gallantly gave up his life in the defense of his country."[33]

While Miller's men penned thoughts in their diaries, Miller's father, unaware that his son had already perished, wrote Miller on December 5. He shared news of family and friends, that his brother Henry had departed for Army training, and hoped that all was well with him in the Pacific. "We think about you constantly,"[34] Henry Miller wrote his son.

"For God's Sake, Those're Carlson's Boys"

Carlson led his companies into the perimeter in midafternoon after completing the trip down Mount Austen without further incident. At the point Pl. Sgt. Rhel Cook of F Company emerged from the jungle to see a sentry in the distance. The guard requested they send in a recognition party, at which Carlson and another officer strolled forward.

"The Marine sentries had no idea who we were," Cook recalled. "They had given us up for lost and were starting to close our records out. They figured we got wiped out."[35]

Carlson's dramatic flair showed during their reentry. Despite their disheveled appearance after spending so much time in the bush, he wanted the men to maintain a military bearing. The men emerged from the jungle with heads high and stepped with as firm a gait as their weakened frames permitted.

"The grapevine spread the news that the Raiders were out of the long bush, the jungle," said Cook. "When we came out to the Marine lines, the colonel who had the right flank offered to call up transportation for us to get to Henderson Field, and Carlson thanked him but said, 'The Raiders walked in. The Raiders will walk out.' That's pride, isn't it?"[36]

Marines inside the perimeter reacted with astonishment and joy that the Raiders had returned. One guard shouted, "Jiggers! Here comes Carlson," while another gazed at the gaunt men, Marines who had earned a reputation for being ruthless, fierce fighters, and could only mumble, "Oh my God! The walking dead!" *Newsweek* magazine reported of the incident, "'For God's sake,' said the awed sentry, 'those're Carlson's boys.' Grimy, bearded, and footsore, the men were filtering, Indian fashion, out of the jungle into the clearing."[37] Martin Clemens, away on leave at the time, said that when he heard of the stirring moment, he wished he had been there to salute the brave force.

While ambulances rushed Maghakian and the wounded to the hospital, the rest of the Raiders hiked the final distance to their bivouac on the Tenaru River. Carlson admonished his men against accepting candy or other foods from fellow Marines, as their stomachs required time to adjust.

"He spread the word not to take any candy or food," said Platoon Sergeant Cook. "You can exchange your canteen for a full one, but no chow. He knew our body wouldn't accept the food, and candy especially would harm us. You can imagine how good that canteen tasted. Carlson was always thinking about us. We loved Colonel Carlson so much."[38]

The Raiders marched to the cheers of other Marines. Some had been inside the perimeter since September, withstanding enemy naval bombardments, aerial attacks, and suicidal charges, yet they still possessed enough emotion to honor what they considered an amazing feat. Scuttlebutt listed the Raiders as good as dead, yet here came Carlson, absent for an entire month in Guadalcanal's wilderness, pursuing and killing an elusive foe to relieve pressure on fellow Marines.

"The other Marines were cheering us the whole way in," recalled Cook. "When we got into Henderson Field, my buddy, a tanker, was there and he looked for me. After I got my platoon bunked down, he took me to his mess hall and they fed me. Those tankers are rough men, but they're standing around watching me and started crying. That's love. There's nothing like a Marine."

Colonel Edson, Carlson's antagonist, provided a lukewarm greeting. He stood quietly to the side as the Raiders marched by, reserving his welcome for those men he had been asked to transfer, such as Captain Washburn and Platoon Sergeant Cook. Carlson received only a formal nod.

"I was one of Edson's men," said Cook. "When Edson saw me, he turned to Carlson, and said, 'Evans, there's one of those men you stole off of me at Quantico.' Carlson said, 'Yes, I got a good one, too.' Red Mike said, 'I know you did.'"[39]

Relief at being inside friendly lines overwhelmed the Raiders, who for the first time permitted themselves to let down their guard. According to Private Bulger, after existing in the jungle, where their concentration could not waver, they reentered a near-forgotten realm, "where it was not even necessary to carry a weapon. What a luxury after a month on the trail with a pack and a weapon as constant companions, day and night, every minute of a twenty-four-hour day. The lean, gaunt, hollow-eyed Raiders had trekked over 120 miles through steaming hot jungles, burning sudans of open kunai grass, crossing dozens of rivers, streams and swamps intermingled with a series of battle with the enemy east of the perimeter. Daily tropical downpours were alternated with long periods of burning hot sun and no water." He added, with a sense of relief mixed with satisfaction, "I realized that I was one of those who had finished this grueling thirty day patrol."[40]

Despite the hazards and tribulations, Carlson had attained each of his goals. His battalion had cleared the eastern sectors of Guadalcanal, had harried the enemy into fleeing west of the perimeter, had obtained valuable intelligence about the Japanese, and had swept the foe from Mount Austen. In the process his Raiders showed that the American soldier was more than a match for the Japanese and proved the value of his gung ho methods. Carlson, the Marine who had pushed and prodded for a battalion organized according to his unconventional beliefs and who had tolerated abuse from

fellow officers, with satisfaction concluded in his official report, "mission accomplished."[41]

One day later Captain Washburn led his three companies into the perimeter.
After departing the higher elevations, Washburn veered north down the
Lunga River and entered Marine lines to the west of Carlson's entrance.
Though just as weary and as soiled as the brethren who had preceded
them, Washburn's group did not enjoy as raucous a welcome as those on the
previous day. That mattered little compared to the hot food and comfortable
cots that awaited. Celebration could come later.

"A Seedy Looking Lot"

The Raiders required time to recoup from the lengthy ordeal. Men shuffled to
their bivouac like zombies, eyes cast straight ahead. Some had difficulty re-
membering different events of the Long Patrol, and all badly needed to add
weight. Sergeant McCullough's weight dropped from 146 to ninety-one
pounds. Captain Peatross lost twenty-two pounds, while John Mather, who had
been accustomed to torrid conditions in the Solomons, was stunned to learn
that his waistline had shrunk from forty-two inches to thirty-two inches.

Of the original 266 men who landed on Guadalcanal with Carlson on
November 4—after one major encounter and numerous smaller skirmishes
with the enemy; after a lack of food and a host of jungle diseases sapped their
strength; after long days patrolling in the jungles, along ridges, through rivers
and streams, and up perilous cliffs—only fifty-seven of those men walked into
the Marine perimeter at Henderson Field.

Captain Washburn, who shed thirty pounds during the patrol, lost two-
thirds of his company to death, wounds, and disease. One of his officers,
Lieutenant Early, stated that of thirty-two men who started out with him, only
eighteen remained, and those men "probably never have recovered from that
ordeal."[42]

Capt. Garrett Graham encountered some members of Carlson's Raiders
after their patrol and noticed two features—weary exteriors belied spirited
interiors. He claimed, "They were definitely a seedy looking lot. Virtually all
the survivors of that solid month in the jungle had malaria, many were a

bright yellow with jaundice, all were haggard and worn from what they had been through, but in spirit they were still a cocky and self-confident outfit."[43]

Most Raiders followed Carlson's advice and guarded what they ate for a few days. Some had little choice. Pvt. Dean Voight walked into the mess at Henderson for his first meal but turned away when the cooks dished out Spanish rice. Rice was the last food he wanted to see. After subsisting on rice and raisins, Private Leeman's stomach had shrunk so much that he could only swallow a few bites of regular Marine chow.

Others ignored precautions and devoured whatever they could. One group of Raiders dug into plates of sauerkraut and sausage, then spent the next twenty-four hours regretting their decision.

The Raiders appreciated two things above the rest—civilized living, and the welcome from other Marine units. For the first time since early November, Raiders could write loved ones back home, take showers, shave, get a haircut, and enjoy normal life. The Red Cross delivered bags containing razors, toothbrushes, and playing cards—everyday utilities with which they had been forced to do without.

The amity created by the rousing welcome lasted beyond the first twenty-four hours. A few days after returning with Captain Washburn, Sgt. Arthur Beth of E Company walked to the Tenaru River to wash out his clothes. A Marine manning a machine gun warned Beth to look out for Japanese, at which a second Marine shouted, "It's safe. The Raiders have cleaned them all out."[44]

The compliment was another way of saying mission accomplished. Carlson, whose theories about guerrilla warfare passed their test in Guadalcanal's jungle, would have loved hearing the words.

"Your Son Was Tops"

Eleven days after returning to the perimeter, the Raiders filed aboard the USS *Neville* for the trip back to Espiritu Santo. Men relished the chance to once again feel comfortable bunks and to again enjoy hot meals whose main entrée did not consist of rice.

Christmas of 1942 at Espiritu Santo was certainly different than the one a year prior for the Raiders. Men painted coconuts in varying colors and strung them on trees, attended religious services, and thought of home.

Meanwhile, the families of the sixteen Raiders killed in action coped with their first holiday without a loved one. On December 26, a delivery boy pedaled his bicycle from the telegraph office to the Miller home to hand over the official government notification of Lieutenant Miller's death. The telegram, bearing the name of the commandant, Lt. Gen. Thomas Holcomb, read:

DEEPLY REGRET TO INFORM YOU THAT YOUR SON FIRST
LIEUTENANT JACK MILLER US MARINE CORPS RESERVE
DIED OF WOUNDS RECEIVED IN ACTION IN THE PER-
FORMANCE OF HIS DUTY AND IN THE SERVICE OF HIS
COUNTRY. TO PREVENT POSSIBLE AID TO OUR ENEMIES
PLEASE DO NOT DIVULGE THE NAME OF HIS SHIP OR
STATION. PRESENT SITUATION NECESSITATES INTERN-
MENT TEMPORARILY IN THE LOCALITY WHERE DEATH
OCCURRED AND YOU WILL BE NOTIFIED ACCORDINGLY.
ACCEPT MY HEARTFELT SYMPATHY.[45]

Since only Mrs. Miller was at home, the delivery boy remained with her until another family member arrived. Carmen Miller and her father, Henry, noticed the bicycle parked out front when they pulled up, and prepared themselves for the worst.

"My mother cried and cried," related Carmen Miller years later. "She never got over Jack's death."[46] Interestingly, about one week earlier Carmen had had a nightmare in which a boy on a bicycle delivered a message informing the family of her brother's death. She told a friend about it, but kept the occurrence from her parents.

Jack Miller did not storm a hill or eliminate a stubborn enemy nest in John Wayne fashion. Hollywood never made a film of his life. He spent less than two weeks in combat, yet his sacrifice meant no less than the loss of a Medal of Honor recipient with three years' service. He represented the young men who put their careers and lives on hold to serve in the war. Miller faced a bright future, most probably in business, but the hopes for marriage, a family, and a bounteous life ended on Guadalcanal. The measure of a man is neither how long he served in combat nor how many foes he had slain. It is best measured in the fact that he answered the call.

Upon learning of his friend's death on Guadalcanal, which followed only by months the news that another friend, Joe, had been killed in the Battle of the Coral Sea, Lt. Barnett Shaw wrote a poem about the trio of buddies who

joined the military. Titled "Joe and Jack and I," the powerful verses express
Shaw's reaction to an inevitable result of war.

> Three Pals we were when the war began,
> Joe and Jack and I.
> Our hearts were free, a fact that we
> Would certainly not deny.
>
> We looked on war as a glamorous game
> Like the shows you sometimes see;
> We all agreed the war had need
> Of Joe and Jack and me.
>
> So both of my friends became Marines
> But I was too old by a year;
> I went my own way and joined that day
> As a ditch-digging Engineer.
>
> It wasn't my stars but those of my pals
> That shone with an ominous spell;
> The plans they made and prayers they prayed
> Were suddenly blasted to hell.
>
> For Joe was lost on the Carrier *Wasp*
> And lost forever will be
> His body and soul in a bottomless hole
> Where only God can see.
>
> Then Jack was killed at Guadalcanal;
> All riddled and torn he fell
> In the oozing mud and slimy blood
> Of the Japs he sent to hell.
>
> So many Joes and many Jacks
> With never a question "Why?",
> In arctic lands and desert sands
> Will fight and curse and die.

A curse on the lands of the Japs and the Huns;
A curse on their souls so black.
Their burning homes and bleaching bones
Is the price they will pay for Jack.

Wherever I go, whatever I do
It's not for myself I act;
For now I know it's double for Joe
And double the same for Jack.

The Casualty lists are just routine
Till the messenger strikes at home;
It's not the same when you read the name
Of one of your very own.[47]

Carlson, whose finely crafted military reports read with the ease of novels, struggled to convey his sympathies when writing letters to the wounded or, most especially, to the families of the men he lost in battle. Though each letter to the wounded Raiders varied in some details, Carlson sent the same message to each. He stated that they were "a living symbol of the courage, fortitude and fearless devotion to duty which we recognize as the basic qualities of men who believe in the justice and efficacy of democratic processes and are determined to attain and retain them regardless of the cost." Carlson claimed his battalion would continue the work toward peace, and ended his letter with, "Gung Ho and Chin up."[48]

His most difficult letter might have been the one Carlson sent to Lieutenant Miller's parents. Everyone, including Carlson and James Roosevelt, who called Miller "a swell kid,"[49] had taken Miller under their wing. Carlson seemed particularly moved by Miller's loss.

"It is with deep regret and a profound sense of personal loss," Carlson began, "that I inform you of the death of your son, Jack, on 4 December 1942, from wounds received in action against the enemy on Guadalcanal on 3 December." Carlson claimed that "Jack was one of my most promising officers," and that "Every officer and man of this outfit feels Jack's loss. He was universally popular because of his quiet, friendly way with people and because of his able and efficient leadership." The colonel ended by stating, "I know how futile are words at a time such as this. Please know that your son was both a man and a hero, and that he died for a cause in which he believed. We are all better Americans for having known him."[50]

In a sign of the regard in which Miller was held, other Raiders, enlisted and officers, sent condolences to the Miller family. Dr. Stephen Stigler, who remained with Lieutenant Miller as he died, wrote Miller's parents, "I can't say enough good about him. He was always smiling and cheerful. Even when things were at their worst he never complained." Stigler added that their son's "men were crazy about him and wept openly when he died. From such battle-tried men as these, that is a great tribute."[51]

A fellow Dallas native, Capt. Joseph Griffith, referred to what Jack's example and leadership would mean for the war. "I am proud to have been associated with him as closely as I was. His memory will serve as an inspiration in the tough times ahead. For Jack was never better than when the going was tough. I know, I have been with him."[52]

The most moving, however, came not surprisingly from Platoon Sergeant Maghakian. He wrote Miller's father that their different ranks meant nothing to his son, as "he always treated me like his own brother we got along swell. He would give me his shirt off of his back and I would do the same for him." Maghakian added, "I have never served under a finer officer in my 7 years of service. I thought the world of him. He was a man all of the way with lots of guts."

Maghakian ended his letter with words of encouragement. "So Mr. Miller all I can say I wish they had more men in the Marine Corps like your son he was tops he had lots of guts and he led his men with plenty of skill in a fight. . . . I will never forget him you should be proud of him."[53]

Once I Walked with Giants

"America's First Trained Guerrillas"

While Maghakian and the Raiders recuperated from their lengthy patrol, the nation's press heaped accolades on the battalion and their leader. "Carlson's boys—officially known as a Marine Raider Battalion—were something new in American warfare," proclaimed *Newsweek*. "They were America's first trained guerrillas, whose boast was that they 'know how to do anything,' and who could prove it. . . . Hand-picked from Marine volunteers, the Raiders took 'graduate work' in military mayhem, at camps and for periods which still remain a strict secret," where Carlson implemented his gung ho philosophy. "Methods used in the Pacific battles today were forged on the Chinese anvil five years earlier."[1]

Reporters who once wondered whether the military could match the victorious Japanese army changed their tunes, for the men on Guadalcanal, including Carlson, had indisputably shown that the American soldier was anyone's equal. "And now, since we started our first large-scale, full-panoplied land offensive on November 1, we have proved capable of generating plenty in the way of a 'Made in the U.S.A.' *blitz*,"[2] wrote the correspondent Ira Wolfert, who accompanied American forces in the Solomons.

To the chagrin of some Marine officers, like Colonel Edson, whose men had spent more time in Guadalcanal and staged a stirring battle at Edson's Ridge near Henderson Field, Carlson's Raiders became the most-publicized and well-known outfit in the Corps. Carlson, with his unique style of leadership, became the darling of the press, who likened the Raider colonel to famed pre–Revolutionary War major Robert Rogers of Roger's Rangers. Writers compared him to Abraham Lincoln and to the actor Gary Cooper and claimed that "Lt. Col. Evans Fordyce Carlson writes books, kills Japs, plays the harmonica and speaks Chinese. He can deliver polished lectures on Asiatic problems, swim an ice-flocked river naked and exist on a half-sock of rice a day. He wears five rows of campaign ribbons and decorations, including three Navy Crosses. He is a fighter, a philosopher, a man of action and an intellectual." The same writer quoted Platoon Sergeant Maghakian as boasting, "I have been to hell and back, and I will go to hell and back again. If I can follow one man—Col. Carlson."[3]

"We Swept Everything Before Us"

Acclaim after the Makin Raid rang hollow, for Carlson knew that he had not performed up to his standards. Not so in December.

Everything he uttered, from his official reports to letters to press briefings, emphasized that Carlson considered the Long Patrol a triumphant success, far beyond a listing of munitions destroyed, which Carlson estimated to be 318 weapons of varying sizes, 45,000 rounds of ammunition, and large amounts of food and medical supplies. His Raiders had traveled 150 miles to cover a straight-line distance of forty miles from Aola Bay to Henderson Field, through some of the worst jungles and sharpest peaks seen to date. He conservatively estimated that in their near daily engagements, they killed 488 Japanese soldiers against sixteen dead and eighteen wounded Raiders. In the process they so neutralized Shoji's forces that he never again mounted an offensive against the Marines guarding Henderson Field, removed the Japanese threat on the perimeter's eastern flank, destroyed Pistol Pete, and strengthened Vandegrift's long-exposed enclave at Henderson Field.

Due to the combined efforts of Marine and Army units at Henderson Field, the swift turnaround at sea brought about when Admiral Halsey assumed command, plus Carlson's electrifying thirty-day patrol, fewer than twenty-five thousand scattered, debilitated Japanese troops lingered in the jungles near Henderson Field or to its west. The succession of defeats caused Tokyo officials to reassess strategy in Guadalcanal and recommend evacuation in a December 31 meeting with Emperor Hirohito.

Though Carlson never mentioned the island in his December report on the Long Patrol, Makin's impact is undeniable. This report, when compared to the harsher ones issued in Makin's aftermath, shows that Carlson learned from his errors in August. He began by emphasizing a trait Nimitz and others criticized as lacking at Makin—aggressiveness.

Carlson repeatedly referred to the offensive approach he took at Guadalcanal. "The enemy must invariably be attacked boldly and swiftly so as to seize from him the initiative" preceded "But there should be prompt movement, and it should be in the direction of the enemy." He argued that in such a brutal war, American troops must "Be tenacious, persistent, aggressive, ruthless," and that the best way to counter the Japanese "is boldly assume the offensive and so condition and train troops that they can out-infiltrate, outflank, out-wit, and *out-fight* the enemy."

The Japanese, he wrote, did not expect the United States to leave the perimeter and strike the Japanese rear, as Carlson had repeatedly and successfully executed during the Long Patrol, so "Seek that back door." He added that American forces had to constantly focus on surprising and outwitting their opponent. Carlson labeled the patrol "guerrilla in nature,"[4] and strongly urged the Marine Corps to adopt his gung ho methods and his version of the fire team.

He claimed the low number of casualties suffered—the combat loss ratio stood at thirty to one in favor of the Raiders—was a direct result of his ability to surprise the Japanese combined with the powerful weaponry of his fire teams. The ratio dropped when adding attrition from disease—125 Raiders had to be evacuated due to malaria, twenty-nine from dysentery, and seventy-one from ringworm (jungle rot). Washburn's E Company and Pete Arias's C Company arrived with a total of 266 men; they departed with only fifty-seven men, although, as Captain Peatross pointed out, "none of us who survived to complete the patrol was exactly in the pink of health."[5]

Another indication that Carlson considered the Long Patrol the high point of his military career comes in the letters he wrote to friends in the patrol's aftermath. On December 11, only days after reemerging from the jungle, Carlson wrote Raymond Swing to thank him for mentioning the Raiders on his radio broadcast the previous November 11. Carlson's evident pride in his battalion came through when he attempted to describe what the Raiders had done for the past month.

"For thirty days they lived in the jungle in native fashion—cooked their own meals (rice, bacon, raisins, tea), made their own shelters from boughs and leaves, and constantly sought the enemy and defeated him. Only men with deep spiritual conviction can endure the hardship incident to this type of campaigning."[6]

More telling are the letters he sent to his former executive officer. Jimmy Roosevelt, the officer who helped form the Raider Battalion, had read the biting comments directed at Carlson by fellow officers and heard his friend castigated as being a communist. He had read the same caustic reports in the Makin Raid's aftermath. Like few people, Jimmy Roosevelt could most share Carlson's joy.

"We swept everything before us," Carlson boasted in a December 10 letter to Roosevelt. "And we found Pistol Pete, the artillery chap who used to pound the air field, and located the . . . east-west trail."

After gushing about the Raiders' performance, Carlson declared, "This operation confirmed my ideas on organization & equipment, Jim. Our best new idea is the fire group." Of the gung ho philosophy that both men had labored to instill, Carlson wrote, "The Gung Ho push came into its own."[7]

Five days later Carlson sent a lengthier letter to Roosevelt. "I wish you could see our Raiders now. You would be proud of your handiwork and mine," he penned, clearly paying homage to their partnership in forming the battalion. "Your advice, comradeship and council I have sorely missed."

In typical Carlson fashion, the officer then allowed his idealistic, quixotic approach to take over. "Gung Ho is here to stay—proved in the crucibles of protracted jungle fighting. Even Vandegrift is unstinting in his praise and vows he will have his whole division trained this way. This campaign proved conclusively the superiority of our method of discipline based on knowledge, reason and individual volition. Even our own doubting officers are convinced."

Carlson added, "A division, an army with this spirit would be unbeatable and could not be denied," and wondered if the battalion should be sent back to the United States for a short time to "give the folks at home an opportunity to see a first class fighting outfit and to stimulate more actively the sentiment in favor of this manner of training and fighting."[8]

Carlson had written no similar letters in August. Despondency over his performance that month had been buried by his command of the Long Patrol at Guadalcanal, where in thirty-one days Carlson lost sixteen dead, fewer than the number killed in two days at Makin.

"We Did Our Job"

Carlson's system also reduced the incidence of psychiatric breakdowns. While Marines in other units and Army infantrymen filled back-area hospitals with mental cases, only one of Carlson's Raiders had to be evacuated with a psychiatric disorder. "You tried to keep your mind off the fear and nerves," said Sergeant McCullough. "It seemed everyone settled down. No post-stress traumatic and all that jazz like we got now. I don't know of a soul, even on the Long Patrol when we all got sick with malaria and everything, I don't know of anybody that couldn't take it."[9]

The Raiders' mental attitude at Guadalcanal impressed the editors of *Fortune* magazine. In a December 1943 article, the magazine studied psychiatric cases in the U.S. military and stated that about one-third of all casualties being returned to the United States were due to neuropsychiatric causes. The magazine concluded, "Breakdown incidence depends largely on the quality of leadership and the conditions of combat," and claimed that the soldier who performs best and most avoids breakdowns "is the one who knows why he is fighting."

The magazine recalled the trauma suffered by British soldiers after their evacuation from Dunkerque, which it labeled the starkest example of traumatic war neurosis of the early war, and added, "Psychiatrically, the American Dunkerque was Guadalcanal," where a harsh combination of factors, including stress, disease, exhaustion, and insects, subjected America's soldiers to near unimaginable tribulations.

Of the Guadalcanal units the magazine studied, *Fortune* stated that the Second Raider Battalion registered the best record, where Carlson had only one case of traumatic war neurosis, "despite the fact that the Raiders fought under the same conditions as the other Marines." The magazine credited Carlson's unique selection and training process, where he not only screened the men he accepted but explained clearly what they were about to face, as factors contributing to his success in reducing psychiatric cases.

The magazine praised Carlson's rigorous training, not only in the military and physical aspects of war, but in its focus on individual initiative and in working together in small teams. "Perhaps more than any other American officer in this war, he has practiced his conviction that training must foster not stifle a soldier's individual initiative." According to the magazine, this training paid off at Guadalcanal, where small groups often had to work on their own, away from officers and other teams.

The magazine heartily endorsed Carlson's system as beneficial to all soldiers who face combat. "Carlson believes that because he prepared the men for what they might expect; because he considered their opinions and feelings; because they were convinced he would never sacrifice a man needlessly; because he provided an outlet for terror and tension; because his men understood what they were fighting for; because the Raiders trusted him implicitly—they suffered virtually no psychiatric casualties."

Fortune then turned to Marine Corps indifference to Carlson. "Despite the success of Carlson's methods, no steps have since been taken to use them elsewhere in the Marine Corps, or in any other unit of the armed forces for that matter." Rather than seeing his methods imitated, Carlson became the focal point of service jealousy and bitterness. "Thus there would seem to be no field command for an officer with Evans Carlson's proven qualities of leadership and with his respect for the dignity of man."[10]

The *New York Times* agreed with *Fortune*'s assessment. After calling his men "A band of the Marine Corps' grimmest killers—tough, jungle-hardened raider troops," the publication lauded the colonel as well as the men. "Most significant, though, was the demonstration of the ability of American troops, properly trained and indoctrinated, to operate independent of established supply lines in the jungle."[11] Carlson, who had spent years battling against mainline Corps doctrine, had to be pleased that his methods and men gained such praise.

Acclaim came from the Raiders themselves, who, like Carlson, understood they had accomplished something unique. Captain Peatross called the Long Patrol "his greatest achievement," and bluntly avowed that "Carlson's outfit was the only battalion that could have made that hike, really a combat patrol, and it did it because it had been trained to move afoot, live off the land, and spend night after night on the ground, in the field, without a burdensome logistics train."[12]

Even Carlson's superior officer at Guadalcanal, General Vandegrift, heaped accolades on the battalion, a group that, as he put it, "accomplished everything I hoped for by the time it returned to the perimeter in early December."[13]

Private Dean Voight stated it more simply. "We did our job."[14]

Captain Washburn could have sent Voight's statement to Connecticut. Ever since December 7, 1941, as he rode the train from Hartford to Quantico and attempted to respond to those civilians who asked if he felt the American soldier was fit for the task of defeating the Japanese, Washburn searched for an answer. One year later, he found it. The Long Patrol, in which he and so many other Raiders had distinguished themselves and vanquished a once-victorious enemy, had supplied the reply.

"We Salute You, Comrades"

In recognition that the patrol was not the result of one man, but of many, Vandegrift awarded the battalion a unit citation for their performance at Guadalcanal. "For a period of thirty days this battalion," declares the citation, "moving through difficult terrain, pursued, harried and by repeated attacks, destroyed an enemy force of equal or greater size and drove the remnants from the area of operations. During this period, the battalion, as a whole or by detachments, attacked the enemy whenever and wherever he could be found in a series of carefully planned and well executed surprise attacks. In the latter phase of these operations, the battalion destroyed the remnants of enemy forces and bases on the upper Lunga River and secured valuable information of the terrain and enemy line of operations."[15]

Individuals throughout the battalion received accolades. For his actions throughout the patrol, particularly during the fierce fighting at Asamana, Captain Washburn earned a Silver Star, as did Platoon Sergeant Maghakian, the bearer of two wounds in two battles. Though in combat for such a brief time, in death Lieutenant Miller earned a Navy Cross for directing the action atop Mount Austen, while Pvt. Joseph Auman received a posthumous Navy Cross for his exploits in providing covering fire at Asamana and Cpl. John Yancey for wiping out the Japanese encampment late in the patrol.

Carlson received his third Navy Cross. Despite harsher conditions than at Makin, presented by both the Japanese army and by the island, Carlson skillfully led his Raiders to success.

Shortly after the Raiders returned to Camp Gung Ho at Espiritu Santo, they assembled for a memorial service to honor Lieutenant Miller and the other comrades who perished in the jungles of Guadalcanal. Carlson's eloquent eulogy conveyed what most felt that day as they gathered in honor of their slain friends, fellow Raiders who sacrificed their lives so that the Long Patrol could succeed.

Carlson told his Raiders that those bodies "remain on the soil of Guadalcanal where they perpetuate the determination of free men to remain free." He added, "It is not given to us to know the process by which certain of us are chosen for sacrifice while others remain," but the Raiders can honor them by remaining "dedicated to the ruthless extermination of the forces of dictatorship which would enslave us. . . ."

Carlson claimed that those who died, like those alive, "loved life. Only yesterday their voices were heard among us as they joined in our songs, rejoiced over letters from home or rang out with lusty exuberance as they participated in contests of sport. When the time came to face the enemy they did not flinch or hold back. Boldly and aggressively they advanced, confident of their superior skill and intelligence, determined in their decision to vanquish these squirming prongs of Japanese militarism and oppression. They knew the nature of the risk they took, but they knew also that human progress inevitably entails human sacrifice."

The commander then addressed the issue of what those deaths meant for those who remained. "With the memory of the sacrifices of our brothers still fresh, let us dedicate again our hearts, our minds and our bodies to the great task that lies ahead. The future of America—yes, the future condition of all peoples, rests in our hands."

Carlson emphasized that each Raider faced a duty that lasted beyond war's end, that they had to assure "that the peace which follows this holocaust will be a just and equitable and conclusive peace." Then, in homage to his friend, President Roosevelt, he stated, "And beyond that lies the mission of making certain that the social order which we bequeath to our sons and daughters is truly based on the four freedoms for which these men died. Any resolutions less than this will spell betrayal of the faith which these staunch comrades reposed in us."

Carlson closed by asking his men to rise and repeat the final Raider benediction, "We salute you, comrades, as Raiders, as Marines, as Americans, as men. God bless you."[16]

Admiral Nimitz, a man who had listened to more than his share of such speeches, later claimed this eulogy was the most powerful he had ever heard. The government apparently agreed. The Office of War Information recorded the eulogy, read by the noted actor Fredric March, for broadcast to troops stationed overseas.

Publicity can be a two-edged sword. Marines besides Carlson's men had been fighting and dying in Guadalcanal since August, repelling a series of attacks without drawing much notice by the nation's press. They had to watch as Carlson's Raiders, fresh off their much-hyped Makin Raid, rushed in, disappeared behind enemy lines for a month, then emerged to great acclaim. Veteran Guadalcanal Marines asked why Carlson's battalion should receive such adulation when they had bled far longer.

Some wondered if the Raider leader sought the publicity. What else could explain the photograph of Carlson, sitting on top of a jeep, chatting with a flock of reporters about the patrol like a messiah? Other Marines on Guadalcanal joked, not without bitterness, that Carlson's slogan, *gung ho*, actually meant "Which way's the photographer?"[17]

Carlson, though, knew where the true victory rested. A mountain of accolades followed him after the Makin Raid, yet they meant little. No matter how vicious the criticism now, Carlson left Guadalcanal confident that his system and theories worked.

Infused with an assurance bred from the successful mission, Carlson spoke to his battalion on February 2, 1943, to mark the one-year anniversary of the Raiders. He took the occasion to remind his men why they had gathered and what made them unique among military units. He mentioned that one year ago "the Marine Raider Battalion came into being, the first organization in the history of American armed forces to be organized and designed purely for raiding and guerrilla missions." For that reason the men should be proud, "you who proved to the world the value of democratic practices in connection with military operations, and who further gave proof of the practicability and deep significance of what we are pleased to call the Gung Ho spirit. . . ."

Carlson listed the traits of a Raider—leadership, honesty, sharing equally in the hardships—and boasted that the battalion had given birth to an enhanced fire team concept. "Most important, though, was the development of what we call the Gung Ho spirit; our ability to cooperate—work together. Not only was it imperative to understand this spirit; it was even more imperative to apply it to daily actions no matter how unimportant they might seem."

Carlson asserted that the battalion triumphed because they marched to a motivation that many military organizations lacked, "a deep spiritual conviction in the righteousness of the cause for which he fights and in the belief that victory will bring an improved social pattern wherein his loved ones and the loved ones of future generations will enjoy a greater measure of happiness and well being than was his lot. And so it has been an unfailing policy in this organization to articulate for you and constantly to remind you of the reasons why we endure and fight and sacrifice."

Carlson admitted to lapses along the way, even hinting of the turmoil surrounding the Makin Raid performance. "Do you suppose these past months since we first came together have been without discouragement for me? I hesitate to tell you how low my spirits have been at times, or how thin my faith has worn."[18]

"Worthy of More Generous Treatment"

Carlson's jubilation lasted only until the following month, when Marine headquarters reorganized the battalion and made it part of the new First Marine Raider Regiment. Another officer, Lt. Col. Alan Shapley, took over Carlson's battalion, while Carlson left to serve as executive officer of the regiment.

The loss of their leader devastated the Raiders. "I stumbled with them up the beach, tears in their eyes, and heard them curse the fate that had robbed them of their old man," wrote the correspondent Jim Lucas. "I sat in their tents and heard them cry like babies."[19]

Carlson attempted to soothe feelings. In a gung ho meeting he explained that his successor would be a strong leader to whom the Raiders owed allegiance. Privately, however, he raged at what he viewed as an injustice. In a March 26 letter to Helen Snow, Carlson confided, "I have been kicked upstairs to the No. 2 job in the regiment. It means that I lost my command."[20]

In large measure, Carlson lost his battalion because of military politics. He paid a price for ruffling feathers inside the Marine Corps corridors of power. Influential officers resented it when he resigned to speak against the nation's China policy, or when they learned of his close bonds with the president. They argued that he stubbornly insisted on his own style of leadership, and were suspicious of his friendly ties to communist military leaders. Worse, Carlson wanted to create an elite unit based not on Corps doctrine but on a Lincolnesque egalitarianism. Jealousy deepened each time a headline featured Carlson's name.

The chief of staff of the First Marine Division, Lt. Col. Merrill B. Twining, observed events from inside channels, yet held a favorable view toward Carlson. In his memoirs, Twining credited Carlson's innovative method of command and wondered if superiors nudged him aside because of his unpopular stances: "If this Byzantine maneuver was conducted to relieve Carlson of command, it gives a momentary glimpse of the dark side of the upper levels of the Marine Corps showing its inflexibility of thought and a compulsive suspicion of all things new and untried. Evans Carlson was worthy of more generous treatment than he received."[21]

Colonel Shapley promptly discarded the gung ho philosophy, declaring in his first meeting with the men his intent to return to a more conventional approach. With that promulgation, the battalion that had been born with such hope in February 1942 came to a sudden end. According to Captain Washburn, "we became pretty military, saluting, dress, military courtesy, and all the rest of that."[22]

Carlson received orders sending him Stateside during the summer of 1943, ostensibly to treat the effects of malaria and other diseases. After a brief stay at a San Diego military hospital, Carlson traveled to Washington, D.C., where he lunched with President Roosevelt and confided to him that his son "has done a good piece of work and you can justifiably be proud of him."[23]

He vented his frustrations in lengthy letters to Raymond Swing. He told his friend, "Suffice to say that the work of the past year has been washed out by the top-side of the Marine Corps—reaction has won a temporary victory." He claimed that in the Raider regiment, "An orthodox line man was sent to command" his battalion, with orders to "wipe out the 'Gung Ho' spirit and reorganize," and that he was given a position "where I had no authority." In more vigorous words, he hinted at postwar turbulence. "I cannot rid myself of the apprehension, which almost amounts to a conviction, that a war of revolution must follow on the heels of this war." He added that the men who are now fighting want more than the same ineffectual leadership and that they will resent that what they sacrificed for is not in sight, which according to his view was "to pattern a society on truth and justice."[24]

Despite his disappointment, Carlson could smile. He received letters from his former Raiders proclaiming how much they wished he were still their commander. "We have a very beautiful camp," wrote one man, "but the boys would chuck it all for a dirty sack of rice and the privilege to be Raiders and shout, '*Gung ho!*' and 'Ahoy, Raider!'"[25]

Hollywood featured Carlson's contribution by filming the battalion's story in a major 1943 release, *Gung Ho!* Though Carlson, Lieutenant Le Francois, and Platoon Sergeant Maghakian served as advisers on the movie, and James

Roosevelt's newly formed Fourth Raider Battalion appeared as Marines, not surprisingly the film, starring Randolph Scott in Colonel Carlson's role and Sam Levene as Transport Maghakian, bore little resemblance to actual conditions. To a man, Raiders dismiss the movie, but during the war it proved to be a powerful recruiting tool for the Marine Corps and, again to the chagrin of prominent Marine officers, a public pedestal for Carlson and his gung ho philosophy.

Finally, Carlson could take solace from the Marine Corps itself. In a 1943 pamphlet titled *Fighting on Guadalcanal*, printed by the government and restricted to the armed forces, Marine officers and enlisted discussed the lessons they learned while combating the enemy for the first time. Many of the ideas could have been drawn from Carlson's manual. A frequent suggestion was that future soldiers and Marines, who might often be isolated in the thick jungles of the southwest Pacific, had to be trained to take the initiative. In his foreword to the book, General Vandegrift mirrored Carlson's thoughts when he suggested that the best move "in training for this type of warfare is to go back to the tactics of the French and Indian days. This is not meant facetiously. Study their tactics and fit in our modern weapons, and you have a solution. I refer to the tactics and leadership of the days of Roger's Rangers."[26]

"A General with the Heart of a Buck Private"

Though Carlson returned to the Pacific and served with distinction, particularly as an observer at the brutal three-day assault at Tarawa in November 1943 and in the June 1944 invasion of Saipan, where he was wounded while rescuing an injured private, he never again commanded troops in battle. Even in a subordinate post, however, he garnered criticism. When a photographer snapped a picture of Edson and Carlson chatting with the onshore commander of the Tarawa forces and labeled it "leaders of the assault," an irate Edson wrote the editor that Carlson had nothing to do with planning the attack.

Being denied a combat command devastated Carlson. Helen Snow wrote that "After 1943 he was never again permitted to command troops in World War II and it nearly broke his already overstrained heart."[27]

Vandegrift delivered another blow in early 1944 when, as the new commandant, he disbanded the First Marine Raider Regiment in favor of a more conventional infantry regiment called the Fourth Marines. In what some viewed an insult, the other three Raider battalions of the discarded First Raider Regiment became self-sufficient battalions in the new outfit, while Carlson's Second Raider Battalion was dismantled and either divided among the other three or placed in a weapons company.

Captain Peatross expressed the emotions most Raiders felt at the dissolution of their once-proud battalion. "The initial reaction was sheer disbelief, then came indignant resentment at what was felt to be betrayal, and finally bitter resignation. The bitterness was especially strong among the 2d Raiders, for they were losing their battalion as well as their elite status." Peatross continued that it was bad enough to be shuffled around in this manner, "but the ultimate humiliation would be the downgrading of Carlson's Raiders to a muscle-bound, comparatively immobile weapons company with lumbering 75mm self-propelled guns and 37mm antitank guns—towed where there were roads; otherwise, manhandled."[28]

Even without the insulting reorganization, the war had bypassed the Raider concept. Carlson and his men provided a welcome highlight early in the war, before America's factories mass-produced tanks and planes and guns. Without the resources to mount massive operations, the United States military relied on speedy operations like Makin to pester the enemy and to give the home front reason to smile.

Once American industry delivered sleek carriers, speedy cruisers, and agile aircraft, the fortunes of war changed. Rather than improvised assaults, the military could stage colossal enterprises, complete with air cover and artillery, and pound the enemy out of their island fortresses. Sheer power and numbers superseded surprise and speed. Direct, large-scale assaults replaced diversionary, commando-style raids or guerrilla operations.

As far as the Pacific War was concerned, Carlson and his Raiders had become an anachronism.

The Saipan wounds sent Carlson home for good. When President and Mrs. Roosevelt visited Carlson at a San Diego hospital in July, the two saw each other for the final time. Within a year Franklin Roosevelt was dead from a cerebral hemorrhage.

"You know how dearly I loved your father and how devoted I was to him and to his ideals," Carlson wrote James Roosevelt on April 12, the same day Roosevelt's father succumbed. "It is tragic that he could not have lived to see the peace he had labored so hard to attain become reality." He confided, "Your father's friendship is the greatest inspiration of my life," and that while the world knew him as great, "only his family and those who had the privilege of being intimately associated with him know how great he really was."[29]

Evans Carlson retired from the military in the summer of 1946. Disillusioned with battling the Marine Corps, he raised more controversy by lending his name to the Committee for a Democratic Far Eastern Policy, a group of citizens working to improve relations with the Chinese Communists. When critics charged Carlson with being a communist, he issued a strong denial in *Time* magazine. James Roosevelt came to his mentor's defense by calling Carlson a patriot, not a communist, who had inspired his men with words and deeds.

After the controversy cooled, Carlson headed to his retirement home in Oregon. His health failing, Carlson suffered a heart attack shortly before Christmas. On May 27, 1947, the fifty-one-year-old Raider died in Portland.

Even in death Carlson proved to be a lightning rod. When James Roosevelt contacted Carlson's widow, Peggy, to offer condolences, he learned that the Marine Corps, according to procedure, had no funds to pay for the shipment of Carlson's body to Washington and burial at Arlington National Cemetery. Upset by what he considered an insult, Roosevelt collected the necessary $812 to defray the costs. "The man had been a patriot, regardless of his politics," Roosevelt later wrote. "His men loved and respected him and were pleased he received, as he deserved, this burial with honors."[30]

Though a Marine honor guard stood at attention as the caisson, containing the flag-draped coffin, wound through Arlington, only a handful of top-echelon Marine officers dotted the sparse crowd. The commandant and fellow Guadalcanal officer, General Vandegrift, paid his respects, along with a small group of other Marine dignitaries, but many Marine officers, including Merritt Edson, declined to participate.

Lavish praise came from the press, if not from the Marine Corps. One article stated, "A gaunt, leathery-skinned Marine general with the heart of a buck private passed quietly across his last line of departure Tuesday, and with him died a small part of every enlisted man."[31]

Carlson may even have found it appropriate that his life should end with such histrionics. After all, it garnered publicity for him and his Raider concept, as well as fit nicely with his flamboyance. Helen Snow claimed that "Evans lived a theatrical life and he was aware of it. He did things with style and had a flair for the dramatic, though always underplaying it as part of the drama. He knew how handsome and commanding he looked in his blues on parade. He loved it when the movie 'Gung Ho' [sic] was made in 1943 with Randolph Scott taking his part and a script by Lucien Hubbard."[32]

In the issue of the *New Republic* published the week after Carlson's death, his friend from China, Edgar Snow, explained Carlson's significance to him and to his countrymen. "Carlson suffered deeply for humanity in his mind as well as his body to come to his truths by painful thought and unflinching self-analysis. He was above everything a man on whom knowledge imposed a duty to act. He spent his courage and great heart lavishly and finally fatally to lead others within spheres where he was guided by certainties attained down a long road of honest doubts and struggles. We have lost an important citizen and great friend whose life, like Roosevelt's, must renew our tattered faith in man."[33]

The man who combined the stirring audacity of Lawrence of Arabia with the lofty nobility of Don Quixote would have relished being compared to his idol, Franklin Roosevelt. He also left the stage with unfinished business. As Agnes Smedley had so astutely observed during their China days, Carlson strove for the stars without reaching them.

It was a fitting end to a turbulent saga.

"They Were the First"

The question whether Carlson and Roosevelt first created the notion of a Raider Battalion is not only difficult to answer but irrelevant. The credit goes to a number of men, including Merritt Edson. One can assert, however, that Carlson and Roosevelt, at a minimum, contributed significantly to the Raider concept. It may not have been theirs alone, but the Second Marine Raider Battalion and its gung ho methods were their unique creation, the only battalion in U.S. military history to so creatively blend military rigidity with democratic practices. In doing so they left an imprint on the Marine Corps.

Also undeniable are Carlson's notable contributions to Marine organization. He altered the basic squad into a three-unit structure consisting of fire teams packing the most potent weapons. Captain Peatross stated in 1995, "In spite of the fact that practically all other units hated and were jealous of the raiders, all Marine infantry squads were organized on the . . . fire team concept by the middle of WWII, and, as you know, are still organized that way today."[34]

Beyond those immediate concerns, Carlson contributed to Marine tactics in a later war. Merrill Twining, the First Marine Division's chief of staff during Guadalcanal, claimed that the widespread utilization of helicopters during the Vietnam War, where they lifted troops and supplies to the fighting arenas and shuttled infantry units to enemy flanks, was a direct result of Carlson's enveloping actions and his use of native carriers during the Long Patrol.

"We can attribute some of the plan's origin to the imagination and initiative inherent in Evans Carlson's speed and mobility through the employment of his native scouts during his classic raid on Guadalcanal," Twining wrote. He added that the helicopter "gained warm acceptance when it first appeared on the battlefields flying Marines of the 1st Division in and out of combat. Today, helicopters are indispensable to all of our armed forces."[35]

Since World War II different special forces units have carried on in the tradition established by Carlson's Raiders and the other Raider battalions. The Green Berets in Vietnam, long-range reconnaissance Marines, Army airborne units, and Marine force reconnaissance companies all trace their heritage to World War II. "Sure, we were the forerunners to special operations," asserted Lieutenant Burnette. "There wasn't much else like it at the time."[36]

Larry Brown entered Marine special forces in 1964, earning a Silver Star and two Purple Hearts for his service in the Vietnam War. Each year for the past several years he has attended the Raider reunions, not so much to laugh and share memories with the World War II warriors as to pay homage to men who influenced who he became.

"Our drill instructors used to mention the Raiders," he explained at the 2007 Raider reunion in San Diego. "We were their future. They were stressed. When we did hand-to-hand combat, they were stressed. They used the Raider legacy as part of the training. Every bit of jungle training we had, the night fighting, sneaking up on people. They were the first to do it, and now we were doing it. It's an honor to sit here with these guys today. They are walking examples of what the Marine Corps is. They were one of the first special operations unit. We were told that. They are something any Marine will cherish—the name Raider. They had to be special to be in that unit. They were the first."[37]

With his gung ho philosophy and his skillful command, especially at Guadalcanal, Carlson proved that special forces units have their place in the military. In arenas where stealth, speed, and cunning are required, special forces can play a dominant role.

Carlson may have battled his windmills, but the world needs Don Quixotes, individuals who prod and nudge us with their words and deeds. Brown's quote shows that what Carlson and the other Raider battalions accomplished had a lasting effect and that his ideals, and the example of men like Washburn, Miller, and Maghakian, live on.

Raiders continue the legacy. Following Word War II, Private Arias fought in two subsequent wars. He survived one of the bloodiest actions of the Korean War at the dreaded Chosen Reservoir, then served two tours in Vietnam with the Pathfinders, a long-range scout unit that, like the Long Patrol, disappeared into the wilds of Vietnam to scout and harass the enemy. Despite those actions, during which he battled beside other men in desperate situations, he does not hesitate when selecting his most memorable time. "I remember my proudest moments were when I served in Carlson's Raiders,"[38] he recalled in 1986.

Private Carson claims that Raider training taught him to never give up, precepts that prodded Private Loveland and Sergeant McCullough to complete promises made to family by gaining their high school diplomas in 2004 and 2006, respectively. Loveland also talks to Air Force personnel undergoing survival training, and uses the Long Patrol as his example of how best to outlast the jungle.

"In that short span of 9 months," offers Pvt. Ashley Fisher of B Company, "I began the development of a mature personality that is with me today and has been all of my life. I learned such things as 'the open door policy'—now considered routine. As I met life's challenges, and there have been many and some pretty tough, I have drawn upon the guidance first set forth in my life by Carlson of Carlson's Raiders."[39]

Part of that legacy is to share what they have with the other Long Patrol participants, the native scouts and carriers who so ably assisted them on their epic mission. Since 1968 the United States Marine Raider Association has sent a steady stream of school supplies to assist the island's children in their educational needs, as well as money in the form of the Sgt. Maj. Jacob Vouza Scholarship Fund.

Honors have rebounded to Carlson's men. In addition to the many Navy Crosses, Silver Stars, and other medals, five men have had warships named in their honor, including Lieutenant Miller and Sergeant Thomason. In 2004, the Navy launched the USS *Makin Island* (LHD 8), a multipurpose amphibious assault vessel. In the ceremony Dr. Philip A. Dur, president of the Northrop Grumman Ship Systems, explained that the ship received such an acclaimed name because "The Makin assault was a precursor to what we call special warfare, or special operations, today."[40]

The same year the Marine Corps dedicated a new building at the Naval Amphibious Base in Coronado, California, after Sergeant Thomason. Commanders at the base selected him because he and the other Raiders represented the type of men they wanted their students to imitate. Across the nation at Quantico, Virginia, the Marines established the Raider Museum at its Marine Martial Arts Center of Excellence to maintain the heritage of Carlson, Edson, and the other Raiders, and on Memorial Day 2007, in Wyandotte, Michigan, the Marine Corps League honored one of the town's citizens killed on the Makin Raid by erecting a monument after Pfc. William Gallagher.

"We Have a Bond Which Is Priceless"

Raiders enjoyed varied careers after 1942. Roosevelt followed his stint as Carlson's executive officer by commanding the Fourth Marine Raider Battalion, a post where he again served with distinction. He received the Army's Silver Star Medal for the Gilbert Islands operation in November 1943, when he willingly headed to the hottest spots of the fighting. He retired after the war as a colonel, and was later promoted to brigadier general due to his combat citations. In the 1950s he began a string of twelve consecutive years as a member of Congress, where he represented his home state of California.

None of the successes matched his time with Carlson. According to his widow, Mary Roosevelt, up to his August 13, 1991, death in Newport Beach, California, Roosevelt claimed that his service with the Raiders was "absolutely the love of his life. He liked the fact that everybody was in this together, with no favorites. To some extent I imagine he enjoyed the anonymity. Not that he was completely anonymous, but he liked that there were no favorites."[41] She repeated James's assertion that if he were to be remembered for one achievement, he would want it to be his work for and with the Raiders.

Numerous examples show Roosevelt's love for the Raiders. Men maintained a correspondence with Roosevelt, and his wife recalls numerous times when a Raider in trouble called her husband for assistance. Roosevelt frequently contributed his thoughts to the "Bull Sheet" section of the Raider Association's newsletter, *Raider Patch*, where Raiders shared information and reminiscences. There you will find Brig. Gen. James Roosevelt's name resting proudly among those of privates and corporals who also sent in news of Raider buddies.

"We Raiders have a bond which is priceless," he wrote with gratification in 1978, "and while I am sure none of us will be overly boastful, I believe we should be full of pride that we are Marine Raiders and of our contribution to the finest military outfit in the world . . . the United States Marine Corps!!!"[42] The triple exclamation points emphasize Roosevelt's bond with the Raiders and how much his service with that group meant to a man whose life had formerly been marred by controversy.

The Marine Corps reciprocated the feeling. When Mary arranged his funeral service on a Sunday to accommodate family, each Marine in the Corps Honor Guard, which normally is not active on Sunday, volunteered his time to ensure that James Roosevelt had the military trappings he deserved. The commander of the Marine Corps at El Toro personally folded the flag and handed it to Mary Roosevelt.

The then commandant of the Marine Corps, Gen. Carl E. Mundy, Jr., wrote Mary a letter in which he explained Roosevelt's value to the Marine Corps. The words illustrate that, unlike Roosevelt's failed business dealings in the 1930s, he embarked upon an amazing turnaround that proved to his father—and to himself—he was deserving of praise.

"Your husband personified the image of a 'Marine,' especially in his active service during World War II. Always leading from the front, his selfless courage and personal fortitude placed him in eminent [sic] danger, but accomplishing his mission and protecting the lives of those serving with him on Makin Island, nonetheless came first."[43]

Captain Washburn returned to Connecticut after the war, where he embarked on a profitable business career crafted on the same trademarks he developed in commanding the men of E Company—decency, trust, hard work, and equity. In a 1980 interview he credited Carlson for showing him how to handle his employees.

"I tried to make them as aware of everything that was going on around them and the ramifications of what we were doing, and why we were doing it. People don't always do that. Communications is a very difficult thing. Carlson was an expert at communications."[44]

The Navy recognized Lieutenant Miller's sacrifice by launching the USS *Jack Miller* (DE 410), a destroyer escort, in January 1944. Fifty-five years later Southern Methodist University honored Miller and the other 133 graduates who died in the war by dedicating a World War II Memorial Plaza. The memorial, which rests in a shady locale on the campus, was a gift from Carmen and Henry Miller in memory of their brother.

Bereft at losing a son and brother at such a young age, the family has labored since 1942 to locate and return home for burial Jack's remains. The specter that he lies along an overgrown trail in Guadalcanal, forever beyond their reach, haunts them, but they have so far enjoyed little success. Frequent requests to the government produced little substantive information. A 1945 letter from Maj. Gen. T. E. Watson of the Marine Corps reported that since Miller's death in 1942, "the growing vegetation on Guadalcanal has undoubtedly aided in helping to conceal the last resting place of your son. It is extremely doubtful if the grave will ever be found."[45]

Other attempts throughout the years failed to locate the rude cross and burial spot of Lieutenant Miller, despite the efforts of friends and government agencies to find it. Platoon Sergeant Maghakian informed the family that he was willing to return to Guadalcanal and, with Jacob Vouza's help, search for the grave, and various government teams explored the region about Mount Austen, without success.

In 1990, Carmen Miller Michael implored Lt. Col. Joseph Mueller, one of the officers assigned to locate burial locations in the Solomons, to do what he could. She had a potent reason. "It was only yesterday that my mother, who will be 98 in June, asked me if I thought there was anything else we could do to try to find him." She added, "We understand that the chances of gaining any new information are very slim, but still would like to take advantage of your willingness to investigate."[46]

Colonel Mueller replied that he would certainly do what he could, but not to raise their hopes. "You see the jungle over here reclaims everything so quickly." He explained that he revisited a location he had searched only three years before, and "I could not even recognize the area anymore." He added,

"The jungle grew so quickly that there was absolutely no trace of us ever having been there."[47]

As of this writing, the Miller family has yet to experience closure. While not abandoning hope, they realize that after six decades, chances are slim of returning Jack to Dallas.

"On an intellectual level I know it doesn't matter where his remains are," explained Carmen Miller Michael in 2008, "but on an emotional level I do. I want my brother back home."[48]

Miller's friend from A Company, Platoon Sergeant Maghakian, returned to the United States after the Long Patrol to recuperate from his two wounds—one suffered at Makin and the other at Guadalcanal—and to help instruct fresh troops at Camp Pendleton, close to where he had trained for Carlson at Jacques Farm. The veteran Marine applied every wile he learned in the southwest Pacific to prepare the young men for battle with the Japanese, but felt empty being back home while his friends in the battalion remained overseas. "I was afraid I'd forgotten how to fight,"[49] he mentioned to a reporter.

Not surprisingly, the twice-wounded Maghakian sought combat. He told Lieutenant Miller's father that he was more than ready to head to the Pacific, because "I have lots making up to do. My wife can't stand me going over again in fact I never mention it in front of her even though I am half cripple in my left arm but they don't know anything about it. So I will have another crack at them even if I did get more than my share."

Some people, especially his wife, tried to caution him that he had already tempted fate by surviving two wounds, but their efforts proved futile. Transport intended to rejoin his buddies in the Pacific, even if it meant he would not return. "I guess we all have our days numbered. I guess I have been lucky twice but they tell me the third time is a charm. Well I don't mind. I know they need men like me overseas, so I am ready to go."[50]

For his heroics at Eniwetok in early 1944, where he rescued a trapped platoon by outflanking the Japanese and dispatching them with a grenade, Transport earned the Silver Star, then followed that with a Bronze Star for action at Tinian in July 1944. At war's end Maghakian retired at 60 percent disability.

For much of his life Maghakian worked as an executive and security consultant for a Las Vegas hotel. The film actor Lee Marvin, who trained under Maghakian and asserted that he was the toughest Marine he had ever met, claimed Transport's valuable lessons during training saved his life on more than one occasion when he reached the battlefield.

Maghakian died in 1977, satisfied that he had exacted payback for Japanese atrocities in China. In 1981, a California state representative introduced legislation naming the new outpatient clinic at the Fresno Veterans Administration Medical Center after Transport. At the clinic's dedication, a speaker read a message from Lee Marvin. Though unable to attend, Marvin wanted the audience to know what Transport meant to him and other Marines. Marvin stated of Maghakian, "Most of us stayed alive because of his excellent training. He was truly a sergeant who cared for his men." The noted actor, who gained fame from military roles, including that of a crusty officer of a specially trained commando unit in *The Dirty Dozen*, claimed that "His memory is burned in my mind forever."[51]

A tapestry of individual gallantry weaves the story of the Second Raider Battalion. The Raiders could not have fashioned their tale without Carlson and Roosevelt's calm guidance at the helm, but the pair could not have registered their lofty deeds without the contributions of men like Captain Washburn, Lieutenant Miller, and Transport Maghakian.

"Once I walked with giants," proclaimed Pvt. John Cotter of D Company. "Nowhere have I known men like the Raiders!"[52]

Endnotes

Chapter 1—Reaching for the Stars but Never Touching Them

1. Navy Department Press Release, August 27, 1942; James Gleason, *Real Blood! Real Guts!* (Irvine, CA: Raider Publishing, 2003), p. 23.
2. All quotes came from www.quotationspage.com.
3. Michael Blankfort, *The Big Yankee* (Nashville: The Battery Press, 2004), p. 93.
4. Ibid., p. 113.
5. Ibid., p. 121.
6. Ibid., p. 125.
7. Herb Richardson, "Giants of the Corps," *Leatherneck*, March 1977, p. 4, found at http://pqasb.pqarchiver.com/mca-members.
8. Brig. Gen. Samuel B. Griffith Interview with Headquarters Marine Corps, November 1968, pp. 204–05.
9. C. F. Mathews, Letter from the Commanding Officer to the Secretary of the Navy, "Recommendation in the Case of First Lieutenant Evans F. Carlson, U.S. Marine Corps, for Award of a Distinguished Service Medal," May 12, 1931, p. 1, in the Evans Carlson Collection, Marine Corps Research Center, Quantico, Virginia.
10. Henry Berry, *Semper Fi, Mac: Living Memories of the U.S. Marines in World War II* (New York: Arbor House, 1982), pp. 113–14.
11. Lt. Col. Jon T. Hoffman, *Chesty* (New York: Random House, 2001), p. 74.
12. Berry, *Semper Fi, Mac,* p. 113.
13. Evans F. Carlson, "The Guardia Nacional de Nicaragua," *Marine Corps Gazette*, August 1937, found at: http://pqasb.pqarchiver.com/mca-members, p. 1.
14. Blankfort, *The Big Yankee,* p. 172.

15. Letter from Evans Carlson to Missy LeHand, June 17, 1937, Correspondence with Evans Carlson, PPF 4951, Franklin D. Roosevelt Presidential Library, Hyde Park, New York.
16. Blankfort, *The Big Yankee*, p. 173.
17. Maj. Gen. Oscar F. Peatross, USMC (Ret.), *Bless 'Em All: The Raider Marines of World War II* (Irvine, CA: ReView Publications, 1995), p. 6.
18. Blankfort, *The Big Yankee*, p. 167.
19. Geoffrey Perret, "Warrior Mao," *MHQ: The Quarterly Journal of Military History* 19, no. 3 (Spring 2007), p. 6.
20. Evans Fordyce Carlson, *Twin Stars of China* (New York: Dodd, Mead & Company, 1940), pp. 65–66.
21. Letter from Evans Carlson to Franklin D. Roosevelt, December 24, 1937, Correspondence with Evans Carlson, PPF 4951, Franklin D. Roosevelt Presidential Library, Hyde Park, New York (hereafter cited as Letter from Carlson to Roosevelt).
22. Letter from Carlson to Roosevelt, December 24, 1937.
23. Letter from Carlson to Roosevelt, March 4, 1938; letter from Carlson to Roosevelt, April 15, 1938; letter from Carlson to Roosevelt, December 24, 1937.
24. Blankfort, *The Big Yankee*, p. 220.
25. Agnes Smedley, *China Fights Back* (New York: The Vanguard Press, 1938), p. 249.
26. Blankfort, *The Big Yankee*, p. 222.
27. Letter from Carlson to Roosevelt, December 24, 1937.
28. Letter from Carlson to Roosevelt, April 15, 1938.
29. Letter from Carlson to Roosevelt, November 29, 1938.
30. Letter from LeHand to Carlson, December 23, 1937; letter from Roosevelt to LeHand, April 26, 1938.
31. Letter from Carlson to LeHand, December 24, 1937; letter from Carlson to LeHand, January 1, 1939.
32. George W. Smith, *Carlson's Raid* (Novato, CA: Presidio Press, Inc., 2001), p. 206.
33. Letter from Carlson to Roosevelt, March 17, 1939.
34. Smith, *Carlson's Raid*, p. 35.
35. Blankfort, *The Big Yankee*, p. 224.
36. Janice R. MacKinnon and Stephen R. MacKinnon, *Agnes Smedley: The Life and Times of an American Radical* (Berkeley: University of California Press, 1988), p. 42.
37. Letter from Carlson to LeHand, March 9, 1940.
38. Lt. Col. David D. Barrett to the War Department, "Comments on Current Events," December 31, 1940, in the Evans Carlson Collection, Marine Corps Research Center, Quantico, Virginia.
39. Blankfort, *The Big Yankee*, p. 285.

Chapter 2—Specially Trained Troops of the Hunter Class

1. Blankfort, *The Big Yankee*, p. 291, pt. 1, chap. 2.
2. Robert J. Casey, *Torpedo Junction: With the Pacific Fleet from Pearl Harbor to Midway* (Indianapolis: The Bobbs-Merrill Company, 1942), p. 25.
3. James Ladd, *Commandos and Rangers of World War II* (New York: St. Martin's Press, 1978), p. 17.
4. Russell Miller, *The Commandos* (Alexandria, VA: Time-Life Books), 1981, p. 21.
5. Ibid., p. 22.
6. James Roosevelt, *Affectionately, F.D.R.* (New York: Harcourt, Brace & Company, 1959), pp. 3, 5, 12.
7. Ted Morgan, *FDR: A Biography* (New York: Simon and Schuster, 1985), p. 283.
8. Roosevelt, *Affectionately, F.D.R.*, pp. 121, 215.
9. Ibid., pp. 4, 144–45.
10. Ibid., pp. 204–06.
11. Ibid., p. 5.
12. Morgan, *FDR: A Biography*, p. 463.
13. Alva Johnston, "Jimmy's Got It," *Saturday Evening Post*, July 2, 1938, pp. 9, 57.
14. J. J. Perling, *Presidents' Sons* (New York: The Odyssey Press, 1947), pp. 318–19.
15. "Salesman's Reply," *Time*, August 22, 1938, found at www.time.com, pp. 1–2.
16. Author's interview with Mary Roosevelt, October 26, 2007.
17. Roosevelt, *Affectionately, F.D.R.*, p. 308.
18. Morgan, *FDR: A Biography*, pp. 462, 466.
19. James Roosevelt Interview with the Marine Historical Center, October 25, 1979.
20. James Roosevelt, *My Parents: A Differing View* (Chicago: A Playboy Press Book, 1976), p. 267.
21. Mary Roosevelt interview, October 26, 2007.
22. Roosevelt, *My Parents: A Differing View*, p. 270.
23. Letter from Capt. James Roosevelt to Maj. Gen. Thomas Holcomb, "Development Within the Marine Corps of a Unit for Purposes Similar to the British Commandos and the Chinese Guerrillas," January 13, 1942, Raider Battalion Correspondence Files, Marine Corps Research Center, Quantico, Virginia.
24. Joseph H. Alexander, *Edson's Raiders: The 1st Marine Raider Battalion in World War II* (Annapolis, MD: Naval Institute Press, 2001), p. 19.
25. R. E. Mattingly, "'The Worst Slap in the Face,'" *Marine Corps Gazette*, March 1983, p. 7, found at: http://pqasb.pqarchiver.com/mca-members.
26. Blankfort, *The Big Yankee*, p. 8.
27. Author's interview with Raymond Bauml, October 22, 2007.
28. Lt. Col. Evans Carlson, "Notes on the Organization of Raider Battalions," to Commanding General, IMAC, December 28, 1942, in the Evans F. Carlson Personal Files Collection, Marine Corps Research Center, Quantico, Virginia.

29. Letter from Evans Carlson to the Commandant of the Marine Corps, January 27, 1943, in the Evans F. Carlson Personal Files Collection, Marine Corps Research Center, Quantico, Virginia.

30. Author's interview with Joseph Griffith, March 7, 2007.

31. Author's interview with Kenneth McCullough, October 10, 2007.

32. Author's interview with Ben Carson, May 30, 2007.

33. Janet Ragland, "Lt. Jack Miller: A Family Bond," found at www.smu.edu/cul/memorial/familybond.htm, p. 1.

34. Ibid., p. 2.

35. Ibid.

36. Ibid.

37. Janet Ragland, "Lt. Jack Miller: A War Heats Up," found at www.smu.edu/cul/memorial/warheats.htm, p. 1.

38. Ibid.

39. Ibid.

40. Letter from Jack Miller to Carmen Miller, December 7, 1941; letter from Jack Miller to his mother, December 1941, in the Jack Miller Collection, DeGolyer Library, Southern Methodist University, Dallas, Texas.

41. Letter from James C. Jones to Henry Miller, February 1, 1943, in the Jack Miller Collection, DeGolyer Library, Southern Methodist University, Dallas, Texas.

42. Author's interview with Virginia Garabedian, February 27, 2008.

43. John H. Aroian, "A Visit with Capt. Vic Maghakian W.W. II Hero," *Armenian Reporter*, May 20, 1971, p. 2.

44. "Lee Marvin's 'Dirty Dozen' Recalls Carlson's Raiders 'Transport' Maghakian," *Showbiz*, undated magazine in the Victor Maghakian Personal File, Marine Corps Research Center, Quantico, Virginia.

45. Ibid.

46. Berry, *Semper Fi, Mac*, p. 121.

Chapter 3—We Could Have Taken on John Dillinger

1. Blankfort, *The Big Yankee*, p. 11.

2. Brian J. Quirk, "Reflections of Carlson's Raiders," *Marine Corps Gazette*, August 2001, pp. 1–2, found at http://pqasb.pqarchiver.com/mca-members.

3. Blankfort, *The Big Yankee*, p. 10.

4. Ibid., p. 12.

5. McCullough interview, May 25, 2007.

6. Griffith interview, March 7, 2007.

7. Mary Roosevelt interview, October 26, 2007.

8. Griffith interview, March 7, 2007.

9. Letter from John Apergis to Archie Rackerby, June 10, 1991, in the John Apergis Personal File, Marine Corps Research Center, Quantico, Virginia.

10. Letter from Lt. Col. Merritt A. Edson to Maj. Gen. Charles F. B. Price, February 20, 1942, in the Merritt A. Edson Collection, Library of Congress.

11. Carson interview, May 30, 2007.

12. Ibid.

13. Blankfort, *The Big Yankee*, p. 22.

14. Quirk interview, October 5, 2007; William Douglas Lansford, "Carlson of the Raiders," *Saga*, February 1961, p. 100.

15. Author's interview with Darrell A. Loveland, October 9, 2007.

16. Carson interview, May 30, 2007.

17. Berry, *Semper Fi, Mac*, p. 121; John Apergis letter to Merritt Edson, February 19, 1942, in the Merritt A. Edson Collection, Library of Congress, Washington, D.C.

18. Peatross, *Bless 'Em All*, p. 16.

19. James Roosevelt, "Evans Carlson: A Personal Memoir," in Craig Symonds, ed., *New Aspects of Naval History* (Annapolis, MD: Naval Institute Press, 1981), p. 389.

20. Smith, *Carlson's Raid*, p. 56.

21. McCullough interview, May 25, 2007.

22. Loveland interview, October 9, 2007.

23. Letters from Jack Miller to his mother, March 1, 1942, and March 1942, in the Jack Miller Collection, DeGolyer Library, Southern Methodist University, Dallas, Texas.

24. Ben Carson interview with the Admiral Nimitz National Museum of the Pacific War, September 21, 2001.

25. Lt. Col. Evans Carlson, "Methods of the U.S. Marine Raiders," undated manuscript in the Evans F. Carlson Collection, Marine Corps Research Center, Quantico, Virginia.

26. 1st Lt. W. S. Le Francois, "We Mopped Up Makin Island," *Saturday Evening Post*, Part I—December 4, 1943, p. 20.

27. Blankfort, *The Big Yankee*, p. 27.

28. Janet Ragland, "Lt. Jack Miller: An Officer and a Friend," found at www.smu.edu/cul/memorial/warbio.htm, pp. 3–4.

29. Letter from Jack Miller to his mother, March 17, 1942, in the Jack Miller Collection, DeGolyer Library, Southern Methodist University, Dallas, Texas.

30. Lieutenant John Apergis letter to Merritt Edson, February 19, 1942, in the Merritt A. Edson Collection, Library of Congress, Washington, D.C.

31. Author's interview with Lathrop Gay, May 28, 2008.

32. "Leatherneck Raiders," Division of Public Relations, Headquarters, U.S. Marine Corps, 1942, in the Evans F. Carlson Collection, Marine Corps Research Center, Quantico, Virginia.

33. Loveland interview, October 9, 2007.

34. Author's interview with Richard Favinger, June 5, 2008.

35. Robert Sherrod, *Tarawa: The Story of a Battle* (New York: Duell, Sloan and Pearce, 1944), p. 37.

36. Carson interview, May 30, 2007.

37. "The First Line," CBS Radio Program script, January 11, 1945, in the Jack Miller Collection, DeGolyer Library, Southern Methodist University, Dallas, Texas.

38. Lucien Hubbard, "Colonel Carlson and His Gung Ho Raiders," *Reader's Digest*, December 1943, p. 67.

39. Blankfort, *The Big Yankee*, p. 21.

40. McCullough interview, May 25, 2007.

41. Letter from Maj. Gen. Oscar F. Peatross to Michael Zak, December 1979, in the Michael J. Zak Collection.

42. Author's interview with Ervin Kaplan, October 3, 2007.

43. Author's interview with Dean Voight, October 9, 2007.

44. "Two Carlson Heroes Make Pastor Proud," *Hartford Courant*, April 13, 1943.

45. Peatross, *Bless 'Em All*, p. 14.

46. Gay interview, May 28, 2008.

47. Sherrod, *Tarawa: The Story of a Battle*, pp. 36–37.

48. McCullough interview, May 25, 2007.

49. Jim Lucas, *Combat Correspondent* (New York: Reynal & Hitchcock Publishers, 1944), p. 101.

50. Ibid., p. 100.

51. Blankfort, *The Big Yankee*, p. 36.

52. Murrey Marder, "Raider Carlson—Maverick Marine," *Washington Post*, June 1, 1947, p. 3B.

53. Joseph P. Lash, *Eleanor and Franklin* (New York: W. W. Norton & Company, Inc., 1971), p. 655.

54. Anonymous, "The Makin Island Raid," *Marine Corps Gazette*, March/April 1943, p. 2.

55. "Doctrine of the Raider Battalion," found in a Raider scrapbook located at the United States Marine Raider Museum, Quantico, Virginia.

56. Brig. Gen. Samuel B. Griffith Interview with Headquarters Marine Corps, November 1968, pp. 53–54.

57. James Roosevelt Interview with the Marine Historical Center, October 25, 1979.

58. Griffith interview, February 20, 2008.

59. Griffith interview, February 20, 2008; Ben Carson interview with the Admiral Nimitz National Museum of the Pacific War, September 21, 2001.

60. Maj. Samuel B. Griffith to Gen. Holland M. Smith, May 7, 1942, found in the Evans F. Carlson Personal File, Quantico, Virginia; Brig. Gen. Samuel B. Griffith Interview with Headquarters Marine Corps, November 1968, p. 54.

61. SSgt. Samuel R. Stavisky, "Raiders in Pacific Not Supermen but Highly Specialized Marines," Marine Corps Press Release, March 29, 1943, pp. 1–2, in "Marine Raiders: Publications, Articles, and Biographies" Folder, Marine Personal Files, Quantico, Virginia.

62. Roosevelt, "Evans Carlson: A Personal Memoir," p. 395.

63. General A. A. Vandegrift, as told to Robert B. Asprey, *Once a Marine* (New York: W. W. Norton & Company, Inc., 1964), p. 100.

64. Gen. Merrill B. Twining, USMC (Ret.), *No Bended Knee* (Novato, CA: Presidio, 1994), p. 142.

65. Berry, *Semper Fi, Mac*, p. 114.

66. Brig. Gen. Samuel B. Griffith Interview with Headquarters Marine Corps, November 1968, pp. 50, 56.

67. Quirk, "Reflections of Carlson's Raiders," p. 1; author's interview with Brian Quirk, February 13, 2007.

68. Quirk, "Reflections of Carlson's Raiders," p. 1.

69. Peatross, *Bless 'Em All*, p. 17.

70. Letter from Carlson to Roosevelt, March 2, 1942.

71. Voight interview, October 9, 2007.

72. Letter from Carlson to Roosevelt, March 2, 1942.

73. Letter from Roosevelt to Carlson, March 12, 1942.

74. Letter from Adm. Chester Nimitz to Adm. Ernest King, April 23, 1942, in the Evans F. Carlson Personal File, Quantico, Virginia.

75. Letter from Carlson to Roosevelt, April 29, 1942.

76. Peatross, *Bless 'Em All*, p. 17.

Chapter 4—We Were Itching for a Fight

1. Blankfort, *The Big Yankee*, pp. 34–35.

2. Author's interview with Jesse Vanlandingham, February 14, 2008.

3. Loveland interview, October 16, 2007.

4. Peatross, *Bless 'Em All*, p. 19.

5. Loveland interview, October 16, 2007.

6. Hiroyuki Agawa, *The Reluctant Admiral* (Tokyo: Kodansha International Ltd., 1979), p. 302.

7. Letter from John Apergis to Archie Rackerby, June 10, 1991, in the John Apergis Personal File, Marine Corps Research Center, Quantico, Virginia.

8. Vanlandingham interview, February 14, 2008.

9. Author's interview with Virgil Leeman, February 15, 2008.

10. Author's interview with Thomas Tobin, October 5, 2007.

11. Loveland interview, October 16, 2007.

12. Lash, *Eleanor and Franklin*, p. 654.

13. Walter Lord, *Incredible Victory* (New York: Harper & Row, Publishers, 1967), p. 48.

14. Ralph Shawlee's account of Midway, *Raider Patch*, May 1989, pp. 2–3.

15. Loveland interview, October 16, 2007.

16. Leeman interview, February 15, 2008.

17. Lt. Col. Robert D. Heinl, Jr., *Marines at Midway* (Headquarters U.S. Marine Corps: Historical Section Division of Public Information, 1948), p. 25.

18. Lord, *Incredible Victory*, p. 95.

19. Gordon W. Prange, with Donald M. Goldstein and Katherine V. Dillon, *Miracle at Midway* (New York: Penguin Books, 1982), p. 204.

20. Apergis to Rackerby, June 10, 1991; Naval Historical Center's Oral History, Battle of Midway, "Recollections of Commander John Ford," found at www.history.navy.mil, p. 3.

21. Leeman interview, February 15, 2008.

22. James Van Winkle, "Bull Sheet," *Raider Patch*, November 1994, p. 20.

23. Favinger interview, June 5, 2008.

24. Leeman interview, February 15, 2008.

25. Apergis to Rackerby, June 10, 1991.

26. "Recollections of Commander John Ford," p. 3.

27. Apergis to Rackerby, June 10, 1991.

28. "Recollections of Commander John Ford," pp. 2–4.

29. Lord, *Incredible Victory*, p. 108.

30. Robert Sherrod, *History of Marine Corps Aviation in World War II* (Washington, D.C.: Combat Forces Press, 1952), p. 64.

31. E. B. Potter and Fleet Admiral Chester W. Nimitz, USN, eds., *Triumph in the Pacific: The Navy's Struggle Against Japan* (Englewood Cliffs, NJ: Prentice-Hall, Inc., 1963), p. 20.

32. Casey, *Torpedo Junction*, p. 398.

33. Berry, *Semper Fi, Mac*, p. 122.

34. Peatross, *Bless 'Em All*, p. 20.

35. Letter from Jack Miller to his parents, July 5, 1942, in the Jack Miller Collection, DeGolyer Library, Southern Methodist University, Dallas, Texas.

36. Handwritten notes about Maj. Gen. Omar T. Pfeiffer Oral History, Marine Corps

Oral History Collection, found in the Evans F. Carlson Collection, Marine Corps Research Center, Quantico, Virginia.

37. Blankfort, *The Big Yankee*, p. 38.
38. Ray Bauml, *The Diary of Ray Bauml, July 2, 1942 to December 19, 1942*, July 30, 1942 entry, from the Ray Bauml Collection.
39. Carson interview, October 11, 2007.
40. Letter from Ray Bauml to Henry Miller, September 8, 1953, in the Jack Miller Collection, DeGolyer Library, Southern Methodist University, Dallas, Texas.
41. *The Diary of Ray Bauml*, July 30, 1942.
42. Ibid.
43. Peatross, *Bless 'Em All*, p. 48.
44. Ibid., p. 51.
45. Berry, *Semper Fi, Mac*, p. 117.
46. Smith, *Carlson's Raid*, p. 90.
47. Carson interview, October 11, 2007.

Chapter 5—It Seemed That Confusion Reigned Supreme

1. Adm. Chester W. Nimitz to Commander in Chief, U.S. Pacific Fleet, "Solomon Islands Campaign—Makin Diversion," October 20, 1942, in the Evans F. Carlson Collection, Marine Corps Research Center, Quantico, Virginia.
2. Ben Carson interview with the Admiral Nimitz National Museum of the Pacific War, September 21, 2001.
3. Letter from Sgt. Victor Maghakian to Henry Miller, July 12, 1943, in the Jack Miller Collection, DeGolyer Library, Southern Methodist University, Dallas, Texas.
4. *Argonaut*, "Report of Second War Patrol, August 8, 1942 to August 26, 1942," in the Evans F. Carlson Collection, Marine Corps Research Center, Quantico, Virginia.
5. Rear Adm. R. E. English, Commander Task Force Seven, "Operations Order No. 71-42," August 5, 1942.
6. Author's interview with Brian Quirk, October 23, 2007.
7. Lt. Col. Evans Carlson, "Operations Order 1-42," On Board *Nautilus*, August 7, 1942; Lt. Col. Evans Carlson, "Operations Order 2-42," On Board *Nautilus*, August 7, 1942.
8. Bauml, *The Diary of Ray Bauml, July 2, 1942 to December 19, 1942*, August 9 entry.
9. Peatross, *Bless 'Em All*, p. 52.
10. Oscar Peatross, "The Makin Raid," *Marine Corps Gazette*, November 1979, pp. 2–3, found at http://pqasb.pqarchiver.com/mca-members.

11. Carson interview, October 11, 2007.

12. Le Francois, "We Mopped Up Makin Island," December 4, 1943, p. 20.

13. Quirk interview, October 23, 2007.

14. Voight interview, October 16, 2007.

15. James Roosevelt interview with the Marine Historical Center, October 25, 1979.

16. Jack Miller letter to his mother, August 17, 1942, in the Jack Miller Collection, DeGolyer Library, Southern Methodist University, Dallas, Texas.

17. Carson interview, October 11, 2007.

18. Peatross, *Bless 'Em All*, p. 54.

19. Ibid.; Brian J. Quirk and Howard A. Young, "Carlson's Raiders on Makin, 17–18 August 1942," *Marine Corps Gazette*, August 2003, p. 1, found at http://pqasb .pqarchiver.com/mca-members.

20. McCullough interview, May 30, 2007.

21. Carson interview, October 11, 2007.

22. Patrick K. O'Donnell, *Into the Rising Sun* (New York: The Free Press, 2002), p. 28.

23. Griffith interview, February 20, 2008; Voight interview, October 16, 2007.

24. Le Francois, "We Mopped Up Makin Island," December 4, p. 21.

25. Carson interview, October 11, 2007.

26. Quirk interview, October 23, 2007.

27. Author's interview with Julius Cotten, April 14, 2008.

28. Lt. Col. Evans Carlson, "Operations on Makin, August 17–18, 1942," On Board *Nautilus*, August 21, 1942, in the Evans F. Carlson Collection, Marine Corps Research Center, Quantico, Virginia.

29. Bauml interview, January 21, 2008.

30. Carson interview, October 18, 2007.

31. Voight interview, October 16, 2007.

32. Carlson, "Operations on Makin, August 17–18, 1942."

33. O'Donnell, *Into the Rising Sun*, p. 29.

34. Cotten interview, April 14, 2008; O'Donnell, *Into the Rising Sun*, p. 29.

35. Peatross, *Bless 'Em All*, p. 56.

36. *Nautilus* War Diary, August 17, 1942.

37. "The Raid on Makin Island, 17–18 August 1942," draft of a chapter on the Makin Raid, Marine Historical Center, August 23, 1956, in the Evans F. Carlson Collection, Marine Corps Research Center, Quantico, Virginia, p. 16.

38. Peatross, *Bless 'Em All*, p. 69.

39. Carlson, "Operations on Makin, August 17–18, 1942."

40. Le Francois, "We Mopped Up Makin Island," December 4, p. 109.

41. Ibid.

42. Peatross, *Bless 'Em All*, p. 72.

43. Cotten interview, April 14, 2008.

44. Le Francois, "We Mopped Up Makin Island," December 4, p. 109.
45. Col. R. G. Rosenquist, Martin J. Sexton, and Robert A. Buerlein, *Our Kind of War* (Richmond, VA: The American Historical Foundation, 1990), p. 54.
46. *Los Angeles Times*, January 25, 1943, article found in the Victor Maghakian Personal File, Quantico, Virginia.
47. *Fresno Bee*, August 19, 1977, article found in the Victor Maghakian Personal File, Quantico, Virginia.
48. September 25, 2000, letter from Stephen Stigler to Virginia Garabedian, found in the Virginia Garabedian Collection.
49. Peatross, *Bless 'Em All*, p. 57.
50. Griffith interview, February 20, 2008.
51. Carlson, "Operations on Makin, August 17–18, 1942."
52. Ben Carson interview with the Admiral Nimitz National Museum of the Pacific War, September 21, 2001.
53. Le Francois, "We Mopped Up Makin Island," December 4, p. 110.
54. Author's interview with Neal Milligan, April 11, 2008.
55. Joseph J. Woodford, "Jungle Fighting as Marine Raiders Know It," Civilian Defense radio program airing over KCMO, Kansas City, March 9, 1944, in the Joseph Woodford Collection.
56. Le Francois, "We Mopped Up Makin Island," December 4, p. 110.
57. Letter from Victor Maghakian to June and Joan Gaston, November 17, 1943, found in the Virginia Garabedian Collection.
58. Gleason, *Real Blood! Real Guts!*, p. 58.
59. McCullough interview, October 10, 2007; Milligan interview, April 11, 2008.
60. Carson interview, October 18, 2007.
61. Griffith interview, February 20, 2008.
62. "White House Hails Raid," *New York Times*, August 28, 1942, p. 1.
63. "Being a Hero Can Get in the Way," *Las Vegas Sun*, p. 3, undated article in the Victor Maghakian Personal File, Marine Corps Research Center, Quantico, Virginia.
64. "Bull Sheet," *Raider Patch*, June 1975, p. 10.
65. McCullough interview, October 10, 2007.

Chapter 6—It Will Forever Remain a Ghastly Nightmare

1. Blankfort, *The Big Yankee*, p. 48.
2. Quirk interview, October 5, 2007.
3. McCullough interview, April 10, 2008.
4. Richard Haller, "First Eyewitness Story of Gilbert Isle Raid," *New York Journal American*, August 28, 1942, p. 2.

5. Evans Carlson letter to Franklin Roosevelt, August 27, 1942, found in the James Roosevelt Papers, Franklin D. Roosevelt Presidential Library, Hyde Park, New York.

6. "The Raid on Makin Island, 17–18 August 1942," draft of a chapter on the Makin Raid, Marine Historical Center, August 23, 1956.

7. Untitled 1943 article by Evans Carlson reprinted in *Raider Patch*, May 1993, p. 20.

8. "Statement made by James C. Green, Private first class, USMC," included in *Nautilus*, "Report of Second War Patrol, August 8, 1942 to August 25, 1942," August 17.

9. Author's interview with Denton Hudman, April 9, 2008.

10. Comdr. J. M. Haines, Commander Task Group G 7.15, "Report of Marine-Submarine Raider Expedition," August 24, 1942, located at the National Archives and Records Administration, College Park, Maryland, p. 9.

11. Peatross, *Bless 'Em All*, p. 76.

12. Cotten interview, April 14, 2008.

13. Peatross, *Bless 'Em All*, p. 78.

14. McCullough interview, October 10, 2007.

15. Peatross, *Bless 'Em All*, p. 78.

16. Sgt. Merle Miller, "Transport Maghakian's Revenge," *Yank*, April 28, 1944, p. 8.

17. Carlson, "Operations on Makin, August 17–18, 1942."

18. "The Raid on Makin Island, 17–18 August 1942," draft of a chapter on the Makin Raid, Marine Historical Center, August 23, 1956, in the Evans F. Carlson Collection, Marine Corps Research Center, Quantico, Virginia, p. 19.

19. Nimitz, "Solomon Islands Campaign—Makin Diversion," October 20, 1942, p. 4.

20. Rosenquist, Sexton, and Buerlein, *Our Kind of War*, p. 51.

21. McCullough interview, April 10, 2008.

22. Carson interview, October 18, 2007.

23. Le Francois, "We Mopped Up Makin Island," December 11, p. 28; Carlson, "Operations on Makin, August 17–18, 1942."

24. Milligan interview, April 11, 2008.

25. McCullough interview, April 10, 2008; Bauml interview, January 28, 2008.

26. Quirk interview, October 23, 2007.

27. Peatross, *Bless 'Em All*, pp. 79–80.

28. Cotten interview, April 14, 2008.

29. Peatross, *Bless 'Em All*, p. 60.

30. Ibid., p. 61.

31. Griffith interview, February 20, 2008.

32. Carlson, "Operations on Makin, August 17–18, 1942."

33. McCullough interview, April 10, 2008.

34. Carlson, "Operations on Makin, August 17–18, 1942."

35. Cotten interview, April 14, 2008.

36. Roosevelt, *My Parents: A Differing View*, pp. 271–72.

37. Milligan interview, April 11, 2008; author's interview with William Nugent, April 15, 2008.

38. Smith, *Carlson's Raid*, p. 153.

39. Bauml interview, January 28, 2008; McCullough interview, April 10, 2008.

40. Roosevelt, "Evans Carlson: A Personal Memoir," p. 398.

41. Blankfort, *The Big Yankee*, pp. 60–61.

42. Griffith interview, February 20, 2008.

43. Kenneth Seaton, "Bull Sheet," *Raider Patch*, March 1982, p. 18; Buck Stidham, "Comments on Returning from the Makin Raid," *Raider Patch*, January 1993, pp. 12–13.

44. Blankfort, *The Big Yankee*, p. 60.

45. Carlson, "Operations on Makin, August 17–18, 1942."

46. Blankfort, *The Big Yankee*, p. 61.

47. Peatross, *Bless 'Em All*, p. 80.

48. Roosevelt interview, October 26, 2007.

49. The surrender account is found in Peatross, *Bless 'Em All*, pp. 81–82.

50. Smith, *Carlson's Raid*, p. 155.

51. Ibid., p. 158.

52. Quirk interview, October 23, 2007.

53. McCullough interview, April 10, 2008.

54. Voight interview, October 16, 2007.

55. Roosevelt interview, October 26, 2007.

56. Le Francois, "We Mopped Up Makin Island," December 11, p. 29.

57. *Nautilus* War Diary, August 17–18, 1942.

58. Peatross, *Bless 'Em All*, pp. 63–66.

59. Letter from Carlson to Roosevelt, August 27, 1942, in the James Roosevelt Papers, Franklin D. Roosevelt Presidential Library, Hyde Park, New York.

60. Rosenquist, Sexton, and Buerlein, *Our Kind of War*, p. 55.

61. Smith, *Carlson's Raid*, p. 160.

62. Bauml interview, January 28, 2008.

63. Roosevelt, *My Parents: A Differing View*, p. 272.

64. Le Francois, "We Mopped Up Makin Island," December 11, p. 41.

65. Adm. Chester W. Nimitz to Commanding General, Amphibious Corps, "Comments on Makin Raid," September 21, 1942, in the Evans F. Carlson Collection, Marine Corps Research Center, Quantico, Virginia.

66. O'Donnell, *Into the Rising Sun*, p. 32.

Chapter 7—A Poor Fit with the Map

1. Carlson, "Operations on Makin, August 17–18, 1942."
2. Le Francois, "We Mopped Up Makin Island," December 11, p. 43.
3. O'Donnell, *Into the Rising Sun*, p. 32.
4. Le Francois, "We Mopped Up Makin Island," December 11, p. 43.
5. Carlson, "Operations on Makin, August 17–18, 1942."
6. October 8, 2007, e-mail from Kenneth McCullough to author.
7. Le Francois, "We Mopped Up Makin Island," December 11, p. 48.
8. Cotten interview, April 14, 2008.
9. Rosenquist, Sexton, and Buerlein, *Our Kind of War*, p. 55.
10. Peatross, *Bless 'Em All*, p. 84.
11. Ibid.
12. Comdr. J. M. Haines, Commander Task Group G 7.15, "Operations Order No. 1-42," August 6, 1942, in the National Archives and Records Administration, College Park, Maryland.
13. Cotten interview, April 14, 2008.
14. Smith, *Carlson's Raid*, p. 156.
15. Ibid., p. 157.
16. James Roosevelt Interview with the Marine Historical Center, October 25, 1979.
17. O'Donnell, *Into the Rising Sun*, p. 35.
18. Cotten interview, April 14, 2008.
19. Blankfort, *The Big Yankee*, p. 71; Buck Stidham, "Comments on Returning from the Makin Raid," *Raider Patch*, January 1993, pp. 12–13.
20. "Eulogy Delivered by Lt. Col. Evans F. Carlson at the Memorial Services for the Members of the 2nd Raider Battalion Who Fell at Makin, 17 and 18 August 1942," copy resting on the wall of the Raider Museum, Quantico, Virginia.
21. Roosevelt, "Evans Carlson: A Personal Memoir," p. 397.
22. Jack Miller letter to his mother, September 3, 1942, in the Jack Miller Collection, DeGolyer Library, Southern Methodist University, Dallas, Texas.
23. "Col. Roosevelt, He See Eye-To-Eye, Says Carlson," *Waterbury Republican*, June 9, 1943.
24. James Roosevelt Interview with the Marine Historical Center, October 25, 1979.
25. Stidham, "Comments on Returning from the Makin Raid," p. 13.
26. "Forty Hours on Makin," *Time*, September 7, 1942, p. 33.
27. Undated newspaper article found in "Marine Raiders: Press Releases," in the Evans Carlson Personal Files, Marine Corps Research Center, Quantico, Virginia; "Marine Corps 'Raider' Battalions Employed in Solomons Offensive," *New York Times*, August 25, 1942; Wesley Price, "Raider Carlson," *New York Picture News*, January 2, 1944, p. 2; Marine Press Release, Division of Public Relations, September 3, 1942.

28. F. Tillman Durdin, "The Roughest and the Toughest," *New York Times*, November 8, 1942, p. SM13.

29. Lucas, *Combat Correspondent*, p. 99.

30. Samuel E. Stavisky, *Marine Combat Correspondent* (New York: Ivy Books, 1999), p. 37.

31. "Jimmy Roosevelt's Part in Makin Attack Comes as Complete Surprise to President," *Cincinnati Post*, August 22, 1942.

32. "Roosevelt Boys Are Making Good," *Springfield* (MA) *News*, August 25, 1942.

33. Drew Pearson, "Major Roosevelt, Marine Raider," undated news article found in the Joseph J. Woodford Collection.

34. "Marine Sizes Up Jimmy," *Newark Evening News*, March 11, 1943, quoting a letter written the previous November.

35. *Boston American*, August 26, 1942.

36. Letter from Carlson to Roosevelt, August 27, 1942.

37. James Roosevelt's Navy Cross citation.

38. Admiral Matome Ugaki, *Fading Victory: The Diary of Admiral Matome Ugaki, 1941–1945* (Pittsburgh: The University of Pittsburgh Press, 1991), pp. 185, 194.

39. 1943 Evans Carlson article reprinted in *Raider Patch*, January 1994, p. 12; Peatross, *Bless 'Em All*, p. 83.

40. F. Tillman Durdin, "Foe Belted on Isle," *New York Times*, August 22, 1942, pp. 1, 3.

41. Holland M. Smith and Percy Finch, *Coral and Brass* (New York: Charles Scribner's Sons, 1949), p. 132.

42. Lt. Col. Charles T. Lamb, "Comments on the Raid on Makin Island Manuscript," August 23, 1956, in the Evans F. Carlson Collection, Marine Corps Research Center, Quantico, Virginia.

43. Peatross, *Bless 'Em All*, p. 89.

44. Berry, *Semper Fi, Mac*, p. 122.

45. Carlson, "Operations on Makin, August 17–18, 1942," p. 5.

46. This account is found in three places. James Roosevelt described it in "Evans Carlson: A Personal Memoir," p. 396; Maj. Gen. Omar T. Pfeiffer Oral History, Marine Corps Oral History Collection, 1968, Marine Corps Research Center, Quantico, Virginia; handwritten notes pertaining to the Omar T. Pfeiffer Oral History found in the Evans F. Carlson Collection, Marine Corps Research Center, Quantico, Virginia.

47. Carlson, "Operations on Makin, August 17–18, 1942."

48. Comdr. J. M. Haines, Commander Task Group G 7.15, "Report of Marine-Submarine Raider Expedition," August 24, 1942, located at the National Archives and Records Administration, College Park, Maryland.

49. Nimitz, "Solomon Islands Campaign—Makin Diversion," October 20, 1942.

50. Stidham, "Comments on Returning from the Makin Raid," pp. 12–13; Roger Conee, "Raiders Not Welcome, But Very Effective," *Raider Patch*, July–September 2004, p. 14.

51. Michael J. Zak, "A Short History of Evans Carlson and the Carlson Raiders," p. 11, Discussion notes for Harvard Business School, 1981; Michael J. Zak, "Evans Carlson and the Carlson Raiders," thesis written for Harvard Business School, 1981, in the Michael J. Zak Collection.

52. Author's interview with Robert Burnette, March 4, 2008.

53. Griffith interview, February 20, 2008.

54. McCullough interview, April 10, 2008.

55. Roosevelt, "Evans Carlson: A Personal Memoir," p. 398; Roosevelt interview, October 26, 2007.

56. McCullough interview, April 10, 2008.

57. Brian J. Quirk, "Epilogue: The 12 Missing in Action," *Marine Corps Gazette*, November 2003, p. 1, found athttp://pqasb.pqarchiver.com/mca-members.

58. Tripp Wiles, *Forgotten Raiders of '42* (Washington, D.C.: Potomac Books, Inc., 2007), p. 128.

Chapter 8—We Rode to the Sound of the Guns

1. Leeman interview, February 15, 2008.

2. Peatross, *Bless 'Em All*, p. 125.

3. Burnette interview, January 31, 2008.

4. Letter from Jack Miller to his parents, October 10, 1942, in the Jack Miller Collection, DeGolyer Library, Southern Methodist University, Dallas, Texas.

5. Author's interview with Rhel Cook, April 9, 2008.

6. Letter from Evans Carlson to James Roosevelt, October 17, 1942, in the James Roosevelt Papers, Franklin D. Roosevelt Presidential Library, Hyde Park, New York.

7. Loveland interview, October 26, 2007.

8. Lowell V. Bulger, "The Second Marine Raider Battalion on Guadalcanal, 4 November–12 December 1942," *Raider Patch*, March 1981, p. 5.

9. Hoffman, *Chesty*, p. 181.

10. "We Are Losing the War," *Time*, September 7, 1942, p. 30.

11. Hoffman, *Chesty*, p. 180.

12. John Toland, *The Rising Sun* (New York: Random House, 1970), pp. 455–56.

13. John Hersey, *Into the Valley* (New York: Alfred A. Knopf, 1943), p. 56.

14. James Jones, *WWII* (New York: Ballantine Books, 1975), p. 28.

15. Richard Washburn, "Bull Sheet," *Raider Patch*, November 1981, p. 21.

16. Bulger, "The Second Marine Raider Battalion on Guadalcanal, 4 November–12 December 1942," March 1981, pp. 7–8.

17. Burnette interview, January 31, 2008.

18. Loveland interview, October 26, 2007.

19. Bulger, "The Second Marine Raider Battalion on Guadalcanal, 4 November–12 December 1942," March 1981, p. 8; Martin Clemens, *Alone on Guadalcanal* (Annapolis, MD: Naval Institute Press, 1998), p. 278.

20. Berry, *Semper Fi, Mac*, p. 123.

21. Bulger, "The Second Marine Raider Battalion on Guadalcanal, 4 November–12 December 1942," March 1981, p. 9.

22. Letter from John Apergis to Archie Rackerby, June 10, 1991, in the John Apergis Collection, Marine Corps Research Center, Quantico, Virginia.

23. William Douglas Lansford, "We Caught Them with Their Pants Down: The Battle at Asamana," *Leatherneck*, November 2007, p. 60.

24. Clemens, *Alone on Guadalcanal*, p. 293.

25. Bulger, "The Second Marine Raider Battalion on Guadalcanal, 4 November–12 December 1942," March 1981, p. 11.

26. Peatross, *Bless 'Em All*, p. 135.

27. Ibid.

28. Ibid., p. 138.

29. Gay interview, May 28, 2008.

30. Cleland Early, "Col. Richard Washburn," *Raider Patch*, May 1991, p. 26; letter from Bob Burnette to June Washburn, March 10, 1991, from the June Washburn Collection.

31. Lowell Bulger, "Bloody Plains Brief," *Raider Patch*, May 1980, p. 12.

32. Ibid., pp. 12–13.

33. John Mather, "The Need for Training as Demonstrated by an Operation on Guadalcanal—1942," a paper found in the Eric Hammel Collection, Marine Corps Research Center, Quantico, Virginia, p. 10.

34. Bulger, "Bloody Plains Brief," p. 13.

35. Bob Tutt, "Guerrilla-Like Carlson's Raiders 'Rode to the Sound of the Guns,'" *Houston Chronicle*, July 1, 1995, pp. 1–3, found at www.chron.com, p. 1.

36. "W. H. Youth in Record Breaking Guerilla [sic] Raid," undated newspaper article in the June Washburn Collection.

37. Vanlandingham interview, June 2, 2008.

38. Gay interview, May 28, 2008.

39. Letter from Richard Washburn to Eric Hammel, September 22, 1963, in the Eric Hammel Collection, Marine Corps Research Center, Quantico, Virginia.

40. Lansford, "We Caught Them with Their Pants Down," p. 64.

41. Gay interview, May 28, 2008.

42. Jim Lucas, Marine Corps Press Release, July 17, 1943, in the Evans F. Carlson Personal Files, Marine Corps Research Center, Quantico, Virginia.
43. Bulger, "Bloody Plains Brief," p. 13.
44. Author's interview with Pete Arias, June 3, 2008.
45. Bill Onstad with Jayson Lowery, *Trust. Truth. Evil* (Victoria, BC: Trafford Publishing, 2005), p. 71.
46. Mather, "The Need for Training as Demonstrated by an Operation on Guadalcanal—1942," pp. 11–12.
47. Lt. Col. Evans Carlson, "Report of Operations of this Battalion on Guadalcanal between 4 November and 4 December, 1942," December 20, 1942, in the Evans F. Carlson Collection, Marine Corps Research Center, Quantico, Virginia, p. 6.
48. Untitled newspaper article found in the June Washburn Collection.
49. Sherrod, *Tarawa: The Story of a Battle*, p. 37.
50. Art McGinley, "Good Afternoon," an undated article found in the June Washburn Collection.
51. Raymond Gram Swing radio broadcast, November 11, 1942, in the Jack Miller Collection.
52. Letter from Evans Carlson to Raymond Swing, December 11, 1942, in the Raymond Gram Swing Collection, Library of Congress, Washington, D.C.

Chapter 9—The Law of the Jungle

1. Ed Fischer, "Close Call," *Raider Patch*, May 1993, p. 5.
2. Gay interview, May 28, 2008.
3. Kaplan interview, October 3, 2007; Burnette interview, February 5, 2008.
4. Loveland interview, June 4, 2008; Gay interview, May 28, 2008.
5. Letter from Evans Carlson to Raymond Gram Swing, December 15, 1942.
6. TSgt. Jim Lucas, undated Marine press release, in the Evans F. Carlson Personal Files, Marine Corps Research Center, Quantico, Virginia.
7. Carlson, "Report of Operations of this Battalion on Guadalcanal between 4 November and 4 December, 1942," pp. 17–18.
8. Author's interview with Nathan Lipscomb, June 4, 2008; Loveland interview, June 4, 2008.
9. Author's interview with Edward Hammer, June 13, 2008.
10. Tobin interview, October 5, 2007.
11. Quirk interview, October 23, 2007.
12. Arthur D. Gardner, "Diary of a Marine Raider: The Cream of the Corps," *Soldier of Fortune*, January 1981, p. 61.
13. Washburn letter to Hammel, September 22, 1963.

14. Herbert Christian Merillat, *The Island* (Boston: Houghton Mifflin Company, 1944), p. 221.
15. McCullough interview, June 6, 2008.
16. Lowell Bulger, "The Second Marine Raider Battalion on Guadalcanal, 4 November–12 December 1942," *Raider Patch*, September 1981, p. 12.
17. Ibid., p. 14.
18. Berry, *Semper Fi, Mac*, p. 125.
19. Apergis letter to Rackerby, June 10, 1991.
20. Twining, *No Bended Knee*, p. 144.
21. McCullough interview, June 6, 2008.
22. Carlson, "Report of Operations of this Battalion on Guadalcanal between 4 November and 4 December, 1942," p. 15.
23. Onstad and Lowery, *Trust. Truth. Evil*, p. 65.
24. Quirk interview, October 23, 2007.
25. Onstad and Lowery, *Trust. Truth. Evil*, p. 67.
26. Letter from Martin Clemens to Michael J. Zak, March 8, 1982.
27. Author's interview with Eugene Hasenberg, June 12, 2008.
28. Marine Corps Press Release, June 1943, found in "Marine Raiders: Press Releases," in the Evans F. Carlson Personal Files Collection, Marine Corps Research Center, Quantico, Virginia.
29. Gay interview, May 28, 2008.
30. Ashley W. Fisher, "Reflection," *Marine Corps Gazette*, August 2001, p. 1, found at http://pqasb.pqarchiver.com/mca-members.
31. Burnette interview, March 4, 2008; Cook interview, April 9, 2008.
32. Don Richter, *Where the Sun Stood Still!* (Calabasas, CA: Toucan Publishing, 1992), p. 343.
33. Bulger, "The Second Marine Raider Battalion on Guadalcanal, 4 November–12 December 1942," March 1981, p. 3.
34. Kaplan interview, June 5, 2008.
35. Carson interview, June 5, 2008.
36. Loveland interviews, October 26, 2007, June 4, 2008.
37. Gay interview, May 28, 2008.
38. Griffith interview, February 20, 2008.
39. Cook interview, April 9, 2008.
40. Berry, *Semper Fi, Mac*, p. 124.
41. Hersey, *Into the Valley*, p. 49.
42. Ibid., p. 48.
43. Tamera Newman, *A Survivor's Story* (Logan, UT: Watkins Printing, 2007), p. 23.
44. Cook interview, April 9, 2008.
45. Author's interview with Frank Kurland, October 3, 2007.

46. Loveland interviews, October 26, 2007, June 4, 2008; Burnette interview, January 31, 2008.

47. Gay interview, May 28, 2008.

48. Loveland interview, June 4, 2008.

49. Leeman interview, June 4, 2008.

50. Hasenberg interview, June 12, 2008.

51. Kurland interview, October 3, 2007.

52. Lipscomb interview, June 4, 2008.

53. Foster Hailey, *Pacific Battle Line* (New York: The Macmillan Company, 1944), p. 255.

54. Quirk interview, October 23, 2007.

55. Leeman interview, June 4, 2008; Gay interview, May 28, 2008.

56. Martin Miller, "A Latino Veteran Finally Shares His Battlefield Tales," *Los Angeles Times*, September 21, 2007, p. 2, found at http://pqasb.pqarchiver.com/latimes.

57. Gay interview, May 28, 2008.

58. Statement found in the Earl Wilson Papers, Marine Corps Research Center, Quantico, Virginia.

59. Berry, *Semper Fi, Mac*, p. 123.

60. Leeman interview, June 4, 2008.

61. Vanlandingham interview, June 2, 2008.

62. Loveland interview, June 4, 2008.

63. Loveland interview, October 26, 2007.

64. Voight interview, October 26, 2007.

65. Cook interview, April 9, 2008.

66. Mather, "The Need for Training as Demonstrated by an Operation on Guadalcanal—1942," p. 13; Loveland interview, October 26, 2007.

67. John W. Studer, "Just Thinkin'," *Raider Patch*, May 1976, p. 4.

68. Loveland interview, October 26, 2007.

69. Peatross, *Bless 'Em All*, p. 150.

70. Ervin Kaplan, M.D., "A Personal View of the Guadalcanal Long Patrol," found at www.us.marineraiders.org/longpatrolview.htm, p. 5; Carlson, "Report of Operations of this Battalion on Guadalcanal between 4 November and 4 December, 1942," p. 7.

71. Griffith interview, February 20, 2008; Washburn letter to Hammel, September 22, 1963.

72. Gay interview, May 28, 2008.

73. Ibid.

74. Ibid.

75. Ben Carson interview with the Admiral Nimitz National Museum of the Pacific War, September 21, 2001.

76. Bulger, "The Second Marine Raider Battalion on Guadalcanal, 4 November–12 December 1942," March 1981, p. 9.
77. Gay interview, May 28, 2008.
78. Kaplan, "A Personal View of the Guadalcanal Long Patrol," p. 5; Burnette interview, March 4, 2008.
79. Hasenberg interview, June 12, 2008.
80. Voight interview, October 30, 2007.
81. Lipscomb interview, June 4, 2008.
82. Peatross, *Bless 'Em All*, p. 153.
83. Carlson letter to James Roosevelt, December 10, 1942.
84. Leeman interview, June 4, 2008.

Chapter 10—Where No Other Marines Have Ever Been

1. Bulger, "The Second Marine Raider Battalion on Guadalcanal, 4 November–12 December 1942," September 1981, p. 16.
2. Letter from Henry Miller to Jack Miller, November 26, 1942, in the Jack Miller Collection, DeGolyer Library, Southern Methodist University, Dallas, Texas.
3. John Schoch, "Bull Sheet," *Raider Patch*, November 1981, p. 24.
4. Letter from Victor Maghakian to Mr. Miller, July 12, 1943, in the Jack Miller Collection, DeGolyer Library, Southern Methodist University, Dallas, Texas.
5. Peatross, *Bless 'Em All*, p. 159.
6. Bulger, "The Second Marine Raider Battalion on Guadalcanal, 4 November–12 December 1942," November 1981, p. 11.
7. Carson interview, June 5, 2008.
8. Bulger, "The Second Marine Raider Battalion on Guadalcanal, 4 November–12 December 1942," November 1981, p. 11.
9. Ibid.
10. Carlson, "Report of Operations of this Battalion on Guadalcanal between 4 November and 4 December, 1942," p. 10.
11. Vanlandingham interview, June 2, 2008.
12. Peatross, *Bless 'Em All*, p. 164.
13. Carlson, "Report of Operations of this Battalion on Guadalcanal between 4 November and 4 December, 1942," p. 11.
14. Bulger, "The Second Marine Raider Battalion on Guadalcanal, 4 November–12 December 1942," November 1981, p. 13.
15. Twining, *No Bended Knee*, p. 164.
16. Letter from Stephen Stigler to Mr. and Mrs. Miller, December 22, 1942, in the Jack Miller Collection, DeGolyer Library, Southern Methodist University, Dallas, Texas.

17. Carlson, "Report of Operations of this Battalion on Guadalcanal between 4 November and 4 December, 1942," p. 11.

18. Vanlandingham interview, June 9, 2008.

19. Letter from Gy. Sgt. Victor Maghakian to Henry Miller, July 12, 1943, in the Jack Miller Collection, DeGolyer Library, Southern Methodist University, Dallas, Texas.

20. Letter from Ray Bauml to Henry Miller, September 8, 1953, in the Jack Miller Collection, DeGolyer Library, Southern Methodist University, Dallas, Texas.

21. Bauml interview, August 10, 2006.

22. Letter from Ray Bauml to Henry Miller, September 8, 1953, in the Jack Miller Collection, DeGolyer Library, Southern Methodist University, Dallas, Texas.

23. Peatross, *Bless 'Em All*, p. 165.

24. Letter from Gy. Sgt. Victor Maghakian to Henry Miller, July 12, 1943, in the Jack Miller Collection, DeGolyer Library, Southern Methodist University, Dallas, Texas.

25. Peatross, *Bless 'Em All*, p. 165.

26. Letter from Capt. John Apergis to Henry Miller, May 10, 1943, in the Jack Miller Collection, DeGolyer Library, Southern Methodist University, Dallas, Texas.

27. Gy. Sgt. Victor Maghakian letter to Henry Miller, July 12, 1943, in the Jack Miller Collection, DeGolyer Library, Southern Methodist University, Dallas, Texas.

28. Ibid.

29. Peatross, *Bless 'Em All*, p. 166; Griffith interview, February 20, 2008.

30. Marder, "Raider Carlson—Maverick Marine," p. 3B.

31. Private First Class Robert N. Herriott, "Beside the Trail," *Leatherneck*, March 1943.

32. "Ambush!" a poem found in the Jack Miller Collection, DeGolyer Library, Southern Methodist University, Dallas, Texas.

33. Navy Cross citation, in the Jack Miller Collection, DeGolyer Library, Southern Methodist University, Dallas, Texas.

34. Letter from Henry Miller to Jack Miller, December 5, 1942, in the Jack Miller Collection, DeGolyer Library, Southern Methodist University, Dallas, Texas.

35. Cook interview, April 9, 2008.

36. Ibid.

37. Lucas, *Combat Correspondent*, p. 99; Gay interview, May 28, 2008; "Carlson's Boys," *Newsweek*, December 28, 1942, p. 24.

38. Cook interview, April 9, 2008.

39. Ibid.

40. Bulger, "The Second Marine Raider Battalion on Guadalcanal, 4 November–12 December 1942," November 1981, p. 9; Richter, *Where the Sun Stood Still!*, p. 351.

41. Carlson, "Report of Operations of this Battalion on Guadalcanal between 4 November and 4 December, 1942," p. 12.
42. Bulger, "The Second Marine Raider Battalion on Guadalcanal, 4 November–12 December 1942," March 1981, p. 6.
43. Garrett Graham, "Back to Makin," *Marine Corps Gazette*, February 1944, p. 1, found at http://pqasb.pqarchiver.com/mca-members.
44. Author's interview with Arthur Beth, May 28, 2008.
45. Telegram from Lt. Gen. Thomas Holcomb to the Miller Family, December 26, 1942, in the Jack Miller Collection, DeGolyer Library, Southern Methodist University, Dallas, Texas.
46. Author's interview with Carmen Miller Michael, February 18, 2008.
47. Lt. Barnett Shaw, "Joe and Jack and I," in the Jack Miller Collection, DeGolyer Library, Southern Methodist University, Dallas, Texas.
48. Draft of a proposed letter, March 3, 1943, in the Evans F. Carlson Collection, Marine Corps Research Center, Quantico, Virginia.
49. Undated letter from Maj. Gen. Joseph Fegan to Laurence Kahn, in the Jack Miller Collection, DeGolyer Library, Southern Methodist University, Dallas, Texas.
50. Letter from Lt. Col. Evans Carlson to Mrs. Miller, January 2, 1943, in the Jack Miller Collection, DeGolyer Library, Southern Methodist University, Dallas, Texas.
51. Letter from Stephen Stigler to Mr. and Mrs. Miller, December 22, 1942, in the Jack Miller Collection, DeGolyer Library, Southern Methodist University, Dallas, Texas.
52. Letter from Joseph Griffith to Mrs. Miller, April 1, 1943, in the Jack Miller Collection, DeGolyer Library, Southern Methodist University, Dallas, Texas.
53. Letter from Gy. Sgt. Victor Maghakian to Mr. Miller, July 12, 1943, in the Jack Miller Collection, DeGolyer Library, Southern Methodist University, Dallas, Texas.

Chapter 11—Once I Walked with Giants

1. "Carlson's Boys," *Newsweek*, December 28, 1942, p. 25.
2. Ira Wolfert, *Battle for the Solomons* (Boston: Houghton Mifflin Company, 1943), p. 136.
3. Price, "Raider Carlson," p. 2.
4. Carlson, "Report of Operations of this Battalion on Guadalcanal between 4 November and 4 December, 1942," pp. 17–18; Lt. Col. Evans F. Carlson to The Commandant, U.S. Marine Corps, "Discussion of and suggestions for improve-

ment in the combat efficiency of Raider battalions, based on experience gained in operations against the enemy," January 27, 1943, in the Marine Raider Battalions Collection, Personal Files, Marine Corps Research Center, Quantico, Virginia, p. 2.

5. Peatross, *Bless 'Em All*, p. 168.
6. Letter from Evans Carlson to Raymond Swing, December 11, 1942, in the Raymond Gram Swing Collection, Library of Congress, Washington, D.C.
7. Letter from Evans Carlson to James Roosevelt, December 10, 1942, in the James Roosevelt Papers, Franklin D. Roosevelt Presidential Library, Hyde Park, New York.
8. Letter from Evans Carlson to James Roosevelt, December 15, 1942, in the James Roosevelt Papers, Franklin D. Roosevelt Presidential Library, Hyde Park, New York.
9. McCullough interview, October 10, 2007.
10. "The Psychiatric Toll of Warfare," *Fortune*, December 1943, pp. 141, 274–82.
11. *New York Times*, December 7, 1942, found in Michael J. Zak, "Evans Carlson and the Carlson Raiders," thesis written for Harvard Business School, 1981.
12. Letter from Oscar Peatross to Michael Zak, December 8, 1979, in the Michael J. Zak Collection.
13. Vandegrift, *Once a Marine*, p. 202.
14. Voight interview, October 30, 2007.
15. Unit citation found in the Evans F. Carlson Collection, Marine Corps Research Center, Quantico, Virginia.
16. Copy of speech found in the Evans F. Carlson Collection, Marine Corps Research Center, Quantico, Virginia.
17. Smith, *Carlson's Raid*, p. 207.
18. Blankfort, *The Big Yankee*, pp. 363–66.
19. Lucas, *Combat Correspondent*, p. 105.
20. Evans F. Carlson, *The Autobiography of Evans Carlson*, p. 56, Reminiscences told to Helen Snow in China, 1940, in the Evans F. Carlson Personal File, Marine Corps Research Center, Quantico, Virginia.
21. Twining, *No Bended Knee*, p. 146.
22. Zak, "Evans Carlson and the Carlson Raiders," p. 16.
23. Letter from Evans Carlson to Franklin Roosevelt, June 17, 1943.
24. Letters from Evans Carlson to Raymond Swing, February 3, 1943, May 24, 1943, and July 21, 1943.
25. Hubbard, "Colonel Carlson and His Gung Ho Raiders," p. 68.
26. *Fighting on Guadalcanal* (Washington, D.C.: United States Government Printing Office, 1943), p. v.
27. Carlson, *The Autobiography of Evans Carlson*, p. 9.
28. Peatross, *Bless 'Em All*, p. 294.

29. Letter from Evans Carlson to James Roosevelt, April 12, 1945.

30. Roosevelt, *My Parents: A Differing View*, p. 277.

31. Marder, "Raider Carlson—Maverick Marine," p. 3B.

32. Carlson, *The Autobiography of Evans Carlson*, p. 3.

33. Michael Straight, "The Faith of a Raider," *New Republic*, June 9, 1947, p. 15.

34. Letter from Oscar Peatross to Michael Zak, December 8, 1979.

35. Twining, *No Bended Knee*, p. 193.

36. Burnette interview, January 22, 2008.

37. Author's interview with Larry Brown, September 7, 2007.

38. "Bull Sheet," *Raider Patch*, January 1986, p. 21.

39. Fisher, "Reflection," p. 1.

40. *Mississippi Press*, February 15, 2004.

41. Roosevelt interview, October 26, 2007.

42. "Bull Sheet," *Raider Patch*, November 1978, p. 19.

43. Letter from Gen. Carl E. Mundy, Jr., to Mary Roosevelt, August 16, 1991, in the Mary Roosevelt Collection.

44. Michael Zak interview of Richard Washburn, January 4, 1980.

45. Letter from Maj. Gen. T. E. Watson to Henry Miller, September 14, 1945, in the Jack Miller Collection, DeGolyer Library, Southern Methodist University, Dallas, Texas.

46. Letter from Carmen Miller Michael to Lt. Col. Joseph N. Mueller, March 16, 1990, in the Jack Miller Collection, DeGolyer Library, Southern Methodist University, Dallas, Texas.

47. Letter from Lt. Col. Joseph N. Mueller to Carmen Miller Michael, October 1, 1990, in the Jack Miller Collection, DeGolyer Library, Southern Methodist University, Dallas, Texas.

48. Carmen Miller Michael interview, February 18, 2008.

49. Merle Miller, "Transport Maghakian's Revenge," *Yank*, April 28, 1944, p. 9.

50. Letter from Gy. Sgt. Victor Maghakian to Mr. Miller, July 12, 1943, in the Jack Miller Collection, DeGolyer Library, Southern Methodist University, Dallas, Texas.

51. *Fresno Bee*, May 13, 1981.

52. "Bull Sheet," *Raider Patch*, June 1975.

Bibliography

I—MARINE CORPS RESEARCH CENTER

The Marine Corps, proud of its heritage, has assembled an astonishing collection of materials at its Marine Corps Research Center on the grounds of the Marine base at Quantico, Virginia. Diaries, photographs, letters, official reports, and oral histories are a few of the many items available to the researcher.

(1) OFFICIAL REPORTS
General

Unless otherwise indicated, the official reports listed below reside at the Marine Corps Research Center, either in the Evans F. Carlson Collection or the Evans F. Carlson Biographical Files.

Barrett, Lt. Col. David D., to the War Department. "Comments on Current Events," American Embassy, Office of the Military Attaché, Chungking, China, December 31, 1940, in the Evans F. Carlson Collection.

Carlson, Maj. Evans F. Memorandum to All Company Commanders. "Battalion Insignia," May 9, 1942, in the Evans F. Carlson Collection.

Carlson, Lt. Col. Evans. "Methods of the U.S. Marine Raiders," undated manuscript in the Evans F. Carlson Collection.

———. "Notes on the Organization of Raider Battalions," to Commanding General, IMAC, December 28, 1942, in the Evans F. Carlson Personal Files.

Commander Marianas Area. "Record of Proceedings of a Military Commission Convened at United States Pacific Fleet, Commander Marianas, Guam, Mariana Islands," April 5, 1946, located at the National Archives and Records Administration, College Park, Maryland. These records of the trial of Vice Adm. Koso

Abe include many examinations, statements, and depositions, including those of Lejena Lokot, Capt. Koichi Hiyashi, Capt. Yoshio Obara, and other key participants.

Griffith, Capt. S. B., and Capt. W. M. Greene to the Special Naval Observer. "Report on the British Commandos," January 6, 1942, in the Evans F. Carlson Personal Files.

Griffith, Maj. Samuel B. "Recommendations on Raider Battalions," May 7, 1942, letter to Gen. Holland M. Smith, CG, Amphibious Corps, Atlantic Fleet, in the "Marine Raider Battalions" Folder, Marine Corps Research Center, Quantico, Virginia.

Mathews, C. F. Letter from the Commanding Officer to the Secretary of the Navy, "Recommendation in the Case of First Lieutenant Evans F. Carlson, U.S. Marine Corps, for Award of a Distinguished Service Medal," May 12, 1931, in the Evans F. Carlson Collection.

Nimitz, Adm. Chester W. April 23, 1942, letter to Adm. Ernest J. King, found in the "Marine Raider Battalions" Folder, Marine Corps Research Center, Quantico, Virginia.

Rabinovitz, 2nd Lt. Aaron. "Translation of Correspondence Between Prisoner of War Information Bureau and Second Demobilization Ministry (Navy Ministry)," 11 March 1946, in the Evans F. Carlson Collection.

Roosevelt, Capt. James. Letter to Maj. Gen. Thomas Holcomb, "Development Within the Marine Corps of a Unit for Purposes Similar to the British Commandos and the Chinese Guerrillas," January 13, 1942, "Raider Battalion Correspondence Files," Marine Corps Research Center, Quantico, Virginia.

Zimmerman, John. "Notes on an Inspection of the Records of the Trial for Murder of Vice Admiral Abe," 30 June 1947 in the Evans F. Carlson Collection.

The Makin Raid

Argonaut, "Report of Second War Patrol, August 8, 1942, to August 26, 1942," in the Evans F. Carlson Collection.

Carlson, Lt. Col. Evans. "Operations Order 1-42," On Board *Nautilus*, August 7, 1942, in the Evans F. Carlson Collection.

———. "Operations Order 2-42," On Board *Nautilus*, August 7, 1942, in the Evans F. Carlson Collection.

———. "Operations on Makin, August 17–18, 1942," On Board *Nautilus*, August 21, 1942, in the Evans F. Carlson Collection.

English, Rear Adm. R. E., Commander Task Force Seven. "Operations Order No. 71-42," August 5, 1942, located at the National Archives and Records Administration, College Park, Maryland.

———. "Report of Raider Expedition against Makin—comments on," to Commander in Chief, U.S. Pacific Fleet, September 3, 1942, in the Evans F. Carlson Collection.

Haines, Comdr. J. M., Commander Task Group G 7.15. "Operations Order No. 1-42," August 6, 1942, at the National Archives and Records Administration, College Park, Maryland.

———. "Report of Marine-Submarine Raider Expedition," August 24, 1942, located at the National Archives and Records Administration, College Park, Maryland.

Lamb, 2nd Lt. Charles T. "Battalion Training Memorandum, Number 22-42," 20 July 1942, in the Evans F. Carlson Collection.

Lamb, Lt. Col. Charles T. "Comments on the Raid on Makin Island Manuscript," August 23, 1956, in the Evans F. Carlson Collection.

Nautilus, "Report of Second War Patrol, August 8, 1942, to August 25, 1942," in the Evans F. Carlson Collection.

Nautilus War Diary, August 1942, in the Evans F. Carlson Collection.

Nimitz, Adm. Chester W., to Commanding General, Amphibious Corps. "Comments on Makin Raid," September 21, 1942, in the Evans F. Carlson Collection.

Nimitz, Adm. Chester W. to Commander in Chief, U.S. Pacific Fleet. "Solomon Islands Campaign—Makin Diversion," October 20, 1942, in the Evans F. Carlson Collection.

The Long Patrol

Carlson, Lt. Col. Evans. "Preliminary Report on Operations of this Battalion from 24 November to 4 December (2d Phase of the operation which commenced on 5 November)," December 13, 1942, in the Evans F. Carlson Collection.

———. "Report of Operations of this Battalion on Guadalcanal between 4 November and 4 December, 1942," December 20, 1942, in the Evans F. Carlson Collection.

Carlson, Lt. Col. Evans F., to The Commandant, U.S. Marine Corps. "Discussion of and suggestions for improvement in the combat efficiency of Raider battalions, based on experience gained in operations against the enemy," January 27, 1943, in the "Marine Raider Battalions Collection," Personal Files, Marine Corps Research Center, Quantico, Virginia.

Mather, John. "The Need for Training as Demonstrated by an Operation on Guadalcanal—1942," a paper found in the Eric Hammel Collection, Marine Corps Research Center, Quantico, Virginia.

(2) ORAL HISTORIES

The following interviews were conducted by Headquarters Marine Corps with various World War II Marine personalities:

Brig. Gen. Samuel B. Griffith, November 1968
Maj. Gen. Omar T. Pfeiffer, 1968

James Roosevelt, October 25, 1979
Gen. Alan Shapley, January 19, 1971
Gen. Merrill B. Twining, February 1, 1967

(3) COLLECTIONS

John Apergis Collection
Joseph N. Bell Collection
Evans F. Carlson Collection
Arthur Claffy Collection
George F. Good, Jr., Collection
Brig. Gen. Samuel B. Griffith Collection
Peder Gustavson Collection
Eric Hammel Collection
Maj. Gen. Commandant Thomas Holcomb Collection
Herbert C. Merillat Collection
A. George Noran Collection
Raymond W. Poppelman Collection
Robert Strehl Collection
Karl E. Voelter Collection
Earl Wilson Collection

(4) PERSONAL FILES

Evans F. Carlson
Evans C. Carlson, Jr.
Ralph Coyte
Charles Lamb
Victor Maghakian
Marine Raider Battalions
Marine Raiders: Publications, Articles, Biographies
John Mather
Jack Miller
Oscar Peatross
Merwyn Plumley
Mitchell Red Cloud
James Roosevelt
Clyde Thomason
Hal Throneson
Jacob Vouza
Richard Washburn

II—FRANKLIN D. ROOSEVELT LIBRARY, HYDE PARK, NEW YORK

Eleanor Roosevelt Papers
  "General Correspondence: Ca, 1941," Box 735.
  "General Correspondence: Ca, 1943," Box 779.
  "Letters from Servicemen: Ca-Ch, 1944," Box 835.
Franklin D. Roosevelt Papers
  "President's Personal File 4951, Carlson, Capt. Evans F."
James Roosevelt Papers
  "U.S. Marine Corps: Carlson, Evans," Box 76.
  "U.S. Marine Corps: Makin Island, 1942," Box 75.

III—OTHER COLLECTIONS

Merritt A. Edson Collection, Library of Congress, Washington, D.C.
Jack Miller Collection, DeGolyer Library, Southern Methodist University, Dallas, Texas.
Raymond Gram Swing Collection, Library of Congress, Washington, D.C.
United States Marine Raider Museum, Quantico, Virginia.

IV—INDIVIDUAL COLLECTIONS

The owners of the following private collections graciously gave me access to the material contained in the collections:
Ray Bauml Collection
Virginia Garabedian Collection
Kenneth McCullough Collection
Mary Roosevelt Collection
June Washburn Collection
Joseph Woodford Collection
Michael J. Zak Collection

V—INTERVIEWS

I would like to thank the following individuals for their assistance in providing information for this book. Their help proved invaluable.

ARIAS, PETE
Private, C Company
Long Patrol
Telephone interview on June 3, 2008

BAUML, RAYMOND
Private first class, A Company
Makin, Long Patrol
Telephone interviews on August 10, 2006; October 22, 2007;
January 21, 2008; January 28, 2008

BETH, ARTHUR
Sergeant, E Company
Long Patrol
Telephone interview on May 28, 2008

BROWN, LARRY
Marine Vietnam Veteran
Personal interview on September 7, 2007

BURNETTE, ROBERT
Lieutenant, E Company
Long Patrol
Telephone interviews on January 22, 2008; January 31, 2008; February 5, 2008
Personal interview on March 4, 2008

CANNISTRACI, FRANK
Raider photographer
Personal interview on March 5, 2008

CARSON, BEN
Private, B Company
Makin, Long Patrol
Telephone interviews on May 24, 2007; May 30, 2007; June 5, 2007; October 11,
    2007; October 18, 2007; June 5, 2008
Interview with the Admiral Nimitz National Museum of the Pacific War, September
    21, 2001

COOK, RHEL
Platoon sergeant, F Company
Long Patrol
Telephone interview on April 9, 2008

COTTEN, JULIUS
Corporal, A Company
Makin
Telephone interviews on April 10, 2008; April 14, 2008

DEVORE, CHESTER
World War II Marine Raider veteran
Telephone interview on May 27, 2008

FAVINGER, RICHARD
Pharmacist's mate, third class
Long Patrol
Telephone interview on June 5, 2008

GARABEDIAN, VIRGINIA
Sister of Victor Maghakian
Telephone interview on February 27, 2008

GAY, LATHROP
Private, E Company
Long Patrol
Telephone interview on May 28, 2008

GRIFFITH, JOSEPH
Captain, B and D companies
Makin, Long Patrol
Telephone interviews on March 7, 2007; May 29, 2007
Personal interview on February 20, 2008

HAMMER, EDWARD
Private first class, D Company
Long Patrol
Telephone interview on June 13, 2008

HASENBERG, EUGENE
Private, B Company
Long Patrol
Telephone interview on June 12, 2008

HUDMAN, DENTON
Private, B Company
Makin, Long Patrol
Telephone interview on April 9, 2008

KAPLAN, ERVIN
Private first class, C and E companies
Long Patrol
Telephone interviews on February 8, 2008; June 5, 2008
Personal interview on October 3, 2007

KURLAND, FRANK
Corporal, E Company
Long Patrol
Personal interview on October 3, 2007

LANSFORD, WILLIAM
Private first class, E Company
Long Patrol
Telephone interview on October 31, 2007

LEEMAN, VIRGIL
Private, C Company
Midway, Long Patrol
Telephone interviews on February 15, 2008; June 4, 2008

LIPSCOMB, NATHAN
Sergeant, E Company
Long Patrol
Telephone interview on June 4, 2008

LOVELAND, DARRELL A.
Private, C Company
Midway, Long Patrol
Telephone interviews on October 9, 2007; October 16, 2007; October 26, 2007; June 4, 2008
Interview with David Morrell, October 15, 2003, courtesy of Darrell A. Loveland.

MAZZANTI, ANTHONY
Private, F Company
Long Patrol
Telephone interviews on August 15, 2006; June 5, 2008

McCULLOUGH, KENNETH
Sergeant, B Company
Makin, Long Patrol
Telephone interviews on March 7, 2007; May 25, 2007; May 30, 2007; October 10, 2007; April 10, 2008; June 6, 2008

MICHAEL, CARMEN MILLER
Sister of Jack Miller
Personal interview on February 18, 2008

MILLIGAN, NEAL
Private, B Company
Makin
Telephone interview on April 11, 2008

NUGENT, WILLIAM
Private first class, B Company
Makin
Telephone interview on April 15, 2008

ONSTAD, WILLIAM
Private first class, D Company
Long Patrol
Telephone interview on October 11, 2007

QUIRK, BRIAN
Private first class, B Company
Makin, Long Patrol
Telephone interview on February 13, 2007
Personal interviews on October 5, 2007; October 23, 2007

ROOSEVELT, MARY
Widow of James Roosevelt
Telephone interview on October 26, 2007
Personal interview on March 7, 2008

TOBIN, THOMAS
Private first class, C Company
Midway, Long Patrol
Personal interview on October 5, 2007

VANLANDINGHAM, JESSE
Private first class, B and E companies
Long Patrol
Telephone interviews on February 14, 2008; June 2, 2008; June 9, 2008

VOIGHT, DEAN
Private, B Company
Makin, Long Patrol
Telephone interviews on October 9, 2007; October 16, 2007; October 26, 2007; October 30, 2007

WASHBURN, JUNE
Widow of Richard Washburn
Telephone interview on November 19, 2007
Personal interview on January 14, 2008

ZAMPERINI, LOUIS
Prison camp inmate
Telephone interview on May 24, 2007
Personal interview on March 6, 2008

   Elsewhere
ROOSEVELT, JAMES
Interview with the Marine Historical Center, October 25, 1979

WASHBURN, RICHARD T.
Interview with Michael J. Zak, January 4, 1980

VI—NEWSPAPERS AND MAGAZINES USED

Albuquerque Journal
Armenian Reporter
Atlanta Journal
Baltimore Sun
Boston American
Boston Daily Record
Chicago Tribune
Cincinnati Post
Columbia (SC) *State*
Exodus

Fall River (MA) *Herald News*
Fresno Bee
Grand Rapids Herald
Hartford Courant
Honolulu Star-Bulletin
Jamestown Post-Journal
Las Vegas Sun
Los Angeles Daily News
Los Angeles Examiner
Los Angeles Times

Louisville Courier-Journal
Marine Corps Chevron
Marines
Mobile Register
National Amvet
New Republic
Newark Evening News
New York Herald Tribune
New York Journal American
New York Picture News
Newsweek
New York Times

Raider Patch
San Diego Union
Santa Ana (CA) Register
Saturday Evening Post
Showbiz
Springfield (MA) News
Sioux City Journal
Time
Washington Daily News
Washington Post
Waterbury (CT) Republican
Yank

VII—BOOKS

Agawa, Hiroyuki. *The Reluctant Admiral*. Tokyo: Kodansha International Ltd., 1979.

Alexander, Joseph H. *Edson's Raiders: The 1st Marine Raider Battalion in World War II*. Annapolis, MD: Naval Institute Press, 2001.

Bauml, Ray. *The Diary of Ray Bauml, July 2, 1942 to December 19, 1942*. Undated manuscript in the Ray Bauml Collection.

Beau, Major Jerome J. C., USMC (Ret.), edited by Robert A. Buerlein. *The U.S. Marine Raiders of WWII: Those Who Served*. Richmond, VA: The American Historical Foundation, 1996.

Berry, Henry. *Semper Fi, Mac: Living Memories of the U.S. Marines in World War II*. New York: Arbor House, 1982.

Blankfort, Michael. *The Big Yankee*. Nashville: The Battery Press, 2004.

Brown, Anthony Cave. *The Last Hero: Wild Bill Donovan*. New York: Times Books, 1982.

Buell, Thomas B. *The Quiet Warrior*. Boston: Little, Brown and Company, 1974.

Burns, James MacGregor. *Roosevelt: The Soldier of Freedom*. New York: Harcourt Brace Jovanovich, Inc., 1970.

Carl, Maj. Gen. Marion E., with Barrett Tillman. *Pushing the Envelope*. Annapolis, MD: Naval Institute Press, 1994.

Carlson, Evans Fordyce. *Twin Stars of China*. New York: Dodd, Mead & Company, 1940.

———. *The Chinese Army*. New York: Institute of Pacific Relations, 1940.

———. *The Autobiography of Evans Carlson*. Reminiscences told to Helen Snow in China, 1940.

Casey, Robert J. *Torpedo Junction: With the Pacific Fleet from Pearl Harbor to Midway*. Indianapolis: The Bobbs-Merrill Company, 1942.

Clark, George B. *With the Old Corps in Nicaragua.* Novato, CA: Presidio, 2001.

Clemens, Martin. *Alone on Guadalcanal.* Annapolis, MD: Naval Institute Press, 1998.

Collier, Peter, with David Horowitz. *The Roosevelts: An American Saga.* New York: Simon & Schuster, 1994.

Cook, Blanche Wiesen. *Eleanor Roosevelt, Volume Two: 1933–1938.* New York: Viking, 1999.

Costello, John. *The Pacific War, 1941–1945.* New York: Quill Books, 1982.

Davis, Burke. *Marine!* Boston: Little, Brown and Company, 1962.

DeNevi, Don. *The West Coast Goes to War, 1941–1942.* Missoula, MT: Pictorial Histories Publishing Company, Inc., 1998.

Feldt, Commander Eric A. *The Coastwatchers.* New York: Oxford University Press, 1946.

Fighting on Guadalcanal. Washington: United States Government Printing Office, 1943.

Frank, Richard B. *Guadalcanal.* New York: Random House, 1990.

Garrett, Richard. *The Raiders.* New York: Van Nostrand Reinhold Company, 1980.

Gleason, James. *Real Blood! Real Guts!* Irvine, CA: Raider Publishing, 2003.

Griffin, W. E. B. *Call to Arms.* New York: Jove Books, 1987.

Hailey, Foster. *Pacific Battle Line.* New York: The Macmillan Company, 1944.

Healy, Mark. *Midway 1942.* Oxford, UK: Osprey Publishing, 1993.

Heinl, Lt. Col. Robert D., Jr. *Marines at Midway.* Headquarters U.S. Marine Corps: Historical Section Division of Public Information, 1948.

Hersey, John. *Into the Valley.* New York: Alfred A. Knopf, 1943.

Hoffman, Major Jon T. *Once a Legend.* Novato, CA: Presidio, 1994.

———. *From Makin to Bougainville: Marine Raiders in the Pacific War.* Washington, D.C.: History and Museums Divisions, Headquarters, U.S. Marine Corps, 1995. I have used the online version found at www.nps.gov/wapa/indepth/extContent/ usmc/pcn-190-003130-00/index.htm.

Hoffman, Lt. Col. Jon T. *Chesty.* New York: Random House, 2001.

Hough, Lieutenant Colonel Frank O., USMCR, Major Verle E. Ludwig, USMC, and Henry I. Shaw, Jr. *Pearl Harbor to Guadalcanal, History of U.S. Marine Corps Operations in World War II, Volume I.* Washington, D.C.: Historical Branch, G-3 Division, Headquarters, U.S. Marine Corps, 1958.

Hoyt, Edwin P. *Raider Battalion.* Los Angeles: Pinnacle Books, 1980.

Ickes, Harold L. *The Secret Diary of Harold L. Ickes, Volume II: The Inside Struggle, 1936–1939.* New York: Simon and Schuster, 1954.

Jones, James. *WWII.* New York: Ballantine Books, 1975.

Jones, Wilbur D., Jr., and Carroll Robbins Jones. *Hawaii Goes to War: The Aftermath of Pearl Harbor.* Shippensburg, PA: White Mane Books, 2001.

Karig, Captain Walter, USNR, and Commander Eric Purdon, USNR. *Battle Report,*

Volume III: Pacific War: Middle Phase. New York: Rinehart and Company, Inc., 1947.

Ladd, James. *Commandos and Rangers of World War II*. New York: St. Martin's Press, 1978.

Lash, Joseph P. *Eleanor and Franklin*. New York: W. W. Norton & Company, Inc., 1971.

Layton, Rear Admiral Edwin T., USN (Ret.), with Captain Roger Pineau, USNR (Ret.), and John Costello. *"And I Was There": Pearl Harbor and Midway—Breaking the Secrets*. New York: William Morrow and Company, Inc., 1985.

Leckie, Robert. *Strong Men Armed: The United States Marines Against Japan*. New York: Da Capo Press, 1997.

Lord, Walter. *Lonely Vigil: Coastwatchers of the Solomons*. New York: The Viking Press, 1977.

———. *Incredible Victory*. New York: Harper & Row, Publishers, 1967.

Lucas, Jim. *Combat Correspondent*. New York: Reynal & Hitchcock Publishers, 1944.

MacKinnon, Janice R., and Stephen R. MacKinnon. *Agnes Smedley: The Life and Times of an American Radical*. Berkeley: University of California Press, 1988.

MacKinnon, Stephen R., and Oris Friesen. *China Reporting: An Oral History of American Journalism in the 1930s and 1940s*. Berkeley: University of California Press, 1987.

Manchester, William. *Goodbye, Darkness*. Boston: Little, Brown and Company, 1979.

Martial Arts Center of Excellence. *One Mind, Any Weapon*. Quantico, VA, 2008 edition.

Mason, John T., ed. *The Pacific War Remembered*. Annapolis, MD: Naval Institute Press, 1986.

Merillat, Herbert Christian. *The Island*. Boston: Houghton Mifflin Company, 1944.

———. *Guadalcanal Remembered*. New York: Dodd, Mead & Company, 1982.

Mersky, Peter B. *U.S. Marine Corps Aviation: 1912 to the Present*. Annapolis, MD: The Nautical & Aviation Publishing Company of America, 1983.

Miller, Donald L. *The Story of World War II*. New York: Simon & Schuster, 2001.

Miller, Russell. *The Commandos*. Alexandria, VA: Time-Life Books, 1981.

Millett, Allan R. *Semper Fidelis: The History of the United States Marine Corps*. New York: Macmillan Publishing Co., Inc., 1980.

Morgan, Ted. *FDR: A Biography*. New York: Simon and Schuster, 1985.

Musicant, Ivan. *The Banana Wars*. New York: Macmillan Publishing Company, 1990.

Newman, Tamera. *A Survivor's Story*. Logan, UT: Watkins Printing, 2007.

Noran, A. George. "Journal of A. George Noran, January 1943."

O'Donnell, Patrick K. *Into the Rising Sun*. New York: The Free Press, 2002.

Onstad, Bill, with Jayson Lowery. *Trust. Truth. Evil.* Victoria, BC: Trafford Publishing, 2005.

Parshall, Jonathan B., and Anthony P. Tully. *Shattered Sword: The Untold Story of the Battle of Midway.* Washington, D.C.: Potomac Books, 2005.

Peatross, Maj. Gen. Oscar F., USMC (Ret). *Bless 'Em All: The Raider Marines of World War II.* Irvine, CA: ReView Publications, 1995.

Perling, J. J. *Presidents' Sons.* New York: The Odyssey Press, 1947.

Potter, E. B. *Nimitz.* Annapolis, MD: Naval Institute Press, 1976.

Potter, E. B., and Fleet Admiral Chester W. Nimitz, USN, eds. *Triumph in the Pacific: The Navy's Struggle Against Japan.* Englewood Cliffs, NJ: Prentice-Hall, Inc., 1963.

Prange, Gordon W., with Donald M. Goldstein and Katherine V. Dillon. *Miracle at Midway.* New York: Penguin Books, 1982.

Price, Ruth. *The Lives of Agnes Smedley.* New York: Oxford University Press, 2005.

Richter, Don. *Where the Sun Stood Still!* Calabasas, CA: Toucan Publishing, 1992.

Roosevelt, Eleanor. *The Autobiography of Eleanor Roosevelt.* New York: Harper & Brothers Publishers, 1961.

Roosevelt, James. *Affectionately, F.D.R.* New York: Harcourt, Brace & Company, 1959.

———. *My Parents: A Differing View.* Chicago: A Playboy Press Book, 1976.

Roscoe, Theodore. *United States Submarine Operations in World War II.* Annapolis, MD: Naval Institute Press, 1949.

Rose, Lisle A. *The Ship That Held the Line.* Annapolis, MD: Naval Institute Press, 1995.

Rosenquist, R. G., Col. Martin J. Sexton, and Robert A. Buerlein. *Our Kind of War.* Richmond, VA: The American Historical Foundation, 1990.

Salisbury, Harrison E. *The Long March: The Untold Story.* New York: Harper & Row, Publishers, 1985.

Schaller, Michael. *The U.S. Crusade in China, 1938–1945.* New York: Columbia University Press, 1979.

Sexton, Col. Martin J., USMC (Ret.). *The Marine Raiders' Historical Handbook.* Richmond, VA: The American Historical Foundation, undated.

Sherrod, Robert. *Tarawa: The Story of a Battle.* New York: Duell, Sloan and Pearce, 1944.

———. *History of Marine Corps Aviation in World War II.* Washington, D.C.: Combat Forces Press, 1952.

Smedley, Agnes. *China Fights Back.* New York: The Vanguard Press, 1938.

Smith, George W. *Carlson's Raid.* Novato, CA: Presidio Press, Inc., 2001.

Smith, Holland M., and Percy Finch. *Coral and Brass.* New York: Charles Scribner's Sons, 1949.

Snow, Edgar. *The Battle for Asia.* Cleveland, OH: The World Publishing Company, 1942.

Spector, Ronald H. *Eagle Against the Sun*. New York: The Free Press, 1985.

Stavisky, Samuel E. *Marine Combat Correspondent*. New York: Ivy Books, 1999.

Stidger, Dr. William L. *These Amazing Roosevelts*. New York: MacFadden Book Company, Inc., 1938.

Symonds, Craig, ed. *New Aspects of Naval History*. Annapolis, MD: Naval Institute Press, 1981.

Toland, John. *The Rising Sun*. New York: Random House, 1970.

Tuchman, Barbara W. *Stilwell and the American Experience in China, 1911–45*. New York: The Macmillan Company, 1971.

Twining, Gen. Merrill B., USMC (Ret.). *No Bended Knee*. Novato, CA: Presidio, 1994.

Ugaki, Admiral Matome. *Fading Victory: The Diary of Admiral Matome Ugaki, 1941–1945*. Pittsburgh: The University of Pittsburgh Press, 1991.

United States Strategic Bombing Survey. *Interrogations of Japanese Officials, Volume I and II*. Washington, D.C.: Naval Analysis Division, 1946.

Interrogations used:

———"Interrogation No. 11: Interrogation of Captain Susumu Kawaguchi, Air Officer on the *Hiryu*," pp. 4–6.

———"Interrogation No. 65: Interrogation of Captain Y. Watanabe Kawaguchi, Gunnery Officer on Admiral Yamamoto's staff," pp. 65–70.

———"Interrogation No. 60: Interrogation of Captain Yasumi Toyama, Chief of Staff, Second Destroyer Squadron," pp. 249–54.

Updegraph, Charles L., Jr. *U.S. Marine Corps Special Units of World War II*. Washington, D.C.: History and Museums Division, Headquarters, U.S. Marine Corps, 1972.

Vandegrift, General A. A., as told to Robert B. Asprey. *Once a Marine*. New York: W. W. Norton & Company, Inc., 1964.

Wheeler, Richard. *A Special Valor: The U.S. Marines and the Pacific War*. New York: New American Library, 1983.

Wilder, Margaret Buell. *Since You Went Away . . . : Letters to a Soldier from His Wife*. New York: McGraw-Hill Book Company, Inc., 1943.

Wiles, Tripp. *Forgotten Raiders of '42*. Washington, D.C.: Potomac Books, Inc., 2007.

Wolfert, Ira. *Battle for the Solomons*. Boston: Houghton Mifflin Company, 1943.

Zamperini, Louis, with Helen Itria. *Devil at My Heels*. New York: E. P. Dutton & Company, Inc., 1956.

VIII—ARTICLES

Thanks to the generosity of two Raiders, Dr. Ervin Kaplan and Frank Kurland, I enjoyed access to past issues of the official newsletter for the United States Marine

Raider Association, *Raider Patch*. The newsletter, one of the best I have seen, contains a vast number of helpful articles, photographs, and reminiscences. I cannot thank Dr. Kaplan and Frank Kurland enough for their kindness. Rather than list every issue or article used, I have cited specific ones in my footnotes.

Aroian, John H. "A Visit With Capt. Vic Maghakian W.W. II Hero," *Armenian Reporter*, May 20, 1971, p. 2; May 27, 1971, pp. 8, 10.

"Being a Hero Can Get in the Way," *Las Vegas Sun*, p. 3, undated article in the Victor Maghakian Personal File, Marine Corps Research Center, Quantico, Virginia.

Bel, Cpl. Aubrey. "A Legacy of Valor," *Marines*, October 1999.

Blatchford, Nicholas. "They Did Right by Gen. Carlson," *Washington Daily News*, June 5, 1947, p. 20.

Blum, Deborah. "Outpatient Center at VA Hospital Honors War Hero Victor Maghakian," *Fresno Bee*, May 20, 1981, pp. D1, D4.

Brooks, B. K. "Carlson's *'Gung Ho'* Knife," *Knife World*, September 2007.

Bulger, Lowell V. "Bloody Plains Brief, Asamana," *Raider Patch*, May 1980, pp. 12–14.

———. "The Second Marine Raider Battalion on Guadalcanal, 4 November–12 December 1942," *Raider Patch*, March, May, September, November 1981.

Camp, Dick. "Valiant Sacrifice," Part I, *Leatherneck*, January 2008, pp. 30–35; Part II, February 2008, pp. 32–35.

Carlson, Evans Fordyce. "Strategy of the Sino-Japanese War," *Far Eastern Survey*, May 19, 1941, pp. 99–105.

"Carlson's Boys," *Newsweek*, December 28, 1942, pp. 24–25.

"Carlson's Heroes," *Time*, January 25, 1943, p. 60.

"Col. Roosevelt, He See Eye-To-Eye, Says Carlson," *Waterbury Republican*, June 9, 1943.

Crowther, Bosley. "*'Gung Ho!'* a Lurid Action Film About the Makin Island Raid," *New York Times*, January 26, 1944, pp. 1–2, found at http://movies2.nytimes.com.

Devine, Danny. "The Great Debate," *National Amvet*, Fall 1992, pp. 16–17.

Durdin, F. Tillman. "Foe Belted on Isle," *New York Times*, August 22, 1942, pp, 1, 3.

———. "The Roughest and the Toughest," *New York Times*, November 8, 1942, p. SM13.

"Editorial," *Boston American*, August 26, 1942.

"Fighting Carlsons of Plymouth," *Hartford Courant*, April 14, 1943.

"Forty Hours on Makin," *Time*, September 7, 1942, pp. 32–33.

"F.D.R.'s Son Tells of Raid," *Los Angeles Times*, undated article found in the James Roosevelt Papers.

Gardner, Arthur D. "Diary of a Marine Raider: The Cream of the Corps," *Soldier of Fortune*, January 1981, pp. 58–62, 91.

"Gen. Holcomb Likens Marines to Commandos," *New York Herald Tribune*, February 24, 1942, p. 17.

Hailey, Foster. "George—and Captain Merillat—Report on Guadalcanal," *New York Times*, October 29, 1944, p. BR5.

Haller, Richard. "First Eyewitness Story of Gilbert Isle Raid," *New York Journal American*, August 28, 1942, p. 2.

Herriott, Pfc. Robert N. "Beside the Trail," *Leatherneck*, March 1943.

"His Son's Part in Raid Is News to President," *New York Herald Tribune*, no date.

"How to Get to Heaven," *Time*, August 31, 1942, p. 26.

Hubbard, Lucien. "Colonel Carlson and His Gung Ho Raiders," *Reader's Digest*, December 1943, pp. 63–68, in the Ray Bauml Collection.

Hull, Michael D. "Marine Colonel Evans F. Carlson," *WWII History*, January 2003, pp. 18–27.

"In Front Line," *Fall River* (MA) *Herald News*, August 25, 1942.

"James Roosevelt Helps Lead Marine Raid on Jap-Held Isle," *Washington Post*, August 22, 1942.

"James Roosevelt, Leatherneck!" *Mobile Register*, September 7, 1942.

"Japanese Communique," *New York Times*, August 22, 1942, p. 2.

Jensen, Ellen. "Heroic Vegan Recalls War Experiences," *Las Vegas Sun*, January 8, 1967, pp. 5–6.

———. "Profile of a Hero," *Exodus*, January–February 1972, pp. 1, 4–5, 11.

"Jimmy Roosevelt's Part in Makin Attack Comes as Complete Surprise to President," *Cincinnati Post*, August 22, 1942.

"Jimmy's Got It," *Sioux City Journal*, August 24, 1942.

Johnston, Alva. "Jimmy's Got It," *Saturday Evening Post*, July 2, 1938, pp. 8–9, 57, 60.

Kaplan, Ervin, M. D. "A Personal View of the Guadalcanal Long Patrol," found at www.us.marineraiders.org/longpatrolview.htm.

Lansford, William Douglas. "Carlson of the Raiders," *Saga*, February 1961, pp. 20–25, 98–104.

———. "We Caught Them with Their Pants Down: The Battle at Asamana," *Leatherneck*, November 2007, pp. 60–64, 94.

"Lee Marvin's 'Dirty Dozen' Recalls Carlson's Raiders 'Transport' Maghakian," *Showbiz*, undated article found in the Victor Maghakian Personal File, Marine Corps Research Center, Quantico, Virginia.

Le Francois, 1st Lt. W. S. "We Mopped Up Makin Island," *Saturday Evening Post*, Part I—December 4, 1943, pp. 20–21, 109–10; Part II—December 11, 1943, pp. 28–29, 41, 43, 45, 48.

Liston-Wakefield, Col. K. R. "A Fond Farewell," *Marine Corps Gazette*, June 1984, pp. 70–72.

"Major Jim Roosevelt Leads Raid on Japs," *Boston Daily Record*, August 22, 1942.

Marder, Murrey. "Raider Carlson—Maverick Marine," *Washington Post*, June 1, 1947, p. 3B.

"Marine Corps 'Raider' Battalions Employed in Solomons Offensive," *New York Times*, August 25, 1942.

"Marine Sizes Up Jimmy," *Newark Evening News*, March 11, 1943.

McCarthy, John. "Carlson's Makin Raid: Last Chapter," *Marine Corps League*, Winter 2004, pp. 24–33.

McCullough, Kenneth L. "The Makin Raid," *Marine Corps Gazette*, August 2006, p. 64.

———. "The Myths of Makin," unpublished article mailed to the author.

———. "Reflections of a Carlson's Marine Raider," unpublished article mailed to the author.

McKnight, Jason. "Training Facility Named for Medal of Honor Hero," *Navy Compass*, January 14, 2005, found at www.navycompass.com.

McWilliams, Carey. "The Education of Evans Carlson," *Nation*, December 1, 1945, pp. 577–79.

Miller, Martin. "A Latino Veteran Finally Shares His Battlefield Tales," *Los Angeles Times*, September 21, 2007, pp. 1–2, found at http://pqasb.pqarchiver.com/latimes.

Miller, Merle. "Transport Maghakian's Revenge," *Yank*, April 28, 1944, pp. 8–9.

Naval Historical Center's Oral History, Battle of Midway, "Recollections of Commander John Ford," found at www.history.navy.mil.

"No Swivel Chairs," *Columbia* (SC) *State*, August 24, 1942.

O'Neil, Frank. "Relics of Heroic Past Uncovered," *Santa Ana* (CA) *Register*, August 4, 1963.

"Optional Embargo of Japan Is Urged," *New York Times*, January 13, 1940.

Park, Edwards. "Raiders' Carlson: He was the Original Gung-ho Marine," *Marine Corps League*, Summer 1996, pp. 13–17.

Pearson, Drew. "Major Roosevelt, Marine Raider," Washington Merry-Go-Round column, undated article found in the Joseph Woodford Collection.

Perret, Geoffrey. "Warrior Mao," *MHQ: The Quarterly Journal of Military History* 19, no. 3 (Spring 2007), pp. 6–15.

"President's Son Fired Upon, but Unhurt at Makin," *Grand Rapids Herald*, August 29, 1942.

Price, Wesley. "Raider Carlson," *New York Picture News*, January 2, 1944, pp. 2–3.

"The Psychiatric Toll of Warfare," *Fortune*, December 1943, pp. 141–43, 268–87.

Quirk, Lt. Col. Brian J., USMC (Ret.). "Flashes of Brilliance," *Marine Corps Gazette*, August 2006, p. 64.

Ragland, Janet. A series of articles about Jack Miller, including:
"Lt. Jack Miller: Introduction," pp. 1–2
"Lt. Jack Miller: A Family's Bond," pp. 1–3
"Lt. Jack Miller: A War Heats Up," pp. 1–2
"Lt. Jack Miller: Jack Miller a Hero," pp. 1–3

"Lt. Jack Miller: An Officer and a Friend," pp. 1–5, found at www.smu.edu/cul/memorial/warbio.htm, pp. 1–5.

"Raider Commander Tells Strategy for Beating Japanese," *Marine Corps Chevron*, June 5, 1943, p. 1.

Rejcek, Peter. "Searching for Missing Marines," *Eagle*, February 2002, pp. 6–7.

Robinson, David. "The Raiders—50 Years and Still Gung Ho," *Marine Corps League*, Spring 1992, pp. 16–27.

"Roosevelt Boys," *Albuquerque Journal*, August 25, 1942.

"Roosevelt Boys Are Making Good," *Springfield* (MA) *News*, August 25, 1942.

"Roosevelt Son's Exploits Give Thrill at White House," *Jamestown Post-Journal*, August 22, 1942.

"Roosevelt's 3 Busy Days of Visiting at San Diego Revealed," *Chicago Tribune*, August 11, 1944, p. 3.

"Roosevelts at War," *Time*, December 29, 1941, p. 8.

"Roosevelts Get News," *New York Times*, August 23, 1942, p. 16.

Scheuer, Philip K. "'Gung Ho' Action-Filled Saga of Leathernecks," *Los Angeles Times*, April 1, 1944, p. 5.

Schwab, Ernest L. "The Gung-Ho Rubber Boat Raiders," *Amphibious Warfare Review*, November 1985, pp. 27–31, 67.

Seacrest, William B., Jr. "'Transport' Maghakian Served His Country Well as a Marine," *Fresno Bee*, May 25, 1996.

Setencich, Eli. "Gorilla Warfare," *Fresno Bee*, June 12, 1982.

Sexton, Col. Martin J. "Sgt. Maj. Vouza," *Marine Corps League*, Autumn 1988, pp. 32–36.

Shawlee, Ralph. "Midway," *Raider Patch*, May 1989, pp. 2–3.

"Somebody Always Spoils the Fun," *Louisville Courier-Journal*, August 23, 1942.

Stavisky, SSgt. Samuel S. "Raiders in Pacific Not Supermen But Highly Specialized Marines," Marine Corps Press Release, March 29, 1943.

Straight, Michael, "The Faith of a Raider," *New Republic*, June 9, 1947, pp. 14–15.

Tregaskis, Richard. "The Best Soldier I Ever Knew," *Saga*, February 1960, pp. 17–19, 84–87.

Trumbull, Robert. "U.S. Marines Strike Again at the Japanese," *New York Times*, August 22, 1942, p. 1.

Tutt, Bob. "Guerrilla-Like Carlson's Raiders 'Rode to the Sound of the Guns,'" *Houston Chronicle*, July 1, 1995, pp. 1–3, found at www.chron.com.

"Two Carlson Heroes Make Pastor Proud," *Hartford Courant*, April 13, 1943.

"U.S. Raids Island in Gilbert Group," *New York Times*, August 22, 1942.

"We Are Losing the War," *Time*, September 7, 1942, p. 30.

"Where I Stand," *Las Vegas Sun*, July 6, 1981, p. 2.

"White House Hails Raid," *New York Times*, August 22, 1942, p. 3; August 28, 1942, pp. 1, 7.

Whitman, Edward C. "Submarine Commandos: 'Carlson's Raiders' at Makin Atoll," pp. 1–7, found at www.chinfo.navy.mil/navpalib/Cno/n87/usw/issue_10/makin_13.gif.

Wright, Jim. "To Sgt. Maj. Vouza!" *Dallas Morning News*, May 28, 1984.

Zak, Michael J. "Evans Carlson and the Carlson Raiders," thesis written for Harvard Business School, 1981

———. "A Short History of Evans Carlson and the Carlson Raiders," Discussion notes for Harvard Business School, 1981.

ARTICLES FROM *MARINE CORPS GAZETTE* WEB SITE

Many articles were found at the Web site created by *Marine Corps Gazette* and *Leatherneck* magazines. The Web site is found at http://pqasb.pqarchiver.com/mca-members.

The articles used from this Web site are:

Anonymous. "The Makin Island Raid," *Marine Corps Gazette*, March/April 1943, pp. 1–2.

Anonymous. "How to Beat the Japs," *Marine Corps Gazette*, July 1943, pp. 1–2.

Anonymous. "Carlson & Leadership," *Marine Corps Gazette*, December 1987, pp. 1–2.

Bartlett, Tom. "Sir Jacob Vouza," *Leatherneck*, May 1984, pp. 1–2.

Carlson, Evans F. "The Guardia Nacional de Nicaragua," *Marine Corps Gazette*, August 1937, pp. 1–16.

Dalton, Robert J. "The Legacy of Evans Carlson," *Marine Corps Gazette*, August 1987, pp. 1–3.

Doying, George. "Red Mike and His 'Do or Die Men,'" *Leatherneck*, March 1944, pp. 1–5.

Edson, Merritt A. "The Coco Patrol," *Marine Corps Gazette*, August 1936, pp. 1–19; November 1936, pp. 1–8; February 1937, pp. 1–19.

Fisher, Ashley W. "Reflection," *Marine Corps Gazette*, August 2001, pp. 1–2.

Graham, Garrett. "Back to Makin," *Marine Corps Gazette*, February 1944, pp. 1–7.

Greene, Wallace M., Jr. "Fire Team—Comrades in Battle," *Marine Corps Gazette*, December 1984, pp. 1–6.

Griffith, Samuel B. "North China, 1937," *Marine Corps Gazette*, December 1938, pp. 1–6.

———. "Guerrilla Warfare in China," *Marine Corps Gazette*, June 1941, pp. 1–10.

———. "The U.S. Crusade in China, 1938 to 1945," *Marine Corps Gazette*, July 1979, pp. 1–2.

Heinl, R. D., Jr. "The Last Banana War," *Marine Corps Gazette*, November 1960, pp. 1–7.

Hoffman, Jon T. "The Legacy and Lessons of the 2d Matanikau," *Marine Corps Gazette*, January 1993, pp. 1–4.

Holmes, Lee M. "Birth of the Fire Team," *Marine Corps Gazette*, November 1952, pp. 1–9.

Keene, R. R. "James R. Roosevelt, Raider and Son of President," *Leatherneck*, October 1991, pp. 1–2.

———. "Gung Ho: The Long Patrol," *Leatherneck*, November 1992, pp. 1–5.

Kopets, Keith. "The Origins of the Fire Team," *Marine Corps Gazette*, December 2000, pp. 1–2.

Lewis, Jack. "A Search for Shadows," *Leatherneck*, December 1999, pp. 1–7.

———. "Marine Raiders Return Home," *Leatherneck*, March 2000, pp. 1–3.

Mattingly, R. E. "'The Worst Slap in the Face,'" *Marine Corps Gazette*, March 1983, pp. 1–9.

Meyers, Lewis. "Developing the Fire Team," *Marine Corps Gazette*, February 1946, pp. 1–3.

Moore, R. Scott. "Small War Lessons Learned," *Marine Corps Gazette*, February 1993, pp. 1–5.

Peatross, Oscar. "The Makin Raid," *Marine Corps Gazette*, November 1979, pp. 1–8.

———. "The Raid on Makin Island," *Leatherneck*, August 1992, pp. 1–11.

———. "The Raid on Makin Island, Part II," *Leatherneck*, September 1992, pp. 1–12.

Pettus, Francis C. "A Four Day Patrol," *Marine Corps Gazette*, June 1944, pp. 1–6.

Quirk, Brian J. "Epilogue: The 12 Missing in Action," *Marine Corps Gazette*, November 2003, pp. 1–2.

———. "Reflections of Carlson's Raiders," *Marine Corps Gazette*, August 2001, pp. 1–2.

———. "Brig. Gen. Evans Fordyce Carlson," *Marine Corps Gazette*, August 2001, p. 1.

Quirk, Brian J., and Howard A. Young. "Carlson's Raiders on Makin, 17–18 August 1942," *Marine Corps Gazette*, August 2003, pp. 1–3.

Richardson, Herb. "Giants of the Corps," *Leatherneck*, March 1977, pp. 1–5.

Russell, W. H. "Before the Fire Team," *Marine Corps Gazette*, November 1984, pp. 1–7.

Smith, J. C. "Guardia Nacional," *Marine Corps Gazette*, November 1965, pp. 1–4.

Tolbert, Frank. "Chinese Army: Japan's Deadliest Foe," *Leatherneck*, June 1942, pp. 1–14.

Twining, Merrill B. "'Head for the Hills!'" *Marine Corps Gazette*, August 1987, pp. 1–7.

Utley, Harold H. "An Introduction to the Tactics and Technique of Small Wars," *Marine Corps Gazette*, May 1931, pp. 1–5.

———. "The Tactics and Technique of Small Wars," *Marine Corps Gazette*, August 1933, pp. 1–7.

———. "The Tactics and Technique of Small Wars," *Marine Corps Gazette*, November 1933, pp. 1–6.

Young, Donald J. "Phantom Japanese Raid on Los Angeles During World War II," *World War II*, September 2003, found at thehistorynet.com, pp. 1–7.

———. "Japanese Submarines Prowl the U.S. Coastline in 1941," *World War II*, July 1998, found at thehistorynet.com, pp. 1–8.

Zimmerman, Phyllis A. "Braiding the Cord: The Role of Evans F. Carlson's 2d Marine Raider Battalion in Amphibious Warfare," *Marine Corps Gazette*, November 1994, pp. 1–6.

ARTICLES FROM *TIME* MAGAZINE WEB SITE

Many articles were found at the Web site created by *Time* magazine. The Web site is found at www.time.com

The articles used from this Web site are:

"Jimmy Gets It," July 4, 1938, pp. 1–2.
"Letters," March 21, 1938, pp. 1–10.
"Letters," May 19, 1941, pp. 1–10.
"Milestones," October 10, 1969, pp. 1–2.
"Modern Mercury," February 28, 1938, pp. 1–6.
"One of the Largest Frauds," December 11, 1972, pp. 1–4.
"Patronage Squabbles," September 25, 1933, pp. 1–2.
"People," September 5, 1932, pp. 1–2.
"People," September 17, 1934, pp. 1–2.
"People," November 18, 1940, pp. 1–3.
"People," May 23, 1969, pp. 1–3.
"Potent Postscript," July 11, 1938, pp. 1–2.
"Salesman's Reply," August 22, 1938, pp. 1–2.
"Shorts," December 26, 1938, pp. 1–2.

IX—WEB SITES

www.pbs.org/thewar/
Ken Burns interviewed some of Carlson's Raiders about the Long Patrol for a section of his multi-episode history *The War*.

www.smu.edu/cul/memorial/warbio.htm
The Web site for the Lt. Jack Miller Collection, Southern Methodist University, Dallas Texas.

www.usmcraiders.com/
An excellent Web site for obtaining additional information on the Raiders.

http://www.usmarineraiders.org/index2.html
The official Web site for the United States Marine Raider Association.

X—MOVIES & DOCUMENTARIES

The Battle of Midway, 1942.

"The First Line," CBS Radio Program script, January 11, 1945, in the Jack Miller Collection, DeGolyer Library, Southern Methodist University, Dallas, Texas.

Gung Ho! Ray Enright, director, 1943.

"In the Shadow of Heroes, USS Makin Island, August 17–18, 1942," from the Kenneth McCullough Collection.

"Jungle Fighting as Marine Raiders Know It," Civilian Defense radio program airing over KCMO, Kansas City, March 9, 1944, in the Joseph Woodford Collection.

Marine Raiders. Harold D. Schuster, director, 1944.

The War. Ken Burns, director and producer, 2007.

"World War II: Makin Island Raid," NBC Radio Broadcast on the show *Cited for Valor*, featuring Col. James Roosevelt, undated broadcast during the war.

Index